T0177273

Communications in Computer and Information Science 2026

Rationale

The CCIS series is devoted to the publication of proceedings of computer science conferences. Its aim is to efficiently disseminate original research results in informatics in printed and electronic form. While the focus is on publication of peer-reviewed full papers presenting mature work, inclusion of reviewed short papers reporting on work in progress is welcome, too. Besides globally relevant meetings with internationally representative program committees guaranteeing a strict peer-reviewing and paper selection process, conferences run by societies or of high regional or national relevance are also considered for publication.

Topics

The topical scope of CCIS spans the entire spectrum of informatics ranging from foundational topics in the theory of computing to information and communications science and technology and a broad variety of interdisciplinary application fields.

Information for Volume Editors and Authors

Publication in CCIS is free of charge. No royalties are paid, however, we offer registered conference participants temporary free access to the online version of the conference proceedings on SpringerLink (http://link.springer.com) by means of an http referrer from the conference website and/or a number of complimentary printed copies, as specified in the official acceptance email of the event.

CCIS proceedings can be published in time for distribution at conferences or as post-proceedings, and delivered in the form of printed books and/or electronically as USBs and/or e-content licenses for accessing proceedings at SpringerLink. Furthermore, CCIS proceedings are included in the CCIS electronic book series hosted in the SpringerLink digital library at http://link.springer.com/bookseries/7899. Conferences publishing in CCIS are allowed to use Online Conference Service (OCS) for managing the whole proceedings lifecycle (from submission and reviewing to preparing for publication) free of charge.

Publication process

The language of publication is exclusively English. Authors publishing in CCIS have to sign the Springer CCIS copyright transfer form, however, they are free to use their material published in CCIS for substantially changed, more elaborate subsequent publications elsewhere. For the preparation of the camera-ready papers/files, authors have to strictly adhere to the Springer CCIS Authors' Instructions and are strongly encouraged to use the CCIS LaTeX style files or templates.

Abstracting/Indexing

CCIS is abstracted/indexed in DBLP, Google Scholar, EI-Compendex, Mathematical Reviews, SCImago, Scopus. CCIS volumes are also submitted for the inclusion in ISI Proceedings.

How to start

To start the evaluation of your proposal for inclusion in the CCIS series, please send an e-mail to ccis@springer.com.

KC Santosh · Aaisha Makkar · Myra Conway ·
Ashutosh K. Singh · Antoine Vacavant ·
Anas Abou el Kalam ·
Mohamed-Rafik Bouguelia · Ravindra Hegadi
Editors

Recent Trends in Image Processing and Pattern Recognition

6th International Conference, RTIP2R 2023
Derby, UK, December 7–8, 2023
Revised Selected Papers, Part I

 Springer

Editors
KC Santosh 🆔
University of South Dakota
Vermillion, SD, USA

Myra Conway 🆔
University of Derby
Derby, UK

Antoine Vacavant 🆔
University of Clermont Auvergne
Aubière, France

Mohamed-Rafik Bouguelia 🆔
Halmstad University
Halmstad, Sweden

Aaisha Makkar 🆔
University of Derby
Derby, UK

Ashutosh K. Singh 🆔
Indian Institute of Information Technology
Bhopal, India

Anas Abou el Kalam 🆔
ENSA - Cadi Ayyad University
Marrakesh, Morocco

Ravindra Hegadi 🆔
Central University of Karnataka
Kalaburagi, India

ISSN 1865-0929   ISSN 1865-0937 (electronic)
Communications in Computer and Information Science
ISBN 978-3-031-53081-4   ISBN 978-3-031-53082-1 (eBook)
https://doi.org/10.1007/978-3-031-53082-1

This Springer imprint is published by the registered company Springer Nature Switzerland AG
The registered company address is: Gewerbestrasse 11, 6330 Cham, Switzerland

Paper in this product is recyclable.

Preface

We are delighted to present this compilation of research papers in Springer's Communication in Computer and Information Science (CCIS) series from the 6th International Conference on Recent Trends in Image Processing and Pattern Recognition (RTIP2R 2023). RTIP2R 2023 was hosted in-person at the University of Derby, UK, from December 07–08, 2023, in collaboration with the Applied AI Research Lab at the University of South Dakota, USA (URL: https://rtip2r-conference.org/).

As highlighted in the call for papers, RTIP2R 2023 attracted a wealth of current and recent research in image processing, pattern recognition, and computer vision across diverse applications, including document understanding, IoT, biometrics, healthcare informatics, and security. With a total of 216 submissions, we carefully selected 62 papers for presentation during the conference. Unlike the last event, we diligently reviewed revised submissions to arrive at final decisions, resulting in an acceptance rate of 28.70%. Each selected/accepted paper underwent a rigorous evaluation process with an average of three single-blind reviews per selection.

In essence, the conference provided a valuable platform that brought together research scientists, academics, and industry practitioners. We firmly believe that the event encapsulated a wealth of innovative ideas. We extend our gratitude to Girijesh Prasad from the School of Computing, Engineering, and Intelligent Systems at Ulster University, UK for delivering an insightful keynote address. During the conference, KC Santosh spearheaded a workshop titled "AI for Good - How about the Carbon Footprint?," featuring speakers including Vinaytosh Mishra (Gulf Medical University, UAE), Wajahat Ali Khan (University of Derby, UK), and Mabrouka Abuhmida (University of South Wales, UK).

Our heartfelt thanks go out to all contributors who made RTIP2R 2023 a success.

November 2023

KC Santosh
Aaisha Makkar
Myra Conway
Ashutosh K. Singh
Antoine Vacavant
Anas Abou el Kalam
Mohamed-Rafik Bouguelia
Ravindra Hegadi

Organization

Patrons

Warren Manning   University of Derby, UK
Louise Richards   University of Derby, UK
Stephan Reiff-Marganiec   University of Derby, UK

Honorary Chairs

Farid Meziane   University of Derby, UK
Alistair McEwan   University of Derby, UK
Xi-zhao Wang   Shenzhen University, China
Laurent Wendling   Université Paris Cité, France
KC Santosh   University of South Dakota, USA

General Chairs

Aaisha Makkar   University of Derby, UK
Myra Conway   University of Derby, UK
Ashutosh Kumar Singh   IIIT Bhopal, India

Program Chairs

Antoine Vacavant   University of Clermont Auvergne, France
Anas Abou el Kalam   Cadi Ayyad University, Morocco
M.-R. Bouguelia   Halmstad University, Sweden
Ravindra Hegadi   Central University of Karnataka, India

Special Track Chairs

Mickael Coustaty   Université de La Rochelle, France
Yassine Sadqi   University Sultan Moulay Slimane, Morocco
Abdul Wahid   University of Galway, Ireland
Aditya Nigam   IIT Mandi, India

Deepika Saxena	University of Aizu, Japan
Jitendra Kumar	NIT Tiruchirappalli, India
Longwei Wang	University of South Dakota, USA
Abdelkrim Haqiq	Hassan 1st University, Morocco

Workshop Chairs

Hubert Cecotti	California State University, Fresno, USA
Rodrigue Rizk	University of South Dakota, USA
Alice Othmani	Université Paris-Est Créteil, France
Nibaran Das	Jadavpur University, India
Manju Khari	JNU, India
Gaurav Jaswal	IIT Mandi, India
Satish K. Singh	IIIT Allahabad, India
Sushma Venkatesh	AiBA AS, Norway

Local Workshop Chairs

Alaa AlZoubi	University of Derby, UK
Maqbool Hussain	University of Derby, UK
Wajahat Ali Khan	University of Derby, UK
Asad Abdi	University of Derby, UK

Core Technical Program Committee (TPC)

Abdul Wahid	University of Galway, Ireland
Abdullah Kaleem	MPGI SOE, Nanded, India
Abhilasha Jain	MIET, India
Abhinav Muley	SVPCET, India
Abhishek Verma	PDPM IIITDM, Jabalpur, India
Abhishek Hazra	IIIT Sri City, India
Agha Husian	ITS Engineering College, India
Ajay Kumar	MIET, India
Akhilesh Pandey	MIET, India
Ali Nazarizadeh	Islamic Azad University Central Tehran Branch, Iran
Alok Aggarwal	UPES, India
Amarpreet Singh	Chandigarh University, India
Amit Saini	MIET, India

Amol Vibhute	SICSR, Symbiosis International (Deemed University), India
Anas Abou El Kalam	Cadi Ayyad University, Morocco
Aniket Muley	Swami Ramanad Teerth Marathwada University, India
Ankur Nagori	CIAE Bhopal, India
Antoine Vacavant	Université Clermont Auvergne, France
Anurag Malik	Uttaranchal University, India
Arkajyoti Mitra	University of Texas at Arlington, USA
Ashutosh Dhar Dwivedi	Aalborg University, Denmark
Badr Hssina	Hassan II University of Casablanca, Morocco
Bhanu Chander	IIIT Kottayam, India
Bimal Mandal	IIT Jodhpur, India
Bouchaib Cherradi	CRMEF Casablanca-Settat (S. P. d'El Jadida), Morocco
Brian Keith Norambuena	Universidad Católica del Norte, Chile
Chetan Pattebahadur	Dr. B.A.M. University, India
Chitra Gaikwad	Government College of Engineering Aurangabad, India
Dattatray Sawat	HCLTech, India
Deepak Sharma	University of Petroleum and Energy Studies, India
Deepak Gupta	GIIT, India
Deepak Rakesh	University of Economics and Human Sciences in Warsaw, Poland
Deepika Saxena	University of Aizu, Japan
Digvijay Singh	Uttaranchal University, India
Dipak Sah	IITISM Dhanbad, India
Gaurav Yadav	IAMR Group, India
Ghanshyam Bopche	NIT Tiruchirappalli, India
Gurjot Gaba	Linköping University, Sweden
Harsimran Kaur	Chitkara University, India
Himadri Mukherjee	West Bengal State University, India
Jatinder Kumar	National Institute of Technology Kurukshetra, India
Joana Sousa	NOS Inovação, Portugal
João Baptista Cardia Neto	UNESP, Brazil
Kalman Palagyi	University of Szeged, Hungary
Kamaljeet Kaur	Star Academy, India
Kaushik Roy	WBSU, India
Kavita Chaudhary	ABESEC, India
Kishu Gupta	National Institute of Technology Kurukshetra, India
Lorenzo Putzu	University of Cagliari, Italy

Madhu Arora   Sri Balaji University, India
Mahadev Patil   Bharati Vidyapeeth's Abhijit Kadam Institute of
                                   Management and Social Sciences, Solapur,
                                   India
Maheswaran S.   Kongu Engineering College, India
Mallikarjunaswamy M. S.   JSSSTU, India
Mansi Poonia   IAMR Group, India
Manwinder Singh   Lovely Professional University, India
Midhula Vijayan   National Institute of Technology, Tiruchirappalli,
                                   India
Mohamed-Rafik Bouguelia   Halmstad University, Sweden
Mohammod Naimul Islam Suvon   University of Sheffield, UK
Mohan Rawat   Chameli Devi Group of Institutions, India
Mohd. Saifuzzaman   Daffodil International University, Bangladesh
Muhammad Adeel Hafeez   University of Galway, Ireland
Mukesh Khandelwal   Govt. Women Mahila Engineering College
                                   Ajmer, India
Muntazir Mehdi   University of Derby, UK
Nahid Sami   University of Derby, UK
Narottam Patel   VIT Bhopal, India
Navjot Rathour   Chandigarh University, India
Navneet Kaur   Guru Nanak Dev Engineering College, India
Neeraj Joshi   MIET, India
Neeraj Kumar   GNIOT, India
Niharika Singh   University of Helsinki, Finland
Onel López   University of Oulu, Finland
Pankaj Dhiman   JUIT, India
Parbhat Gupta   SRM Institute of Science and Technology
                                   Modinagar, India
Parminder Kaur   Guru Nanak Dev University, India
Peter Dolan   University of Minnesota, Morris, USA
Pooja Janse   Dr. B.A.M. University, India
Pooja Rani   National Institute of Technology, Kurukshetra,
                                   India
Pooja S.   Galgotias University, India
Prabhakar S.   ITSEC, India
Prabhakar C. J.   Kuvempu University, India
Prakash Hiremath   KLE Technological University, India
Pranav Kumar Singh   Central Institute of Technology Kokrajhar, India
Prashant Kumar   National Institute of Technology Durgapur, India
Prasun Tripathi   University of Sheffield, UK
Rahul Kumar   BIT Meerut, India

Rajat Singh	Uttaranchal University, India
Rajat Balyan	Uttaranchal University, India
Ranit Kishore	Tula's Institute, India
Ravi M.	GFGC, Raichur, India
Ravinder Kumar	Guru Nanak Dev University, India
Ravindra Hegadi	Central University of Karnataka, India
Ravindra Sharma	Swami Rama Himalayan University, India
Rimjhim Rimjhim	Jain University, India
Rodrigo Nava	AstraZeneca, UK
Rodrigue Rizk	University of South Dakota, USA
S. S. Patil	University of Agricultural Sciences, Bangalore, India
Sachin Kumar	Vidya College, India
Samson Anosh Babu Parisapogu	Chaitanya Bharathi Institute of Technology, India
Sandeep Arora	Lovely Professional University, India
Sandhya Pundhir	DSEU, India
Sanjay Jain	ITM University Gwalior, India
Sara Arezki	University Hassan First, Morocco
Satender Kumar	National Institute of Technology Kurukshetra, India
Saurabh Singhal	Chandigarh University, India
Shaik Vaseem Akram	SRU, India
Shalini Aggarwal	Graphic Era Hill University, India
Sharad Saxena	Thapar Institute of Engineering and Technology, India
Shashank Agnihotri	MIET, India
Shilpa Sharma	JIMSEMTC, India
Shivam Chaudhary	MIET, India
Shubham Mahajan	Ajeenkya DY Patil University, India
Shweta Pandey	Uttaranchal University, India
Siddharth Dabhade	National Forensic Sciences University, India
Smruti Swain	National Institute of Technology, Kurukshetra, India
Sumanth Sharma	Government College for Women, Kolar, India
Sumit Sharma	National Institute of Technology Kurukshetra, India
Sunil Nimbhore	Dr. Babasaheb Ambedkar Marathwada University, India
Swarnika Swarnika	NGI, India
Thomas Monoth	Mary Matha Arts & Science College, Kannur University, India
Uruj Jaleel	Alliance University, India

V. Malemath	KLE Dr. M. S. Sheshgiri College of Engg. and Technology, Belagavi, India
Vikas Humbe	SRTM University, India
Vinay Singh	UPES, India
Vinay T. R.	Nitte Meenakshi Institute of Technology, India
Vinaytosh Mishra	Gulf Medical University, UAE
Vineet Vishnoi	Shobhit University Meerut, India
Vivek Singh	Sharda University, India
Yusera Khan	Shri Mata Vaishno Devi University, India
Zakaria Rguibi	FST Settat, Morocco

Conference Secretaries

| Jose David Cortes | Applied AI Research Lab, USA |
| Siddhi K. Bajracharya | Applied AI Research Lab, USA |

Webmaster

| KC Santosh | Applied AI Research Lab, USA |

Contents – Part I

Applied Image Processing and Pattern Recognition

Biometrics and Applications

Contents – Part II

Healthcare Informatics

Pattern Recognition in Blockchain, Cyber and Network Security, and Cryptography

Artificial Intelligence and Applied Machine Learning

Building a Heroin Abuse Prediction Model: A Generalized Machine Learning Approach

Divya Kumari[1]([⊠]) [iD] and Aleena Swetapadma[2]

[1] New Horizon College of Engineering, Bangalore 560103, India
divya.nov30@gmail.com
[2] KIIT University, Bhubaneswar 751024, Odisha, India

Abstract. Aims: In the modern era, substance abuse is a global problem. CDC's (Centre for Disease Control) National Center for Health Statistics reported in July 2021 that, more than 93000 drug overdose deaths occurred alone in the United States. **Design:** A cohort study. **Setting:** The drug consumption data is collected online in United Kingdom. Total 2000 records are present, out of which, 1885 records are considered for the work after initial data processing. The dataset has the drug consumption output outcome of 18 drugs, heroin is one of them. **Measurements:** In this work, an intelligent approach has been proposed for detecting abuse of one of the most illicit substances - heroin. A random forest-based machine learning model is proposed which can predict heroin abused individuals with very high accuracy. For the abuse prediction, various supervised machine learning methods are applied, and their performance is compared. These algorithms are applied to different sets of features. Among the applied five algorithms, feature importance score is calculated for logistic regression, ensemble learning (gradient boosting) and random forest. The feature importance score for each feature is calculated for all applied algorithms k-nearest neighbour and naïve bayes. The ranking of all features is done based on the obtained score. **Findings:** It is found in the study that the heroin-abuse dataset collected from UCI, two-classification based on random forest (RF) and gradient boosting (GB) achieved more than 90% accuracy as well as more than 90% sensitivity, specificity, precision, and f-score. The proposed model gave the best accuracy 94.697% for heroin-use detection. **Conclusions:** The assessment of the proposed framework on all possible feature sets shows that the framework works well for heroin abuse prediction as different give satisfactory results.

Keywords: Artificial Intelligence · Demography · Ensemble learning · Illicit Drugs · Personality Features

1 Introduction

Substance abuse is one of the most prominent issues of today's generation. Hence substance abused individuals should be monitored constantly to overcome the abuse. Most of the substance abuse is related to drugs like alcohol, heroin, cocaine, opioids, cannabis, volatile substances etc. Among these substances, heroin is the highly used drugs by

KC Santosh et al. (Eds.): RTIP2R 2023, CCIS 2026, pp. 3–13, 2024.
https://doi.org/10.1007/978-3-031-53082-1_1

individuals. Heroin induces direct toxic effects on the brain and heroin intake leads to endocarditis, renal diseases, pulmonary diseases, various skin and soft tissues problems, hepatitis and other medical problems [1]. There is short term and long-term consequences of using heroin on academic performance of high school students. [2]. The teenagers are prone to drug usage because of various reasons like peer pressure, urge to seek validation from peers and mainly because their brains are still physically developing. Their academic performance is hugely impacted if they consume heroin. This drug is adulterated to be distributed in Switzerland [3]. Here, 3476 samples of heroin from 721 seizures are analyzed. In several ways, individuals consume heroin. It can be consumed via inhalation or intravenous route. Various case studies have found that when heroin is substituted for cocaine especially in opioid naive patients, it can result in multi organ failure [4]. Various factors affect heroin-related overdose [5]. The focus is made on the components of the United States illicit drug market. These components include the source or type of heroin, its price, and the purity of the sample. The stress factor also has a role in heroin addiction [6]. Results show that there is a strong relationship of stress with exposure to drug use triggers, craving and mood. For drug use confirmation, fingerprints are considered to play a major role. For drug testing from a single fingerprint, an environmental cutoff concept is proposed to be used as environmental contamination from fingertips is always possible [7]. There is a difference between fingerprints of heroin users and non-users. In one of the studies, the self-administration of cocaine, cannabis and heroin in the human laboratory is described [8]. Its merits and demerits are analyzed. This study helps to address various factors that lead to cocaine, marijuana, and heroin intake. The early detection of the illicit drug abused individuals correctly is crucial for better monitoring. For detection of substance abuse, in some cases, clinical tests and magnetic resonance imaging have been used. In previous works, machine learning has been used for the detection of substance abuse. Linear discriminant analysis and artificial neural networks are used to predict pharmacological treatments received by intravenous drug users [9]. The best accuracy obtained is 62.7%. For the prediction of the heroin abused individuals, the decision tree-based model is used, and the sensitivity and specificity obtained respectively are 82.55 and 72.98 [10]. The demographic features used for prediction are age and gender. Impulsivity is taken as the personality feature for this prediction. Heroin abused individuals are detected on a data sample from Bulgaria using an elastic net method [11]. Result is shown using the performance metric receiver operating characteristic (ROC) in which area under the curve is 0.863. A review of prediction of drug abuse using machine learning techniques is done [12]. It also includes the studies done on heroin abuse prediction.

Most of the above-described methods use clinical tests or image processing to detect substance abuse. Some of them machine learning methods like decision tree, linear discriminant analysis, nearest neighbour, support vector machine is used for the detection of heroin abuse using personality traits and demographic features, but the accuracy of the method is not good i.e., below 80%. The goal of the work is to design an efficient method for detection of heroin abuse using personality and demographic features, so that the method can be used for monitoring the abuse without any clinical test. Hence in this work, an intelligent approach has been proposed for substance abuse detection.

2   Materials and Methods

The proposed method consists of various steps as shown in Fig. 1. The steps are input selection, input processing, feature extraction, abuse detection and performance analysis.

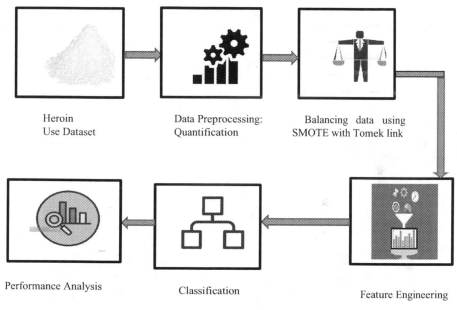

Fig. 1. Methodology

2.1   Dataset Details

The dataset used in this work was gathered from UCI repository [13]. There are 12 attributes in this dataset. The dataset has 1885 records, among which 942 are females and 943 are males of different ages belonging to various countries of different races and educational backgrounds. In the dataset, 11.24% consume heroin and 88.76% do not consume heroin.

2.2   Data Preprocessing

The dataset consists of many categorical features with many levels. It is important to quantify these features to get continuous data so that the suitable data mining methods can be further applied to it. The features age and education are quantified from ordinal original. As the categories of features such as gender, country of location and ethnicity are unordered, the technique of nonlinear CatPCA [14] is used. Other attributes like five traits dimensions: NEOAC (Neuroticism, Extraversion, Openness, Agreeableness, Conscientiousness), impulsivity and sensation seeking are quantified from interval original. For exploratory data analysis (EDA), Python version 3.8.5 has been used. SMOTE

(Synthetic minority oversampling technique) with Tomek link is used to balance the imbalanced data.

2.3 Performance Evaluation Metrics

Various supervised machine learning algorithms are applied to the heroin-use dataset to find the algorithm which is the most efficient. The accuracy and other performance metrics are compared using LOOCV (Leave-one out cross validation). The applied algorithms were logistic regression (LR), gaussian naive bayes (NB), K-nearest neighbour (KNN), random forest (RF) and gradient boosting (GB). The comparison between all algorithms is done on various performance evaluation metrics.

LOOCV (Leave-one-out cross validation) is used to train and test the model. In this approach, model fitting and prediction is done using one observation validation set. Each observation is considered as the validation set and the remaining N-1 observations are assumed to be the training set. Figure 2 represents how LOOCV works.

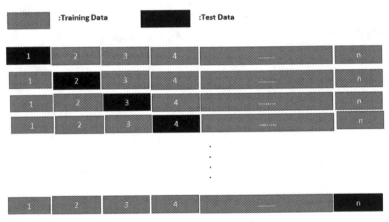

Fig. 2. Representation of Leave-One-Out Cross Validation

2.4 Methods Used

Intelligent methods such as artificial intelligence-based methods are more frequently used in many applications. Intelligent methods have many advantages over statistical methods. Two most important aspects of designing an intelligent classification approach are selection of feature extraction techniques and selection of classifiers. Various machine learning methods are used to build the system which assesses and predicts the user's physical and mental well-being. The various techniques used in this study are discussed below.

2.4.1 Synthetic Minority Oversampling Technique

It is required to make unbalanced datasets balanced, so that the machine learning classification algorithms can be fit successfully. Synthetic minority oversampling technique (SMOTE) is one of the traditional approaches used for balancing such datasets [15]. In this work, SMOTE with Tomek link techniques has been used. It was introduced in 2016 [16]. Table 1 shows the distribution of samples in original data. Figure 3 shows the distribution of samples of heroin before and after application of SMOTE.

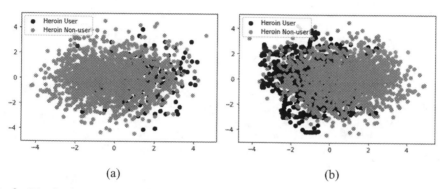

(a)   (b)

Fig. 3. Distribution of sample (a) Original samples of heroin (b) Samples after using SMOTE Tomek of heroin

Table 1. Sample distribution of heroin

Heroin	
User	Non-user
11.24%	88.76%

2.4.2 Supervised Machine Learning Techniques

In this work, various machine learning techniques such as logistic regression (LR), Gaussian naïve bayes (NB), gradient boosting (GB) [17] and nearest neighbour (k-NN) [18] have been used.

2.5   Feature Importance

In the machine learning field, feature importance and its visualization play a very significant role as an analysis method. Among the used classifiers in the work, apart from NB and k-NN, feature importance score is calculated for all classification algorithms. Figure 4 is a heat map which represents the correlated values and correlation between all the features in the heroin-use dataset.

3   Results

3.1   Result of Exploratory Data Analysis (EDA)

To better understand the dataset and get the proper insights from it, exploratory data analysis is performed on the dataset. Figure 5 is grouped box and whiskers plot of the personality feature: 'impulsivity' vs. demographic feature: 'country' and the output heroin users are represented with orange color and heroin non-users are represented in blue color. It is evident that these features are important, and the use of heroin varies in different countries according to the impulsivity of the individuals.

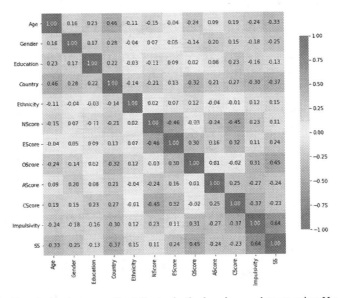

Fig. 4. Correlation between all attributes in the heroin-use dataset using Heat map.

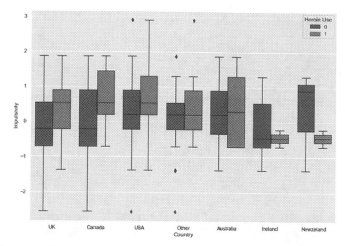

Fig. 5. Grouped box and whiskers plot of Impulsivity vs. Country and Heroin Use

3.2 Result of Machine Learning Analysis

For this study, heroin-abuse dataset has been processed. Table 2 depicts the classification result of different classification algorithms using all twelve features for heroin-use. Table 1 shows the details of all twelve used features. The performance outcome parameters used are sensitivity, specificity, precision, F-score, and accuracy. GB and RF give maximal results for all used performance outcome parameters. k-NN gives better results than NB and LR.

Table 2. Heroin abuse prediction: Performance with all 12 features

Method used	Sensitivity/Recall (%)	Specificity (%)	Precision (%)	F-score (%)	Accuracy (%)
NB	79.75	71.599	73.74	76.63	75.67
LR	81.07	71.42	73.93	77.34	76.24
kNN	99.70	72.08	78.12	87.60	85.89
GB	91.37	91.01	91.04	91.21	91.19
RF	95.15	94.25	94.299	94.72	94.697

Table 3 shows the result of applying various machine learning algorithms using all personality features, which are the seven features namely five factor model NEOAC (Neuroticism, Extraversion, Openness, Agreeableness, Conscientiousness), impulsivity and sensation seeking.

Table 3. Heroin abuse prediction: Performance with 7 features (NEOAC, SS,Imp)

Method used	Sensitivity/Recall (%)	Specificity (%)	Precision (%)	F-score (%)	Accuracy (%)
NB	76.31	65.06	68.59	72.25	70.69
LR	74.56	67.17	69.43	71.90	70.87
kNN	99.52	69.03	76.27	86.36	84.27
GB	89.597	90.08	90.03	89.81	89.84
RF	94.89	93.02	93.15	94.01	93.96

Classification results using only selected features for heroin-use is shown in Table 4. Age, impulsivity, and gender are selected for heroin use prediction. The same set of selected features is used in [10].

Table 4. Heroin abuse prediction: Performance with only selected features (age, impulsivity and gender)

Method used	Sensitivity/Recall (%)	Specificity (%)	Precision (%)	F-score (%)	Accuracy (%)
NB	74.36	62.28	66.35	70.12	68.32
LR	70.83	66.05	67.59	69.18	68.44
kNN	60.43	84.46	79.54	68.68	72.44
GB	87.69	68.68	73.68	80.08	78.18
RF	87.69	68.44	73.53	79.99	78.06

According to the result, random forest is the best performer, followed by gradient boosting, k-nearest neighbour, logistic regression and naïve bayes. To know among all used features, feature importance score is calculated for the applied algorithms: logistic regression, gradient boosting, and random forest. The importance score of all features for the mentioned classification algorithms to predict heroin use is calculated. Figure 6 shows its graphical representation. Based on the feature importance score, the ranking of features is done for each used classification algorithm. It is found that for heroin use data, N-Score ranks first for logistic regression whereas the feature country ranks first for both random forest and gradient boosting algorithms. NScore or Neuroticism refers to the tendency to have negative emotions or have anxiety and depression. An individual who has more negative emotions is thus more prone to become heroin addict. The location of an individual also influences the factor of becoming a heroin addict as in few countries' heroin is more easily accessible. This result depicts clearly that both personality features and demographic information play a vital role in prediction of heroin consumption.

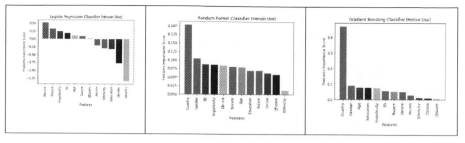

Fig. 6. Graphical representation of feature importance score

4   Discussion

This paper explored the relevance of personality traits and demographic information in illicit drug abuse detection using an intelligent approach. Heroin is the illicit drug on which this work is done. Our work is inspired by these two ideas: i) there is a relationship between the heroin use and the personality profile of the user. ii) The heroin consumption may also be dependent on the demographic data. To assess this idea, a generalized machine learning model is proposed that takes various sets of features. The first feature set includes all personality and demographic information. The second feature set includes only personality features that are components of the five-factor model (NEOAC -neuroticism, extraversion, openness to experience, agreeableness, conscientiousness). The third set includes all personality traits (five factor model, impulsivity and sensation seeking). The fourth set includes selected features that are used in the previous work. Our results showed: i) the most important features in heroin-use detection are neuroticism and country. iii) various classification algorithms like Gaussian naïve bayes, nearest neighbour, gradient boosting and random forest are used, and the performance metrics used for the determination are sensitivity, specificity, precision, f-score and accuracy iv) the most accurate and efficient result is obtained when personality traits along with demographic data are used as attributes and fed to the random forest-based machine learning model. Machine Learning algorithms have been employed in the previous work to detect if an individual consumes psychoactive drug like alcohol [19, 20] and drug abuse. As a small dataset has been used to validate the proposed method, it can be considered as a limitation of the method. In the future work, more test cases will be considered for validation of the proposed work for getting reliable results in detecting drug abuse without clinical test, more input features will be investigated which will have significant contribution to build a robust method. The proposed intelligent method can be outlined as follows:

- A novel framework for detecting illicit drug –heroin abuse is proposed.
- Much better result in terms of sensitivity, specificity, precision, f-score and accuracy than previous studies which used machine learning for the prediction of abuse.
- It can be used effectively for early detection of illicit-drug heroin abuse and monitoring abused individuals and thus will be immensely helpful for counseling adolescent persons without performing any clinical test. Heroin abuse is detected with accuracy of 94.697%

References

1. McCann, U.D., Ricaurte, G.A.: Drug abuse and dependence: hazards and consequences of heroin, cocaine and amphetamines. Curr. Opin. Psychiatry **13**(3), 321–325 (2000). https://doi.org/10.1097/00001504-200005000-00014
2. Paolini, A.C.: Heroin usage: impact on student performance and truancy among high school students. J. Drug Issues **2**(1), 853–861 (2016). https://doi.org/10.21767/2471-853X.100011
3. Morelato, M., Franscella, D., Esseiva, P., Broséus, J.: When does the cutting of cocaine and heroin occur? The first large-scale study based on the chemical analysis of cocaine and heroin seizures in Switzerland. Int. J. Drug Policy **73**, 7–15 (2019). https://doi.org/10.1016/j.drugpo.2019.07.025
4. Becker, T., Papathomas, E., Chan, B.S.: Harm of heroin substitution for cocaine in opioid Naïve patients. Forensic Sci. Addict. Res. **2**(4) (2018). https://doi.org/10.31031/FSAR.2018.02.000541
5. Unick, G., Rosenblum, D., Mars, S., Ciccarone, D.: The relationship between US heroin market dynamics and heroin-related overdose, 1992–2008. Addiction **109**(11), 1889–1898 (2014). https://doi.org/10.1111/add.12664
6. Preston, K.L., Epstein, D.H.: Stress in the daily lives of cocaine and heroin users: relationship to mood, craving, relapse triggers, and cocaine use. Psychopharmacology **218**, 29–37 (2011). https://doi.org/10.1007/s00213-011-2183-x
7. Ismail, M., Stevenson, D., Costa, C., Webb, R., De Puit, M., Bailey, M.: Noninvasive detection of cocaine and heroin use with single fingerprints: determination of an environmental cutoff. Clin. Chem. **64**(6), 909–917 (2018). https://doi.org/10.1373/clinchem.2017.281469
8. Haney, M.: Self-administration of cocaine, cannabis and heroin in the human laboratory: benefits and pitfalls. Addict. Biol. **14**(1), 9–21 (2009). https://doi.org/10.1111/j.1369-1600.2008.00121.x
9. Grassi, M.C., Caricati, A.M., Intraligi, M., Buscema, M., Nencini, P.: Artificial neural network assessment of substitutive pharmacological treatments in hospitalised intravenous drug users. Artif. Intell. Med. **24**(1), 37–49 (2002). https://doi.org/10.1016/S0933-3657(01)00093-8
10. Fehrman, E., Muhammad, A.K., Mirkes, E.M., Egan, V., Gorban, A.N.: The five factor model of personality and evaluation of drug consumption risk. In: Palumbo, F., Montanari, A., Vichi, M. (eds.) Data Science. Studies in Classification, Data Analysis, and Knowledge Organization, pp. 231–242. Springer, Cham (2017). https://doi.org/10.1007/978-3-319-55723-6_18
11. Ahn, W.Y., Vassileva, J.: Machine-learning identifies substance-specific behavioral markers for opiate and stimulant dependence. Drug Alcohol Depend. **1**(161), 247–257 (2016). https://doi.org/10.1016/j.drugalcdep.2016.02.008
12. Mak, K.K., Lee, K., Park, C.: Applications of machine learning in addiction studies: a systematic review. Psychiatry Res. **1**(275), 53–60 (2019). https://doi.org/10.1016/j.psychres.2019.03.001
13. Fehrman, E., Muhammad, A.K., Mirkes, E., Egan, V., Gorban, A.: Drug Consumption (quantified) Data Set (2016). [WWW Document]. https://archive.ics.uci.edu/ml/datasets/Drug+consumption+%28quantified%29
14. Linting, M., van der Kooij, A.: Nonlinear principal components analysis with CATPCA: a tutorial. J. Pers. Assess. **94**(1), 12–25 (2012). https://doi.org/10.1080/00223891.2011.627965
15. Fernández, A., Garcia, S., Herrera, F., Chawla, N.V.: SMOTE for learning from imbalanced data: progress and challenges, marking the 15-year anniversary. J. Artif. Intell. Res. **61**, 863–905 (2018). https://doi.org/10.1613/jair.1.11192
16. Zeng, M., Zou, B., Wei, F., Liu, X., Wang, L.: Effective prediction of three common diseases by combining SMOTE with Tomek links technique for imbalanced medical data. In: 2016 IEEE International Conference of Online Analysis and Computing Science (ICOACS), pp. 225–228, IEEE, 28 May 2016. https://doi.org/10.1109/ICOACS.2016.7563084

17. Hastie, T., Tibshirani, R., Friedman, J.H., Friedman, J.H.: The Elements of Statistical Learning: Data Mining, Inference, and Prediction. Springer, New York (2009). https://doi.org/10.1007/978-0-387-84858-7
18. Peterson, L.E.: K-nearest neighbor. Scholarpedia **4**(2), 1883 (2009)
19. Kumari, D., Kilam, S., Nath, P., Swetapadma, A.: Prediction of alcohol abused individuals using artificial neural network. Int. J. Inf. Technol. **10**, 233–237 (2018)
20. .Kumari, D., Swetapadma, A.: A novel method for predicting time of alcohol use based on personality traits and demographic information. IETE J. Res. 1–10 (2022)

Fake News Detection Using Transfer Learning

Jagendra Singh[1(✉)], Dinesh Prasad Sahu[1], Tanya Gupta[1], Dev Singhal[1], Bechoo Lal[1,2], and Anil V. Turukmane[1,3]

[1] School of Computer Science Engineering & Technology, Bennett University, Greater Noida, India
jagendrasngh@gmail.com
[2] Department of Computer Science Engineering, Konenru Lakshmaiah Education Foundation, Vaddeswaram, India
[3] School of Computer Science and Engineering, VIT - AP University, Amaravati, India

Abstract. In this innovative study, multi-task transfer study and Natural Language Processing or NLP join forces to fight the ever-growing challenge of identifying fake news. By simultaneously training a model on an array of related tasks sentiment analysis, language modeling, and fake news detection, it unlocks the potential to deeply comprehend natural language structures and patterns. This not only bolsters accuracy and effectiveness but also unlocks a treasure trove of advantages, including enhanced precision, efficiency, and adaptability to new data. Fearlessly pitted against fake-news detection tactics, the proposed method emerges victorious, showcasing superior accuracy and agility in computation times. Tested on a battlefield of news articles, it demonstrates the power of multi-task transfer learning and NLP in the fight against misinformation. In the grand scheme of things, this study offers a novel and creative approach, revolutionizing the study of identifying fake-news, and paving the way for diverse applications, from social media monitoring to news filtering and beyond. In the vast, interconnected world of NLP, this groundbreaking method emerges as a beacon of hope, guiding us towards a future where truth prevails, and fake news is vanquished.

Keywords: Artificial Intelligence · Deep Learning · Natural Language Processing · Sentiment analysis · Fake news detection

1 Introduction

Fake news has proliferated so much in last few years that many people are concerned about how it can harm democracy and public dialogue. Due to the widespread use of social networks and the internet, the prevalence of fake news has increased, which poses a challenge for individuals in discerning between what is true and false. The use of NLP and Multitask Transfer Learning is a feasible way to identify fake news since it allows the model to harness ideas from related tasks and improve its performance [1]. A vital technique used in spotting fake news is natural language processing (NLP).The area of Artificial Intelligence known as Natural Language Processing is centered on educating computers to comprehend and converse using natural language.

© The Author(s), under exclusive license to Springer Nature Switzerland AG 2024
KC Santosh et al. (Eds.): RTIP2R 2023, CCIS 2026, pp. 14–24, 2024.
https://doi.org/10.1007/978-3-031-53082-1_2

To identify patterns, extract information, and make predictions based on language, Natural Language Processing helps computers to understand and analyze the context, syntax and semantics of the language and allows computers to analyze and comprehend human language. Researchers are using machine learning techniques known as multi-task transfer learning to increase the accuracy of NLP models in several tasks such as language translation, sentiment analysis, and text classification. This method improves the model's performance on individual tasks by allowing it to simultaneously learn from several challenges [2, 3]. The problem statement is to identify fake news accurately, which can make a substantial difference in people's lives and society as a whole. Identifying false news is a challenging task because it frequently calls for a thorough comprehension of the context and purpose of the item. False information can have serious consequences, including riots, political unrest, and even fatalities. Thus, it is crucial to build an effective system for detecting bogus news. Misinformation has the potential to seriously affect people's lives by influencing their beliefs, actions, and decisions [4].

The fast-paced nature of social media makes it easy for fake information to spread, and it can be difficult to tell it apart from real news [5]. Several organizations and people share the goal of identifying and eliminating fake news. Some examples of social media platforms that have created tools and algorithms to recognise fraudulent information and eliminate it from their platforms include Facebook and Twitter. Factchecking agencies like PolitiFact and FactCheck.org also try to confirm news accounts and ensure that the public is given correct information. We plan to leverage a pre-trained BERT model as a foundation for our multi-task transfer learning approach to improve the performance of our model [6].

BERT is a modern language model that has demonstrated exceptional proficiency in various NLP tasks due to its training on a vast corpus of text. We intend to use a collection of labeled false news stories to train our model and enhance the pre-trained BERT model's performance on this dataset by employing multi-task transfer learning techniques. We will use statistical formulas such as F1-score, recall, accuracy, and precision to compare the performance of both models [7]. We will assess how well our multi-task transfer learning technique performs in comparison to a baseline model that is trained exclusively using the fake news dataset.

2 Problem Statement

In today's digital age, social media platforms reign supreme in the realm of news consumption. Alas, with great power comes great responsibility, and the rampant spread of falsified information on these platforms poses a severe threat to society. Our research intends to address this pressing problem head-on by creating a system that proactively assesses the veracity of news items shared on social media [4].

We utilize the supplemental data present on social media to categorise news articles in order to accomplish this admirable goal. The two fundamental components of the social media news ecosystem are news articles and users, including publishers and readers. Our approach goes beyond merely validating news content against authenticated sources. We take into account various other crucial factors, such as user engagement, publisher bias towards the news topic, and the user's historical credibility, to make a justifiable classification of the news content.

Our innovative methodology provides a comprehensive and nuanced approach to fake news detection, addressing the complexities and challenges posed by the social media landscape. By harnessing the collective intelligence of social media users and utilizing cutting-edge technology, we can promote a more informed and truthful discourse online. With this research, we take a significant step towards safeguarding society against the perils of misinformation and disinformation in the digital age [8].

At a high level, our system computes the News-News relationship from social media using the User-News relationship. We then derive the News Content Vector using the BERT Library, which is then fed into a Graph Attention Networks (GATs) scheme for prediction. The machine learning model Identify applicable funding agency here. If none, delete this. We use is based on a semi-supervised technique, which continuously learns the volatile social relationships and is prone to changing user-credibility scores before making a prediction. By considering the reliability of the user sharing the news as well as the overall social media engagement of the news, our method seeks to be more accurate than current fact-checking systems. This will assist to lessen the spread of incorrect information by giving news items on social media sites a more accurate classification [9].

Last but not least, the goal of our research is to address the pressing issue of the increase of incorrect information on online platforms. Our suggested approach would employ supplemental data from social media to categorize news content while considering user trustworthiness and news consumption behavior. By doing this, we intend to give news items a more legitimate classification and stop the propagation of incorrect information on social networking networks.

3   Methodology

We intend to compare the effectiveness of transfer learning (TL) to models generated under low resource restrictions using a few-shot learning-based technique. Initially, we establish a baseline model to serve as a benchmark for comparison. Subsequently, we showcase two TL methods that we have customized for the purpose of detecting fake news. Siamesen neural networks are used in the foundational or base-line model that we are exploring. These networks have a unique architecture that allows them to assess how similar input samples are to one another [10].

Following network optimization, we may use the discriminative features to expand the model's predictive power to encompass not only fresh data but also novel classes with unknown distributions (Fig. 1).

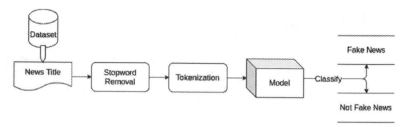

Fig. 1. Proposed framework for fake news classification

3.1 ULMFiT (Universal Language Model Fine-tuning)

With the help of this LM model, we were able to employ transfer learning and attain acceptable accuracy with very few labelled data points. The ULMFiT technique tries to improve a computer's understanding of natural language by modifying an existing language model to suit a particular purpose. This is comparable to how people acquire new talents by expanding upon their existing knowledge. Having prior knowledge and skills can facilitate learning new concepts, just like knowing how to cook rice can simplify the process of making fried rice. In the context of language interpretation, an AWD-LSTM is a pre-trained model commonly used in ULMFiT, Which has undergone training with an enormous amount of textual data to enhance its language comprehension abilities. It resembles giving the model a head starts on the new task before it begins to learn it. The AWD-LSTM model is then in two steps tailored to a particular purpose [11].

We often begin by fine-tuning a pre-trained language model on the specific text data associated with that task when we want to apply it for a new task. This procedure aids the model's performance improvement and adaptation to the new task. This aids the model's acquisition of the particular lingo used for that task. The model is then enhanced for the particular classification task by adding a classification layer. ULMFiT employs several strategies during this process to stop the model from forgetting what it has already learned [12].

It is advantageous to utilize ULMFiT in low-resource scenarios since it produces impressive results even with little amounts of data. A pre-trained language model can perform exceptionally well in text categorization tasks even with a minimal amount of data, as few as 1000 samples. ULMFiT is a potent technique for teaching computers to comprehend language better overall. ULMFiT is a fascinating development in natural language processing that can achieve exceptional outcomes with small amounts of data by fine-tuning a pretrained model for a specific purpose. This technique has broad potential applications, particularly in low-resource settings where obtaining sufficient data could be a challenge.

Bert. To comprehend the meaning of the words in a phrase, the language model BERT leverages deep learning. It can be adjusted to execute a range of jobs, including text classification, sentiment analysis, and question answering. The model, which was unveiled in 2018, has excelled in numerous standards for language comprehension [13]. The utilization of a mechanism termed "Attention" by BERT is one of its benefits. By paying attention, the model can evaluate each word's significance in a phrase while also taking into account the surrounding context. This is especially helpful because a word's meaning can vary depending on the words that surround it. Compared to other language models like recurrent neural networks, BERT can employ attention to refer to many points in a sentence at once, even if they are far apart (Fig. 2).

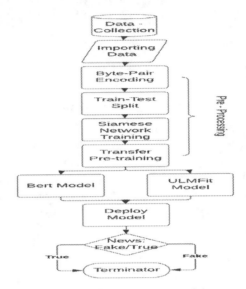

Fig. 2. Flow Chart of our Methodology

An additional benefit that BERT has over other language models, such as ULMFiT, is its bidirectionality. This means that it can comprehend the connotation of a word based on its use by examining the words both preceding and following it (Fig. 3).

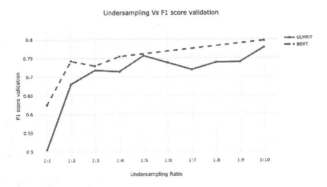

Fig. 3. Under sampling Ratio.

This is achieved by BERT using the pretraining technique known as "Masked Language Modeling.". Here, some of the words in a sentence are randomly masked, and the model is assigned with predicting the meaning of those words in light of the context of the rest of the sentence. As a result, the model is compelled to consider the words that come before and after the word that is being hidden.

In addition to being deep, BERT is also multilayered. BERT is available in two sizes: BERT-Base consists of 12 tiers, whereas BERT-Large comprises 24 tiers. The model can recognize the meaning of longer phrases and record more complicated links between words by having more layers. There are 110 million parameters in BERT-Base and 340 million in BERT-Large. In conclusion, BERT is an effective language model that can infer a word's meaning from the context in which it appears. This is accomplished by using attention, depth, and bidirectionality. It regularly produces great results in several natural language processing tasks as a result of these properties [13].

Challenges

One of the main challenges in using transfer learning models such as BERT and ULMFiT for fake news detection is the limited availability of labeled training data. Fake news detection often calls for a substantial amount of labeled information to train models effectively, but this may be difficult to obtain due to the cost and time required to label data manually. Additionally, fake news detection requires not only detecting false information but also identifying the intent behind the message, which is a complex task that may require additional contextual information. Using transfer learning models for fake news detection presents an additional hurdle in the form of potential data bias. When the training dataset exhibits bias towards specific categories of fake news or particular groups, the resulting model might struggle to perform effectively on novel data that deviates from these predefined categories [14]. This, in turn, can lead to unreliable predictions and hinder the model's ability to generalize across different contexts.

Moreover, the intricate and ever-evolving nature of fake news poses challenges in pinpointing the essential features necessary for accurate classification. These crucial identifying features may undergo alterations as new forms of fake news surface, and their relevance can also fluctuate based on the platform or target audience.

This means that the models need to be continually updated and retrained to keep up with these changes. Lastly, the transferability of the models to different languages and cultures may be limited. Fake news often takes different forms in different languages and cultures, and a model trained on data from one linguistic background or cultural context may not perform as effectively on data from another linguistic background or cultural context. This highlights the need for diverse and representative training data for transfer learning models to be effective in detecting fake news across different languages and cultures.

4   Experimental Setup

The experimental framework for this investigation encompasses multiple phases, such as data pre-processing, language model pre-training, fine-tuning for counterfeit news classification, and benchmark evaluation. Initially, we collect and cleanse the datasets, which comprise news articles tagged as authentic or fabricated. Subsequently, we pre-train an array of language models on vast quantities of textual data, utilizing unsupervised learning methodologies. Following that, we refine these tools to use to generate misleading information classification, leveraging labeled features to instruct the models in discerning between genuine and fraudulent news pieces. Ultimately, we gauge the fine-tuned models' performance against a benchmark dataset and scrutinize the outcomes to determine the efficacy of transfer learning in detecting fabricated news (Fig. 4).

Fig. 4. Stages of the Experimental Setup.

4.1   Fake News Dataset Pre-processing

We implemented tokenization on the counterfeit news dataset by employing a specific technique called"Byte-Pair Encoding" (BPE), as introduced in a 2018 research paper by Cherry. Byte Pair Encoding, a variety of tokenizing lowercase words, assigns a single token to the most frequently occurring words in the vocabulary, where as rarely occurring common terms are split in two or more lowercase word symbol, akin to the function of sub word based tokenization algorithms. This method enables the model to effectively represent words absent from its lexicon, which is particularly beneficial for languages with complex morphology. We adopted a 30–70 division to partition database into testing and training subsets to refine and enhancing the classifiers.

By importing the entire dataset into a Pandas data frame and utilizing the sample function, we randomly shuffled the data to generate these splits. To ensure repeatability, we set the frac parameter to 1.0 and the random seed to 42. Rather than modifying or reducing the model's vocabulary during the fine-tuning stage for Transformer-based strategies, we aimed to match the model's vocabulary with the dataset's language by using the model's original vocabulary from pre-training.

Pretraining Corpora
To train BERT and ULMFiT, a substantial amount of training data which in particular should be unlabeled, would be required. The training data we used was from ISOT Fake News Dataset.

In our research, we utilized a dataset of 172,815 articles from ISOT, to train BERT, and AWD-LSTM language models for ULMFiT. To create training-validation-test splits, we loaded the entire dataset into Pandas and shuffled it to form 70 for training and 30 for validation and testing. We divided the remaining 30 of the dataset in half to create separate validation and test sets. To avoid including tokens from the validation set in the vocabulary of the training set, we made sure to eliminate them before computing the dataset statistics. We presplit the text using the Moses Tokenizer (Koehn et al., 2007) before tokenization to make space-splitting easier in later tasks. However, we tokenized the dataset using Byte-Pair Encoding as a light step before processing for pretraining.

Transfer Pretraining

We carried out pretraining on a cased BERT-Base model, utilizing Google's pretraining scripts in conjunction with our unique unlabeled text corpora. The objective of pretraining the masked language model included a probability of 0.15 for a word to be masked, a maximum of 20 masked language model predictions, and an upper limit of 512 for sequence length. We ran the model through 1,000,000 steps of training, setting the learning rate at 1e-4 and the batch size at 256. We dedicated 157 h to train the model on a Google Cloud Tensor Processing Unit (TPU) v3-8, with an initial learning rate warmup period of 10,000 steps. ULMFiT utilized a 3-tier AWD-LSTM architecture, with an embedding dimension of 400 and a hidden dimension of 1150 for pretraining. For the embedding, RNN input, hidden-to-hidden transition, and RNN output, we employed dropout with the subsequent ratios: (0.1, 0.3, 0.3, 0.4). The recurrent weight matrices of the LSTM were dropped out by a factor of 0.5. During the 30 epochs of training, the model was trained with a weight decay of 0.1, a batch size of 128, and a learning rate of 1e-3. Slanted triangular learning rate schedules were used, and the Adam optimizer was used (Howard and Ruder, 2018). On a device featuring a single NVIDIA GEFORCE GTX GPU, the model underwent an 11-h training session.

Fine-Tuning

In our research, we sought to flourish a computer program which recognizes fictitious news stories with accuracy. To achieve this, we utilized a technique called fine-tuning, this entails customizing already-trained algorithms for a fresh assignment. The models used that were previously trained had already been trained on a huge body of text data, allowing them to learn the data's fundamental structures as well as trends. By using these pre-trained models as a starting point, we could save time and computational resources, as we didn't have to train our models from scratch. To modify the previously developed algorithms with the purpose of specifically identifying misleading information, we added a new classification layer or head to the existing model architecture. This freshly added tier would be the one in charge of figuring out if a specific news piece is true or not. The prediction model was then adjusted using an accumulation of labelled articles from newspapers, allowing the new classification layer to learn from the data and employ the fundamental trends of the model that was previously trained to the misleading issue of categorization. The benefit of this approach is that it allowed us to leverage the knowledge and expertise contained within the pre-trained weights and apply this to enhance the model's functionality for the given assignment. By adding the classification layer, we were able to tailor the model specifically to the given categorization task of misleading information, while still retaining the underlying architecture and knowledge of the pre-trained weights.

In our study, we utilized BERT, a widely used transformer-based language model, to perform fake news classification. To adapt BERT to the task at hand, The already trained BERT-Base model received an identification head that consists of just one linear layer from us (Fig. 5).

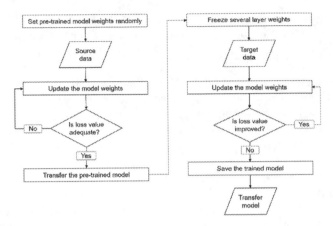

Fig. 5. Flowchart of the model transfer and the fine-tuning procedure.

We employed the fine-tuning technique to train our model on the fake news classification task. The job-specific data was used to train the added categorization head with the weights that were previously trained constant. We trained the model over three epochs with a 32 batch and a 0.000002 learning rate. Our findings showed that the BERT model's refined design performed better in classifying fake news than the BERT model that was already previously trained. The incorporation of the classification head allowed the model to better capture the nuances of the task at hand, resulting in improved performance. Overall, our results highlight the effectiveness of BERT in performing fake news classification and the importance of fine-tuning the model for task-specific applications.

During the research, we utilized ULMFiT, a transfer learning approach for NLP, for the purpose of misleading information classification. Initially, we adjusted the language frameworks for the counterfeit dataset for news, totaling to 10 epochs, implementing a 0.01 learning rate, 80 batches per batch, and a 0.3 weight decline. During this phase, we did not incorporate any additional classification heads into the model. In the concluding stage of fine-tuning, we integrated a composite classification head into the model, comprising a linear layer followed by batch normalization, ReLU activation, another linear layer, and an additional batch normalization layer.

5   Results

The baseline model, a Siamese recurrent network, underwent testing on a counterfeit news classification task and secured an accuracy of 79% on the test set. We investigated transfer learning (TL) methodologies as a strategy to enhance performance. Our findings indicate that Transfer Learning techniques surpassed the Siamese network baseline. We fine-tuned a couple of distinct pre-trained language models: BERT and ULMFiT. BERT attained a final accuracy of 89%, representing an 11% improvement over the Siamese network's performance. ULMFiT reached a final accuracy of 93%, signifying a 15% improvement over the Siamese network. We theorize that the superior performance of the TL models can be attributed to the preserved pre-trained knowledge in the language models utilized for fine-tuning. The pretraining phase aids the models in forming relationships between text, enabling improved performance on stylometric-based tasks with minimal fine-tuning.

6 Conclusion

After researching extensively, we have concluded that it is extremely vital to distinguish fake news because it circulates quickly through the internet. However, it can be difficult to do so in languages where there is limited data available. To solve this problem, we have studied various methods to create accurate classifiers using only a small amount of data. Our research shows that using transfer learning methods can be very effective in creating strong fake news classifiers. Moreover, we have also shown that transformer-based techniques can be adapted to different writing styles by using multitask learning. Our study provides valuable insights into how these techniques can be used to identify fake news in languages where resources are limited.

References

1. Mall, S.: Heart diagnosis using deep neural network, accepted in 3rd International Conference on Computational Intelligence and Knowledge Economy ICCIKE 2023, Amity University, Dubai, 2023
2. Sharma, N., et al.: A smart ontology-based IoT framework for remote patient monitoring. Biomed. Signal Process. Control **68**(March), 102717 (2021). https://doi.org/10.1016/j.bspc.2021.102717
3. Kumar, S., Pathak, S.K.: A comprehensive study of XSS attack and the digital forensic models to gather the evidence. ECS Trans. **107**(1) (2022)
4. Sharan, A.: Term co-occurrence and context window based combined approach for query expansion with the semantic notion of terms. Int. J. Web Sci. (IJWS) Inderscience **3**(1) (2017)
5. Upreti, K., Gupta, A.K., Dave, N., Surana, A., Mishra, D.: Deep learning approach for hand drawn emoji identification. In: 2022 IEEE International Conference on Current Development in Engineering and Technology (CCET), Bhopal, India, pp. 1–6 (2022). https://doi.org/10.1109/CCET56606.2022.10080218
6. Yadav, C.S., et al.: Malware analysis in IoT & android systems with defensive mechanism. Electronics **11**, 2354 (2022). https://doi.org/10.3390/electronics11152354
7. Kumar, R.: Lexical co-occurrence and contextual window-based approach with semantic similarity for query expansion. Int. J. Intell. Inf. Technol. (IJIIT) IGI **13**(3), 57–78 (2017)
8. Berghout, T., Benbouzid, M., Muyeen, S.M.: Machine learning for cybersecurity in smart grids: a comprehensive review-based study on methods, solutions, and prospects. Int. J. Crit. Infrastruct. Prot. **38**(May), 100547 (2022). https://doi.org/10.1016/j.ijcip.2022.100547
9. Sajid, M., Rajak, R.: Capacitated vehicle routing problem using algebraic particle swarm optimization with simulated annealing algorithm. In: Artificial Intelligence in Cyber-Physical Systems. CRC Press (2023)
10. Bohat, V.K.: Neural network model for recommending music based on music genres. In: 10th IEEE International Conference on Computer Communication and Informatics (ICCCI -2021), Coimbatore, INDIA, 27–29 January 2021
11. Goswami, A., Sharma, D., Mathuku, H., Gangadharan, S.M.P., Yadav, C.S.: Change detection in remote sensing image data comparing algebraic and machine learning methods. Electronics Article id: 1505208 (2022)

12. Lin, C.T., et al.: IoT-based wireless polysomnography intelligent system for sleep monitoring. IEEE Access **6** (2017)
13. Yadav, A., Kumar, S., Singh, J.: A review of physical unclonable functions (PUFs) and its applications in IoT environment. In: Hu, Y.C., Tiwari, S., Trivedi, M.C., Mishra, K.K. (eds.) Ambient Communications and Computer Systems. LNNS, vol. 356, pp. 1–13. Springer, Singapore (2022). https://doi.org/10.1007/978-981-16-7952-0_1
14. Prasad, M., Daraghmi, Y., Tiwari, P., Yadav, P., Bharill, N.: Fuzzy logic hybrid model with semantic filtering approach for pseudo relevance feedback- based query expansion. In: 2017 IEEE Symposium Series on Computational Intelligence (SSCI) (2017)

Deep Learning Envisioned Accident Detection System

Intekhab Alam, Ayush Verma, and Manju Khari$^{(\boxtimes)}$

Jawaharlal Nehru University, New Delhi 110067, India
{intekh31_scs,ayushv34_scs}@jnu.ac.in, manjukhari@yahoo.co.in

Abstract. The conflict between computational overhead and detection accuracy affects nearly every Automated Accident Detection (AAD) system. Although the accuracy of detection and classification approaches has recently improved dramatically, the systems' high computational resource requirements make them unsuitable for deployment in situations when immediate feedback is required. This paper suggests a strategy for developing an accurate, cost-efficient automatic collision identification system that can be deployed with a minimal amount of hardware. The AAD system is divided into three key phases—Detection, Tracking, and Classification and offers computationally reduced intensive algorithms for each of these stages. For the detection phase, YOLOv3, it uses a deep learning model that has been trained through knowledge distillation. Its accuracy is on par with that of YOLO (You-Only-Look-Once). On the basis of the information inference and data mining techniques COCO (Common Objects in Context) dataset, YOLOv3 surpasses all other identification techniques considering runtime complexity, averaging an astounding 30 frames/second on a low-end system. It attains an Average Precision (AP) mark of 44.8. For the tracking phase, the system makes use of SORT (Simple Online Real-time Tracking). Since a radial basis kernel with a support vector machine works efficiently, an area under the curve (or AUC) score of 0.92 is achieved. Alongside this, this paper examines a number of machine-learning techniques for the classification stage.

Keywords: Automatic Accident Detection · Computer Vision · Deep Learning · YOLO · Vehicle Tracking

1 Introduction

Moving both individuals and possessions from one place to another requires efficient and effective transportation in today's world. However, there are also major risks associated with transportation, most notably in terms of accidents. Traffic accidents cause millions of deaths and injuries each year, posing a severe threat to global public health. Traffic accidents have a substantial social and economic impact as well, costing an estimated $518 billion annually throughout the globe [1]. The causes of traffic accidents are complex and multifaceted, involving a combination of human, environmental, and technological factors. Human factors, such as driver behavior and error, are the most

KC Santosh et al. (Eds.): RTIP2R 2023, CCIS 2026, pp. 25–38, 2024.
https://doi.org/10.1007/978-3-031-53082-1_3

common cause of accidents, accounting for up to 90% of all accidents [2]. Accidents can also be caused by environmental variables, like as weather and road design. Technological factors, such as vehicle design and safety features, can help mitigate the risk of accidents but can also introduce new risks, such as distracted driving. To address the issue of traffic accidents, researchers and engineers have been exploring various approaches to develop intelligent transportation systems that can detect and prevent accidents in real-time. These systems can help reduce the number of accidents and improve overall road safety, ultimately leading to more efficient and sustainable transportation systems. Advanced technologies like artificial intelligence and computer vision enable the development of intelligent solutions capable of real-time accident detection and prevention, ultimately saving lives and improving the overall efficiency of our transportation systems. In addition to the human and economic costs of traffic accidents, there are also broader societal implications to consider.

Traffic accidents can lead to significant disruptions in transportation systems, causing delays and inefficiencies that can have a ripple effect on other aspects of society, such as commerce and healthcare. Additionally, accidents involving vehicles can harm the environment, particularly through air pollution and greenhouse gas emissions. To address these broader societal implications, it is essential to take a holistic approach to transportation and accident prevention. This approach should involve a combination of technological solutions, such as intelligent transportation systems, as well as policy and regulatory measures, such as improved road safety regulations and enforcement of traffic laws. Additionally, public education and awareness campaigns can help raise understanding about the risks of traffic accidents and encourage safer driving behaviors. In conclusion, transportation and accidents are inextricably linked, with traffic accidents posing significant risks to public health, the economy, and the environment. By investing in research and development in this field, we can develop innovative solutions that can help reduce the number of accidents and improve overall road safety, ultimately leading to more efficient and sustainable transportation systems. Additionally, by taking a holistic approach to transportation and accident prevention, we can address the broader societal implications of traffic accidents and create a safer, more sustainable future for all.

The rest of this paper is organized as follows: Sect. 2 discusses about literature survey and previous works related to accident detection systems. Section 3 explains the methodology followed for implementation of algorithms. Section 4 discusses the results and validation measures for comparison among various algorithms. Section 5 concludes the paper with overview of the paper and future directions.

2   Literature Survey

Kapri et al. [3] devised a system which states that in a remote location when no one is present for reporting it, an accident could happen. High-end vehicles now come equipped with hardware elements that may detect and record accidents. Unfortunately, these gadgets are immovable and pricey.

A system using HDy Copilot, an Android app, was recommended by Fernandes et al. [4] for detecting accidents related to multimodal alert dissemination. The user can also access the app, get notifications from nearby vehicles for potential road dangers, and stop the countdown timer if a false collision is discovered by using an android phone, which is also used to access the app. When a car crash happens, an alert is sent out to all nearby vehicles, and texts and phone calls are also made to the rescue number. This is demonstrated on the e-Call platform. However, the core problem—phone breakage or signal loss—remains unchanged, making the gadget ineffective.

Piedad et al. [5] analysis is based on Hungarian algorithm information inference and data mining techniques. It developed a paradigm that outlines a smart system that detects traffic problems across vehicle networks quickly, warns of them, and evaluates their seriousness. The authors have created and used a prototype towards automated accidents. After a careful examination of all pertinent characteristics, the results demonstrated that a vehicle's speed is a significant contributing element in front collisions. The explored classification algorithms do not significantly differ from one another, and they do demonstrate that the efficiency of the model can be markedly improved unless accidents are classed according to the impacts, especially in front crashes in which the vehicle is usually the one that strikes.

According to Priyanka et al. [6] description of this technique, aims to avoid accidents by identifying the driver's circumstances, such as when they are too tired or unfit to drive. Infrared Radiation reflecting obstacle sensors are used to determine the positioning of the eyes. The sensor transmits to the controller a weak signal as soon as the eyes open, and a high signal after the eyes have been closed for at least four seconds. Input from the sensor is processed by the PIC controller to turn on or off the alarm system and, if the alarm sound is ON, display "Driver Slept" on the display. The low or high signal is processed by the controller. The low or high signal is processed by the controller. As therefore, driver is informed possibly avoiding a serious collision. Since fatigue plays a large role in accidents, this kind of technology offers an especially efficient way of preventing such occurrences. Although the system offers a means of preventing accidents brought on by drunkenness, the fact that it does not offer damage detection means that there may be further reasons that are not discovered and the emergency contacts are not informed would be a serious drawback.

According to Bewley et al. [7], the primary goal of this study's measured approach of multiple item detection and tracking is to effectively connect objects for usage in actual time as well as online applications. For this reason, it is shown that tracking performance is greatly influenced by detection quality and that improving the algorithm can improve tracking up to 18.9%. Even though the tracking components of this system are only tracked using a straightforward combination of well-known methods, which include the Kalman Filter with Hungarian algorithm, it nonetheless achieves tracking accuracy on par with other online trackers. The tracker changes at an average rate of 260 Hz, which is around 20x faster with respect to other cutting-edge trackers.

Dogru et al. [8] proposed system broadcasts traffic alerts to the drivers using simulated data obtained from vehicular ad-hoc network (VANETs) relying on the velocity as well as position of the cars. Additionally, it demonstrates how ITS may use machine learning methods to detect collisions on freeways. In order to develop a model that can identify between accident cases and usual cases, supervised machine learning methods like random forest models (RF), Artificial Neural Networks (ANN), and support vector machine are used to traffic data. In terms of accuracy, the RF algorithm was found to perform superior to the ANN and SVM algorithms. With 91.56% accuracy, the RF algorithm performed better than the SVM (88.71%) and the ANN (90.02%) algorithms.

Chand et al. [9] presented a cutting-edge support system for self-driving automobiles that can detect collisions using a dashboard camera. The system uses the centroid tracker technique for recognizing the observed vehicle and the Mask R-CNN framework to detect cars. In order to determine whether an accident has taken place amongst all of the recognized vehicles, the approach additionally computes a number of factors, including as speed, momentum, and trajectory.

Tsuji et al. [10] address the construction of an extensive pedestrian detecting system. They discuss the placement of the cameras, coordinate systems, simple IR-based recognition, surveillance, computing relative movement vectors, and collision evaluation standards.

Wakim et al. [11] propose a Markovian hypothesis to explain pedestrian behavior. Using a hidden Markov model, the dynamics of pedestrians are represented by four states: sitting still, strolling, jogging, and running. The likelihood of changing states is shown on a model transition diagram. The probability distributions of absolute speed and change in direction were modeled as truncated Gaussians for each state. Collision probabilities are forecasted using Monte-Carlo simulations.

In their Probabilistic framework for multi-object tracking, Antonini et al. [12] used this setup to analyze pedestrian trajectory and assign marks for doing so. The way a pedestrian's body is oriented frequently reveals important details about the direction of movement to come. Therefore, determining the pedestrian orientation may help with motion prediction and provide more accurate collision probability predictions. Support Vector Machines based on Hartley wavelet coefficients are used by Poggio et al. [13] to estimate a person's orientation and classify amongst various orientations. To extract the automobile's characteristics (velocity, momentum, and direction), Zu et al. [14] use the Mean Shift algorithms for tracking as well as a motion detection using the Gaussian Mixture Model (GMM). Ren et al. [15] suggestion is to first extract segments of road and line positions before applying background subtraction for obtaining moving objects. Then a time and space graphic with a traffic tracking graph is produced. For classification and accident recognition, a Support Vector Machine (SVM) was employed.

3   Methodology

Our system is designed to automate incident detection in real-time using a three-phase process: detection, tracking, and classification. In the detection phase, we employ the You Only Look Once (YOLO) method [16], a popular deep learning algorithm, to identify and categorize moving cars in images and video frames. YOLO divides the input into a grid-like arrangement of cells and predicts box boundaries and class likelihoods for each cell. This approach is faster than traditional object detection algorithms and allows for the detection of multiple items in a single pass. The YOLO method has proven to be versatile and can be applied to various tasks beyond accident detection, including traffic monitoring, vehicle counting, and license plate recognition [17]. The data generated by these systems can be valuable for traffic management and law enforcement organizations. To track the detected cars over time, we utilize the Simple Online and Realtime Tracking (SORT) algorithm. SORT combines well with YOLO, as it focuses on object tracking while YOLO excels at object identification and categorization. Studies have demonstrated that the YOLO and SORT algorithms achieve high accuracy and reliability in object detection and tracking [18]. In the classification stage, we evaluate different machine learning techniques to classify the segmented automobile images from the detection phase into damaged and undamaged classes. This step allows us to assess the state of damage for each detected car. By employing less computationally intensive algorithms for each stage, we aim to create a reliable and economically affordable real-time incident alert system that requires minimal equipment. In addition to accident detection, other related works have explored the application of deep learning techniques for driver safety. For instance, a real-time driver drowsiness detection model based on facial features has been proposed [19]. This system quickly detects signs of drowsiness in drivers and provides warnings to ensure their safety. The YOLO developers have provided a range of trained models with different backbone classifiers. Table 1 showcases the model size, performance, parameter quantity, and layer depth for several backbone classifiers on the ImageNet validation benchmark. Among these classifiers, MobileNet-v2 stands out for its competitive performance and minimal memory and processing requirements. Therefore, we have employed the pretrained YOLO-v3 model, which utilizes MobileNet-v2 as the backbone, for both the teacher and student models. Figure 1 represents the top-level design of the proposed methodology.

Table 1. Multiple backbone classifier model's depth, parameter count and size.

Classifier	Size	Parameter	Depth	Accuracy
VGG19	543 MB	143 M	26	72%
ResNet50	100 MB	25 M	20	74.6%
ResNet101	175 MB	44 M	20	76.9%
MobileNet	16 MB	4 M	90	71%
MobileNetV2	14 MB	3 M	90	72.5%

3.1 Phase 1 - Vehicle Detection

In view of the necessity for significant recall and computing lightness, we used the YOLO v3 vehicle recognition method, which is computationally light and has a high recall. YOLO v3 is ahead of the pack for a number of reasons, including its:

- Quickness
- Detection precision
- Excellent generalization
- Freely available

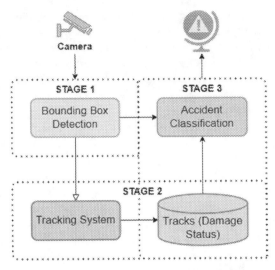

Fig. 1. Top-level design of the suggested system

Implementing the following four methods, the algorithm operates:

1. **Grid blocks:** In this first step, uniformly shaped N × N cell grids are created from the original image (A). The class of every grid cell and the confidence value of probability value should be predicted locally. This is done along with the coverage of the item of grid cell.

2. **Bounding box:** The next step is to localize the borders of the bounding box. These boxes are the rectangles that cover/bound every article present in the image. It is possible to have several box boundaries as there are items in each image. All the final bounding boxes are stored in Y which is the final matrix/vector form of each bounding box.

$$Y = [px, bc, bd, bh, bw, C1, C2] \tag{1}$$

This is especially important when the model is being trained.

- The value of px denotes the object's square's likelihood value.
- The x and y location coordinates of the center of the bounding box with respect to the adjacent grid cell - bc and bd.
- The letters bh and bw stand for the bounded box's height and breadth in reference to the adjacent grid cell.
- The classes $C1$ and $C2$ serve as substitutes for Player or Ball, respectively. More classes are available if your use cases require them.

IOU (Intersection Over Union): The IOU's (a value within 0 and 1) purpose is to eliminate such grid boxes and retain only the necessary ones. Here is the reasoning for it:

The IOU selection threshold is set by the user and can be, for example, 0.5.

The IOU, which is the the intersection Region divide by the Union Area, is then calculated for each grid cell using YOLO.

Finally, it considers grid cells with an an IOU > limit rather than those predicted to have an IOU threshold.

Non-Maximum Suppression: Setting an IOU ceiling isn't always enough because an item could have many boxes with IOU that's over the limit, and if all of those boxes are left open, noise might get in. It can be used in this situation to conserve only the items having the best chance of being found.

Dataset

For YOLOv3 training, made use of the Boxy Automobiles Dataset [20]. Since the primary purpose of the Boxy cars dataset was to train vehicle identification algorithm in self-driving systems, the majority of the dataset's photos include automobiles in traffic and on roads. Given that our system receives CCTV footage from scenes of busy highways and traffic, for our use case, this dataset works out exactly right. This files include 200,000 1232×1028-pixel photos with 1,990,806 automobiles tagged with 2D and 3D bounding rectangles. During the distillation training phase, annotated images (ground truth) which are two-dimensional are used as hard labels. Figure 2 represents a sample image of the dataset which is used for YOLOv3 training.

Fig. 2. Two-dimensional bounding boxes with annotations

Preprocessing

The dataset's images are all down scaled to 512×512 resolution, and the trained YOLO v3 using ResNet152 backbone classifier is used to generate the custom annotation or soft labels. A three-dimensional tensor with the shape 19*19*85 that recognizes and categorizes items from the MS-COCO dataset that correspond to 80 different classes is predicted of the trained model (teacher model). Here only exists one class, "Vehicle," that has to be identified by our system. As a result, our model's (the student model's) output is a 3D tensor with the shape 19*19*6 as represented in Fig. 3. From the 80 potential subclasses in the MS-COCO dataset, only four classes are predicted—"motorcycle," "car," "truck," and "bus"—are used to produce soft labels for each image.

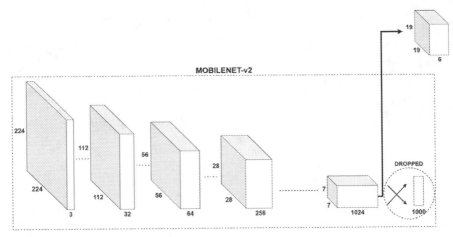

Fig. 3. Yolo architecture. A 19*19*6 tensor replaces MobileNet-v2's last classification

Training

During training, when an object is identified in bounding box, the loss of classification (Eq. 2) in each cell equals the squared variance of the category's conditional probability for every class:

$$L_1 = \sum_{i=0}^{s^2} 1_i^{obj} \sum_{c \in classes} \left(p_i(c) - \hat{p}_i(c) \right)^2 \tag{2}$$

where $1_i^{obj} = 1$ if an object shows up in cell i, otherwise 0. p̂i(c) signifies the conditional likelihood for class c in cell i.

Localization loss (Eq. 3): Localization loss calculates the variances in expected sizes aa well as placements of the boundary boxes.

$$L_2 = \lambda_{coord} \sum_{i=0}^{s^2} \sum_{j=0}^{B} 1_{ij}^{obj} \left[\left(x_i - \hat{x}_i \right)^2 + \left(y_i - \hat{y}_i \right)^2 \right]$$
$$+ \lambda_{coord} \sum_{i=0}^{s^2} \sum_{j=0}^{B} 1_{ij}^{obj} \left[\left(\sqrt{w_i} - \sqrt{\hat{w}_i} \right)^2 + \left(\sqrt{h} - \sqrt{\hat{h}_i} \right)^2 \right] \tag{3}$$

where λ_{coord} in order to compensate up for the loss of boundary box coordinates, increase the weight. $1_{ij}^{obj} = 1$ if the object's identity is determined by the jth border box in cell i, else 0, x, and y represent box offsets. Box dimensions are w and h, respectively.

Confidence loss (Eq. 4): If a box-containing object is found, the following degree of confidence loss occurs:

$$L_3 = \sum_{i=0}^{s^2} \sum_{j=0}^{B} 1_{ij}^{obj} \left(C_i - \hat{C}_i \right)^2 \tag{4}$$

where $1_{ij}^{obj} = 1$ Ci is the border box's rating of the box j in cell i, if the jth border box in cell i is responsible for detecting the object, otherwise 0. The degree of degree of confidence loss is following in the absence of an object being found in the box. (Eq. 5):

$$L_4 = \lambda_{noobj} \sum_{i=0}^{s^2} \sum_{j=0}^{B} 1_{ij}^{noobj} \left(C_i - \hat{C}_i \right)^2 \tag{5}$$

where is 1_{ij}^{noobj} is complement of 1_{ij}^{obj}

When identifying the background, λ_{noobj} weighs down the loss by using the box confidence value of boxes j in cell i, or C_i.

Equation 1: For truth predictions, combined training loss: $Lg = L1 + L2 + L3 + L4$.

Equation 2: Soft label loss:

$$L_s = \sum_{i=1}^{19} \sum_{j=1}^{19} \sum_{k=1}^{6} \left(y_{ijk} - \hat{y}_{ijk}\right)^2 \tag{6}$$

where y_{ijk} denotes the expectation of the student YOLOv3model.

and $\hat{y}_{ijk}$ denotes the expectation of the teacher YOLOv3model.

Equation 3: Combined YOLOv3 training loss:

$$L = L_s * \alpha + (1 - \alpha)L_g \tag{7}$$

where $\alpha \in [0,1]$ is a hyperparameter used to measure soft label loss.

Evaluation Metrics: We computed the AP value on the preprocessed dataset to assess the detection ability of our model. The accuracy of detectors for objects is frequently assessed using the AP, or average precision score.

$$AP = \int p(r)dr \tag{8}$$

3.2   Phase 2 - Vehicle Tracking

The major goal of SORT's pragmatic approach to tracking many objects is to associate them effectively for online as well as real-time applications. Despite merely employing a simple combination of well-known methods for the tracking components, like the Kalman Filter along with Hungarian algorithm, this method achieves an accuracy on par with cutting-edge online trackers. Additionally, relative to other competing methods, it delivers exceptional runtime speed because of its simplicity. The localization and velocity of each vehicle's bounding box were considered by the writers in SORT, and in order to approximate values from previously collected data, they employed Kalman filtering. Then, depending on the Euclidean distance between each of the bounding boxes, they utilized the Hungarian assignment algorithm to assign each one to previously established tracks or, if the distance was too great, to initialize a new track. A recursive method called the Kalman filter determines the current state of a system using noisy measurements. The system's state shows the position and motion of an object in a video stream when it comes to online real-time tracking. The measurements of an object's position, its noise characteristics, and the current state estimation are all inputs to the Kalman filter. The updated state estimate is then generated, considering the fresh measurements, and dampening the impact of measurement noise. The process is described in Fig. 4.

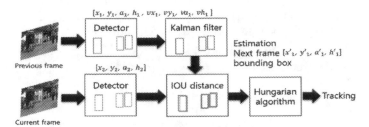

Fig. 4. SORT Tracking

The object detections are assigned to the tracks using Hungarian algorithm. The assignment issue, which is the challenge of assigning a set of items to a set of targets, is solved by a combinatorial optimization algorithm. In the framework of online real-time surveillance, the targets are the previously established tracks, and the objects represent detected in the current frame. Hungarian algorithm places each detection on the line of track that is physically closest to it. The overall distance between each of the detection and the tracks is calculated for this assignment to be as short as possible. The shape 19*19*6 of image which the algorithm allocates detections to tracked objects in a way that reduces the overall distance between them, whereas the Kalman filter offers precise state estimations of the object across time. In computer vision applications like tracking objects in CCTV cameras, autonomous cars, and robotics, this strategy is frequently utilized.

3.3   Phase 3 - Accident Classification

The images of the detected vehicles are extracted using the bounding box obtained from the input frame. After that, each image is categorized based on the extent of damage. An accident was caused by a damaged automobile, according to higher damage status. To categorize identified vehicle photos for damage state, a SVM was trained using a radial basis kernel. The training methodology is covered in detail in the section that follows.

Dataset Used

The classification model was trained using the Accident dataset (Pasheai al., 2019). There are 10,480 photos of both damaged and undamaged autos in the dataset. The majority of the samples in the repository were downloaded from websites. This results, a larger share is made up of excellent photos. The size of the dataset is roughly 1.5 GB. The photos are 640 × 480 pixels in size and in the JPEG format. Each image in the collection is given a class label (damaged or undamaged) that corresponds to it.

Preprocessing

Every picture in this data set is transformed to grayscale color space and down sampled to 224*224 resolution. Given that the majority of the database's photos were directly.

Most of the content was taken from the internet and was of great quality. We have included nominal noise in Gaussian form to simulate inputs directly acquired from lower-resolution CCTVs to boost the generalization of the model's results in deployment. Such a process has demonstrated a notable improvement in accuracy at the inference time.

Fig. 5. Label 1 for "damaged vehicle" & Label 2 for "undamaged vehicle"

Training

For the purpose of categorising vehicle photos into damaged and undamaged categories, we trained the SVM using radial basis kernel. The standard configuration in scikit-learn, a Python language tool that is used for training the SVM, is 1.0 for the most important SVM parameter, slackness, and 0.1 for the gamma value of the radial basis function. Figure 5 represents the classification for vehicles.

Evaluation Metrics

To assess the classification performance of the SVM classifier, recall and precision were evaluated. Accuracy and memory are important factors to consider when evaluating models. Precision is with regard to of runtime complexity defined as the group of correctly classified positive instances amongst all occurrences, whereas recall is the percentage of every instance in the positive category that were correctly labelled.

4 Results

YOLOv3 surpasses all other detection methods on the MS-COCO datasets. Therefore, driver is informed runtime complexity as well averaging a startling 30 frames per second on a low-end PC. This results in an average precision (AP) value of 44.8. Simple Online Real Time Tracking, or SORT, is used for the tracking step, and for the stage of classification, various machine learning techniques are compared and shown that the support vector machine technique with a radial basis kernel excels over the opposition with an AUC. Table 2 shows the AP score and runtime of various models when used with ResNetv2 as backbone classifier. Table 3 shows the Precision, Recall and F-score of various classification algorithms.

Table 2. Performance evaluation of several detection algorithms

Model	AP score	Run Time(fps)
Faster R-CNN	34.7	15
Single Shot Detectors	31.2	19
Yolo v3	44.8	30

Table 3. The accident classification model's performance

Model	Precision	Recall	F1-score
Random Forest	0.85	0.79	0.82
Decision Tree	0.70	0.69	0.70
SVM(linear) Classifier	0.82	0.81	0.82

4.1 AUC-ROC Analysis

A typical statistic for assessing the efficacy of binary classification algorithms is the area under a curve (AUC). It evaluates the model's ability to distinguish between positive and negative categories. AUC has a range of 0 to 1, with 0.5 suggesting that the algorithm is no better than guessing at random and 1 suggesting perfect classification. Here we are classifying between two labels accident vs non-accidents. Figure 6 represents the AUC using various algorithms - decision tree attains 0.91, random forest attains 0.70, linear SVM achieves 0.91 and SVM achieves 0.92.

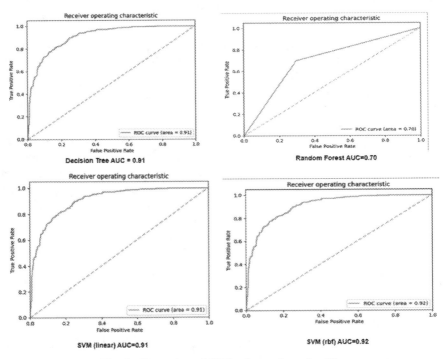

Fig. 6. Illustration of AUC using various algorithms

5 Conclusion

The relationship between computational overhead and detection accuracy affects nearly every AAD system. The study offers a way for creating a real-time, AAD system that is both reliable and affordable in terms of computing. The suggested system seeks to address the trade-off between computing overhead and detection accuracy by segmenting the model into three phases – Detection phase, tracking phase, and classification phase) and employing unique algorithm for each stage. YOLO v3 for the Detection stage are introduced. SORT is used for the tracking stage. The research evaluates various machine learning methods for the classification stage and determines that the SVM, which employs a radial basis kernel, is the best performance. Overall, the proposed method offers a viable solution to the problems of processing overhead and detection precision in AAD systems. The suggested method strikes a balance between computational effectiveness and accuracy, opening the door for the creation of useful and affordable real-time accident detection technologies. Future research directions in this field may include exploring the integration of other data sources, such as LiDAR and radar, to enhance the system's performance and robustness. Additionally, the development of more efficient and lightweight deep learning models, such as those based on neural architecture search, can help address the computational challenges associated with real-time processing. Finally, the incorporation of reinforcement learning and other advanced machine learning techniques can enable the system to adapt and improve its performance over time, further enhancing its effectiveness in detecting and preventing accidents.

As we continue to explore the possibilities of vision-based accident detection systems using deep learning, it is important to consider their broader implications and applications. These systems can be integrated with intelligent transportation systems (ITS), such as traffic signal control and dynamic traffic routing, leading to more efficient traffic management and improved road safety. Real-time accident detection enables faster emergency response, potentially saving lives and reducing the severity of injuries. The data collected by these systems is valuable for insurance companies and law enforcement agencies, aiding in determining accident causes and liability assessment. With the rise of autonomous vehicles, vision-based accident detection systems can ensure their safe operation by proactively detecting and avoiding potential accidents. Additionally, the data gathered can provide insights for urban planning and infrastructure development, helping design safer and more efficient transportation networks.

References

1. Road traffic injuries. World Health Organization, 21 June 2021. https://www.who.int/newsroom/fact-sheets/detail/road-traffic-injuries. Accessed 20 June 2023
2. Caroselli, Beachler & Coleman, L.L.C., 22 September 2021. https://www.cbmclaw.com/what-percentage-of-car-accidents-are-caused-by-human-error. Accessed 01 July 2023
3. Kapri, P., Patane, S., Shalom, A.: Accident Detection & Alert System, IEEE (2018)
4. Fernandes, B., Gomes, V., Ferreira, J., Oliveira, A.: Mobile Application for Automatic Accident Detection and Multimodal Alert, IEEE (2015)

5. Fogue, M., Garrido, P., Martinez, F.J.: System for Automatic Notification and Severity Estimation of Automotive Accidents, IEEE (2014)
6. Sankpal, P.M., More, P.P.: Accident avoidance system using IR transmitter. IJRASET 5(IV) (2017)
7. Bewley, A., Ge, Z., Ott, L., Ramos, F., Upcroft, B.: Simple online and realtime tracking. In: 2016 IEEE International Conference on Image Processing (ICIP), pp. 3464–3468 (2016). https://doi.org/10.1109/ICIP.2016.7533003
8. Dogru, N., Subasi, A.: Traffic accident detection using random forest classifier. In: 2018 15th Learning and Technology Conference (L&T), pp. 40–45 (2018). https://doi.org/10.1109/LT.2018.8368509
9. Chand, D., Gupta, S., Kavati, I.: Computer vision based accident detection for autonomous vehicles. In: 2020 IEEE 17th India Council International Conference (INDICON), pp. 1–6 (2020). https://doi.org/10.1109/INDICON49873.2020.9342226
10. Tsuji, T., Hattori, H., Watanabe, M., Nagaoka, N.: Development of night-vision system. IEEE Trans. Intell. Transp. Syst. 3(3), 203–209 (2002)
11. Wakim, C., Capperon, S., Oksman, J.: A Markovian model of pedestrian behavior. In: Proceedings of the IEEE International Conference on Systems, Man, and Cybernetics, pp. 4028–4033, October 2004
12. Antonini, G., Venegas, S., Thiran, J.P., Bierlaire, M.: A discrete choice pedestrian behavior model for pedestrian detection in visual tracking systems. In: Proceedings of the Advanced Concepts for Intelligent Vision Systems, Brussels, Belgium, September 2004
13. Shimizu, H., Poggio, T.: Direction Estimation of Pedestrian from Images, AI Memo 2003-020, Massachusetts Institute of Technology, August 2003. http://cbcl.mit.edu/cbcl/publications/aipublications/2003/AIM-2003-020.pdf
14. Hui, Z., Yaohua, X., Lu, M., Jiansheng, F.: Vision-based real-time traffic accident detection. In: Intelligent Control and Automation (WCICA), 2014 11th World Congress on, pp. 1035–1038, June 2014
15. Ren, J., Chen, Y., Xin, L., Shi, J., Li, B., Liu, Y.: Detecting and positioning of traffic incidents via video-based analysis of traffic states in a road segment. IET Intell. Transp. Syst. 10(6), 428–437 (2016)
16. Shafiee, M.J., Chywl, B., Li, F., Wong, A.: Fast YOLO: a fast you only look once system for real-time embedded object detection in video. J. Comput. Vis. Imaging Syst. 3 (2017). https://doi.org/10.15353/vsnl.v3i1.171
17. Lin, C.-J., Jeng, S.-Y., Lioa, H.-W.: A real-time vehicle counting, speed estimation, and classification system based on virtual detection Zone and YOLO. Math. Probl. Eng. 2021, 1–10 (2021). https://doi.org/10.1155/2021/1577614
18. Pillai, M.S., Chaudhary, G., Khari, M., et al.: Real-time image enhancement for an automatic automobile accident detection through CCTV using deep learning. Soft. Comput. 25, 11929–11940 (2021). https://doi.org/10.1007/s00500-021-05576-w
19. Singh, P.K., Gupta, A., Upadhyay, M., Jain, A., Khari, M., Lamba, P.S.: Multimodal driver drowsiness detection from video frames. J. Mob. Multimed. 19(02), 567–586 (2022). https://doi.org/10.13052/jmm1550-4646.19210
20. Behrendt, K.: Boxy vehicle detection in large images. In: 2019 IEEE/CVF International Conference on Computer Vision Workshop (ICCVW), pp. 840–846 (2019)

Revolutionizing Drug Discovery: Unleashing AI's Potential in Pharmaceutical Innovation

Ashish Singh Chauhan[1]([✉]), Samta Kathuria[2], Anita Gehlot[3], and G. Sunil[4]

[1] UIPS, Division of Research and Innovation, Uttaranchal University, Dehradun, India
ashishchauhan.pharmacy@gmail.com
[2] LCD, Division of Research and Innovation, Uttaranchal University, Dehradun, India
[3] UIT, Division of Research and Innovation, Uttaranchal University, Dehradun, India
[4] School of Computer Science and Artificial Intelligence, SR University, Warangal, India

Abstract. Artificial Intelligence (AI) technologies, including machine learning, and deep learning, have enabled the efficient analysis of vast datasets, ranging from molecular structures to clinical trial results. These techniques speed up the initial stages of drug discovery by making it easier to predict possible drug candidates, improve molecular designs, and identify novel targets. The study analyses the AI models to learn complex patterns and relationships, which enables them to make accurate predictions about the efficacy, toxicity, and interactions of drugs. AI algorithms are used in this study to predict the success of drug discovery and to estimate accurate predictions. The study also identified which AI algorithms provide a good predicted result. In conclusion, AI algorithms have evolved into crucial instruments in the search for new drugs, significantly increasing the predictability of the identification of potential drug candidates. The precision and effectiveness of this transformative process promise to be further improved by ongoing developments in AI technology and data accessibility.

Keywords: Drug Discovery · Artificial Intelligence · Deep Learning

1 Introduction

According to the Center for Drug Evaluation and Research (CDER), the key areas and potential policy developments concern the integration of AI in pharmaceutical manufacturing. The focus is on evaluating the current regulatory framework and identifying gaps that need to be addressed. Establishing a regulatory framework for advanced manufacturing evaluation aims to accommodate AI implementation while considering the impact on existing technologies and facilities. Public input through the docket will play a central role in shaping future policy decisions by CDER [1]. Based on this data, a Precedent research data report shows that the market for generative AI in pharmaceuticals is booming, with hundreds of millions of dollars in additional income expected between 2023 and 2032. The relevant UN Sustainable Development Goals in this study are represented by Sustainable Development Goal 3 (SDG3): Make sure everyone lives a healthy life and promote well-being at all ages [2]. The global market for artificial intelligence in the pharmaceutical industry is anticipated to reach USD 1.24 billion in 2022 with a CAGR of 32.3% due to the industry's rapid adoption of AI [3].

KC Santosh et al. (Eds.): RTIP2R 2023, CCIS 2026, pp. 39–50, 2024.
https://doi.org/10.1007/978-3-031-53082-1_4

Artificial Intelligence (AI) is a scientific field that plays a crucial role in the pharmaceutical industry. Some areas where AI is used in pharmaceutical formulation include Drug discovery and design, Virtual screening, Formulation optimization, Predicting drug-excipient compatibility, Personalized medicine, quality control, safety and toxicity assessment and clinical trial optimization. Developing a drug discovery using AI requires deep knowledge of Pharmacokinetics and pharmacodynamics [4].

This study describes the AI techniques used in different areas of Drug discovery. Artificial Intelligence (AI) is transforming the pharmaceutical industry, particularly in drug formulation, by leveraging the power of data analytics, machine learning, and computational modelling. How AI is used in pharmaceutical companies to get to market faster with discoveries.

The above-mentioned areas are covered using emerging technology. To discuss the emerging AI technology used in Drug discovery, and how it is giving a new direction to the pharmaceutical sector. The contribution of the study is as follows:

- The essential concepts and significance of digitisation in drug design are discussed.
- Artificial Intelligence enforcement in Drug stability prediction, Risk Prediction in Drug Discovery Development and reducing animal testing.
- AI's implementation algorithms in Drug Discovery are examined, using machine learning, especially deep learning.
- Future directions in research on drug discovery medicine are discussed, along with a thorough overview of the current research challenges.

The organization of this study is carried out in the following context. Section 2 of the study presents an overview of the use of AI in drug discovery and its potential for pharmaceutical innovation. Section 3 represents enabling AI technologies in drug discovery applications. Section 4 gives a summary of the accuracy of the AI algorithm used in different drug discovery applications and shows the average accuracy data in different applications. Section 5 emphasizes the limitations and challenges in the potential to revolutionize drug discovery. Section 6 concludes the paper by comparing AI algorithm accuracy data and is an active research area with a lot of directions of research for the future reader.

2 Overview of Technology

Drug discovery is a crucial step in drug development, Due to the deployment of computer-aided, high-throughput screening, drug design, and combinatorial chemistry, drug discovery makes up a sizable portion of machine learning applications in pharmaceutical sciences. However, Drug design and discovery face several challenges that can be addressed or improved using Artificial Intelligence techniques [5].

Artificial intelligence can process large amounts of data in a way that humans cannot. AI in drug discovery, more than 1060 molecules form a huge chemical space that support the creation of many different pharmacological compounds. However, the process of developing a drug is constrained by a lack of cutting-edge technologies, making it take time and be a costly endeavour that can be resolved by applying AI. AI can quickly validate hit and lead compounds, as well as expedite therapeutic target validation and structural design optimization [6].

AI can significantly impact Drug discovery by accelerating development, improving drug quality, enabling personalized medicine, and reducing costs. However, it's essential to validate AI models thoroughly and integrate them effectively into the drug development workflow to maximize their benefits in the pharmaceutical industry.

3 Enabling Technology

The development of artificial intelligence (AI) has resulted in a vast expansion in the field of medicine AI plays an important role in pharmaceutical research when it comes to creating new compounds with specific characteristics and functions. Traditional approaches often involve identifying and altering pre-existing molecules, but this can be a labour and time intensive process. On the other hand, AI-based methods can accelerate the process of creating new compounds with desirable properties and activities. For example, recently a deep learning (DL) system has been trained on a dataset of well-known pharmacological molecules and their relevant features to suggest a new therapeutic molecule [7]. AI is applied in medicinal chemistry to predict the effectiveness and toxicity of potential drug compounds. Traditional approaches to drug discovery often rely on time-consuming and labor-intensive experimentation to assess a compound's potential effects on the human body. Multiple data points are analyzed by ML algorithms, which can identify trends and patterns that human researchers might not be able to [8].

Novel approaches to AI in drug discovery can be usefully divided into four parts: drug design, poly-pharmacology, drug repurposing, and drug screening Fig. 1. The use of AI

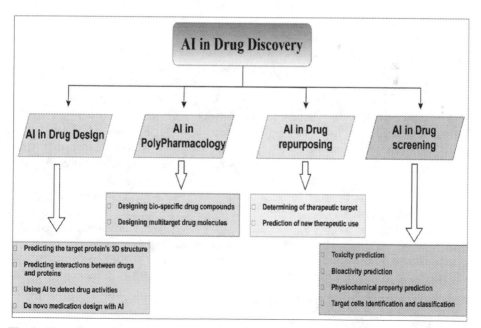

Fig. 1. Drug discovery using artificial intelligence (AI). Various applications of drug discovery can effectively use AI, including drug design, poly-pharmacology, drug repurposing, and drug screening.

in a primary stage is to predict drug properties, which might minimize the requirement for clinical trials, it would be advantageous both financially and ethically [9].

3.1 AI in Drug Design (DD)

AI and ML algorithms can analyse biological data to identify potential drug targets. By processing large-scale genomic and proteomic datasets, AI can highlight specific molecules or proteins that may be crucial in disease pathways and could be targeted by new drugs. AI can analyse databases of approved drugs and their known interactions to find new therapeutic applications for existing medications [9]. This strategy can speed up drug development as repurposing an approved drug often requires less time and cost compared to developing a completely new compound [10]. In silico virtual screening involves using computational methods, often driven by ML models, to analyse the interactions between potential drug candidates and target molecules. This process helps identify promising drug leads before they are physically tested in the laboratory [11].

Binary activity prediction is used by Support Vector Machine (SVMs) with supervised ML algorithms to distinguish between a drug and a non-drug or between a particular molecule and one that is not. To order the database compounds by decreasing activity likelihood, SVM classification is used in LBVS. Optimised special ranking functions are utilized to reduce errors in SVM ranking. A disease subtype can be found using the clustering approach for an unsupervised learning category, whereas a target in a disease can be found using the feature-finding method [12].

The use of the Bayesian algorithm in drug design is growing. It offers a probabilistic framework for making judgements and predictions, incorporating prior knowledge and updating it with new information as it becomes available. Bayesian algorithms are employed in drug design to streamline the process of selecting potential drug candidates, forecasting their properties, and making informed decisions about which compounds to pursue further [13].

Combining publicly available datasets and internal datasets allowed for the successful development of Random Forest models for approximately 200 different kinases. Compared to other machine learning techniques, Random Forest models performed better. With better sensitivity but worse specificity, only a DNN demonstrated comparable performance. However, because they are simpler to train, the authors preferred the Random Forest models [13].

Decision trees can be used for constructing regression models and classification models for both qualitative and quantitative forecasting. Single decision trees are often used because they are simple to read and portray. However, more sophisticated ML algorithms like random forest or gradient-boosting modelling exceed them [14].

Table 1. Technological Benefits

Reference	Algorithm used	Key Benefits	Accuracy
[15]	Support Vector Machine (SVMs)	SVMs exhibit remarkable performance in data analysis, achieving high accuracy, sensitivity, precision, and specificity in predictive models of drug designing	89.78%
[16]	Bayesian	One of the key benefits is that they can update forecasts when new data becomes available and incorporate existing information, improving assessment accuracy	60%
[17]	Random Forest	By merging the predictions from many decision trees, Random Forest may effectively predict molecular characteristics and activities in drug design, offering enhanced accuracy and resilience compared to standalone models	83.3%
[17]	Decision Tree	The effective analysis of intricate correlations between molecular features and biological activities helps in the prediction of possible drug candidates	88.9%

3.2 AI in Poly-Pharmacology (PP)

Poly-pharmacology, another area where AI excels, focuses on drugs with multiple target interactions, providing a more comprehensive approach to treating complex diseases. AI-driven techniques help identify and characterize the intricate network of interactions that drugs have within the human body. This knowledge enables the design of drugs with multifaceted mechanisms of action, potentially leading to more effective and personalized therapies. DL techniques, such as deep neural networks, have also demonstrated their utility in learning complex patterns and representations from biological data [18].

A supervised machine learning, Support Vector Machines (SVMs) used for classification and regression tasks. In the context of poly-pharmacology, which involves studying the interactions between multiple drugs and their effects on multiple targets or pathways, SVMs can be applied to various aspects of the analysis [19].

Naive Bayesian classification is tolerant of noise and can analyse vast volumes of data quickly. It only takes a small amount of training data to estimate the parameters (variable's means and variances) needed for classification [21].

To alleviate the instability of the decision tree model brought on by its hierarchical structure, the random forest algorithm is applied to bag and subset selection procedures. Multiple training sets are randomly sampled to create numerous trees, and the features are then improved using out-of-bag cases [22].

Table 2. Technological Benefits

Reference	Algorithm used	Key Benefits	Accuracy
[20]	Support Vector Machine (SVMs)	To predict bioactivity, SVMs can employ a variety of internal methods (kernels) with the Radial Basis Function (RBF) kernel being the most common	86.2%
[21]	Bayesian	The prediction from pharmacophore mapping and molecular docking were combined to create Bayesian classifiers	74.38%
[22]	Random Forest	Identify targets of several query ligands simultaneously in an RF-QSAR, because it is thought to prevent overfitting and properly handle unbalanced classes, this algorithm is an ensemble of decision trees	73.9%
[23]	Decision Tree	Using a decision tree analysis based on chi-squared automatic interaction detection (CHAID)	79%

3.3 AI in Drug Repurposing (DR)

Drug repurposing is a cost-effective strategy to find new therapeutic applications for existing drugs, which can potentially save time and resources compared to developing entirely new drugs. Support Vector Machine (SVM) can play a role in this process by helping to predict drug interactions prioritize drugs and assist in the discovery of new therapeutic applications [24].

SVMs can analyse vast databases of approved drugs and their known interactions, suggesting new uses for these medications. This approach saves time and resources and reduces the risks associated with developing entirely new compounds from scratch [24]. SVMs used as a data representation, training data, feature selection and extraction, model training, prediction, cross-validation and model evaluation, ranking and prioritization, and integration with other data sources in a drug repurposing [26].

The naïve assumption that the characteristics are independent is what gives the Bayesian classifier its name. The odds of the individual events can be multiplied based on this supposition. The "naive" assumption will be used, as explained: the probability of the individual occurrences will be multiplied, but the probabilities themselves will not be computed using the equation, but rather a Laplacian-corrected estimator [27].

Random Forest contributes to drug repurposing efforts by processing complex, high-dimensional biological data. They can spot subtle patterns and connections that human researchers might not immediately notice. These models can help prioritize drug candidates for further investigation based on their potential efficacy and safety profiles [25].

Table 3. Technological Benefits

Reference	Algorithm used	Key Benefits	Accuracy
[26]	Support Vector Machine (SVMs)	SVM uses linear machine learning to effectively categorise probable interactions and direct drug discovery, providing strong predictive power for therapeutic target indication in repurposing	87.4%
[27]	Bayesian	Predict targets based only on the chemical structure using a Naïve Bayes	77%
[28]	Random Forest	The random forest approach performed more effectively to the other classifiers in terms of accuracy and AUC	90.6%
[29]	Decision Tree	Currently, proposed data integration methods take into account different aspects of diseases and drugs, making assumptions more robust	99.03%

3.4 AI in Drug Screening (DS)

In drug screening, A Random Forest plays a crucial role in in-silico virtual screening, which involves the computational analysis of potential drug candidates and their interactions with target molecules. By employing AI models in this stage, researchers can prioritize the most promising compounds for further investigation, streamlining the experimental process and minimizing the need for exhaustive laboratory testing [32].

In drug screening, SVMs can classify compounds as potential drugs or predict their biological activities. SVMs applied in Feature representation, Data collection and labelling, Data preprocessing, Model training, Kernel functions, Model tuning, Model evaluation, and Predictions [30].

Decision trees (DTs) are easy-to-understand, predictive machine learning techniques. The decision tree-building process typically involves the two basic steps of selecting properties and pruning. The branch represents the molecule's test result, the leaf node serves as a classification label, and the chosen attributes are regarded as internal nodes. The established tree is pruned using the pruning program to avoid the decision tree's complexity [32].

Remember that the choice of algorithm should be based on the characteristics of the data, the problem's complexity, and the available computational resources. It's also a good practice to experiment with multiple algorithms and compare their performances to find the most suitable one for the specific drug screening task at hand [28]. As a result, AI, ML, and DL are invaluable tools in the initial stages of drug discovery, enabling

Table 4. Technological Benefits

Reference	Algorithm used	Key Benefits	Accuracy
[30]	Support Vector Machine (SVMs)	The SVMs demonstrated the feasibility of a fresh approach for foretelling the biological actions of ligands and finding fresh lead compounds	88%
[31]	Bayesian	To screen for drug-induced ototoxicity during the drug development process	90.2%
[32]	Random Forest	The random forest approach is a quick, trustworthy, and efficient in-silico method	81.9%
[32]	Decision Tree	The decision tree approach is a computationally efficient method for searching through large data sets for possible targets for in vitro or in vivo experimental evaluation	75.8%

researchers to prioritize the most promising candidates and accelerate the development of new and more efficient therapies for a wide range of diseases [29].

4 Result

Figure 2 shows the result on the basis of comparable analysis of different algorithms i.e., SVM, Bayesian, random forest and decision tree on the four major aspects in the domain of drug discovery, which are drug design, poly-pharmacology, drug repurposing and drug screening. The analysis is done on the basis of recent year publications from 2018 to 2023 and results are calculated on the basis of average in all four parameters.

SVM gives an accuracy of 89.78% in DD, 86.2% in PP, 87.4% in DR, and 88% in DS, thus the total calculated average of percentage of all four aspects is 87.84%. The second algorithm which is Bayesian, shows an accuracy of 60% in DD, 74.38% in PP, 77% in DR, and 90.2% in DS, and thus gives the accuracy average of all percentages in total is 75.39%. The study analyses the third algorithm in drug discovery is a random forest which gives an accuracy of 83.3% in DD, 73.9% in PP, 90.6% in DR, and 81.9% in DS, and in total it gives the average percentage of all four parameters is 82.42%. The paper further stresses of fourth algorithm i.e., the decision tree in four spheres of drug discovery and gives an accuracy of 88.9% in DD, 79% in PP, 99.03% in DR, and 75.8% in DS, and that's how the average percentage of RF in four aspects is 85.68%.

Figure 3 shows, that the final result concludes that SVM is a better option to be used in drug discovery as it achieves the highest accuracy average of 87.84% because SVMs exhibit remarkable performance in data analysis, sensitivity, precision, and specificity in predictive models of drug designing, also help in predicting bioactivity with highest accuracy. SVM is comparably better in providing strong predictive power for therapeutic target indication in repurposing and also helps in demonstrating the feasibility of a

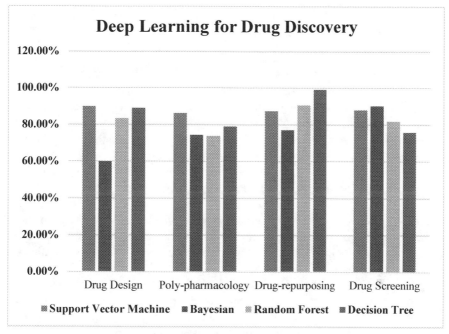

Fig. 2. A comparison of the accuracy rates achieved over the previous years utilizing various machine learning techniques for drug discovery. (SVM: support vector machine, Bayesian: Bayesian methods including naive Bayes classifier, Random Forest, and Decision Tree)

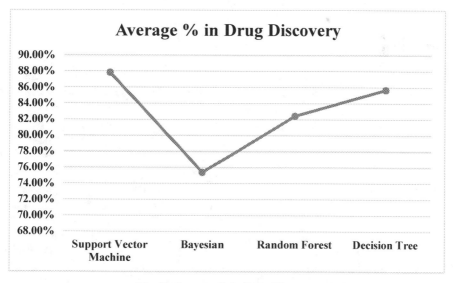

Fig. 3. Average % in Drug Discovery

fresh approach for fore-telling the biological actions of ligands and finding fresh lead compounds.

5 Limitation

AI has the potential to revolutionize drug discovery. However, there are some limitations and challenges that are described below:

When handling sensitive patient data, data privacy and regulatory compliance are top priorities. Data protection and privacy regulations must be followed while using AI for drug discovery. In the United States, we have a regulation called HIPAA that protects information, and in Europe, they have a law called General Data Protection Regulation (GDPR).

AI in drug discovery requires further standardization in data formats, data collection, and analysis. But right now, there are different ways of doing these things, which can make it difficult to compare results from different studies. This makes it difficult for computers to make accurate predictions and models.

The methodologies used in drug discovery need to be more uniformly standardized in terms of data formats, data gathering, and data processing. This can limit the ability to compare the results of different studies and research objectives which limits the effectiveness of AI in making accurate predictions and models.

Despite these challenges, AI is already helping to find new drug discovery. AI can find new targets for drugs, create new molecules for drugs, and predict if new drugs are safe and effective. As AI gets better and we learn more, it will become an even more important role in drug discovery in the future.

6 Conclusion and Future Scope

The ability to precisely forecast pharmacological attributes is one of the biggest benefits of employing AI at the beginning of drug discovery. Researchers are able to make better conclusions about the pharmacokinetic and pharmacodynamic characteristics of a drug candidate by utilizing AI's capacity to learn from various datasets and complex patterns. Through improved medication safety profiles and more exact dosage regimens, this predictive power may ultimately lower the likelihood of negative effects during clinical trials and after the product has been put on the market.

Financially, the time and resources needed to produce new pharmaceuticals can be greatly decreased thanks to AI's capacity to optimize the drug discovery process. Pharmaceutical businesses can invest their time and resources more effectively by quickly selecting the most promising candidates, which will hasten the development and marketing of new drugs. AI can reduce the risks posed to patients during clinical trials by increasing the safety and effectiveness of drugs, according to an ethical point of view. Artificial intelligence (AI) models can assist in avoiding needless human trials for pharmaceuticals that are unlikely to be successful or pose major dangers by precisely predicting pharmacological attributes and probable side effects.

AI is already having a major impact on drug discovery and is an active research area with a lot of directions of research in future. Some of the areas of research related to AI in drug discovery:

Developing a new AI algorithm and models: A researcher upgraded the AI model for a better outcome that could more accurately and efficiently predict drug properties, identify new drug targets, and design new drugs.

Integrating AI with other technologies: Other technologies, such as genomics and big data analytics with AI, create new and powerful tools for drug discovery.

References

1. US Food & Drug Administration (Center for Drug Evaluation and Research): A discussion paper on Artificial intelligence in drug manufacturing (2023). https://www.fda.gov/media/165743/download. Accessed 26 July 2023
2. Precedence research: Generative AI in Pharmaceutical Market 2023. SDG-Goals 3. https://www.precedenceresearch.com/generative-ai-in-pharmaceutical-market. Accessed 28 July 2023
3. PR Newswire: AI in Pharma Global Market Report (2022). https://www.prnewswire.com/news-releases/ai-in-pharma-global-market-report-2022-301542906.html. Accessed 28 July 2023
4. Jiang, J., Ma, X., Ouyang, D., Williams, R.O.: Emerging artificial Intelligence (AI) technologies used in the development of solid dosage forms. Pharmaceutics **14**(11), 2257 (2022). https://doi.org/10.3390/pharmaceutics14112257
5. Damiati, S.A.: Digital pharmaceutical sciences. AAPS PharmSciTech **21**(6), 1–12 (2020). https://doi.org/10.1208/s12249-020-01747-4
6. Paul, D., Sanap, G., Shenoy, S., Kalyane, D., Kalia, K., Tekade, R.K.: Artificial intelligence in drug discovery and development. Drug Discov. Today **26**(1), 80–93 (2021)
7. Blanco-González, A., et al.: The role of AI in drug discovery: challenges, opportunities, and strategies. Pharmac. (Basel Switz.) **16**(6) (2023). https://doi.org/10.3390/ph16060891
8. Hansen, K., et al.: Machine learning predictions of molecular properties: accurate many-body potentials and nonlocality in chemical space. J. Phys. Chem. Lett. **6**(12), 2326–2331 (2015). https://doi.org/10.1021/acs.jpclett.5b00831
9. Patel, V., Shah, M.: Artificial intelligence and machine learning in drug discovery and development. Intell. Med. **2**(3), 134–140 (2022). https://doi.org/10.1016/j.imed.2021.10.001
10. Moingeon, P., Kuenemann, M., Guedj, M.: Artificial intelligence-enhanced drug design and development: toward a computational precision medicine. Drug Discov. Today **27**(1), 215–222 (2022)
11. Luukkonen, S., van den Maagdenberg, H.W., Emmerich, M.T.M., van Westen, G.J.P.: Artificial intelligence in multi-objective drug design. Curr. Opin. Struct. Biol. **79**, 102537 (2023). https://doi.org/10.1016/j.sbi.2023.102537
12. Hessler, G., Baringhaus, K.-H.: Artificial intelligence in drug design. Mol. (Basel Switz.) **23**(10) (2018). https://doi.org/10.3390/molecules23102520
13. Lavecchia, A.: Deep learning in drug discovery: opportunities, challenges and future prospects. Drug Discov. Today **24**(10), 2017–2032 (2019)
14. Talevi, A.: Machine learning in drug discovery and development part 1: a primer. CPT Pharmacometrics Syst. Pharmacol. **9**(3), 129–142 (2020)
15. Arora, G., Joshi, J., Mandal, R.S., Shrivastava, N., Virmani, R., Sethi, T.: Artificial Intelligence in surveillance, diagnosis, drug discovery and vaccine development against COVID-19. Pathogens **10**(8) (2021). https://doi.org/10.3390/pathogens10081048

16. Jaganathan, K., Tayara, H., Chong, K.T.: Prediction of drug-induced liver toxicity using SVM and optimal descriptor sets. Int. J. Mol. Sci. 22(15), 8073 (2021). https://doi.org/10.3390/ijm s22158073

17. Dara, S., Dhamercherla, S., Jadav, S.S., Babu, C.M., Ahsan, M.J.: Machine learning in drug discovery: a review. Artif. Intell. Rev. 55(3), 1947–1999 (2022). https://doi.org/10.1007/s10 462-021-10058-4

18. Chaudhari, R., Fong, L.W., Tan, Z., Huang, B., Zhang, S.: An up-to-date overview of computational polypharmacology in modern drug discovery. Expert Opin. Drug DisCov. 15(9), 1025–1044 (2020)

19. Gupta, R., Srivastava, D., Sahu, M., Tiwari, S., Ambasta, R.K., Kumar, P.: Artificial intelligence to deep learning: machine intelligence approach for drug discov-ery. Mol. Diversity 25, 1315–1360 (2021)

20. Cortés-Ciriano, I., et al.: Polypharmacology modelling using proteochemometrics (PCM): recent methodological developments, applications to target families, and future prospects. MedChemComm 6(1), 24–50 (2015). https://doi.org/10.1039/c4md00216d

21. Tian, S., et al.: Modeling compound-target interaction network of traditional Chinese medicines for type II diabetes mellitus: insight for polypharmacology and drug design. J. Chem. Inf. Model. 53(7), 1787–1803 (2013). https://doi.org/10.1021/ci400146u

22. Lee, K., Lee, M., Kim, D.: Utilizing random Forest QSAR models with optimized parameters for target identification and its application to target-fishing server. BMC Bioinform. 18(S16) (2017). https://doi.org/10.1186/s12859-017-1960-x

23. Trevisan, C.: Decision tree for ward admissions of older patients at the emergency department after a fall: falls and ward admission in older people. Geriatr. Gerontol. Int. 18(9), 1388–1392 (2018)

24. Choudhury, C., Murugan, N., Priyakumar, U.D.: Structure-based drug repurposing: traditional and advanced AI/ML-aided methods. Drug Discov. Today 27(7), 1847–1861 (2022)

25. Prasad, K., Kumar, V.: Artificial intelligence-driven drug repurposing and structural biology for SARS-CoV-2. Curr. Res. Pharmacol. Drug Discov. 2, 100042 (2021). https://doi.org/10. 1016/j.crphar.2021.100042

26. Srivastava, D.: An artificial intelligence based recommender system to analyze drug target indication for drug repurposing using linear machine learning algorithm. J. Algebraic Stat. 13, 790–797 (2022)

27. Nidhi, M., Glick, J.W., Davies, J.L.: Prediction of biological targets for compounds using multiple-category Bayesian models trained on chemogenomics data-bases. J. Chem. Inf. Model. 46(3), 1124–1133 (2006)

28. Kim, E., Choi, A.-S., Nam, H.: Drug repositioning of herbal compounds via a ma-chine-learning approach. BMC Bioinform. 20(10) (2019)

29. Ahmed, F.: SperoPredictor: an integrated machine learning and molecular docking-based drug repurposing framework with use case of COVID-19. Front. Public Health 10 (2022)

30. Fang, J., et al.: Predictions of BuChE inhibitors using support vector machine and naive Bayesian classification techniques in drug discovery. J. Chem. Inf. Model. 53(11), 3009–3020 (2013). https://doi.org/10.1021/ci400331p

31. Zhang, H., Liu, C.-T., Mao, J., Shen, C., Xie, R.-L., Mu, B.: Development of novel in silico prediction model for drug-induced ototoxicity by using naïve Bayes classifier approach. Toxicol. In Vitro 65, 104812 (2020)

32. Hong, H., Tong, W., Xie, Q., Fang, H., Perkins, R.: An in silico ensemble method for lead discovery: decision forest. SAR QSAR Environ. Res. 16(4), 339–347 (2005). https://doi.org/ 10.1080/10659360500203022

Empathy-Driven Chatbots for the Arabic Language: A Transformer Based Approach

Ismail Rabii[✉], Mohamed Boussakssou, and Mohammed Erritali

Data4earth Laboratory, FST Beni Mellal, Sultan Moulay Slimane University, Beni-Mellal,
Morocco
ismail.rabii@usms.ac.ma

Abstract. Developing chatbots for the Arabic language presents unique challenges due to its complex grammar, rich vocabulary, and diverse dialects. Therefore, tailoring chatbot development methodologies and models specifically for Arabic is essential to ensure accurate understanding and generation of responses. This paper presents an empathy-driven chatbot which is a transformer-based model specifically designed for the Arabic language. The model is trained using a corpus of Arabic conversational pairs and is compared against a Seq2Seq model based on Bi-LSTM and attention mechanism. Empathy-driven chatbots aim to understand and respond to users' emotions, needs, and concerns in a sensitive and human-like manner. By integrating empathy into chatbot design, we enhance the conversational experience, making interactions more personalized, engaging, and satisfying for users. While empathy has been extensively studied in English based chatbots, its application in other languages, such as Arabic, presents unique challenges and opportunities. Our research focuses on the development of an empathic chatbot that can understand and respond to user input in a contextually relevant and empathetic manner. The transformer based chatbot exhibits several advantages over the Seq2Seq model, including improved perplexity and BLEU score, indicating enhanced language modeling and generation capabilities.

Keywords: Empathy · Chatbots · Arabic Language · Transformer Model · Seq2Seq Model · Language Modeling · Conversational Agents · Bi-LSTM · Attention

1 Introduction

In the realm of conversational AI, chatbots have become an invaluable tool for interacting with users, providing support, and automating customer service. Although chatbots have made significant progress in recent years especially in this era of large language models (LLM) [1], incorporating empathy into chatbots interactions remains an interesting and challenging area of research. This paper explores the importance of empathy in chatbot interactions and the specific challenges of developing empathetic Arabic chatbots due to the lack of appropriate datasets. Empathy, in the context of human-computer interaction, refers to the ability of a system or entity to understand and respond to the

KC Santosh et al. (Eds.): RTIP2R 2023, CCIS 2026, pp. 51–65, 2024.
https://doi.org/10.1007/978-3-031-53082-1_5

emotional state and needs of the user. It involves perceiving, interpreting, and responding to emotional cues, thereby establishing a connection that goes beyond mere transactional exchanges [2]. Empathy plays a crucial role in building trust, enhancing user satisfaction, and delivering personalized experiences. Empathetic chatbots have the potential to revolutionize a variety of fields, including customer service, mental health support, and language learning [3]. By simulating human empathy, these chatbots can provide a more compassionate and customized interaction experience, making users feel heard, understood and supported. Empathetic chatbots can help users when they need them, provide emotional support, and provide relevant guidance based on the user's emotional state [4]. A major obstacle to developing empathetic chatbots in Arabic is the lack of suitable datasets. Training chatbots to generate empathetic responses relies heavily on large amounts of conversational data capturing various emotional states and corresponding linguistic expressions. However, the availability of such Arabic datasets remains limited, hindering progress in developing empathetic chatbots targeting Arabic speakers. The lack of Arabic datasets limits the ability to train models efficiently and hinders the creation of culturally inclusive and emotion-aware chatbot interactions [7]. This paper is organized as follows. Section 2 provides an overview of related work in the field of chatbot development using deep learning in the Arabic language, highlighting the advancements and techniques used in developing chatbots for the Arabic language. Section 3 details the approach employed to develop the empathic Arabic chatbot, including the proposed model, dataset collection, translation process, and dataset pre-processing techniques. Section 4 presents the experimental setup, including the hyperparameters used, and discusses the results of the model, such as loss, perplexity, and BLEU [10] score. Section 5 discusses a comparison with another seq2seq model provided to evaluate the performance of the proposed approach and the last section summarizes the key findings, discussing the implications of the results, and suggesting future research directions to further enhance the development of Arabic chatbots.

2   Related Work

Despite the abundance of research on English chatbots, there is some scarcity of Arabic chatbots due to challenges in the Arabic language Several research efforts in deep learning are currently focused on developing Arabic bots and generating text. Seq2seq model has been widely utilized in many papers. For instance, Khan and Yassin (2021) [5] proposed SeerahBot, an Arabic chatbot specializing in the biography of the Prophet.

The chatbot was developed using machine learning and natural language processing techniques. Its primary purpose is to assist users in answering questions about the Prophet's hadiths and provide them with essential information regarding his biography. To enhance accessibility, the application was deployed on the Telegram platform. The results of the study demonstrated the effectiveness and superiority of SeerahBot in addressing inquiries related to the Prophet's biography. The evaluation utilized a set of 200 questions specifically designed for this purpose. The data collected for the study was organized and stored in text files. Notably, SeerahBot achieved a high level of precision and accuracy, with a quality and accuracy rating of 35.71% for providing information on the Prophet's biography. Furthermore, Boussakssou and Erritali (2022) [6] introduced an Arabic chatbot application called midoBot, which utilized the Seq2Seq deep learning technique. This application was designed to engage in conversations with humans on various common topics and was trained using approximately 81,659 conversations. The findings of the research indicated that the application exhibited superiority in answering most questions and generating novel responses. The researchers achieved satisfactory results by combining the LSTM (Long Short-Term Memory) [11] and GRU (Gated Recurrent Unit) [12] models. During the training process, they observed that GRU outperformed LSTM in terms of computational efficiency. GRU required approximately 140 s per epoch, while LSTM took significantly longer at 470.78 s. However, despite the computational advantage of GRU, LSTM produced more accurate and appropriate answers. The final accuracy of the LSTM model was recorded as 89%, while the GRU model achieved an accuracy of 85%. Similarly but in the aspect of empathic dialogue machines, Naous et al. (2020) [7] introduced a Bi-LSTM (seq2seq) model based on attention designed for an Arabic Empathetic bot. The model was implemented and evaluated using a dataset consisting of 38,000 samples. The results indicated that the proposed model achieved a BLeU score of 50%, demonstrating its effectiveness in generating empathetic responses. While the model succeeded in generating empathetic responses, it showed an average Relevance score which indicates that the responses can sometimes go off-topic and may not be suitable responses for the emotional context of the input utterance. The limitations of this work were mainly due to the limited size of the dataset. And as a solution to this limitation, the authors used AraBERT [22] a BERT [14] model trained on Arabic text for developing an empathic Arabic BERT2BERT [8] chatbot. This model outperformed the seq2seq model with additional 5 points in the BLeU score and also beat it on the human evaluation which based on the judgment of human subjects by collecting answers of 84 Arabic native speakers on three questions (Empathy: Does the generated response show an ability to infer the emotions in the given utterance? Relevance: How relevant is the generated response to the input utterance?, Fluency: How understandable is the generated response? Is it linguistically correct?).

Likewise for the closed domain bots and especially in healthcare services we found Mohammed Abdelhay et al. (2023) [9] made a significant contribution by introducing MAQA, the largest Arabic Healthcare Q&A dataset. This dataset comprises over 430,000 questions covering 20 medical specializations. The research further explores the performance of three deep learning models, namely LSTM, Bi-LSTM [13], and Transformers [16], in the context of MAQA. The experimental findings reveal that the Transformer model, outperforms the traditional models. It achieves an average cosine similarity [17] of 80.81% and a BLeU score of 58%, showcasing its superior performance compared to the other models tested.

In this work, we adopt a small Transformer model combined with the pre-trained words embedding AraVec on our own translated conversational dataset which is used for the pre-training phase of our model. This last will be fine-tuned with the same empathic dataset used by [7] to get our tiny empathic chatbot model.

3   Proposed Method

The proposed model in this study is a Transformer-based architecture specifically designed for the task at hand. The Transformer model has gained considerable attention in the field of natural language processing due to its ability to capture long-range dependencies and effectively process sequential data.

The Transformer model consists of several key components, including self-attention mechanisms and feed-forward neural networks. Self-attention allows the model to attend to different parts of the input sequence simultaneously, enabling it to capture relevant contextual information effectively. This mechanism enables the model to learn intricate relationships between words and phrases, leading to improved performance in language understanding and generation tasks.

Additionally, the Transformer model incorporates positional encoding to preserve the sequential order of the input data. This encoding scheme provides crucial information about the relative positions of words within the input sequence, helping the model maintain the context and sequence information during processing.

Figure 1 explains the different steps we went through in our proposed approach. First, as a result of the lack of Arabic conversational datasets, we translated a portion the Cornell Movies dataset [?] to Arabic for the pre-training phase and then we also used the dataset used in [7] for the finetuning. For the second step, we clean the dataset and preprocess it for our purpose. in the next step, we build a wordvector dictionary that contained each word in our dataset and its embedding vector representation (embedding matrix). Afterward in adoption to the dictionary that we build as a feeder to our model in the training step which is divided into two main sub-steps: Pre-training and fine-tuning steps. Finally, we evaluate our model in the final step using the BLeU score and we compared our results to the results gained in [7].

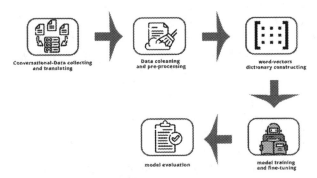

Fig. 1. The General pipeline architecture of the proposed models

3.1   Data Collecting and Translating

In this subsection, we describe the collection and translation process involved in acquiring the dataset for training our proposed model. We initially obtained the Cornell Movie

Dialogs Corpus, a well-known dataset widely used for conversational modeling, in its original English format. However, to accomplish our task we took a portion from this dataset and went through a manual cleaning process based on deleting inappropriate conversational pairs After the cleaning process, we were left with approximately 20,000 lines of conversational pairs from the Cornell dataset. In adopting, the cleaned data we conducted a thorough data translation by employing google translate API as a tool for this purpose. Subsequently, we evaluate our translating dataset using the same evaluation approach used by [7], which is based on taking a sample of 100 translated conversational pairs and checking how many translated pairs from this sample have a correct Arabic meaning, we found an accuracy of 95% for our translated dataset (95 of 100 pairs have a correct meaning).

3.2   Data Cleaning and Processing

In this subsection, we outline the crucial steps involved in cleaning and pre-processing the acquired dataset to ensure its quality and suitability for training our proposed model.

Removal Tashkil: Tashkil refers to the diacritical marks used in Arabic script to indicate short vowels and other phonetic features (Fig. 2).

مَنْ رَاقَبَ النّاسَ مَاتَ هَماً

من راقب الناس مات هما

Fig. 2. Removing Tashkil

To simplify the text and facilitate better language processing, we removed the tashkil marks from the dataset. This step allowed us to standardize the representation of Arabic words, making them more consistent and improving subsequent analysis and modeling.

Removal of non-Arabic Words: To maintain the integrity of the dataset and ensure that our chatbot focuses exclusively on Arabic conversations, we implemented a filtering process to remove any non-Arabic words present in the dataset (Fig. 3).

احذية اديداس-Adiddass هي الافضل

احذية اديداس هي الافضل

Fig. 3. Non-Arabic words removing

This step involved comparing each word against a predefined Arabic word list and discarding any non-matching words. By eliminating non-Arabic words, we ensured that the subsequent analysis and modeling steps focused solely on the target language.

Standardization of Arabic Letters: Arabic script exhibits variations in letter forms due to different fonts and writing styles (Table 1).

Table 1. Standardization of Arabic letters

Before normalizing	After normalizing
أ،إ،آ	ا
ؤ	و

To enhance the consistency and comparability of the dataset, we standardized the Arabic letters to a common form. This standardization process involved mapping different letter variations to a single representative form, thereby ensuring uniformity across the dataset.

Building the Word Vocabulary: To facilitate further processing and modeling tasks, we performed tokenization, splitting the text into individual words or tokens and for this task, we used tokenization by word which is based on taking each word as a single token. This process results in the end of more than 40000 unique tokens. This tokenization step enabled us to construct a word vocabulary, a comprehensive list of unique words present in the dataset. The word vocabulary served as a foundational component for subsequent text analysis, feature extraction, and modeling stages.

3.3 Word-Vector Dictionary (Embedding Matrix)

In this subsection, we describe the process of creating the embedding matrix, which serves as a word vector dictionary for our proposed model. We utilize the Aravec [18] word embedding model to obtain vector representations for each word in our vocabulary.

To acquire vector representations for each word in our vocabulary, we leverage the Aravec word embedding model. The Aravec model is a pre-trained word embedding model specifically designed for the Arabic language. By utilizing this model, we assign vector representations with a to each word in our vocabulary, capturing semantic and contextual information associated with the words.

To further use this word embedding obtained from AraVec which came with higher dimensions than we need,so the challenge of reducing its dimensionality to make it fit on our task rise in the horizon. Fortunately, Reaunok.(2019) [19] proposed an effective empirical method based on a combination of a post-processing algorithm [23] with Principal Component Analyse PCA. This reduction in dimensionality enables more efficient storage and computation, contributing to improved performance and memory usage in subsequent modeling steps.

This embedding matrix provides enriched and contextually meaningful representations for the words in our vocabulary, enabling the chatbot to better understand and generate responses.

3.4 Model Evaluation

During the pre-training phase, we monitor the model's progress by calculating the cross-entropy loss. The cross entropy loss measures the dissimilarity between the predicted output and the ground truth. By minimizing this loss, our model learns to generate responses that closely match the desired outputs.

Throughout the fine tuning stage, we continue to monitor the cross entropy loss. Additionally, we compute the perplexity metric, which is derived from the cross entropy loss. Perplexity reflects the model's ability to predict the next word in a sequence. A lower perplexity indicates that the model has a better understanding of language patterns and can generate more coherent responses. We used the perplexity metrics to ensure that the model is adapting to the empathetic task generation task. Lower cross-entropy loss and perplexity values signify improved model performance and a better understanding of the task at hand.

To evaluate the accuracy of our model's generated responses, we employ the BLEU (Bilingual Evaluation Understudy) score as a metric. The BLEU score measures the similarity between the generated responses and the ground truth or reference responses. It assesses the degree of overlap in n-grams (sequences of words) between the generated and reference responses. A higher BLEU score indicates that the generated responses align more closely with the reference responses, implying greater accuracy in capturing the intended meaning.

These evaluation metrics allow us to gauge the progress and effectiveness of our model throughout the training and evaluations process, ensuring that it continually improves in generating accurate and coherent responses.

4 Experiments

In this section, we explain the experiments conducted to evaluate the performance of our proposed transformer model. We begin by discussing the hyperparameters employed in the model, including the custom scheduling of the learning rate. Subsequently, we provide an overview of the experimental environment utilized to run our model. Finally, we delve into the training process, which is divided into pre-training and fine-tuning stages. We analyze the improvements in loss, perplexity, and BLEU scores as key evaluation metrics.

4.1 Hyperparameters

To configure our transformer model, we deliberately chose small values for the hyper-parameters to explore the effectiveness of a compact transformer model architecture for our task. By opting for a smaller transformer model, we aimed to investigate if it could outperform larger sequence-to-sequence models traditionally used in similar tasks (Table 2).

Table 2. Training parameters

Hyperparameter	Value
Batch Size	64
Learning Rate	custom scheduling
Number of Encoder Layers	4
Number of Decoder Layers	4
Hidden Dimension (d model)	128
Number of Attention Heads	8
Dropout Rate	0.1
Maximum Sequence Length	40
Warmup Steps	6,000

The number of transformer layers, hidden size, attention heads, and dropout rate were intentionally set at smaller values compared to standard transformer architectures. This choice allowed us to examine the model's performance with limited computational resources while focusing on the efficiency and effectiveness of the model for our specific task.

Additionally, we employed a custom learning rate scheduling strategy tailored to the small-scale model. This strategy involved warm-up steps where the learning rate was gradually increased from an initially low value to the optimal range for training. The warm-up steps aimed to stabilize the training process and help the model converge effectively, particularly during the early stages of training when the model parameters are still being initialized.

Through this deliberate selection of small hyperparameter values, we aimed to investigate the potential benefits of a compact transformer model for our specific task. By comparing its performance against larger sequence-to-sequence models, we aimed to gain insights into the trade-offs between model size and performance in the context of our task (Figs. 4 and 5).

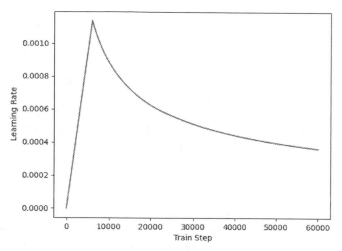

Fig. 4. Learning rate scheduling

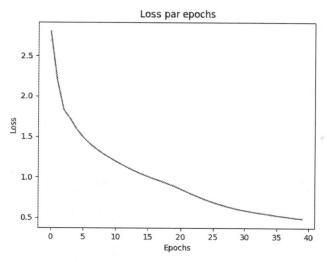

Fig. 5. The loss of the pre-training phase

4.2 Experimental Environment

Our transformer model was trained and evaluated on a local machine with an Intel Core i5-1035G1 CPU running at 1.00 GHz and 8 GB of RAM. The implementation was carried out using TensorFlow 2, a widely-used deep learning framework, in conjunction with Python 3. We employed the Adam optimizer with specific parameter settings, including beta1 = 0.9, beta2 = 0.98, and epsilon = 1e−9. This optimizer choice provided efficient gradient-based optimization during the training process. The choice of a local machine provided fine-grained control over the training process and flexibility in exploring different hyperparameters and model configurations.

4.3   Pre-training

In the pre-training phase, we focus on training our transformer model on a large dataset to capture general language patterns and contextual understanding. We utilized the translated Cornell dataset as the training dataset, which provided a diverse range of conversational data for our model to learn from.

The plots of the loss metric showcased the decreasing trend of Loss as the model learned from the translated Cornell dataset. The decreasing loss indicated that the model was gradually minimizing the dissimilarity between the predicted and ground truth outputs, demonstrating its ability to capture the desired conversational patterns.

4.4   Fine-Tuning

In the fine-tuning phase, we aimed to further refine our transformer model by training it on a more specific task or domain. We maintained the same hyper parameters as in the pre-training phase, including the number of attention heads, to ensure consistency and compare the performance across the two phases (Fig. 6).

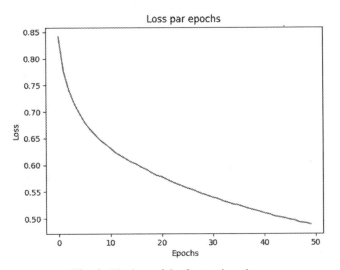

Fig. 6. The loss of the fine-tuning phase

To fine-tune the model, we utilized the empathic dataset (80% of data used for training and the rest of the data used for validation), which provided domain-specific conversational data relevant to our target task. This dataset offered a narrower focus and more specific context for the model to learn from, enabling it to generate responses that aligned closely with the empathic nature of the task.

During the fine-tuning phase, we evaluated the performance of the model using a similar loss metric as in the pre-training phase and also we used the perplexity metric on the validationdataset. We monitored the loss and perplexity to assess the model's adaptation and improvement on the empathic dataset. Additionally, we employed the

BLEU score as a metric to evaluate the accuracy of the model's responses compared to the reference responses from the validation dataset (Figs. 7 and 8).

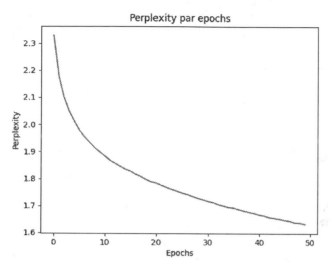

Fig. 7. Perplexity

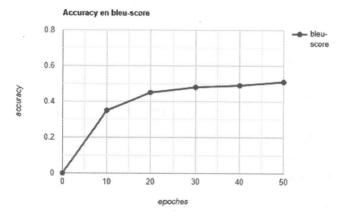

Fig. 8. BLeU score

To provide a more comprehensive analysis of the model's performance, we present in Table 3 a selection of generated responses by the model, and also we compared them to thereal (human-generated) responses from the validation dataset. These responses were generated in response to a set of contextsentences that were intentionally excluded from the training dataset.

By fine-tuning the model with the same hyperparameters and utilizing the empathic dataset, we aimed to enhance the model's performance, ensuring its relevance and effectiveness for the target task.

Table 3. The generated responses by the model compared to the real

Human generated Output	Model Prediction	Input
هذا عظيم	هذا رائع جدا اتمنى ان تحظى بوقت رائع	ذهبت مع مجموعة من الناس من مدرستي
اوه لا هل اكتشفت ذلك	اوه لا هل انت بخى	كسرت بطريق الخطأ ابرق الشاي القديم المفضل لدي والدتي الاسبوع الماضي
لم تخبرني انك تعيش معها	نعم نعم هذا صحيح	البعض منا يحاول النوم
يا الهي هذا راعع	هذا يبدو راءعا	انا محضوظ جدا لاني حصلت على المنحة الدراسية
ما هي فكرتك	هذا رائع حق	شركتي خطت لي لحفلة تقاعد في خلف ضهري
هل كنت في الماء	هل أنت بخير	كنت خائفا
يجب عليك الإتصال بهم و أخبرهم	نا متأكد من أنك ستجد شيئا يعجبك في النهاية	لا أشعر بخيبة أمل شديدة حيال ذلك

The promising results of this fine-tuning phase show the model's ability to express empathetic responses when prompted with input utterances with various emotional states and domain contexts, which also proves its ability to handle open domain conversations.

Despite the results achieved by our model in generating relevant empathetic responses in open-domain settings, it has been observed that the model shows a poorly performance in handling inputs with neutral emotion state like:

كيف يمكنني ان اصلح هاتف ؟

the model answer with:

انا اسف لسماع ذلك

this over-empathetic behavior due to the data used to train our which is a pure-conversationally data and also the size of the empathetic dataset used for the fine-tuning stage, was bigger than the pre-training data. In addition to this performance didn't able to capture the semantics for multi-turn conversation due to the nature of the dataset.

5 Discussion

In the discussion section, we compared the performance of our Transformer model with a Seq2Seq model that utilized attention [7]. The Seq2Seq model employed three different embedding size configurations (100, 300, and 500), while our Transformer model used a smaller embedding size of 128. We evaluated the models based on their perplexity and also compared their BLEU metrics (Table 4).

Table 4. Comparison of perplexity between Seq2seq and Transformer

Model	Embedding Dimension	Perplexity
Transformer (d = 128)	128	1.66
Seq2Seq (d = 100)	100	53.5
Seq2Seq (d = 300)	300	48.7
Seq2Seq (d = 500)	500	38.6

Despite the smaller embedding size, our Transformer model achieved a lower perplexity compared to the Seq2Seq model with the largest embedding size. This indicates that our Transformer model had a better ability to predict the next word in a sequence. The lower perplexity can be attributed to the transformer architecture's attention mechanism, which allows it to effectively capture and incorporate contextual information from the input. Additionally, the positional encoding mechanism used in transformers provides explicit positional information, aiding the model in understanding the sequence better (Table 5).

Table 5. Comparison of bleu score between the transformer model and seq2seq models

Model	Embedding Dimension	Score BLEU
Transformer (d = 128)	128	0.501
Seq2Seq (d = 100)	100	0.11
Seq2Seq (d = 300)	300	0.32
Seq2Seq (d = 500)	500	0.50

The superior performance of the Transformer model can be attributed to its ability to effectively capture contextual information, leverage attention mechanisms, and utilize positional encoding. Despite having a smaller embedding size, our Transformer model outperformed the larger Seq2Seq model in terms of perplexity. This demonstrates the strength of the transformer architecture in modeling language patterns and generating coherent sequences. The BLEU scores of our Transformer model were comparable to those of the larger Seq2Seq model. This suggests that our model was able to generate responses of similar quality despite the smaller embedding size. The results indicate that our Transformer model, with its smaller embedding size, outperformed the Seq2Seq model in terms of perplexity while achieving comparable BLEU scores. The transformer architecture's attention mechanism and positional encoding contribute to its ability to capture contextual information and generate high quality responses.

6 Conclusion

In conclusion, our study demonstrates the effectiveness of the Transformer model in generating good quality responses for chatbot modeling in Arabic. Despite having a smaller embedding size compared to the Seq2Seq model, our Transformer model achieved a lower perplexity while maintaining comparable BLEU scores. The attention mechanism and positional encoding in the transformer architecture contribute to its ability to capture contextual information and generate coherent and contextually appropriate responses.

To further improve our study, future research can focus on generating larger and more diverse datasets specifically tailored for chatbot modeling in Arabic. This can help address the limitations of the current dataset and provide the model with a broader range of conversational patterns and expressions. By incorporating a more extensive dataset, we can enhance the model's ability to understand and generate responses that align with Arabic language nuances and cultural context.

Additionally, leveraging larger models such as DialoGPT [20] for Arabic language can be a promising direction for future research. DialoGPT, with its advanced language generation capabilities, can be fine-tuned on Arabic conversational data to create a more powerful and contextually aware chatbot. This would enable the model to generate more accurate, contextually appropriate, and engaging responses in Arabic conversations.

In conclusion, by generating high quality datasets specifically for chatbot modeling in Arabic and exploring the utilization of advanced models like DialoGPT, we can enhance the performance and capabilities of Arabic chatbot systems. These advancements will contribute to creating more sophisticated and effective chatbots that can better cater to the needs and preferences of Arabic-speaking users.

References

1. Wei, J., et al.: Leveraging large language models to power chatbots for collecting user self-reported data. arXiv preprint arXiv:2301.05843 (2023)
2. Liu, B., Shyam Sundar, S.: Should machines express sympathy and empathy? Experiments with a health advice chatbot. Cyberpsychol. Behav. Soc. Netw. **21**(10), 625–636 (2018)
3. Zhou, L., et al.: The design and implementation fxiaoice, an empathetic social chatbot. Comput. Linguist. **46**(1), 53–93 (2020)
4. Wardhana, A.K., Ferdiana, R., Hidayah, I.: Empathetic chatbot enhancement and development: a literature review. In: 2021 International Conference on Artificial Intelligence and Mechatronics Systems (AIMS). IEEE (2021)

5. Khan, M.Z., Yassin, S.M.: SeerahBot:an arabic chatbot about prophet's biography. In: International Journal of Innovative Research in Computer Science & Technology (IJIRCST) (2021)
6. Boussakssou, M., Ezzikouri, H., Erritali, M.: Chatbot in Arabic language using seq to seq model. Multimed. Tools Appl. **81**(2), 2859–2871 (2022)
7. Naous, T., Hokayem, C., Hajj, H.: Empathy-driven Arabic conversational chatbot. In: Proceedings of the Fifth Arabic Natural Language Processing Workshop (2020)
8. Naous, T., et al.: Empathetic BERT2BERT conversational model: learning Arabic language generation with little data. arXiv preprint arXiv:2103.04353 (2021)
9. Abdelhay, M., Mohammed, A., Hefny, H.A.: Deeplearning for Arabic healthcare: MedicalBot. Soc. Netw. Anal. Min. **13**(1), 71 (2023)
10. Papineni, K., et al.: Bleu: a method for automatic evaluation of machine translation. In: Proceedings of the 40th Annual Meeting of the Association for Computational Linguistics (2002)
11. Hochreiter, S., Schmidhuber, J.: Long short-term memory. Neural Comput. **9**(8), 1735–80 (1997). https://doi.org/10.1162/neco.1997.9.8.1735. PMID: 9377276
12. Cho, K., et al.: Learning phrase representations using RNN encoder-decoder for statistical machine translation. arXiv preprint arXiv:1406.1078 (2014)
13. Huang, Z., Xu, W., Yu, K.: Bidirectional LSTM-CRF models for sequence tagging. arXiv preprint arXiv:1508.01991 (2015)
14. Devlin, J., et al.: BERT: pre-training of deep bidirectional transformers for language understanding. arXiv preprint arXiv:1810.04805 (2018)
15. Vaswani, A., et al.: Attention is all you need. In: Advances in Neural Information Processing Systems, vol. 30 (2017)
16. Lahitani, A.R., Permanasari, A.E., Setiawan, N.A.: Cosine similarity to determine similarity measure: study case in online essay assessment. In: 2016 4th International Conference on Cyber and IT Service Management, Bandung, Indonesia, pp. 1–6 (2016). https://doi.org/10.1109/CITSM.2016.7577578
17. Danescu-Niculescu-Mizil, C., Lee, L.: Chameleons in imagined conversations: a new approach to understanding coordination of linguistic style in dialogs. arXiv preprint arXiv:1106.3077 (2011)
18. Soliman, A.B., Eissa, K., El-Beltagy, S.R.: Aravec: a set of Arabic word embedding models for use in arabic NLP. Procedia Comput. Sci. **117**, 256–265 (2017)
19. Raunak, V., Gupta, V., Metze, F.: Effective dimensionality reduction for word embeddings. In: Proceedings of the 4th Workshop on Representation Learning for NLP (RepL4NLP-2019) (2019)
20. Zhang, Y., et al.: DialoGPT: large-scale generative pre-training for conversational response generation. arXiv preprint arXiv:1911.00536 (2019)
21. Antoun, W., Baly, F., Hajj, H.: AraBERT: Transformer-based model for Arabic language understanding. arXiv preprint arXiv:2003.00104 (2020)
22. Youhadmeathello: How phrasing affects memorability Cristian Danescu-Niculescu-Mizil, Justin Cheng, Jon Kleinberg and Lillian Lee Proceedings of ACL (2012)
23. Mu, J., Bhat, S., Viswanath, P.: All-but-the-top: Simple and effective post-processing for word representations. arXiv preprint arXiv:1702.01417 (2017)

Image Classification Using Federated Learning

Haewon Byeon[1], Ajdar Ullah[2], Ziauddin Syed[3], Alighazi Siddiqui[3](✉), Aasif Aftab[3], and Mohd Sarfaraz[4]

[1] Department of Digital Anti-Aging Healthcare, Inje University, Gimhae 50834, Republic of Korea
bhwpuma@naver.com

[2] School of Mechanical and Manufacturing Engineering, National University of Science and Technology, Islamabad 44000, Pakistan
ajdar.bme20smme@student.nust.edu.pk

[3] Department of Computer Science, College of Computer Science and Information Technology, Jazan University, Jazan 45142, Saudi Arabia
{ziauddin,aaftab}@jazanu.edu.sa, ghazi.siddiqui@gmail.com

[4] Department of Information Technology and Security, College of Computer Science and Information Technology, Jazan University, Jazan 45142, Saudi Arabia
msarfaraz@jazanu.edu.sa

Abstract. Multiple users can jointly train a universal model using federated learning, a revolutionary AI approach, without having to reveal their personal data. With this strategy, anonymity is maintained while a secure learning environment is guaranteed. In contrast to the Workplace 31 dataset, this study presents a brand-new dataset made up of 23,326 photos obtained from eight different corporate sources and painstakingly organised into 31 classifications. It is noteworthy that this dataset is the first image classification dataset created specifically for federated learning. Along with the dataset, we also suggest the revolutionary federated learning algorithms Handled Cyclic and Handled Star. A cycle progression is established via Handled cycle, whereby a user gets weights from a previous user, adjusts them through localised training, and then transmits them to the following user. The essential job of image categorization within the context of computer vision is considerably improved by this novel approach, which highlights the development of federated learning. Traditional centralised deep learning model training requires centralised access to enormous datasets, which raises questions about data security and privacy. Federated learning addresses these issues by facilitating dispersed device collaboration for model training while restricting raw data exposure. This paper highlights the crucial role that federated learning has had in furthering AI research by giving an overview of its use in the context of image categorization.

Keywords: Image · Classification · Federated Learning · Computer Vision

1 Introduction

The foundation of computer vision in the period of information driven innovation and man-made brainpower is image classification. The ability to really order photographs into determined bunches has accelerated improvement in various businesses, from driverless

KC Santosh et al. (Eds.): RTIP2R 2023, CCIS 2026, pp. 66–75, 2024.
https://doi.org/10.1007/978-3-031-53082-1_6

vehicles to clinical finding. Be that as it may, as the intricacy of these calculations wants customized administrations has risen, issues with information protection, security, and proprietorship have come to the front. A lot of information are much of the time unified as a feature of customary image classification methods to prepare profound learning models. Regardless of whether it works, this methodology presents serious protection and security gambles, particularly when delicate information is in question. Federated learning has turned into a state of the art way to deal with adjusting the interest for complex models with the necessity to safeguard information security.

Lately, profound learning applications have put a high need on security and information insurance. Applying profound learning procedures to areas requires taking client protection (like individual wellbeing information) into account. Federated learning has been recommended as a method for utilizing private information while expanding information utility. League learning can prepare the organization without direct admittance to private nearby information via preparing on neighborhood gadgets (clients) and helpfully learning an entire federated model through total neighborhood information.

The main goal of this research is to enhance the area of artificial intelligence (AI) through the investigation and use of federated learning, a novel strategy that permits cooperative model training without the requirement for centralised data exchange. The production of a fresh image dataset specifically created for federated learning as well as the suggestion of cutting-edge federated learning algorithms are the main contributions of this work. Novel Dataset Creation: This work presents a fresh and painstakingly curated image dataset in an effort to improve federated learning approaches. These 23,326 photos, drawn from a variety of commercial sources, have been painstakingly arranged into 31 different classes. Being the first of its kind and designed exclusively for image categorization in the context of federated learning, this dataset closes a significant gap. Innovative Federated Learning Algorithms: This work advances federated learning algorithms beyond just creating datasets. It introduces the Handled Cyclic and Handled Star federated learning algorithms. Improved collaborative model learning is made possible by the Handled Cyclic method, which offers a cyclic mechanism for weight transmission and localised fine-tuning among users. Another cutting-edge method for federated learning is the Handled Star algorithm, which might provide special advantages for federated training.

The results of this study contribute to the larger AI landscape by solving the problems with data privacy and security that are present in conventional centralised deep learning models. In addition to improving the effectiveness of model training across distant devices, the application of federated learning approaches to image classification also strengthens the process's general security and privacy. As a result, the work is ready to advance the field of AI research and spur new ideas for federated learning approaches.

2   Review of Literature

McMahan (2017) This ground-breaking work introduces the idea of federated learning and offers a method for deep network training on dispersed data sources that is communication-efficient. The authors suggest Federated Averaging, a technique that enables individual devices to change model parameters locally before aggregating them in a way that protects privacy. The paper shows how federated learning may be used to train deep networks with little communication overhead, making it appropriate for situations where communication and data privacy are important considerations.

Li et al.'s (2019) Thorough analysis of federated learning covers its difficulties, approaches, and future prospects. The review discusses issues including model aggregation methods, applications, and communication effectiveness. It also explores unanswered research topics, such as processing non-IID data, device heterogeneity, and security implications. Researchers and practitioners interested in learning about the landscape of federated learning can use the paper as a thorough reference.

Kairouz and others (2019) The developments and difficulties of federated learning are explored in this article. It addresses important concerns like security, system architecture, and heterogeneity. The authors give insights into the convergence characteristics of federated learning algorithms and examine trade-offs between various strategies for aggregating model updates. The report also suggests future research topics, highlighting the significance of tackling outstanding issues to guaranteethe viability and robustness of federated learning in varied applications.

Bagdasaryan et al. (2018) explores a crucial component of federated learning's security, talking about the potential for malicious actors to introduce backdoors to the model during the aggregation process. The paper identifies possible weak points in the federated learning pipeline and offers details on how attackers can abuse the aggregation technique to jeopardize the integrity of the global model. The significance of preserving model security in federated learning environments is brought home by this work.

Smith et al. (2017) investigate the application of federated learning in the context of multi-task learning. The authors suggest a federated optimization method that enables devices to work together on a variety of connected tasks while protecting data privacy. The performance of the model as a whole is improved using this method while still protecting the privacy of individual devices.

Yang and others (2019) This study gives a conceptual overview of federated machine learning and emphasizes its importance in the age of distant data sources and data privacy issues. The authors talk about federated learning's uses in several industries, including healthcare, the Internet of Things (IoT), and edge computing. In situations where centralized data gathering is unfeasible or unwanted, the study highlights the potential of federated machine learning to offer effective and privacy-preserving model training.

3   Proposed Methods

3.1   Objective

In federated learning (FL), various clients (suppose K clients) cooperate without expecting to trade their information to get familiar with a worldwide model. The loads of such a model ought to be set to w, and the misfortune worth ought to be set to L(xi, yi; w) for test (xi, yi). The ongoing objective is to decide ideal w to achieve the accompanying objective:

$$\min \frac{1}{|D|} \sum_{i=1}^{|D|} L(x_i, y_i; w) \tag{1}$$

where D addresses the amount of the multitude of information that different clients own, as seen underneath:

$$D = \bigcup_{k=1}^{k} D_k \tag{2}$$

where Dk represents the information that has a place with the k-th client. We can alter our objective capability as continues considering this:

$$\min \frac{1}{|D|} \sum_{k=1}^{k} \sum_{i=1}^{|D_k|} L(x_i, y_i; w) \tag{3}$$

In the event that we use Lk to address the kth client's typical neighborhood misfortune,

$$L_K = \frac{1}{|D_k|} \sum_{i=1}^{|D_k|} L(x_i, y_i; w) \tag{4}$$

which suggests that we want to lessen the weighted all out of neighborhood misfortunes endured by our clients, and that the loads depend on the quantity of information tests those clients have with them. Like , this goal capability performs comparative assignments. We discussed it with the goal that our paper would remain solitary.FedAvg was enlivened by this detailing to weighted normal the neighborhood model loads and produce was displayed beneath:

$$w = \sum_{K=1}^{K} \frac{|D_k|}{|D|} w_k \tag{5}$$

As demonstrated in Figure 1, this collection happens iteratively, with every emphasis starting with the focal server sending the worldwide model to the nearby clients, who then update their neighborhood models and submit them back to the worldwide server for conglomeration. Up until the worldwide model joins, this happens.

The Fed Avg calculation, be that as it may, can take various correspondence rounds to meet, especially when there is factual heterogeneity in the datasets of the clients. Thus, exactness additionally declines. Moreover, by averaging the boundaries from the nearby clients, Took care of Avg constructs a summed up model. This powers the neighborhood model's measurable heterogeneity to get familiar with a summed up portrayal that may not match the conveyance of its information, bringing about inadequately prepared nearby clients.

In that occurrence, nearby clients are disappointed with the worldwide model. We recommend the Fed-Cyclic and Took care of Star calculations considering the Federal Reserve Avg's downsides. These calculations consider the measurable heterogeneity of information between clients while as yet guaranteeing the agreeable nearby exhibition of worldwide models.

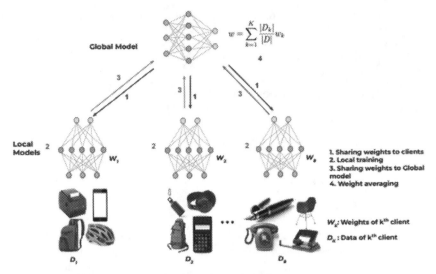

Fig. 1. FedAvg algorithm

4 Proposed Dataset

We offer a dataset with 23,326 images that we've accumulated from 8 different image-facilitating sites. Every one of the 8 sources in our federated learning climate relates to 8 particular clients. There are around 2916 photographs on normal for each source, spread across 31 classifications.

Fig. 2. Sample images from our dataset.

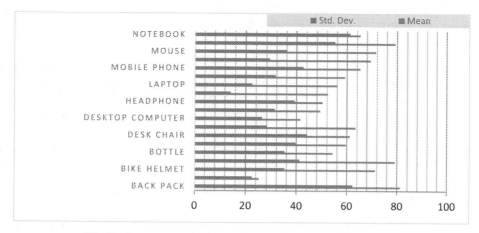

Fig. 3. Average, standard deviation, and quantity of photographs

The Workplace 31 dataset, which incorporates regular office hardware including a console, printer, screen, PC, etc, filled in as the model for this dataset.

The image classifications in our assortment match those in the Workplace 31 dataset. We went above or more to ensure that each source yielded just relevant, incredible photographs. By physically arranging the assortment, we killed photos of low quality, duplication, or superfluity. Figures 2 and 3 give a measurable rundown of the circulation of photographs across sources and across classes. Figure 4 shows the example images.

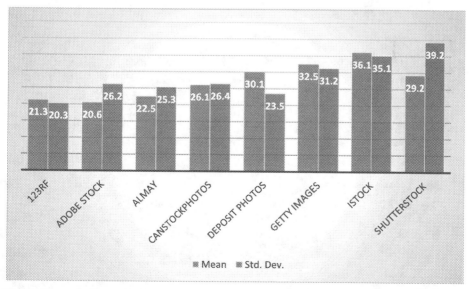

Fig. 4. The normal, standard deviation, and all out number of photographs from each hotspot for each class in the dataset.

5 Experimental Set and Result Analysis

5.1 Implementation Detail

The examinations we hurried to test the adequacy of our Federated image classification calculations are talked about in this segment. We utilize the PyTorch pretrained model library's [33] VGG-19 organization that has been pre-prepared (VGG-19 organization) for instatement. The organization's excess layers are supplanted with three new completely associated layers (estimated 1024, 256, and 31) and a softmax layer, while its convolutional layers are frozen.

We apply ReLU enactment with a dropout pace of 0.5 in the initial two totally connected layers. With a cluster size of 64, we have utilized SGD enhancer. Any client gets the information separated as follows: 80:20 train:test. Despite the fact that classification exactness is the essential assessment metric, we have additionally utilized full scale F1 score and weighted F1 score. 3e-4 (3 x 104) is the standard pace of learning.

5.2 Result Analysis

On our dataset, we test every one of the four techniques (FedAvg ,RingFed , Took care of Cyclic, and Took care of Star).

We kept =0.8 for RingFed since Fig. 4 information exhibits that this worth gave the most noteworthy precision to RingFed.

We present the discoveries from both the worldwide and neighborhood assessments. For nearby assessment, neighborhood test sets are utilized; for worldwide assessment, their association is utilized. Figure 5 overall assessment discoveries show that our two

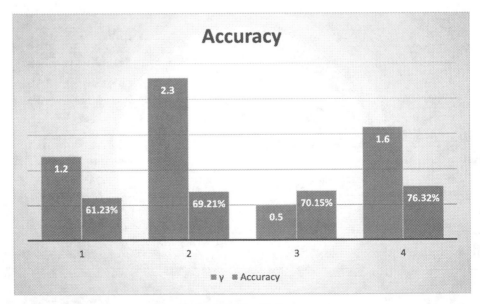

Fig. 5. Against Ring Fed's accuracy

proposed methods, Took care of Cyclic and Taken care of Star, outflank FedAvg and RingFed, as can be shown. Taken care of Star beats the other three, scoring 91.72% exactness. Moreover, our methodologies unite rapidly. Figure 6 expresses that Took care of Star needs 50 worldwide rounds on our dataset. RingFed requires similar number of worldwide rounds as Taken care of Star, yet its precision is lower.

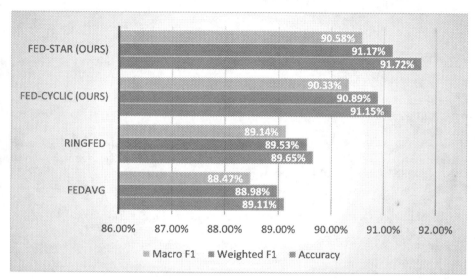

Fig. 6. As indicated by exploratory discoveries, Took care of Star and FedCyclic both accomplish more exactness than FedAvg and F1-scores.

6   Conclusion

A potential strategy to deal with the issues provided by decentralized data sources in the field of machine learning is image categorization using federated learning. This cutting-edge approach makes use of the cooperative capabilities of numerous devices while respecting data localization and privacy issues. In this study, we investigated various federated learning techniques in the context of image classification tasks, such as FedAvg, RingFed, Fed-Cyclic, and Fed-Star. According to the findings, it is clear that these federated learning techniques outperform more established centralized systems. Although FedAvg, a foundational technique, shows respectable accuracy, the succeeding methods build on it to produce even better outcomes. In order to improve accuracy and F1 scores, Ringed provides a cyclic aggregation pattern, stressing the significance of communication patterns in federated systems.

The greatest accuracy, weighted F1, and macro F1 scores are produced by our own contributions, Fed-Cyclic and Fed-Star, demonstrating the efficacy of our suggested improvements. Due to Fed-Cilic's use of cyclic aggregation schedules, model convergence and performance have been improved. While Fed-Star uses a star-topology communication structure, which increases accuracy and total F1 scores. Overall, these results highlight the promise of federated learning as an effective method for solving image classification problems, particularly in situations where data distribution, privacy, and heterogeneity are critical factors. The decentralized structure of federated learning not only protects the privacy of individual data but also makes it possible to train reliable models across a variety of datasets. Further study in this area could concentrate on improving communication tactics, eliminating any biases generated by federated datasets, and expanding the applicability of these techniques beyond image classification. In conclusion, the combination of federated learning with image classification provides the door for a machine learning paradigm that is more collaborative, effective, and privacy-conscious.

References

McMahan, H.B., Moore, E., Ramage, D., Hampson, S., Arcas, B.A.: Communication-efficient learning of deep networks from decentralized data. In: Proceedings of the 20th International Conference on Artificial Intelligence and Statistics (AISTATS), vol. 54, pp. 1273–1282 (2017)

Li, T., Sahu, A.K., Talwalkar, A., Smith, V.: Federated learning: challenges, methods, and future directions. IEEE Signal Process. Mag. **37**(3), 50–60 (2019)

Kairouz, P., et al.: Advances and open problems in federated learning (2019). arXiv preprint arXiv: 1912.04977

Bagdasaryan, E., Veit, A., Hua, Y., Estrin, D., Shmatikov, V.: How to backdoor federated learning (2018). arXiv preprint arXiv:1807.00459

Smith, V., Chiang, Y.J., Sanjabi, M., Talwalkar, A.: Federated multi-task learning. In: Advances in Neural Information Processing Systems (NeurIPS), pp. 4424–4434 (2017)

Yang, Q., Liu, Y., Chen, T., Tong, Y.: Federated machine learning: concept and applications. ACM Trans. Intell. Syst. Technol. (TIST) **10**(2), 1–19 (2019)

Chen, C., Chen, Z., Zhou, Y., Kailkhura, B.: Fedcluster: boosting the convergence of federated learning via cluster-cycling. In: 2020 IEEE International Conference on Big Data (Big Data), pp. 5017–5026. IEEE (2020)

Chen, D., Hong, C.S., Zha, Y., Zhang, Y., Liu, X., Han, Z.: Fedsvrg based communication efficient scheme for federated learning in mec networks. IEEE Trans. Veh. Technol. **70**(7), 7300–7304 (2021)

Chen, W., Bhardwaj, K., Marculescu, R.: Fedmax: mitigating activation divergence for accurate and communication-efficient federated learning. In: Hutter, F., Kersting, K., Lijffijt, J., Valera, I. (eds.) Machine Learning and Knowledge Discovery in Databases: European Conference, ECML PKDD 2020, Ghent, Belgium, September 14–18, 2020, Proceedings, Part II, pp. 348–363. Springer International Publishing, Cham (2021). https://doi.org/10.1007/978-3-030-67661-2_21

De Cristofaro, E.: An overview of privacy in machine learning (2020). arXiv preprint arXiv:2005. 08679

Dekel, O., Bachrach, R.G., Shamir, O., Xiao, L.: Optimal distributed online prediction using minibatches. J. Mach. Learn. Res. **13**(1), (2012)

Deng, Y., Kamani, M.M., Mahdavi, M.: Adaptive personalized federated learning (2020). arXiv preprint arXiv:2003.13461

Drainakis, G., Katsaros, K.V., Pantazopoulos, P., Sourlas, V., Amditis, A.: Federated vs. centralized machine learning under privacy-elastic users: a comparative analysis. In: 2020 IEEE 19th International Symposium on Network Computing and Applications (NCA), pp. 1–8. IEEE (2020)

Duan, M., Liu, D., Chen, X., Liu, R., Tan, Y., Liang, L.: Self-balancing federated learning with global imbalanced data in mobile systems. IEEE Trans. Parall. Distrib. Syst. **32**(1), 59–71 (2020)

Duan, M., et al.: Fedgroup: efficient federated learning via decomposed similarity-based clustering. In: 2021 IEEE International Conference on Parallel & Distributed Processing with Applications, Big Data & Cloud Computing, Sustainable Computing & Communications, Social Computing & Networking (ISPA/BDCloud/SocialComw2/SustainCom), pp. 228–237. IEEE (2021)

Preserving Accuracy in Federated Learning via Equitable Model and Efficient Aggregation

Muntazir Mehdi[1]([✉]), Aaisha Makkar[1], Myra Conway[1], and Lakshit Sama[2]

[1] University of Derby, DE22 1GB Derby, UK
m.mehdi@derby.ac.uk
[2] Capgemini Engineering, Adelaide, Australia

Abstract. Machine learning has revolutionized research by extracting complicated patterns from complex data, particularly in healthcare and medical imaging, where accurate diagnosis is critical. The concept of federated learning has gained popularity in the field of machine learning as a viable technique for addressing privacy issues in distributed settings. This research explores federated learning in healthcare, demonstrating its capability to achieve results comparable to centralized data while enhancing the accuracy of deep learning models for clinical data interpretation. To ensure reliable model performance during federated learning rounds, this study introduces a proactive mechanism for coordinating server updates with equitable client modifications. The equitable model, designed to reduce accuracy fluctuations, consistently improves accuracy across multiple training rounds on a non-IID dataset. We achieved smooth accuracy improvement by implementing the novel Equitable model, resulting in robust model development. As healthcare AI continues to advance, federated learning emerges as a critical tool for developing precise prediction models while preserving patient data privacy and aligning with increasingly strict data standards worldwide, such as GDPR regulations. This strategic approach not only promotes ethical, efficient, and secure progress in medical research and practice, but it also emphasizes the importance of protecting patient data privacy while utilizing machine learning's potential.

Keywords: Federated Learning · Fair Aggregation · Client updates

1 Introduction

Machine learning has sparked widespread interest in a variety of research fields due to its remarkable ability to analyse data effectively. Researchers can extract multi-dimensional characteristics from complex data that would be difficult for humans to recognize by using machine learning techniques. The ability to capture fine details in medical data is essential for improving diagnostic procedures in the field of healthcare and medical imaging, where it has proven of special value. Convolutions, deep neural networks, support vector machines, and clustering

© The Author(s), under exclusive license to Springer Nature Switzerland AG 2024
KC Santosh et al. (Eds.): RTIP2R 2023, CCIS 2026, pp. 76–88, 2024.
https://doi.org/10.1007/978-3-031-53082-1_7

techniques are a few of the algorithms used for machine learning that have been successfully used in the medical field to find correlations in medical data that are challenging for humans to recognize. As a result, various medical specialties and fields, like pathology, radiation therapy, neurological science, genetics, and psychological diseases, have been incorporated into the scope of medical artificial intelligence.

The protection of patients' personal information is currently the top concern in the field of healthcare AI, despite the advancements in diagnosis accuracy brought about by machine learning. Traditional centralized machine learning techniques that rely on collecting and learning from huge amounts of data are no longer appropriate since there are more restrictive data regulations around the world, such as the EU's General Data Protection Regulation, China's Personal Information Protection and California's Privacy Rights Act. Health Insurance Portability and Accountability Act (HIPAA) compliance is essential for preserving patient medical records and private health information that can be identified in the context of medical data. In order to address privacy concerns while using medical data effectively and securely, researchers have looked into a variety of solutions.

The problems with data privacy posed by conventional machine learning techniques are structurally addressed by federated learning. It provides a decentralized learning strategy, eliminating the need to send significant amounts of personal information to a centralized server for model generation. Instead, each collaborating client receives the initial training model from the server, and the model update process happens in each client's local data environment. The server then brings together every single client's result to build a better learning model without compromising the privacy of individual client data.

The adoption of federated learning has the potential to greatly benefit the healthcare sector. It presents a remarkable opportunity for researchers and medical professionals to develop more precise predictive models without the need to directly access or collect patients' personal information. This collaborative approach facilitates efficient information sharing between healthcare institutions, ensuring that patient data remains confidential and secure, thus favoring ethical advancements within the medical field. In our comprehensive study, we explored various aspects of federated learning's application within the healthcare domain. We explored different federated learning techniques tailored to the unique challenges presented by the medical sector, acknowledging the real-world complexities of implementation. Our research specifically addressed the recurring challenge of accuracy decline in federated learning during successive rounds of model updates. To combat this issue, we proposed a novel approach designed to proactively prevent accuracy deterioration. Furthermore, we tackled the critical task of preserving the accuracy and security of federated learning models during the aggregation phase. We introduced a logical technique that assigns appropriate preferences to clients based on their accuracy, ensuring that the most reliable contributions are prioritized in the global model. Our research endeavors contribute to the ongoing evolution of federated learning within the healthcare sector, with the long-term goal of enhancing both the accuracy of predictive models and the security of patient data.

2   Related Work

The concept of "federated learning" has a notable historical trajectory, tracing back to 1976 when Patrick Hill, a philosophy professor, introduced the Federated Learning Community (FLC) with the objective of fostering collaborative learning and addressing challenges related to anonymity and isolation within expansive research universities [3]. Over time, the term "federated learning" has gained substantial prominence. In 2017, Google introduced federated learning (FL) as an innovative approach to privacy-enhanced machine learning (ML) within distributed environments, particularly in sensitive sectors like healthcare and finance [11].

Federated learning presents a significant solution for constructing models in scenarios where disparate entities necessitate data sharing [15]. Its classification is often based on the distribution of training data, encompassing horizontal, vertical, or hybrid forms. The advantages of federated learning manifest for both data providers and consumers. For instance, it facilitates tasks such as predicting hospital readmission risks using patients' Electronic Health Records (EHR) [12], and enables activities like screening for atrial fibrillation through electrocardiograms captured by smartwatches [14]. Throughout the federated model learning process, the confidentiality of sensitive patient data is effectively maintained within local institutions or individual consumers, thereby ensuring the highest degree of privacy protection.

Since machine learning has become an essential piece in diagnosis diseases and evaluating patients' conditions, especially with the rapid advancement in image classification performance. Machine learning models have shown effectiveness in predicting severe diseases that have a significant impact on patients' lives through the use of the patient's computer tomography (CT) and magnetic resonance imaging (MRI) data.

For instance, [8] commenced a study using N4 field correction on preprocessed M&M and ACDC datasets. For the purpose of diagnosing hypertrophic cardiomyopathy, their research combined federated learning with the ResNet model, which offered improved accuracy and robustness compared to the traditional Distributed Machine Learning (DML) environment. Another study by [5] focused on classifying paediatric chest radiographs as viral pneumonia, bacterial pneumonia, or normal cases using the ResNet model. This study underlined how federated learning and DML are comparable, along with improved security against inference attacks. In order to improve the generation of medical databases, researchers have also looked into the field of generative models. [7] improved the performance of federated learning by using the generative adversarial network (GAN) algorithm on the Cardiac dataset. Under certain circumstances, the incorporation of GAN has the potential to improve disease diagnosis accuracy. Researchers have expanded their focus beyond accuracy improvement to address issues with communication effectiveness and remote collaboration. In order to enable real-time networking in a federated learning environment, [16] explored optimizing network structures for brain tumor segmentation.

Brophy [1] used generative adversarial networks (GANs) in a unique setting to investigate the connection between arterial blood pressure (ABP) and photoplethysmogram (PPG). Based on PPG data, they developed a time series-to-time series generative adversarial network model for ABP generation. This novel method produced outcomes comparable to those of traditional Distributed Machine Learning (DML) techniques, offering an alternative to pricey ABP measurements. The use of federated learning goes beyond the boundaries of medicine to include disease diagnosis. A real-time emotion state classification system based on multimodal data streaming was introduced by Nandi and Xhafa in 2022 [13]. They used three-layer feed-forward neural networks to train a classifier by utilizing physiological and audiovisual recordings. Federated Real-time Emotion Classifiers (FedREMCs) have the potential to be used in a variety of healthcare domains, as highlighted by the increased number of clients in federated learning that highlighted improved classification accuracy.

Yoo [17] concentrated on developing a classifier for the severity of major depressive disorder using heart rate variability data. They overcame nonidentically distributed (IID) challenges using the Personalized Federated Cluster Model, which produced results with higher accuracy than conventional Federated Averaging. Furthermore, the field of COVID-19 diagnosis has attracted a lot of interest. By utilizing medical image datasets, Zhang [19] introduced a dynamic fusion-based federated learning algorithm for diagnosing COVID-19 infections. Three clients participated in the experiment, which evaluated accuracy and convergence using various training techniques. Similarly, Makkar [9] introduced the SecureFed method using secure Markov chain aggregation for COVID-19 detection.

To further distinguish between chest X-ray images of pneumonia and COVID-19 patients, Liu [7] investigated a federated learning-based Covidnet algorithm. The method showed potential for medical imaging analysis through federated learning despite performing less well than ResNet models. Dayan [2], in contrast to individual-based studies, demonstrated the advantages of federated learning by enlisting several medical institutions for the analysis of COVID-19 patient data. Twenty institutions working together produced classifiers that performed on average 13.9% better than those created solely using data from local institutions.

Additionally, Kumar [6] developed a framework for diagnosing lung CT imaging that combines capsule networks and blockchain-based federated learning. Their method outperformed the benchmark models already in use, boasting improvements in sensitivity and specificity performances of over 7%.

In multi-agent systems, fairness has been a crucial factor in resource allocation. The upholding of agent fairness has been investigated using a variety of policies and strategies. For instance, a maximin sharing policy, as proposed in [18], aims to enhance the performance of the weakest agent. A fair-efficient policy, on the other hand, as discussed in [4], aims to reduce disparities in the utilities of various agents.

Fairness has also been examined in the context of Federated Learning (FL), primarily with the aim of ensuring accuracy among various clients. Agnostic FL [10], which strives to reduce the maximal loss function across all clients, is one notable contribution. Similar to this, q-Fair FL [14] encourages clients to distribute accuracy more evenly. In order to align with the broader idea of fairness in the FL framework, hierarchically fair FL [4] introduces a mechanism in which greater contributions by clients are rewarded.

Nevertheless, the convergence of federated optimization confronts a substantial hurdle due to statistical heterogeneity. The decentralized nature of data introduces inherent imbalances and non-identically distributed (Non-IID) characteristics, while conventional centralized training presupposes independent and identically distributed (IID) data-a consequence of varying sample sizes and device correlations. In light of this challenge, our focus shifts to achieving parity in local model updates and global server aggregation. This endeavor centers on preventing accuracy deterioration during the convergence phase, particularly when confronted with challenges related to client fairness. To address these concerns, we propose an innovative aggregation model for equitable client updating, specifically designed to avert accuracy decline.

3   Methodology

In this section, we will explore the data employed for our research and detail the process of preparing this data into a specific format for training and evaluating our model using various techniques.

3.1   Data

We carefully utilized the well-known MNIST dataset in our research project, using it as the cornerstone for both the training and evaluation phases of our model. The MNIST dataset holds an esteemed reputation within the machine learning community, primarily due to its rich repository of thoughtfully hand-crafted digits. This dataset is regarded as a model and indispensable asset, particularly for its critical role in digit recognition tasks. Our next step involves dividing the centralized data into multiple decentralized datasets.

3.2   Creating Decentralized Datasets

Data is inherently dispersed across multiple clients or devices in the context of Federated Learning. The creation of these decentralized datasets is essential. In order to do this, we carefully divided the MNIST dataset into the appropriate number of segments, which we then acquired. We then created distinct train_loader and test_loader objects for each of these partitions. These custom-built data loaders were critical in facilitating individual client training and evaluation. Our next discussion is about the structure of the neural network to train and test on these decentralized datasets.

3.3 Structure of Neural Networks

In our study, we used a neural network model that was specifically created to accurately extract complex features from input images. This model used a deep architecture with three strategically integrated convolutional layers that excelled at capturing and refining these features. In addition, pooling operations were added to these layers, which worked together to enhance the abilities of feature extraction. The Rectified Linear Unit (ReLU) activation function, which was strategically used to introduce non-linearity and abstraction, was added to a fully connected layer as a crucial component. The final layer of our model was carefully designed to consist of ten neurons, each diligently dedicated to classifying one of the ten distinct digits in the MNIST dataset. This layer expertly utilized the potent SoftMax activation function, which is critical in multiclass classification tasks. It skilfully converted the model's raw outputs into probability distributions across the ten digit classes, enabling the model to perform accurate and reliable image classification. The upcoming section will explain about the aggregation model that how we are going to consider the client models updates for the aggregation.

3.4 Aggregation Model

The central server is essential to federated learning because it aggregates client model updates, which is a vital step in improving the global model's comprehension of distributed data. Our study introduces a sophisticated aggregation model that evaluates and accepts client updates according to predetermined standards. This model acts as a gatekeeper, separating legitimate updates from potentially malicious intrusions. Additionally, it assigns weight to each client update while considering data size and model accuracy, resulting in a thorough and equitable update for the following round.

Our aggregation model includes the following significant improvements:

- **Client Updates Validation:** A client update validation mechanism that compares each client's most recent update to the moving average of its five prior submission has been implemented as shown in equation (1). This process verifies the updates' integrity and looks for any anomalies that might indicate malicious activity based on the difference of dissimilarities.

$$MAU_k = \frac{1}{k} \sum_{i=n-k+1}^{n} U_i \tag{1}$$

Where k indicate the sample width i.e. number of last updates from the client for moving average and in our case we are using the average of last five updates, n indicate the total number of updates and U represents the values of the client update.

- **Protect Against Superfluous Updates:** To preserve the integrity of the aggregation process, we carefully examine incoming updates to spot any extra submissions that go beyond the anticipated number of clients. This preventative measure guards against attempts from outside sources to interfere with the federated learning process.
- **Supplementary Information:** In addition to the gradient updates, our aggregation model includes supplementary information for each client. This additional information includes the ratio of client accuracy to the data size on specific round. This contextual information enables the aggregation model to make informed and equitable decisions when processing updates to prevent the model from over-fitting.
- **Weighted Aggregation:** After carefully verifying and enriching the client updates, we use a weighted aggregation approach. This method estimates the significance of the client's contribution based on the moving average dissimilarity and supplemental information from the client. As a result, we generate a final aggregated update that effectively leverages the value that each client brings to the federated learning process.

We strengthen the security of the federated learning framework by implementing this ground-breaking aggregation technique, preventing potential malicious attacks during the update aggregation procedure. At the same time, we make sure that each client's unique data contribution is appropriately acknowledged, enhancing the performance of the global model in subsequent training cycles.

3.5   Equitably Updating the Clients

In the realm of traditional federated learning, clients routinely receive updates in each training round, resulting in model improvement for subsequent iterations. However, an intriguing challenge arises when these updates fail to outperform their predecessors, potentially leading to a decline in the accuracy of the client model. To address this concern and ensure continuous improvement, our research introduces a novel technique, as illustrated in Fig. 1. A comparator is integrated into each client model, which is the key component of this strategy. This newly introduced component acts as a vigilant overseer, diligently evaluating the model's initial five epochs accuracy following each update and it depends on the computational resources, if we have limited resources then we can take the decision on the average of the initial two epochs.

Here is how the procedure progresses:

- **Post-Update Accuracy Assessment** After receiving an update, the client model begins five training epochs during which the embedded comparator deliberately examines the model's performance.
- **Decision-Making Phase** The analysis of these first five epochs' average accuracy marks the critical turning point in the decision-making process. If this assessment reveals an improvement over the previous version, the most recent update is kept for future training. Conversely, if the accuracy demonstrates a decline, the model intelligently reverts to the prior iteration.

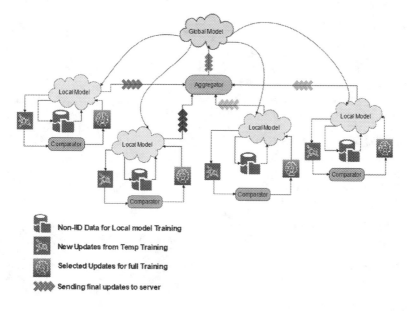

Fig. 1. Equitable Federated Learning framework

This technique ensures that client model optimization will be dynamic and adaptive. It serves as a safeguard against potential accuracy degradation while continuously driving the model towards improvement. Our method strengthens the integrity of client models by encouraging an ongoing cycle of improvement, ultimately adding to the overall success of the federated learning process.

3.6 Comparator Algorithm

This section describes in brief the algorithm used to implement the equitable model, which will ensure its accuracy in subsequent rounds.

Input

- *num_clients*: Number of clients in the federated system
- *num_rounds*: Number of federated learning rounds
- *epochs*: Number of local training epochs per client
- *batch_size*: Batch size for training
- *train_loader*: List of data loaders for training data partitioned among clients
- *test_loader*: Data loader for the global test dataset

Output

- *train_losses*: List of average training losses for each round
- *test_losses*: List of test losses for each round
- *accuracies*: List of test accuracies for each round

Initialization

- $global\_model = InitializeModelOnGPU()$
- $client\_models = [InitializeModelOnGPU() \; for \; in \; range(num\_clients)]$
- $for \; model$ in $client\_models :$
-     Load global model's weights into client models
-     Initialize SGD optimizers for each client model

Federated Learning Loop

1: **for** $round$ in range(num_rounds) **do**
2:     $total\_loss \leftarrow 0$
3:     **for** $client\_id$ in range($num\_clients$) **do**
4:         $client\_model \leftarrow client\_models[client\_id]$
5:         $optimizer \leftarrow optimizers[client\_id]$
6:         $client\_data \leftarrow train\_loader[client\_id]$
7:         $client\_loss \leftarrow ClientUpdate(client\_model, optimizer, client\_data, num\_epochs = epochs)$ ▷ Perform client update
8:             $total\_loss \leftarrow total\_loss + client\_loss$ ▷ Aggregate client loss
9:             **if** $epoch < 5$ **then**   ▷ Check accuracy in the first 5 epochs
10:                 **if** ClientAccuracyImproved($client\_model, client\_data, num\_epochs = epochs$) **then**
11:                     $last\_good\_model \leftarrow client\_model.clone()$
12:                 **else**
13:                     $client\_model.load\_state\_dict(last\_good\_model.state\_dict())$
14:                 **end if**
15:             **end if**
16:         **end for**
17:         $server\_aggregate(global\_model, client\_models)$
18:         $train\_losses.append(total\_loss/num\_clients)$
19:         $test\_loss, test\_accuracy \leftarrow EvaluateGlobalModel(global\_model, test\_loader)$
20:         $test\_losses.append(test\_loss)$
21:         $accuracies.append(test\_accuracy)$
22: **end for**
            return $train\_losses, test\_losses, accuracies$

4   Experimental Evaluations

In our experimental evaluation, we thoughtfully divided our dataset into two distinct formats: IID (Independent and Identically Distributed) and Non-IID (Non-Independent and Non-Identically Distributed) data. This division enabled us to thoroughly evaluate the effectiveness of our federated learning model in various data circumstances. The IID dataset setup mirrored scenarios where all clients had similar data characteristics, enabling us to evaluate model performance when data was uniformly distributed across clients. Conversely, the Non-IID dataset configuration simulated real-world complexities by assigning different data subsets to various clients, reflecting heterogeneous data scenarios. We acquired essential insights into the model's flexibility and stability by running trials on both dataset types, which improved our overall grasp of its strengths and limitations.

4.1 IID Partitioning and Evaluation

The partitioning of the dataset into segments, which ensures that each of the ten clients receives an IID subset of the data, is an important phase in achieving the goal of independent and identically distributed (IID) data distribution. To achieve this, we made use of 'torch.utils.data.random_split,' a tool found in the PyTorch framework. This tool made it easy to divide the MNIST dataset into our required segments, each one intended for a different client. Making sure that these partitions maintain some degree of data uniformity is the key component of IID data distribution. The random_split function was useful in dividing the dataset so that each client's segment had an approximately equal number of samples, effectively balancing the volume of data assigned to each client. It's also noteworthy that the random_split function automatically maintains class distribution. Given that the original MNIST dataset has a balanced class distribution, our approach ensures that each client's data segment also has an equitable distribution across the ten distinct digit classes (0 to 9). This precise data partitioning procedure is critical in ensuring that each client's dataset is both individually representative and collectively homogeneous, in accordance with the fundamental principles of IID data distribution. We achieved an impressive accuracy rate of 98.8% by utilizing IID data. This exceptional performance was complemented by an average training loss of 0.000737 and a test loss of 0.0454. These findings demonstrate how well our model performs when used with an IID data distribution.

4.2 Non-IID Partitioning and Evaluation

We used a non-Independent and Identically Distributed (non-IID) data distribution approach in our study, where each client's dataset was purposefully made up of images from two different categories, which are chosen from predefined pairs like [0, 1], [2, 3], [4, 5], [6, 7], or [8, 9]. A one-hot encoded tensor has been used for "target_labels," which stores image labels, after the MNIST dataset initialization. Images with matching labels were found for each category pair and added to the corresponding category subset within 'target_labels_split.' We used the 'torch.split' function to split the indices of selected images into segments of equal size to ensure fair data distribution among clients. After establishing the distribution of our non-IID dataset, we went on to train a fundamental federated learning model over the course of fifty rounds with the main goal of evaluating accuracy and loss fluctuations over rounds. We discovered that the highest

recorded accuracy plateaued at approximately 93.8% during this iterative process. However, it is important to note that significant differences were observed
from one round to the next. The accuracy and loss trajectories showed this
variability, as depicted in Figs. 2(a) and 2(b). The recurring accuracy declines
observed across multiple rounds of training raised significant concerns regarding
the system's robustness and consistency, especially in sensitive domains such as
medical healthcare where precise decisions are critical. As a result, we decided
to address this issue by developing an Equitable model, which is specifically
designed to improve accuracy maintenance and reduce deterioration over the
successive rounds, ensuring the maintenance of robust client models.

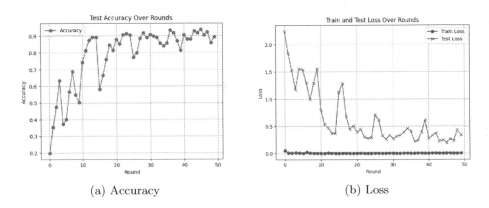

(a) Accuracy   (b) Loss

Fig. 2. Accuracy and Loss before Equitable Model

4.3   Applying Equitable Model

We developed the novel Equitable model to mitigate accuracy declines in
response to the observed accuracy fluctuations in the initial federated learning model. To comprehensively evaluate the impact of the Equitable model on
accuracy stability, we conducted a series of experiments using the same non-
IID dataset and an identical number of training rounds. What we uncovered in
these experiments was a consistent and remarkable trend of accuracy improvement with each successive round, coupled with a simultaneous reduction in loss.
Notably, we achieved an impressive 95.6% accuracy at the end of the 50th round,
with little, if any, variation between rounds, as shown in Fig. 3(a) and 3(b). We
effectively protected the client models against accuracy reductions using our
innovative strategy. Subsequently, this model exhibited either improved or sus-
tained performance levels in subsequent rounds, ensuring the integrity and stability of the federated learning process throughout the optimization phases.This
resilience in the face of accuracy challenges positions our Equitable model as a
promising advancement in the field of federated learning.

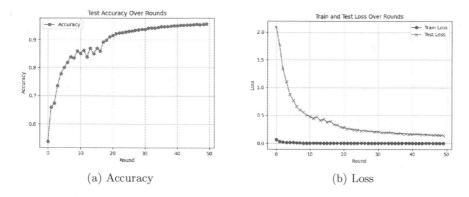

(a) Accuracy   (b) Loss

Fig. 3. Accuracy and Loss after Equitable Model

5   Conclusion

This research explores federated learning, a promising machine learning paradigm that can protect data privacy and security. The study demonstrates that federated learning can produce outcomes that are comparable to those of centralized and Independently and Identically Distributed (IID) data, enabling the development of more accurate and robust deep learning models for clinical image analysis. To enhance the precision of Federated Learning models, a proactive methodology is employed, involving a thorough assessment and coordination of server updates with client modifications. This method establishes a robust defense against malicious updates, thereby ensuring the integrity of the Federated Learning system. A cognate mechanism at the server side ensures accurate models are included in global aggregation due to heterogeneous training data. A client-side technique has been proposed as equitable model to address accuracy reductions caused by server upgrades, which was demonstrated through simulated scenarios. However, it is essential to acknowledge the study's limitations, particularly in the context of the trade-off between enhancing model accuracy and increasing computational complexity. Future research should address this computational complexity and find innovative ways to mitigate it while continuing to improve accuracy. In the long run, federated learning is a crucial tool in healthcare AI, enabling the creation of precise prediction models without compromising patient data privacy.

References

1. Brophy, E., De Vos, M., Boylan, G., Ward, T.: Estimation of continuous blood pressure from PPG via a federated learning approach. Sensors **21**(18), 6311 (2021)
2. Dayan, I., et al.: Federated learning for predicting clinical outcomes in patients with COVID-19. Nat. Med. **27**(10), 1735–1743 (2021)
3. Hill, P.: The rationale for learning communities and learning community models. Research Square (1985)

4. Jiang, J., Lu, Z.: Learning fairness in multi-agent systems. In: Advances in Neural Information Processing Systems, vol. 32 (2019)
5. Kaissis, G., et al.: End-to-end privacy preserving deep learning on multi-institutional medical imaging. Nat. Mach. Intell. **3**(6), 473–484 (2021)
6. Kumar, R., et al.: Blockchain-federated-learning and deep learning models for COVID-19 detection using CT imaging. IEEE Sens. J. **21**(14), 16301–16314 (2021)
7. Li, T., Sahu, A.K., Talwalkar, A., Smith, V.: Federated learning: challenges, methods, and future directions. IEEE Sig. Process. Mag. **37**(3), 50–60 (2020)
8. Linardos, A., Kushibar, K., Walsh, S., Gkontra, P., Lekadir, K.: Federated learning for multi-center imaging diagnostics: a simulation study in cardiovascular disease. Sci. Rep. **12**(1), 3551 (2022)
9. Makkar, A., Santosh, K.C.: Securefed: Federated learning empowered medical imaging technique to detect COVID-19 using chest x-rays. Research Square (2022)
10. Marfoq, O., Neglia, G., Vidal, R., Kameni, L.: Personalized federated learning through local memorization. In International Conference on Machine Learning, pp. 15070–15092. PMLR (2022)
11. McMahan, B., Moore, E., Ramage, D., Hampson, S., y Arcas, B.A.: Communication-efficient learning of deep networks from decentralized data. In: Artificial intelligence and statistics, pp. 1273–1282. PMLR (2017)
12. Min, X., Bin, Yu., Wang, F.: Predictive modeling of the hospital readmission risk from patients' claims data using machine learning: a case study on copd. Sci. Rep. **9**(1), 2362 (2019)
13. Nandi, A., Xhafa, F.: A federated learning method for real-time emotion state classification from multi-modal streaming. Methods **204**, 340–347 (2022)
14. Perez, M.V., et al.: Large-scale assessment of a smartwatch to identify atrial fibrillation. New Engl. J. Med. **381**(20), 1909–1917 (2019)
15. Sahinbas, K., Catak, F.O.: Secure multi-party computation-based privacy-preserving data analysis in healthcare IoT systems. In: Kose, U., Gupta, D., Khanna, A., Rodrigues, J.J.P.C. (eds.) Interpretable Cognitive Internet of Things for Healthcare, pp. 57–72. Springer, Cham (2012). https://doi.org/10.1007/978-3-031-08637-3_3
16. Tedeschini, B.C., et al.: Decentralized federated learning for healthcare networks: a case study on tumor segmentation. IEEE Access **10**, 8693–8708 (2022)
17. Yoo, J.H., et al.: Personalized federated learning with clustering: non-IID heart rate variability data application. In: 2021 International Conference on Information and Communication Technology Convergence (ICTC), pp. 1046–1051. IEEE (2021)
18. Zhang, J., Li, C., Robles-Kelly, A., Kankanhalli, M.: Hierarchically fair federated learning. arXiv preprint arXiv:2004.10386 (2020)
19. Zhang, W., et al.: Dynamic-fusion-based federated learning for COVID-19 detection. IEEE Internet Things J. **8**(21), 15884–15891 (2021)

Fake News Investigation Using Ensemble Machine Learning Techniques

Jai Jain[1], Vansh Dubey[1], Lakshit Sama[2], Vimal Kumar[1]([⊠]),
Simarpreet Singh[1], Ishan Budhiraja[1], and Ruchika Arora[3]

[1] Bennett University, Greater Noida, Uttar Pradesh, India
{vimal.kumar,ishan.budhiraja}@bennett.edu.in
[2] Capgemini Engineering, Melbourne, Australia
[3] SR University, Ananthasagar, Hasanparthy Hanumakonda, Telangana, India

Abstract. The classification of any information as true or false has piqued the curiosity of researchers all around the world. Different types of studies are done to document the impact of misleading and fake news on the general public, as well as people's reactions to such news. Falsified news or fabricated posts are any textual or visual content that is fake/false that is created in order for readers to believe in anything that isn't true. For instance, a news item headlined "Beasts in White Aprons" was recently circulated on the microblogging platform-Facebook, by an acknowledged reporter from Srinagar, J &K, and many began to believe it, despite the fact that it was completely false. Therefore, the main goal of this research is to apply various machine learning models to distinguish between real and fraudulent news. By using several machine learning models to discriminate between authentic and false news, we add to the expanding body of research on identifying fake news in this work. Our model performs better in scenarios in which there is limited data.

Keywords: Artificial Intelligence · decision tree · fake news · gradient boosting · logistic regression · random forest classifier

1 Introduction

Thanks to the social media and internet, it is now simpler and more convenient to access news information. To the social media and internet, it is now simpler and more convenient to access news information. Internet users routinely follow newsworthy events online, and this process is made simpler by the rise in mobile device use.

But enormous potential also entails immense responsibility. Society is greatly influenced by the media. And, as is frequently the case, this may have positive effects on people. To achieve certain objectives, the media may distort information in a number of ways. As a result, news pieces that are not fully genuine, if not entirely fake, are produced. A lot of websites appear to be dedicated almost

KC Santosh et al. (Eds.): RTIP2R 2023, CCIS 2026, pp. 89–100, 2024.
https://doi.org/10.1007/978-3-031-53082-1_8

completely to the distribution of misleading information. They create hoaxes, misinformation, & disinformation that pass for real news, and they typically utilize social media to drive attention & spread their message. Most experts claim that Artificial intelligence (AI) can assist in the fight against fake news. As hardware have become progressively cheaper and larger datasets are starting to become available, AI systems have recently improved their performance on a range of classification tasks (voice detection, picture recognition etc.).

People are finding it easier to find news because of the easy access and multiplication of information available through traditional news sources or social media. As a result, determining the difference between false and true news has become difficult. It encourages the dissemination of misleading information as a result [1].

The term Fake news refers to deceptive journalism and claims that are used to deceive and mislead the public. Presently, the legitimacy of social media networks, where most of this information is shared, is in jeopardy. Misinformation of this nature can have major societal ramifications, hence detecting it has become a hot topic in research. Preventing the spread of fake and misleading knowledge is important [2]. Human involvement, such as the use of the International Fact Checking Network (ICFN) and other manual fact-checking websites like the Washington Post, Snopes, Fact Checker, Fact-Check, and Truth Or Fiction, can be used to verify the veracity of information [3].

Websites may appear reliable and effective, but they have scalability problems when dealing with massive amounts of data. To solve this problem, the automatic fact-checking concept was developed, and it comprises of 3 components: Recognition, validation, and correction are all steps in the identification, verification, and correction process. All 3 components work together to uncover bogus claims, verify their veracity and disseminate updated, accurate information on social platforms [2].

In this study, by using several machine learning models to differentiate between authentic and false news, we add to the expanding corpus of research on spotting fake news. Our approach involves analyzing textual and visual content to find patterns and characteristics that may be used to categorize news stories as either authentic or fake. Our findings can inform the development of more effective tools and techniques for combating the proliferation of misleading information in today's media landscape.

1.1   Novelty

This paper's main goal is to examine and combine various classification and regression models for detecting fake news. There have been previous works in this field but most of them make use of one or two AI models whereas others depend on human input. The objective is to create a separate model that can differentiate between fake and real news without any human intervention to a high degree of accuracy. For this, we have put together 3 classifiers and 1 regression model to create an ensemble method that compares results from these four models and provides an output that gives an accuracy score higher than any of the previous methods (Fig. 1).

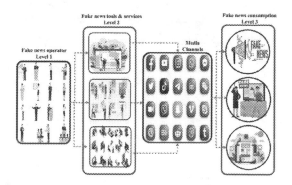

Fig. 1. Fake news levels

1.2 Motivation

Recently, the discussion about fake news and incorrect information has intensified. This is because to the potential harm they might cause in a variety of disciplines, one of which is politics. Various research have built algorithms based on machine learning for identifying false news as a result of the volume of news produced every day. Also, the news that circulates on WhatsApp, are mostly fake but even then, many people (older people in most cases) believe it to be true and then circulate it further with word of mouth. Print media giants have also created their own bespoke web extensions, such as Decodex, to help distinguish between true and false content. Fake news is frequently propagated with the assistance of machine learning algorithms, hence antidote algorithms emerge to assist in recognizing the contents and sources of such misinformation [2]. There are three types of sophisticated algorithms: content-based, message diffusion dynamic-based, & composite. Despite several attempts, every one of these algorithms suffer from the absence of a comprehensive set of data providing multivariate information to help in the effective detection of false news aspects. So, the quest to solve these problems motivates us to do this project.

1.3 Background Knowledge

This project requires the knowledge of how regression and classification models work, especially gradient boosting classification, random forest classification, decision tree classification, logistic regression. Also, it is obvious that we should know data preprocessing. And not only this, but we should also be familiar with the 8 steps of data life cycle.

2　Proposed Methodology

(See Fig. 2).

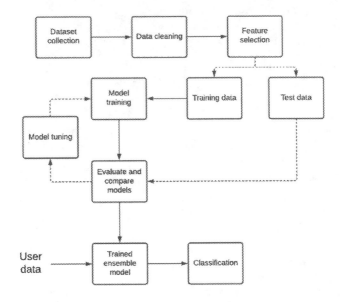

Fig. 2. Project Flow

2.1　Problem Statement Modelling and Research Contributions

Researchers are looking at ways to discern between real and misleading information due to the ubiquity of fake news and its possible detrimental effects on society. Through the use of several machine learning models to categorise news stories as real or fraudulent, this research seeks to solve the issue of false news. The classification process is aided by the identification of patterns and traits through the use of textual and visual content analysis. The study adds to the body of knowledge already available on spotting false news and provides knowledge that may be used to create tools and methods that are more efficient. The investigation of machine learning methods including logistic regression, decision trees, random forest classifiers, and gradient boosting, as well as the identification, validation, and correction of fake news, are significant aspects of this effort. The research's significance lies in its ability to affect journalism and control the dissemination of false information.

2.2　Methodology

As proposed in the workflow above, our fake news detection method will follow the traditional AI/ML life cycle. Data will be collected from various sources on the internet and put together in a collected dataset.

Once the dataset collection is completed, target value and features will be identified, and data pre-processing will take place on these features. Here, the target value will be the "fake/truth" category of the dataset while other columns will serve as features. Data pre-processing includes checking for and removal of null values, duplicate values, standardizing and encoding the independent variables.

Datasets often contain an extensive amount of columns that may be irrelevant to the final prediction and not removing these extra columns may lead to overfitting. In order to avoid this and improve the system's efficiency, dimensionality reduction will be applied.

The data is divided into training and testing sets after pre-processing. Four models- namely decision tree classification, logistic regression, gradient boosting classification and random forest classification- will be made use of in this project. These models will be trained using the dataset then tested on the same dataset.

The models are trained till the final ensemble method obtained by combining the four methods produces desirable results. Criteria such as precision, F1-score, accuracy and coefficient of determination amongst various other scores will be used to judge the models. Once the model is trained, manual user data is entered at the end and the model will classify the given data as either "false" or "true". Data cleaning cycle is demonstrated in Fig. 3.

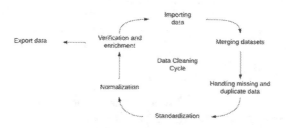

Fig. 3. Data Cleaning Cycle

Datasets are imported and merged (if multiple datasets are present). Null and missing values are either removed or replaced by the average of respective columns. Duplicate values are deleted from each column. Standardization and normalization are methods used for when different features in the dataset have highly varying ranges. Standardization is the rescaling of features so that the mean and standard deviation are 0 and 1 respectively. Normalization is the process of rescaling the features themselves into the range 0–1.

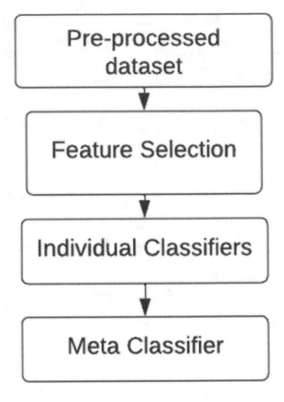

Fig. 4. Ensemble Method Flowchart

Figure 4 shows how ensemble methods work. Each model is trained individually and the averages of the results from each model is taken into account for the final combined method.

Feature selection refers to the process of eliminating 'irrelevant' features in order to avoid overfitting. This falls under 'Dimensionality Reduction'. This is achieved by identifying and selecting a subset of features based on their coefficient of determination values. If two features are found to be highly correlated, the algorithm selects one feature and drops the other. This cycle is repeated till all the remaining features have low correlation with each other.

We have used 4 classification methods -: Gradient boost classification, Decision Tree classification, Logistic regression and Random Forest classification. Then we got the weighted average of each individual method and then returned the answer. Weights were assigned on the basis of accuracy of each method.

2.3   Logistic Regression

Traditional statistics and machine learning both benefit from the usage of the approach known as logistic regression. Similar to linear regression, logistic regression makes predictions about whether something is true or untrue rather than continuous variables like size. And that's precisely what we're doing at this very moment [12].

2.4   Decision Tree Classification

A technique to supervised learning is the decision tree. Both classification and regression issues may be solved with it. It is used most frequently, nonetheless, to address classification-related problems. Dataset properties are included in internal nodes. The branches stand in for judgement calls. In this tree-structured classifier, the conclusion is provided by each leaf node [13].

2.5   Random Forest Classification

It works by combining multiple decision tree classifiers and chooses the output based on voting. The theory is that uncorrelated trees working together as a committee will outperform an individual model The individual decision trees inside have low bias and high variance and after combining their outputs we get a lesser biased or rather a more generalized model [14].

2.6   Gradient Boost Classification

Gradient boost classifier builds fixed size trees from the previous tree's errors. It uses gradients of all unknown hyperparameters to reduce errors. Finally gradient boosting stops when there are no visible changes in the predicted outputs. It initially has high bias but with time the bias error is reduced [13].

3   Experimental Setup and Result Analysis

3.1   Dataset Discription

The project makes use of two datasets containing around 21000 clippings of news articles regarding US politics published in the years 2016–2017. Both datasets have 4 columns each- "title", "text", "subject", "date". Title-string data type, contains the headline of the article text-string data type, contains a snippet of the article subject- string data type, categorical column with values "US News", "Middle-east", "Government News", "left-news", "News" and "politics"; contains the topic of the article date- string data type, contains dates in the format "Month DD, YYYY", contains the date of publication of the article.

3.2   Pre-processing

Pandas library is used to read the dataset and load it in the form of DataFrames. The last ten columns of each dataset are removed and added to a new DataFrame for "manual testing". This manual testing is also known as the validation phase, which usually takes place after training and testing on the dataset is done. As the original datasets do not contain the target column, a new column called "class" is created for this purpose. This category contains integer values "0" or "1", 0 being False and 1 being True. For data pre-processing, the two datasets (False and True) are merged together for efficiency. After the datasets have been combined, to make sure the training and testing sets reflect the data's general distribution, they are mixed at random.

Non-alphanumeric characters such as extra whitespaces, special characters and links are removed from the set using regex. This is done to remove "noise" and clean the dataset so that only relevant keywords are present during model training. Unnecessary categories ("title", "subject" and "date") are manually removed from the DataFrame. This is feature selection done to ensure the model training uses less resources and avoids the risk of overfitting. After the independent and dependent variables are identified, the independent variable (here, category "text") is converted into vectors using sklearn's Tfidf Vectorizer. Every time a word appears in a given article, its TF-IDF value increases, but when it makes an appearance in other articles for the given dataset, the score decreases. During training and testing, this score will be used to associate words with their class (True/False) - if certain words containing a specific range of TF-IDF scores are found in the "False" class during training, the model will be able to classify articles as False if the same terms are recognised with TF-IDF values in the same range during testing phase.

3.3   Results

Each independent model produces its own classification in a binary format, where 0 denotes "Fake" and 1 denotes "Not Fake". These individual reports are compiled and displayed in a presentable format to the user. As multiple models were used, the final accuracy is observed to be higher than the models used themselves. Our model performs better in scenarios where the input data is limited. This is the main differentiator of our research paper (Figs. 5, 6, 7, 8 and Table 1).

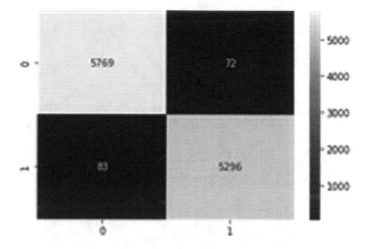

Fig. 5. Confusion matrix for LR model

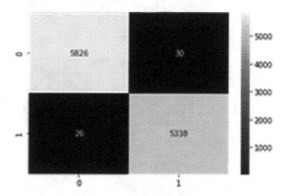

Fig. 6. Confusion matrix for DT model

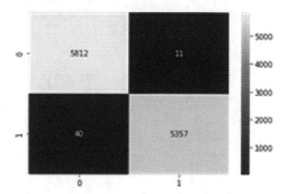

Fig. 7. Confusion matrix for GB model

Table 1. Related Work

Reference	Dataset	Contributions	Accuracy achieved	Challenges
[4]	FakeNewsData1, Fake-OrReal News, TwitterBR, and btv lifestyle	1. Misinformation identification in many languages 2. Each dataset was evaluated using customised features, Word2Vec, DCDistance, BagOfWords, and convulutional neural network(CNN) as a classifier	79%	It is not possible to improve accuracy
[5]	Italian Facebook dataset	Contextual features, consumer features, geometrical characteristics, mindset features, and projected features were considered as features for a classifier	91%	Unable to spot the factor that has a detrimental effect on the data
[6]	Twitter and Weibo datasets	Appropriate & unlabeled samples are used to train CNN. Model results were verified using five-fold cross-validation	90%	The analysis includes more than 1100 Twitter tweets and more than 800 posts on Weibo
[7]	2282 news articles related to the US election	There have been some new additions to the training classifiers	85%	There are only a few data points available. Future datasets should be accessible to researchers in a significant proportion, and deep learning algorithms with more accurate predictions of false news should be feasible
[8]	5800 twitter tweets	BiLSTM-CNN can assess whether tweets are false news or not by comparing them to training characteristics in order to validate them	86.12%	You can only categorize anything as false or authentic using text-based attributes.
[9]	the PolitiFact dataset, BuzzFeed dataset	Using matrix-tensor factorization, the attributes are extracted. Moreover, XGBoost and DNN are implemented to classify the retrieved features	85.86%	The extracted features using content and context was not demonstrated
[10]	Liar dataset	DSSM-LSTM classifies news utilizing semantic features to identify disinformation	99%	Feature extractions based on semantic characteristics were not shown
[11]	Extracted using FakeNewsNet tool	Long short term memory(LSTM), GRU and recurrent neural network (RNN) deep learning techniques were utilized to research binary classification	75%-LSTM 45%-GRU 62%-RNN	It's doesn't achieve greater precision, and it is restricted to a small dataset

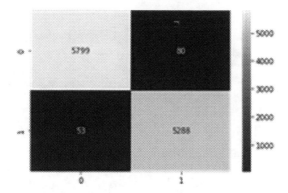

Fig. 8. Confusion matrix for RF model

	precision	recall	f1-score	accuracy
LR	0.98	0.99	0.99	0.9861
DT	0.99	0.99	0.99	0.9950
GB	0.99	0.99	1.00	0.9954
RF	0.99	0.99	0.99	0.9881

3.4 Conclusion

The final model was tested with real-world news articles collected from the internet and produced highly accurate results. As multiple models were used, the final accuracy is observed to be higher than the models used themselves. The model was most accurate when tested for articles containing mentions of "Trump" or keywords closely related to US politics.

3.5 Future Scope

The model can be further refined by switching up the ensemble technique (changing to bagging instead of the basic average-score boosting) or adding more complex models. The introduction of neural networks and deep learning methods such as LSTM and RNN can further boost the accuracy of the final model. By expanding the scope of the training dataset, the fake news detection can also be used for topics outside of US politics.

References

1. Ahmad, I., Yousaf, M., Yousaf, S., Ahmad, M.O.: Fake news detection using machine learning ensemble methods. Complexity **2020**, 1–11 (2020)
2. Rajalaxmi, R., Narasimha Prasad, L., Janakiramaiah, B., Pavankumar, C., Neelima, N., Sathishkumar, V.: Optimizing hyperparameters and performance analysis of LSTM model in detecting fake news on social media. Trans. Asian Low-Resour. Lang. Inf. Process. (2022)

3. Hakak, S., Alazab, M., Khan, S., Gadekallu, T.R., Maddikunta, P.K.R., Khan, W.Z.: An ensemble machine learning approach through effective feature extraction to classify fake news. Futur. Gener. Comput. Syst. **117**, 47–58 (2021)
4. Faustini, P.H.A., Covoes, T.F.: Fake news detection in multiple platforms and languages. Expert Syst. Appl. **158**, 113503 (2020)
5. Vicario, M.D., Quattrociocchi, W., Scala, A., Zollo, F.: Polarization and fake news: early warning of potential misinformation targets. ACM Trans. Web (TWEB) **13**(2), 1–22 (2019)
6. Liu, Y., Wu, Y.-F.B.: FNED: a deep network for fake news early detection on social media. ACM Trans. Inf. Syst.(TOIS) **38**(3), 1–33 (2020)
7. Reis, J.C., Correia, A., Murai, F., Veloso, A., Benevenuto, F.: Supervised learning for fake news detection. IEEE Intell. Syst. **34**(2), 76–81 (2019)
8. Asghar, M.Z., Habib, A., Habib, A., Khan, A., Ali, R., Khattak, A.: Exploring deep neural networks for rumor detection. J. Ambient. Intell. Humaniz. Comput. **12**, 4315–4333 (2021)
9. Kaliyar, R.K., Goswami, A., Narang, P.: DeepFake: improving fake news detection using tensor decomposition-based deep neural network. J. Supercomput. **77**, 1015–1037 (2021)
10. Jadhav, S.S., Thepade, S.D.: Fake news identification and classification using DSSM and improved recurrent neural network classifier. Appl. Artif. Intell. **33**(12), 1058–1068 (2019)
11. Vereshchaka, A., Cosimini, S., Dong, W.: Analyzing and distinguishing fake and real news to mitigate the problem of disinformation. Comput. Math. Organ. Theory **26**, 350–364 (2020)
12. Dutta, H.S., Dutta, V.R., Adhikary, A., Chakraborty, T.: HawkesEye: detecting fake retweeters using Hawkes process and topic modeling. IEEE Trans. Inf. Forensics Secur. **15**, 2667–2678 (2020)
13. Ozbay, F.A., Alatas, B.: Fake news detection within online social media using supervised artificial intelligence algorithms. Phys. A **540**, 123174 (2020)
14. Bali, A.P.S., Fernandes, M., Choubey, S., Goel, M.: Comparative performance of machine learning algorithms for fake news detection. In: Singh, M., Gupta, P.K., Tyagi, V., Flusser, J., Ören, T., Kashyap, R. (eds.) ICACDS 2019, Part II. CCIS, vol. 1046, pp. 420–430. Springer, Singapore (2019). https://doi.org/10.1007/978-981-13-9942-8_40

Deep Learning Based Bug Detection in Solidity Smart Contracts

Jagendra Singh[✉], Dinesh Prasad Sahu, Shreyans Murkute, Ujjwal Yadav, Manish Agarwal, and Pranay Kumar

School of Computer Science Engineering and Technology, Bennett University, Greater Noida, India
jagendrasngh@gmail.com

Abstract. Smart contracts have the potential to revolutionize many sectors by automating difficult procedures and removing the need for middlemen. Smart contracts are self-executing contracts in which the contents of the agreement between the buyer and seller are directly encoded into lines of code. Nevertheless, because smart contracts are immutable, vulnerabilities cannot be easily rectified after they are implemented. For this reason, it is essential to identify and eliminate vulnerabilities before implementation. The Ethereum Blockchain is the primary home of such Contracts which are written in the full-fledged programming language-Solidity. The process of finding these vulnerabilities before deployment is known as Smart Contract Auditing. We propose this new scalable framework of Smart Contract Auditing which promises accuracy and dependability using Deep Learning approaches that can be leveraged for large scale auditing.

Keywords: Artificial Intelligence · Deep Learning · Smart Contract Vulnerabilities · Bytecode Representation

1 Introduction

To Blockchain and smart contracts have taken the Web3 community by storm in recent years. The penetration of smart contracts can be seen in the whole Web3 and Blockchain world and especially in applications such as Decentralized Finance (DeFi), DAOs, real estate, NFTs, etc. [1]. A smart contract can be defined as a set of instructions stored on the Ethereum platform which can automatically execute a certain predefined set of instructions if some well-defined conditions are met [2]. However, smart contracts are certainly not bulletproof. In fact, many people in the Web3 space are of the opinion that smart contracts are only as "smart" as the people that have created it. Malicious actors in the space have exploited smart contract owners many times and sometimes the extent has been in the millions. An infamous example is the DAO hack of 2016 which exploited the smart contract to the tune of $150M using a re-entrancy vulnerability [3].

To safeguard against such attacks, smart contract auditing became an industry of its own with many high-profile projects gaining notoriety on the back of trust gained by the "Audited" label. However, as demand for audits for large-scale projects grew so did wait

KC Santosh et al. (Eds.): RTIP2R 2023, CCIS 2026, pp. 101–109, 2024.
https://doi.org/10.1007/978-3-031-53082-1_9

times and costs for all other players in the community. These players either had to use less than ideal automated tools [4] for their projects or had to skip the auditing process altogether.

After evaluating the advantages and disadvantages of deep learning models [5], we decided to use a Convolutional Neural Network (CNN) for vulnerability detection purposes. In the later years of the last decade special notice was given to the Android Malware Detection problem [6]. Ultimately, the community was able to concentrate its time and efforts to solve this problem through various Machine Learning methodologies, primarily Deep Learning. Ultimately, many models were made that promised and showcased great accuracy using CNN's something that was considered non-conventional at that time. This was because CNN had been used primarily for pure Computer Vision tasks such as Object Detection and various other types of Real-Image analysis.

Researchers were able to show that CNN's can work well even for synthetic data such as Malware Detection in Java Bytecode [4]. We aim to use this approach to solve the problem of Vulnerable Solidity Contracts on the Ethereum Blockchain. The whole data pipeline of the project is based on carrying out Convolutions without Stride. The concerned architecture and the dependent Data lifecycle are explained in the following sections. The primary aim of such an architecture and data lifecycle is to preserve the semantics of the Solidity Code when it is converted into an image.

2   Literature Survey

When approaching this problem, the way to go was with a 2-pronged strategy in the initial phases. We tried to find appropriate resources that highlighted the exact nature of the types of Vulnerabilities found in Smart Contracts and try to find out possible solutions to solving similar problems in the Deep Learning literature. On the second front we found significant success being attained by researchers on the Android Malware Detection systems using a similar approach. Therein as well, a color inspired CNN based solution on the program Bytecode seemed to bring great success. Not only were custom made Models showing great potential but even techniques such as Transfer Learning in which Deep Learning models made for a specific and separate purpose also were found to be applicable [7]. The main motivation to carry out such a study was to find out the potential and ability of a purpose-built CNN network to learn from a Program's Bytecode. This certainly seemed to be the case.

On the first front, we also found out that there exists a very concrete definition and outlines for what is a 'vulnerability' in a Solidity Smart Contract [8]. We were specifically intrigued by 4 specific types of vulnerabilities because of the specific pattern seen in the Contract bytecode which will make it detectable by CNN. These are-

- Re-Entrancy
- Unchecked LL Calls
- Tx.Origin
- Timestamp-Dependency

Re-Entrancy is considered by many to be the most exploitable type of Smart contract vulnerability around. The main idea of Re-Entrancy is very simple. The attacker first of all tries to exploit the Transfer function of a Token Contract. The main idea is to use a fallback function to keep siphoning off funds stored in the Contract before the balance in the contract is updated. The DAO attack is an extremely famous example of a Re-Entrancy Attack (Figs. 1 and 2).

Reentrancy

```
contract SimpleDAO {
  mapping (address => uint) public credit;
  function donate(address to) payable {
    credit[to] += msg.value;
  }
  function withdraw(uint amount) {
    if (credit[msg.sender]>= amount) {
      bool res =
          msg.sender.call.value(amount)();
      credit[msg.sender] -= amount;
    }
  }
  function queryCredit(address to) returns
      (uint){
    return credit[to];
  }
}
```

Fig. 1. Vulnerable Contract

```
contract ReenAttack {
  SimpleDAO public dao =
      SimpleDAO(0xd914...39138);
  address owner;
  function ReenAttack(){owner =
      msg.sender; }
  function() {
      dao.withdraw(dao.queryCredit(this));
      }
  function getJackpot(){
      owner.send(this.balance); }
}
```

Fig. 2. A Re-Entrancy exploiting Attack Contract

This vulnerability where a function that has both deposit and withdraw functionalities and siphoning off funds without balance updation was used to siphon off funds close to $50 Million in Ether of that time. Even though this exploit occurred in 2016, Re-Entrancy continues to be a major problem today [9]. Given below are examples of both the vulnerable contract and the attacker contract.

This is a classic example of a contract containing Re-Entrancy vulnerabilities. As we can see this SimpleDAO contract has both donate and withdraw functionality. But the Re-Entrancy is solely contained in the withdraw function. Here, the usage of msg.sender.call.value is wrong. The usage of this method causes the Ether in this case to be withdrawn without the updation of the balance of the contract. An attacker contract created by a bad actor with nefarious designs is shown below. This ReenAttack Contract can exploit the given contract. In some cases, the entire holding can be siphoned off [10].

Unchecked Low Level Calls is another type of Smart contract vulnerability. It is widely considered to be a type of vulnerability which can cause the Ether of the Vulnerable contract to be "lost" but it is not a contract that can be attacked by an external contract to siphon funds. Nevertheless, loss of Ether is still a major concern. In most cases, the existence of Unchecked Low Level calls is based on the usage of low-level calls such as call(), callcode(), delegatecall() or send(). The vulnerability occurs when an exception occurs during code execution. The behavior of these lower level calls is considered to be anomalous when such a situation occurs. Instead of stopping execution these calls return Boolean value set to false. This can lead to fail-opens causing important functionalities such as send() to fail. In most cases this vulnerability cannot be exploited except for some edge cases where a potential attacker can induce a call to fail on purpose if it leads to some behaviour that is mutually beneficial. Given below is an example of Unchecked Low Level Calls vulnerable contract [11].

Tx.Origin vulnerability was borne out of efforts of the Solidity community to verify transactions and provide a greater sense of security. The use of social engineering to exploit vulnerabilities in financial systems or even other types of systems is almost as old as those systems themselves. The Tx.Origin call method was introduced to verify the Transactors identity when an external contract called a specific function. This identity was verified using the Tx.origin call method. The Tx.Origin method does this with the help of the Transactors address value.

A bad actor can exploit this predictable behaviour by using fallback functions to pose as another for another Tx.Origin using function in the contract which has a different context. Given below are two contracts. The first is a vulnerable contract and the second is an attacker contract.

This is an example of a contract using the Tx.Origin method to verify the transactors' identity. We should keep in mind that instead of using Tx.Origin method we can use the msg.sender call method to perform the function of verification before transfer or any other thing without the vulnerability associated with Tx.Origin. Here we can see that the TxAttackWallet can use the address of TxUserWallet to still use the transferTo function of TxUserWallet.

Timestamp-Dependency is the last type of Smart contract we will be elaborating on. This type of vulnerability from the other 3 as it is largely concerned with the mining operation on the Blockchain and can be exploited due to the public nature of the Blockchain. Just like most other vulnerabilities it is also connected to the usage of a specific method namely block.timestamp. Whenever a certain functionality of the Contract depends on the value of this block.timestamp, the contract can be vulnerable because the exploiter can be aware of the timestamp value that will be expected. This is because of the public nature of that contract [12].

It is clear to see why this contract is vulnerable to the Timestamp-Dependency vulnerability. This is a Lotto contract which rewards users with a "Jackpot" if they guess the correct random value. However, the random variable here is determined by the block.timestamp method. Any miner here can check the hash value of the jackpot variable directly from the blockchain and therefore bypass the random nature of the jackpot and lotto system of the contract [13]. This kind of vulnerability can be easily solved by removing the dependence of contract functions and variables on block.timestamp method [14].

3 Methodology

When building an AI tool, there are 2 primary facets that someone has to focus on particularly when the solution is going to be based on Deep Learning:

- Understanding the data at hand.
- Building a model around it.

Our approach consists of following steps:

- Data pre-processing: Here we maintain the locality of the smart contract for neural net, while converting smart contracts into input images for CNN. We maintain the semantics and context of a smart contract.
- Neural net architecture: Our CNN architecture will be able to differentiate vulnerable smart contracts and verified contracts.

The problem at hand is one which is concerned with data availability, data selection and how we define and rule out a vulnerability.

We begin to solve this issue with the use of Bug Injection technique. Our data set comprises different types of smart contracts across projects like lending, swapping, Tokens, Launchpads, DNS, Vaults, NFTs, etc. The data set also expands across multiple EVM compatible chains. The data was collected in a custom manner from chain-scanning sites such as Etherscan, BSCScan and etc.

3.1 Bug Injection Technique

The basic idea is to collect audited smart contracts, inject bugs into them from an already prepared Bug-Pool and save the ground truth labels. We can then feed this to the Neural Network model for training after performing appropriate pre-processing. The Bug Injection module is illustrated here (Fig. 3):

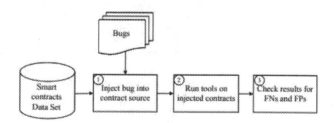

Fig. 3. Contract Injection Timeline

Data selection is something that we have given great importance to as well. The selected contracts are either already audited or are part of high-profile projects which hold funds. Therefore, the assumption that such contracts can at least be 'relatively' vulnerability-free is not far-fetched.

3.2 Data Pre-processing Pipeline

This challenge is primarily transformed into a Computer Vision problem using Image Mapping from related compiled bytecode in the pre-processing pipeline. This strategy has had outstanding success with related issues like Android Malware Detection (Table 1).

Table 1. Proposed Method Algorithm

Algorithm 1 Proposed Method Algorithm
Input: C_{Sol}: Smart contract source code
Output: R : Detection result
1: **procedure** Proposed method(C_{Sol})
2:     C_{OP} = Compile(C_{Sol})
3:     C_T = Transform(C_{OP})
4:     I_C = Image_Mapping(C_T)
5:     R = Predict(I_C)
6:     return R
7: **end procedure**

Our strategy depends on successful image mapping because we will later use this information to feed a computer vision-based model. The primary goal is to condense each Opcode instruction and its associated arguments into a single pixel. This will aid the model's ability to generalise and detect and categorize higher-dimensional patterns.

3.3 Network Architecture

Deep learning methods can provide constant execution time by calculating the product of learned weight values and input values from the smart contract. While these methods have shown good accuracy in classifying malware and vulnerable software codes, most deep learning models, particularly convolutional neural network (CNN)-based detection methods, are designed to classify images, not software codes.

To overcome this challenge, we have adopted an innovative approach of converting the textual representation of software code into images and then by feeding these images to CNN-based deep learning models. By doing so, we can leverage the power of CNN-based models to effectively classify software codes and detect vulnerabilities with high accuracy.

There are however some newer things we had to try to achieve efficiency on such a model. The reason is simple. For our data distribution of course Stride-less convolution makes sense due to the above-mentioned reasons. However, it is also known that stride-less convolution is considered to be quite an expensive operation. The reason is simple to understand. The filter will have to go through all the higher dimensionalities throughout the network without any striding operation (Fig. 4).

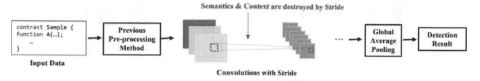

Fig. 4. CNN Architecture with Stride Operation

To tackle this issue, we will be using a layer of Depth wise Separable Convolution. This type of Convolution which is also seen in networks such as MobileNet. Depth wise Separable Convolution is made of 2 separate convolutional operations. The first one known as Depth wise Convolution is based on upon breaking or 'grouping' the Input Feature into separate channels and apply an individual filter to each channel separately. This type of convolution will be ineffective without the Pointwise Convolution that follows it. Pointwise Convolution is basically made up of 1×1 filters which are applied to the concatenated output of the previous layer.

This type of Convolution is actually the basis of popular frameworks such as Efficient-Net. According to authors of EfficientNet usage of Depth wise Separable Convolution is revolutionary. This is because it shows the exact same results as a normal convolutional layer but with only 11% of the FLOPS (Floating Point Operations Per Second). This makes Depth wise Separable convolution extremely useful in cases where training is considered to be already 'inefficient'. For EfficientNet, this was because the model was Deep, but in our case, it is because our model uses stride-less convolution.

4 Results

To comprehensively validate our results, we tested our model against a custom dataset made from Smart Bugs Curated and custom data created for this purpose. Smart Bugs Curated is a special dataset containing Smart contracts labelled with a solid ground truth label. For these initial tests, we only focused on 4 vulnerabilities. Re-Entrancy, Unchecked LL Calls, Tx.Origin and Timestamp-Dependency (Fig. 5).

As VGG and Inception are models created with ImageNet Dataset in mind it requires converting our data into a 2D-RGB image instead of a 1-D RGB image that our In addition to this we compared the performance of our Model against other large CNN models such as Inception and VGGNet or VGG which have shown to have good performance against similar tasks such as Android malware detection. Finally, we tested this performance with the help of 4 separate metrics – Accuracy, Precision, Recall and F1-score model uses. This slightly changed the comparison parameters as the problem changed from being a 1-D Convolutional Operation to a 2-D Convolutional Operation. Also, the size of the image had to be adjusted as the input size for both Inception and VGG are specified.

We implemented the model using the latest PyTorch version – 2.0.0+cu118 and Python version 3.8.1. As for the hardware we used the services of the Cloud Platform-Google Colab. The exact configuration of the system was of two types. We either used the Colab Free Tier to train which has a Nvidia Tesla T4 GPU and 12.7 GB System RAM. In addition, we also used the Premium Tier GPU of Colab a Nvidia A100 and 83.5 GB System RAM for the purpose of training and tuning our model.

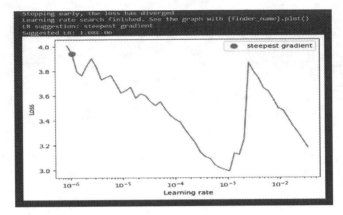

Fig. 5. Learning Rate Optimization for SGD

To compare our model to other baseline models such as Inception and VGGNet we have used TensorFlow version as we found Transfer Learning models to have better performance there with easier integration.

During the model training phases we faced various Hyperparameter search difficulties. We ultimately trained the Model using the SGD optimization algorithm with a Learning Rate chosen after careful consideration.

5   Conclusion

We have developed this model with a vision to enhance the already existing smart contract auditing tools and leverage the public data that has been already audited. The rapid advancements in the fields of machine learning and artificial intelligence have allowed us to develop a tool so efficient and quick that we can now think of eradicating the manual efforts required with auditing.

One of the most exciting features of this tool is the ability to create 'Detectors' of various vulnerabilities in almost no time. As we don't need to create complex Symbolic Rules to detect new vulnerabilities this tool is completely future proof to even new exploits.

Some of the standout features of this Model are:

- Self-learning model that improves its accuracy over time.
- Leveraging the latest advancements in the field of AI/ML.
- Use of a vast dataset that encompasses a variety of smart contracts.
- Invulnerable to even new types of exploits and hacks.
- Fast and consistent execution times.
- Easy to incorporate new vulnerabilities in the future.

We also believe that making such a tool which makes trustable vulnerability detection accessible to ALL players in the Web3 community will also bring with it significant goodwill and recognition. This tool will allow us to foster a community and catch the imagination of all. Being a tool, which is based on AI in the Blockchain space will enable us to tap into both of these communities and lead innovation in addressing other blockchain-related issues with AI.

References

1. Kumar, S., Pathak, S.K.: A comprehensive study of XSS attack and the digital forensic models to gather the evidence. ECS Trans. **107**(1), 7153 (2022)
2. Sharma, N., et al.: A smart ontology-based IoT framework for remote patient monitoring. Biomed. Sig. Process. Control **68**, 102717 (2021). https://doi.org/10.1016/j.bspc.2021.102717
3. Mall, S.: Heart diagnosis using deep neural network. In: 3rd International Conference on Computational Intelligence and Knowledge Economy, ICCIKE 2023. Amity University, Dubai (2023)
4. Sharan, A.: Term co-occurrence and context window based combined approach for query expansion with the semantic notion of terms. Int. J. Web Sci. (IJWS) **3**(1), 32–57 (2017)
5. Yadav, C.S., et al.: Malware analysis in IoT & android systems with defensive mechanism. Electronics **11**, 2354 (2022). https://doi.org/10.3390/electronics11152354
6. Kumar, R.: Lexical co-occurrence and contextual window-based approach with semantic similarity for query expansion. Int. J. Intell. Inf. Technol. (IJIIT) **13**(3), 57–78 (2017)
7. Berghout, T., Benbouzid, M., Muyeen, S.M.: Machine learning for cybersecurity in smart grids: a comprehensive review-based study on methods, solutions, and prospects. Int. J. Crit. Infrastruct. Prot. **38**, 100547 (2022). https://doi.org/10.1016/j.ijcip.2022.100547
8. Upreti, K., Gupta, A.K., Dave, N., Surana, A., Mishra, D.: Deep learning approach for hand drawn emoji identification. In: 2022 IEEE International Conference on Current Development in Engineering and Technology (CCET), Bhopal, India, pp. 1–6 (2022). https://doi.org/10.1109/CCET56606.2022.10080218
9. Sajid, M., Rajak, R.: Capacitated vehicle routing problem using algebraic particle swarm optimization with simulated annealing algorithm. In: Artificial Intelligence in Cyber-Physical Systems. CRC Press (2023)
10. Bohat, V.K.: Neural network model for recommending music based on music genres. In: 10th IEEE International Conference on Computer Communication and Informatics (ICCCI -2021), Coimbatore, India (2021)
11. Yadav, A., Kumar, S., Singh, J.: A review of physical unclonable functions (PUFs) and its applications in IoT environment. In: Hu, Y.C., Tiwari, S., Trivedi, M.C., Mishra, K.K. (eds.) Ambient Communications and Computer Systems, vol. 356, pp. 1–13. Springer, Singapore (2022). https://doi.org/10.1007/978-981-16-7952-0_1
12. Prasad, M., Daraghmi, Y., Tiwari, P., Yadav, P., Bharill, N.: Fuzzy logic hybrid model with semantic filtering approach for pseudo relevance feedback-based query expansion. In: 2017 IEEE Symposium Series on Computational Intelligence (SSCI) (2017)
13. Goswami, A., Sharma, D., Mathuku, H., Gangadharan, S.M.P., Yadav, C.S.: Change detection in remote sensing image data comparing algebraic and machine learning methods. Electronics **11**(3), 431 (2022). Article id: 1505208
14. Lin, C.-T., et al.: IoT-based wireless polysomnography intelligent system for sleep monitoring. IEEE Access **6**, 405–414 (2017)

Comparative Analysis of CNN Pre-trained Model for Stock Market Trend Prediction

Jitendra Kumar Chauhan[1,2(✉)], Tanveer Ahmed[1], and Amit Sinha[2]

[1] Computer Science Department, Bennett University, Plot Nos 8, 11, TechZone 2, Greater Noida 201310, Uttarpradesh, India
{E19SOE817,tanveer.ahmed}@bennett.edu.in
[2] Department of Information Technology, ABES Engineering College, Ghaziabad, India
amit.sinha@abes.ac.in

Abstract. This research offers an in-depth comparative analysis of various pre-trained Convolutional Neural Network (CNN) models such as VGG16, ResNet50, InceptionV3, MobileNetV2, and Xception to predict stock market trends. Our approach involves the conversion of time-series financial data into 2D image-like structures through the application of two distinct techniques: the Gramian Angular Field (GAF) and the Markov Transition Field (MTF). By applying this transformation, we leverage the power of CNNs. We utilize the ideas of transfer learning and try to evaluate the performance of each model using several measures including predictive accuracy, precision, recall, F1-score, and computational efficiency. The analysis highlights the unique advantages and limitations of each model, thereby offering valuable insights into their suitability for stock market prediction tasks. This study is a significant contribution to the current body of literature on financial time series forecasting, providing a novel perspective on using pre-trained CNN models in the Indian Financial Sector. It carries important implications for future work and practitioners in the finance and investment sectors, offering a tool for more e-market predictions.

Keywords: Stock trend classification Deep learning · Trading · Convolutional neural network GAF · MTF

1 Introduction

Stock price prediction is at the heart of the financial world and the broader global economy. Investors, traders, economists, and policymakers closely monitor the fluctuation of stock prices to make informed decisions. Understanding where inventory costs are headed can cause quite a few rewarding opportunities, consisting of strategic funding, hazard management, and macroeconomic making plans. The economic markets are complicated and multifaceted structures

© The Author(s), under exclusive license to Springer Nature Switzerland AG 2024
KC Santosh et al. (Eds.): RTIP2R 2023, CCIS 2026, pp. 110–129, 2024.
https://doi.org/10.1007/978-3-031-53082-1_10

where countless variables have interaction. Global occasions, governmental rules, company decisions, economic signs, mental elements, and climate situations can have an effect on inventory prices. This elaborate interplay of things contributes to the non-linear and non-desk-bound conduct of economic time series, making inventory charge prediction one of the most difficult tasks in finance. Stock fee prediction isn't always a brand-new phenomenon. It dates returned to the early days of inventory exchanges when investors trusted rudimentary evaluation, intuition, and revel in. Over the decades, statistical models, econometric evaluation, technical signs, and quantitative strategies have evolved to research historic charge facts and identify potential trends. Despite advances in mathematics, statistics, and computing, accurate stock price prediction stays elusive. Factors contributing to the mission encompass:

1. Market Noise: Financial markets are rife with noise and extraneous facts that could confound evaluation.
2. Volatility: Markets are regularly having difficulty with surprising and unpredictable adjustments.
3. Emotional Factors: Investor psychology and sentiment play a big role in marketplace actions.
4. Regulatory Changes: Unexpected modifications in governmental or regulatory policies can dramatically affect stock fees.
5. Global Events: Unforeseen international occasions which include herbal disasters, pandemics, or geopolitical tensions can result in abrupt market shifts.

With the advent of computer technology, more sophisticated patterns emerged of Simple linear regression including complex machine learning algorithms, computational methods are irrelevant in the world of finance. However, traditional methods often fail to capture the complex non-linear dynamics of the market. Researchers have been seeking ways to incorporate the non-linear and non-desk bound behavior of monetary time series, yet the problem remains a persistent challenge (Abhyankar et al.,1997) [1]; (Hartman and Hlinka, 2018) [2]. The persistent difficulty in predicting stock prices underscores the need for innovative approaches. There is a continuous quest for models that can better interpret the complexities of financial data, learn from historical trends, and predict future price movements with greater accuracy. Stock price prediction remains a critical yet enigmatic component of financial analysis. The potential rewards are substantial, but so are the risks and challenges.

In this paper, we harness the capabilities of deep learning, notably, Convolutional Neural Networks (CNNs), to forecast stock prices. Focusing on 20 equities from the Indian stock exchange, our methodology employs multiple pre-trained CNN architectures such as VGG16, ResNet50, and InceptionV3 [Simonyan and Zisserman, 2014; He et al., 2015 [3,4]; Szegedy et al., 2016] [5]. Recognizing the inherent temporal sequences in stock prices, we convert a stock's price into two-dimensional imagery via Markov Transition Fields (MTF) and Gramian

Angular Fields (GAF) [Wang and Oates, 2015] [6]. These techniques are adept at spatially encoding temporal patterns, enhancing the CNNs' analytical performance. The resultant 2D images are processed through the pre-trained CNN models. Through extensive numerical examination, spanning over five years of stock data, we have found that the method shows good results in terms of prediction accuracy. This is considering the case of MTF and GAF simultaneously. Leveraging these pre-trained CNN models, we not only demonstrate their potential in real-world stock market scenarios but also highlight their scalability benefits in demanding computational contexts. The rest of the paper is organized as follows:

2   Literature Review

The landscape of economic market forecasting keeps evolving, with various research papers investigating various theories, strategies, and technology. Understanding financial market forecasting begins with the basic tasks of time series analysis and trading regulation. Box and Jenkins (1970) [7] proposed a paradigm shift by introducing the ARIMA model, an important technique in time series forecasting. However, this model operates under the assumptions of linearity and stationarity - conditions that data on financial markets often violate. Subsequently, Nelson (1991) [8] and Taylor (1986) [9] proposed ARCH and GARCH models, respectively, to deal with the inherent volatility commonly found in economic time series data. To bridge the gap between theory and practice, Brock, Lakonishok, and LeBaron (1992) [10] empirically tested the utility of simple industrial trading rules, a cornerstone of financial trading and they emphasized.

Turning to the realm of data transformation techniques, various methods have been proposed to align time series data with advanced machine learning techniques Wang and Oates (2015) [11] use Gramian Angular Field (GAF) - a new technique for time series transformation data for convolutional neural networks (CNNs). A Markov Transition Field (MTF) is introduced, which is a new technique for transforming time series data into a 2D matrix. Guo et al. (2016) [12] engaged visibility graph networks, developing a different approach for visualizing time series data, while Xie, Xu, and Wang (2016) [13] and Lahmiri and Boukadoum (2019) [14] investigated wavelet transform and empirical mode decomposition (EMD) as preprocessing techniques for economic time series data, respectively.

Building a solid foundation of theoretical and variable methodologies, recent research has used pre-trained CNN models to forecast various applications in the financial domain. Sezer and Ozbayoglu (2018) [15] showed the potential of deep learning techniques, especially CNN, in finance for tasks such as credit card fraud detection. In another application, Zhang, Zhou, and Yang (2019) [16] use CNN to predict stock price movements based on financial media, which provided a new perspective on the use of inputs to predict stock prices and Ding, Zhang, Liu, and Duan (2015) [11] demonstrated the forecasting capability of CNN based on textual financial reports. Patel, Shah, Thakkar, and Kotecha (2015)[17] used pre-trained CNN models to evaluate the effectiveness of transfer learning for predicting financial market dynamics. In addition, Li, Li, and Li (2020) [18] demonstrated the capability of transfer learning using previously trained models to predict stock market movements using large-scale classification image models to be used for financial time series forecasting.

To tie the whole thing together, several researchers have conducted comparative analyses and meta-analyses to assess the overall performance of various forecasting techniques. Tsantekidis et al. (2017) [19] supplied a comparative take look at machine studying techniques, including CNNs, for inventory rate prediction. Bao, Yue, and Rao (2017) [20]and Hoseinzade and Haratizadeh (2019) [21] proposed hybrid models that integrate distinct device-gaining knowledge of techniques, providing strong and flexible strategies for inventory prediction. Makridakis, Spiliotis, and Assimakopoulos (2018) [22] provided a complete comparison of statistical and system studying techniques in time series forecasting, providing insights into the strengths and weaknesses of those extraordinary approaches. Lastly, Gu, Kelly, and Xiu (2020) [23] tested a whole lot of gadget learning models for their capability in forecasting stock returns, evaluating their performance based totally on a big dataset of inventory marketplace records.

3   Proposed Methodology

This section expands upon the details of the proposed approach. The overall methodology has been divided into four main parts. They are as follows:

1. The first subsection describes the model architecture in detail.
2. In the second subsection, we discuss the CNN architecture in detail.
3. In the third section a discussion on labeling of stock's close-price.
4. In the last section describe the image generation.

3.1   Model Architecture

In the first step, we download the historical data for 20 distinct shares from Yahoo Finance. These statistics consist of daily data like open price, close fee, excessive, low, quantity, etc., for a selected duration. These prices serve as the basis for our next analysis and version education. Once we have the prices, we rework them into images using distinct techniques: Gramian Angular Fields (GAF) and Markov Transition Fields (MTF). These techniques encode time-collection information into images that could then be processed via convolutional neural networks. GAF captures the temporal correlations among one-of-a-kind time steps, whilst MTF illustrates the probabilistic transitions between unique states inside the time-collection information. We use five different pre-trained Convolutional Neural Network (CNN) models for our purpose: VGG16, ResNet50, Inception, MobileNetv2, and Xception. Each model offers a prediction based totally on the input images. This prediction step is executed one at a time for the images generated via each of the GAF and MTF techniques. To get our very last prediction, we compute a weighted common of the predictions from all five models for each of the 20 shares. This method permits us to leverage the strengths of every model and minimizes the influence of any single version's weaknesses. By doing this separately for the GAF-generated images and the MTF-generated snapshots, we are able to evaluate the performance of the two picture encoding strategies within the context of our particular undertaking (Fig. 1).

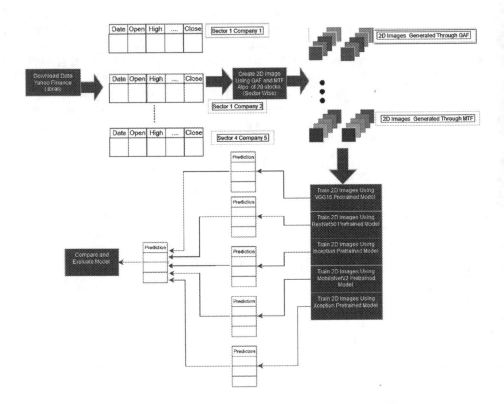

Fig. 1. Proposed framework for Stock trend classification

3.2   CNN Architecture

Convolutional Neural Networks, commonly referred to as CNNs, are a break-through technology in deep learning, particularly geared toward visual recognition tasks. These models have played a pivotal role in achieving state-of-the-art results in areas such as image classification, object detection, and facial recognition. The beauty of CNNs lies in their ability to automatically and adaptively learn spatial hierarchies of features from the input data. The convolution operation involves sliding a kernel across the input data and performing element-wise multiplication followed by summation. Each kernel is tuned to recognize specific characteristics, such as edges, corners, textures, or more complex patterns in higher layers. The output of this operation is known as a feature map or activation map. Strides and padding are critical concepts in convolutional layers. A stride determines how many steps a kernel takes when sliding across the input. Padding, on the other hand, adds extra pixels around the input to control the spatial dimensions of the output feature maps. By tuning these parameters, one can achieve a desirable level of control over the layer's operation. Pooling layers play a vital role in down-sampling or reducing the spatial dimensions of the feature maps. By doing so, they make the model more robust to variations and reduce the computational complexity. Max Pooling selects the maximum value from a group of values within a window, while Average Pooling takes the average. Both methods are effective in preserving essential features while discarding redundant information. The choice between Max and Average Pooling depends on the specific requirements of the task. Fully connected layers act as the final stages of a CNN. They combine the features extracted from previous layers into a more abstract and high-level understanding of the input data. The final fully connected layer often uses a softmax activation function, especially for multi-class classification tasks. The softmax function converts the raw output into probabilities, providing a clear and interpretable prediction for each class.

Various designs of CNNs were proposed over the years, each introducing new thoughts and techniques for enhancing performance. Choosing the right pre-trained version for a specific challenge is hard. For the challenge of stock market trend prediction, the following models are used in this article: VGG 16, ResNet50, InceptionV3, MobileNetV2, Xception.

3.3   Labeling of Stock's Close-Price

The methodology for labeling stock trends is central to our proposed research, as it lays the foundation for the predictive capabilities of our models. This method,

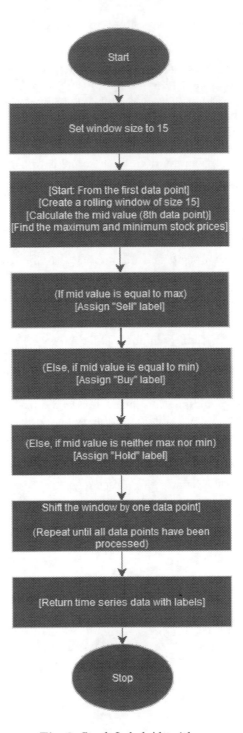

Fig. 2. Stock Label Algorithm

though simple in theory, proves to be highly effective in practice. It employs a window-based algorithm, considering a specific number of data points to assign labels to stock prices. The procedure to accomplish the goal is highlighted in the following text.

Algorithm Description:

1. Window Size Selection: Initially, the window size is set to encompass 15 data points. This size is not rigid and can be adjusted to meet the specific needs of any analysis.
2. Rolling Window Creation: For each stock price dataset, we commence with the first data point and proceed by creating a rolling window of the set size.
3. Midpoint Calculation: Within each window, we identify the midpoint, or the eighth data point in this case.
4. Maximum and Minimum Identification: The maximum and minimum stock prices within the window are identified, and the labeling of the midpoint is executed based on these values.
   a. Sell Label: If the midpoint equals the maximum price, it is labeled as "Sell," indicating that the stock price has reached a peak and may represent an opportune selling moment.
   b. Buy Label: Conversely, if the midpoint corresponds to the minimum price, it is labeled as "Buy," signifying a low in stock price and possibly a favorable buying opportunity.
   c. Hold Label: If the midpoint is neither the maximum nor minimum price, the label "Hold" is assigned, suggesting no significant high or low in stock price and implying a recommendation to defer transactions.
5. Rolling Window Progression: The window is then shifted forward by one data point, and the process is repeated until all data points have been processed.

The final product is a time series of stock prices with corresponding "Buy," "Sell," or "Hold" labels. These labels are primed for further analysis and model training. This methodology, by converting raw stock prices into actionable labels, contributes to the decision-making process in investment strategies. The flexibility in window size and the structured approach to labeling provide a robust tool for financial analysts and researchers. Further exploration may include optimizing the window size based on specific stock behaviors and integrating additional variables into the algorithm to enhance predictive accuracy.

3.4 Image Generation

In this article, we focused our efforts on forecasting price trends. To do this, we converted stock prices into pictures. In this case, we used Gramian angular fields (GAF) and Markov transition fields (MTF). Both methods put time-collection data into picks in a way that gives a time cost based on the total pattern embedded in the series and makes those patterns more visible to algorithms and detection devices

3.4.1   Grammian Angular Field(GAF)

The Gramian angular fields (GAF) approach is an effective means of transforming time-series data into images, which can be employed for machine learning examination. Here is a precise explanation of the steps involved.

1. **Regularization:** Here, we must regularize the time series data $X = [x_1, x_2, \ldots, x_P]$, such that it falls between -1 and 1. This can be achieved by conducting the min-max regularization technique:

$$x_i' = 2 \left(\frac{x_i - \min(X)}{\max(X) - \min(X)} \right) - 1.$$

   This regularization step is paramount as the GAF method relies on arccosine and cosine functions, which necessitate inputs that are within a given boundary.

2. **Polar Coordinate Transformation:** After normalization, each element of x_i' in the temporal dataset is transformed to a polar coordinate. The angle ϕ is then calculated from this data point $\phi_i = \arccos(x_i')$, and the radius r is simply the moment in time at which the datum is recorded.

3. **Gramian Angular Field:**Next, we evaluate the Gramian Angular Field G, a $P \times P$ matrix that chronicles the temporal links of the sequence. This can be either a Gramian Angular Summation Field (GASF) or a Gramian Angular Difference Field (GADF). The elements of the GASF are calculated using the formula:

$$GASF_{i,j} = \cos(\phi_i + \phi_j),$$

   whereas the GADF is calculated as:

$$GADF_{i,j} = \sin(|\phi_i - \phi_j|).$$

4. **Image Representation:** The GAF is visualized as an image, where the color intensity of each pixel corresponds to the value in the GAF. The resulting image retains the complete temporal correlation information from the original time series.

These images, generated from the GAF transformation, can be input into image-based machine learning models, like convolutional neural networks (CNNs), for further analysis. A significant advantage of GAF is its ability to maintain the temporal relationship of the time series, enabling CNNs to recognize sequential patterns within the data, potentially improving predictive performance (Fig. 3).

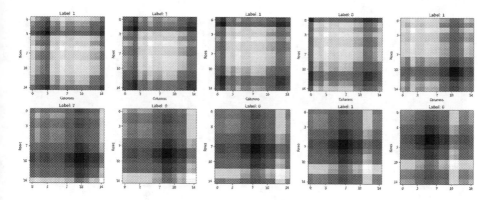

Fig. 3. Stock GAF Images

3.4.2 Markov Transition Field(MTF)

The Markov Transition Field (MTF) is another innovative method for transforming time-series data into an image for use in machine learning analysis. The MTF method specifically captures the temporal dependency in time-series data. The steps involved in the MTF method are as follows:

1. **Discretization:** The first step in this MTF method is to discretize the normalized time series data $X = [x_1, x_2, \ldots, x_P]$. This is basically done using quantile bins, where the bin edges are determined by the quantiles of the data distribution. As a result, each x_i in the series is replaced by its corresponding quantile bin.
2. **Transition Matrix:** After discretization, we calculate the transition matrix T, which is a $P \times P$ matrix where each entry $T_{i,j}$ represents the probability of transitioning from state i to state j in the time series. This transition matrix captures the dynamics of the time series.
3. **Markov Transition Field:** Then, we compute the Markov Transition Field (MTF), which is also a $P \times P$ matrix. Each entry $MTF_{i,j}$ in the MTF is calculated as the probability of transitioning from the state at time i to the state at time j, which is given by T_{x_i, x_j}.
4. **Image Representation:** The MTF matrix can then be visualized as an image, where each pixel's intensity corresponds to the value of the MTF matrix. The resulting image retains the dynamic transitions of the original time series.

The images generated through the MTF transformation can be used as inputs for image-based machine learning models, such as convolutional neural networks (CNNs). A key advantage of MTF over other time-series-to-image transformation methods is its capability to maintain and emphasize the Markov property of the time series, which could potentially improve the performance of time-series prediction or classification tasks (Fig. 4).

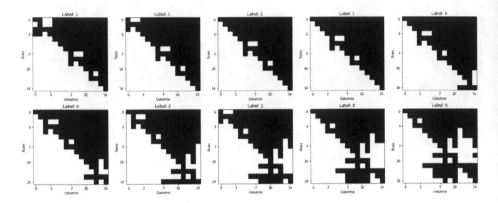

Fig. 4. Stock MTF Images

4   Results

4.1   Dataset and Evaluation Criterion

The dataset used in this study consists of the daily stock prices for the following Indian companies over the past five years: COAL INDIA, CIPLA, BRITTANIA, BPCL, BHARTI AIRTEL, BAJAJ AUTO, AXISBANK, ASIAN PAINTS, ADANI PORTS, ONGC, MARUTI, INFY, ICICIBANK, HINDALCO, HEROMOTOR, HDFCBANK, HCLTECH, GAIL, EICHERMOTOR, DRREDDY. This data has been retrieved from Yahoo Finance, which is a reliable source of historical stock price information.

Each data record in our dataset includes the date, opening price, closing price, highest price of the day, lowest price of the day, the volume of shares traded that day, and the adjusted closing price. The information of the close price is used to generate the image-like structures through the Gramian Angular Fields (GAF) and Markov Transition Fields (MTF) transformations. The labels for the data, which represent the trends we are trying to predict, are generated by a window-based labeling technique shown in Fig. 2. For each window of 15 d, the trend is classified as "Buy" if the mid-window price is the minimum within the window, "Sell" if the mid-window price is the maximum within the window, and "Hold" otherwise.

As for the evaluation criteria, the performance of the CNN models (VGG16, ResNet50, InceptionV3, MobileNetV2, and Xception) on the stock market trend prediction task will be measured using accuracy, precision, recall, and F1 score:

1. Accuracy: This is the proportion of total predictions that are completely correct. It's calculated as

$$(True\ Positives + True\ Negatives)/Total\ Predictions$$

2. Precision: Also called Positive Predictive Value, this is the proportion of positive predictions that are actually correct. It's calculated as Precision

$$\text{True Positives}/(\text{True Positives} + \text{False Positives})$$

3. Recall: Also known as Sensitivity, Hit Rate, or True Positive Rate, this is the proportion of actual positives that are correctly identified. It's calculated as

$$\text{True Positives}/(\text{True Positives} + \text{False Negatives})$$

4. F1 Score: The F1 Score is the harmonic mean of Precision and Recall, and it tries to balance the two in a single number. It's calculated as

$$2 * (\text{Precision} * \text{Recall})/(\text{Precision} + \text{Recall})$$

4.2   Experimentation with Different Pretrained Model

The overall performance comparison of different methods across a diverse variety of stocks is an essential exercise to decide the best model for stock market trend prediction. For each version, we file the accuracy, precision, recall, and F1 rating across 20 stocks, together with COAL INDIA, CIPLA, BRITTANIA, BPCL, BHARTI AIRTEL, BAJAJ AUTO, AXISBANK, ASIAN PAINTS, ADANI PORTS, ONGC, MARUTI, INFY, ICICIBANK, HINDALCO, HEROMOTOR, HDFCBANK, HCLTECH, GAIL, EICHERMOTOR, DRREDDY.

4.2.1   GAF Images Results with Different Pretrained Model

Table 1. Results from AsianPaint Stocks Images through GAF

Image Creation	Pretrained Model	Label	Precision	Recall	F1-Score	Accuracy
GAF	VGG16	Hold	0.44	0.42	0.43	0.55
		Buy	0.6	0.85	0.71	–
		Sell	0.47	0.14	0.21	–
	ResNet50	Hold	0.28	0.28	0.28	0.47
		Buy	0.59	0.61	0.6	–
		Sell	0.43	0.41	0.42	–
	InceptionV3	Hold	0.35	0.48	0.4	0.51
		Buy	0.61	0.73	0.66	–
		Sell	0.6	0.14	0.22	–
	MobileNetV2	Hold	0.41	0.22	0.3	0.54
		Buy	0.55	0.97	0.7	–
		Sell	0.6	0.09	0.16	–
	Xception	Hold	0.31	0.07	0.12	0.54
		Buy	0.57	0.93	0.7	–
		Sell	0.48	0.3	0.37	–

Table 2. Results from Maruti Stocks Images through GAF

Image Creation	Pretrained Model	Label	Precision	Recall	F1-Score	Accuracy
GAF	VGG16	Hold	0.36	0.56	0.45	0.47
		Buy	0.6	0.5	0.55	–
		Sell	0.44	0.33	0.38	–
	ResNet50	Hold	0.5	0.21	0.29	0.52
		Buy	0.54	0.88	0.67	–
		Sell	0.43	0.19	0.26	–
	InceptionV3	Hold	0.52	0.23	0.32	0.55
		Buy	0.56	0.95	0.71	–
		Sell	0.46	0.12	0.2	–
	MobileNetV2	Hold	0.36	0.33	0.35	0.52
		Buy	0.57	0.83	0.68	–
		Sell	0.46	0.12	0.2	–
	Xception	Hold	0.36	0.42	0.38	0.5
		Buy	0.64	0.58	0.61	–
		Sell	0.44	0.44	0.44	–

Table 3. Results from Average of 20 Stocks Images through GAF

Image Creation	Pretrained Model	Label	Precision	Recall	F1-Score	Accuracy
GAF	VGG16	Hold	0.45	0.33	0.36	0.54
		Buy	0.61	0.78	0.67	–
		Sell	0.51	0.3	0.33	–
	ResNet50	Hold	0.44	0.31	0.3	0.49
		Buy	0.58	0.69	0.61	–
		Sell	0.35	0.3	0.29	–
	InceptionV3	Hold	0.43	0.81	0.3	0.5
		Buy	0.57	0.75	0.63	–
		Sell	0.47	0.3	0.32	–
	MobileNetV2	Hold	0.47	0.24	0.28	0.52
		Buy	0.58	0.81	0.66	–
		Sell	0.48	0.29	0.33	–
	Xception	Hold	0.43	0.32	0.34	0.52
		Buy	0.58	0.76	0.65	–
		Sell	0.48	0.29	0.34	–

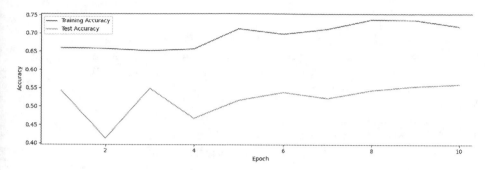

Fig. 5. GAF Maruti Accuracy vs Epoch

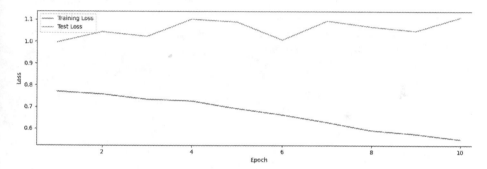

Fig. 6. GAF Maruti Loss vs Epoch

In our study, we investigated the performance of pre-trained AsianPaint stock images processed through GAF. The analysis, as shown in Table 1, reveals remarkable variability in precision, recall, F1-score, and accuracy on different characters. In particular, the VGG16 model had an F1-Score of 0.71 for the Buy line but only 0.21 for the Sell line. In comparison, the MobileNetV2 model achieved the best balance with F1 scores of 0.7 and 0.16 for the Buy and Sell lists, respectively. The data also show significant differences in performance between the models, with Xception showing a surprisingly low F1-Score for Hold labels at 0.12. Through systematic analysis, it is clear that obtaining a well-balanced display of Hold, Buy, and Sell labels is a complex task, and it is important to choose an appropriate pre-trained model In another study, we investigated the application of pre-trained images on Maruti Stocks Images, using GAF for visualization. As described in Table 2, there are some interesting patterns to note. For example, the InceptionV3 model exhibited an impressive F1-Score of 0.71 for Buy labels, while the VGG16 model balanced all three classes ResNet50, although it showed promising performance with a 0.67 F1-Score for Buy labels, its inaccuracies and remember Hold and Sell lines are. Furthermore, Figs. 3 and 4 show the accuracy and loss and epoch graphs for GAF Maruti and MobileNetV2, showing the complex correlation between training achievement and final performance. Finally, we performed a detailed analysis of 20 stock figures using the average GAF and previously trained models. Table 3 summarizes these findings, showing consistency in some areas, and variation in others. For example, the VGG16 instance was able to produce an F1-Score of 0.67 for the Buy label, while Xception had a balanced performance with F1-Scores of 0.65 and 0.34 for the Buy and Sell labels, respectively MobileNetV2 regular performance with almost equal results for all Buy and Sell labels, while F1-Scores were 0.66 and Interestingly, InceptionV3 had an impressive recall of 0.81 for the Hold label but a low F1-Score of 0.3. This detailed analysis highlights the complexity of model selection, emphasizing that optimizing performance requires a fine-grained and thorough understanding of specific dataset characteristics In summary, this study contributes important insights into how the models perform on stock datasets using GAF. They emphasize the importance of careful model selection, tuning, and possibly, fusion in order to obtain the best results across different metrics. Furthermore, these findings can lay the foundation for future studies of robust sampling, transferability, and real-world applications to the complexity of banking research (Fig. 5, 6 and Table 4).

4.2.2 MTF Images Results with Different Pretrained Model

Table 4. Results from Asian Paint Stocks Images through MTF

Image Creation	Pretrained Model	Label	Precision	Recall	F1-Score	Accuracy
MTF	VGG16	Hold	0.72	0.36	0.48	0.66
		Buy	0.67	0.86	0.76	–
		Sell	0.6	0.6	0.6	–
	ResNet50	Hold	0.79	0.22	0.34	0.58
		Buy	0.54	1	0.7	–
		Sell	1	0.16	0.27	–
	InceptionV3	Hold	0.6	0.62	0.61	0.63
		Buy	0.66	0.89	0.75	–
		Sell	0.5	0.13	0.21	–
	MobileNetV2	Hold	0.58	0.62	0.6	0.66
		Buy	0.73	0.74	0.73	–
		Sell	0.59	0.53	0.56	–
	Xception	Hold	0.49	0.34	0.4	0.57
		Buy	0.59	0.8	0.68	–
		Sell	0.6	0.4	0.48	–

Table 5. Results from Maruti Images through MTF

Image Creation	Pretrained Model	Label	Precision	Recall	F1-Score	Accuracy
MTF	VGG16	Hold	0.44	0.58	0.5	0.59
		Buy	0.68	0.69	0.69	–
		Sell	0.63	0.4	0.49	–
	ResNet50	Hold	0.53	0.48	0.51	0.55
		Buy	0.56	0.83	0.67	–
		Sell	0.5	0.1	0.17	–
	InceptionV3	Hold	0.61	0.46	0.52	0.57
		Buy	0.61	0.62	0.62	–
		Sell	0.48	0.58	0.53	–
	MobileNetV2	Hold	0.51	0.44	0.47	0.57
		Buy	0.62	0.68	0.65	–
		Sell	0.49	0.48	0.48	–
	Xception	Hold	0.77	0.5	0.61	0.63
		Buy	0.58	0.91	0.7	–
		Sell	0.86	0.25	0.39	–

Table 6. Results from Average of 20 Stocks Images through MTF

Image Creation	Pretrained Model	Label	Precision	Recall	F1-Score	Accuracy
MTF	VGG16	Hold	0.57	0.47	0.49	0.61
		Buy	0.64	0.73	0.68	–
		Sell	0.62	0.52	0.55	–
	ResNet50	Hold	0.64	0.36	0.42	0.59
		Buy	0.6	0.8	0.68	–
		Sell	0.63	0.42	0.47	–
	InceptionV3	Hold	0.55	0.49	0.5	0.55
		Buy	0.61	0.66	0.62	–
		Sell	0.5	0.43	0.44	–
	MobileNetV2	Hold	0.56	0.41	0.46	0.58
		Buy	0.65	0.76	0.66	–
		Sell	0.63	0.41	0.46	–
	Xception	Hold	0.56	0.42	0.46	0.57
		Buy	0.61	0.73	0.66	–
		Sell	0.57	0.44	0.47	–

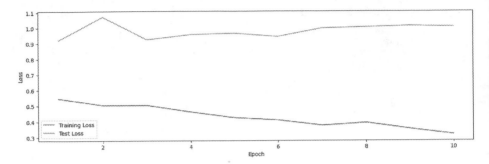

Fig. 7. MTF Maruti Accuracy vs Epoch

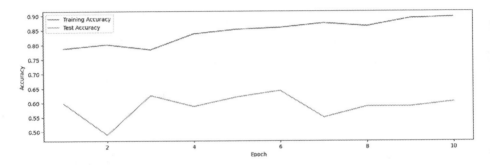

Fig. 8. MTF Maruti Loss vs Epoch

While testing Asian Paint Stocks Images using MTF, we found a significant variation in model performance among the pre-trained models, as shown in Table 5. Using the VGG16 model, we found 0.72, 0.36, and Precision, Recall, and F1-Score 0.48 for the Hold label, indicating a balanced model. On the other hand, using ResNet50, we found a reduced F1-Score of 0.34 for Hold, while obtaining a perfect Recall score for Buy labels. Such a diversity of pre-trained models highlights the sensitivity and robustness of the dataset. Notably, Xception showed the lowest performance with an F1-Score of 0.4 for the Hold label but showed promising results for the Buy and Sell labels. The improvement in performance due to the large amount of heterogeneity in the model emphasizes the importance of careful selection and optimization for specific financial image analysis tasks In analyzing the Maruti coefficients by MTF, as shown in Table 6, we found a large spread of results among the pre-trained models. VGG16 was used to note a slightly more balanced performance, with an F1-Score of 0.5 for Hold and 0.69 for Buy labels. However, with ResNet50, the F1-Score for the Sell label significantly decreased to 0.17, indicating difficulty in classifying this particular label. Using MobileNetV2, the Buy and Sell scores showed nearly identical patterns, indicating how similar the model can be. Xception's performance stood out with a high F1-Score of 0.7 for the Buy label and 0.86 Precision for the Sell label, although the challenges were indicated by a low Recall of 0.25 for the Sell label (Fig. 7 and Fig. 8). The average analysis of the 20 stock images by MTF, as shown in Table 6, presents a relatively consistent pattern between the previously trained models. VGG16 showed a moderate performance with an F1-Score of 0.49 for the Hold label, while ResNet50 showed a slightly better Precision for Hold but a lower F1-Score of 0.42. The InceptionV3 sample showed a balanced view with nearly identical F1 scores for the Hold, Buy, and Sell labels. Both MobileNetV2 and Xception followed a similar trend, with a trend toward better results for Buy labels. The consistency in these results may reflect the nature of the dataset, with an average of 20 stock images. This highlights the importance of a standardized approach that takes into account the specific characteristics of the stock under analysis in order to achieve optimal performance By analyzing three tables detailing the performance of the pre-trained models on stock image datasets we have found unique insights into the behavior of these models Differences in Accuracy, Recall, F1-Score, Accuracy between forms and constructions that need a standardized approach and f emphasize careful consideration of the specific characteristics of the dataset Understanding these nuances financial analysts and data scientists can properly select and refine models and has provided accurate and meaningful predictions in stock image analysis using MTF Corresponding statistics of accuracy vs. accuracy. and loss vs. loss. era further supports the findings, providing visual insight into the models' training dynamics. On average, 20 stock images were analyzed using both GAF and MTF methods. GAF analyses using VGG16, Xception, MobileNetV2, and InceptionV3 models revealed a complex terrain of model selection, with performance variability in different lines MTF method used for Asian Paint Stocks Image and Maruti Image, is explored in detail in the context of the pre-trained model While the GAF analysis emphasized the generic nature of the data set and the importance of standardized design, the MTF analysis emphasized the importance greater if rigorous analysis and targeted changes for optimal performance in stock classes are emphasized. Both approaches emphasize the importance of understanding and adapting to specific dataset characteristics to achieve optimal results.

5   Conclusion

The study's evaluation of the use of pre-trained convolutional neural networks (CNNs) to predict stock market trends shows significant improvements in financial forecasting. Using other data transformation techniques such as Gramian angular fields (GAF) and Markov transition fields (MTF) provides a new perspective on how to capture temporal dependence in stock market data. The efficiency of the MTF transform method and different results in different pre-trained models such as VGG16, ResNet50, etc. Emphasize the importance of the transform method and model selection. Future directions, such as model refinement, exploration of new data transformation techniques, and clustering techniques, mean that we can scale up this approach as we move towards a more data-intensive economy. Integrating these approaches could pave the way for more sophisticated and reliable tools in economic forecasting, and give the region the ability to navigate the ever-changing and complex world of capital markets to the sky.

Declaration of Competing Interest. The authors declare that they have no known competing financial interests or personal relationships that could have appeared to influence the work reported in this paper.

References

1. Abhyankar, A., Copeland, L., Wong, W.: Non-linear dynamics in financial markets: evidence and implications. Econ. J. **107**, 864–880 (1997)
2. Hartman, D., Hlinka, J.: Nonlinear dependencies in international stock market returns: are they predictable? J. Int. Money Financ. **81**, 116–135 (2018)
3. Simonyan, K., Zisserman, A.: Very deep convolutional networks for large-scale image recognition. In: Proceedings of ICLR (2014)
4. He, K., et al.: Deep residual learning for image recognition. In: Proceedings of CVPR (2015)
5. Szegedy, C., et al.: Inception-v3: rethinking the inception architecture for computer vision. In: Proceedings of CVPR (2016)
6. Wang, Z., Oates, T.: Imaging time-series to improve classification and imputation. In: 2015 International Conference on Image Processing (ICIP), pp. 2796–2800 (2015). IEEE
7. Box, G.E.P., Jenkins, G.M.: Time Series Analysis: Forecasting and Control. Holden-Day, ??? (1970)
8. Nelson, D.B.: Conditional heteroskedasticity in asset returns: A new approach. Econometrica (1991)
9. Taylor, S.J.: Modelling financial time series (1986)
10. Brock, W., Lakonishok, J., LeBaron, B.: Simple technical trading rules and the stochastic properties of stock returns. J. Finance **47**(5), 1731–1764 (1992)
11. Wang, Z., Oates, T.: Encoding time series as images for visual inspection and classification using tiled convolutional neural networks. In: AAAI Workshops (2015)
12. Guo, Q., Song, Y., Li, X.: An innovative method for daily traffic flow forecasting using VLNN and GRNN. IEEE Access (2016)
13. Xie, J., Xu, X., Wang, S.: A comparison of denoising methods for chaotic time series with application to short-term traffic flow forecasting. Expert Systems with Applications (2016)
14. Lahmiri, S., Boukadoum, M.: Stock market forecasting using empirical mode decomposition coupled with neural network models. Neural Computing and Applications (2019)
15. Sezer, O.B., Ozbayoglu, M.: Financial time series forecasting with deep learning: A systematic literature review: 2005–2019. Applied Soft Computing (2018)
16. Zhang, W., Zhou, X., Yang, H., Wang, J.: Financial market prediction with a hybrid approach. Information Sciences (2019)
17. Patel, J.S., Shah, S., Thakkar, P., Kotecha, K.: Predicting stock market index using fusion of machine learning techniques. Expert Systems with Applications (2015)
18. Li, L., Li, Q., Li, D.: The ARIMA+GARCH model application in the forecasting of stock index. Mathematical Problems in Engineering (2020)

19. Tsantekidis, A., Passalis, N., Tefas, A., Kanniainen, J., Gabbouj, M., Iosifidis, A.: Forecasting stock prices from the limit order book using convolutional neural networks. In: Business Informatics (CBI), 2017 IEEE 19th Conference on (2017)
20. Bao, W., Yue, J., Rao, Y.: A deep learning framework for financial time series using stacked autoencoders and long-short term memory. PloS one (2017)
21. Hoseinzade, E., Haratizadeh, S.: Deep learning in prediction of stock market indices: A case study of tehran stock exchange. Financial Innovation (2019)
22. Makridakis, S., Spiliotis, E., Assimakopoulos, V.: Statistical and machine learning forecasting methods: Concerns and ways forward. PloS one (2018)
23. Gu, S., Kelly, B., Xiu, D.: Empirical asset pricing via machine learning. The Review of Financial Studies (2020)

Deep Reinforcement Learning Based Energy-Efficient Design for STAR-IRS Assisted V2V Users

Shalini Yadav[✉] and Rahul Rishi

Department of CSE, UIET, MDU Rohtak, 124001 Rohtak, Haryana, India
{shalini.rs.uiet,rahulrishi}@mdurohtak.ac.in

Abstract. Vehicle-to-Vehicle communication (V2V-C) is a cutting-edge technology in the field of 6G networks that improves spectrum utilization and energy efficiency (EE). Despite the potential benefits, there are some considerable difficulties with V2V-C, such as cross-channel interference, co-channel interference and the demand for huge connectivity. To address these challenges, researchers have turned to simultaneous transmitting and reflecting reconfigurable intelligent surfaces (STAR-IRSs) as auxiliary devices to improve wireless network performance. These surfaces allow users on opposite sides to be served at the same time by sending and reflecting signals. However, the existing solution has been limited to either continuous or discrete spaces, limiting optimisation parameters to either continuous or discrete nature. To address these limitations, the proposed scheme use a hybrid space to optimise the EE of the network for the downlink STAR-IRS aided communication system in the presence of vehicle-to-vehicle pairs (V2VPs), allowing one parameter to be continuous and the other to be discrete. In this research work, the proposed scheme uses the parameterized deep Q-network (P-DQN) framework for estimating the beamforming vector and phase shift for EE optimisation. The results from the simulation demonstrate the efficacy of the system proposed by maximising the spectrum usage and energy efficiency.

Keywords: STAR-IRS · P-DQN · V2V-C · EE

1 Introduction

Future wireless sixth-generation (6G) communication networks' performance could be improved by reconfigurable intelligent surfaces (IRSs) [1]. IRSs can be characterized as two-dimensional arrays made up of a lot of inexpensively reconfigurable passive elements. These elements are controlled by a FPGA controller. The propagation of wireless signals that are received can be changed by appropriately altering the amplitude and phase responsiveness of these components. The majority of the current research on IRSs is predicated on the idea that they are capable of only reflecting incident signals, necessitating the placement of both the transmitter and receiver on a singular side of the Intelligent Reflecting surface (IRS). A novel IRS architecture named STAR-IRSs has been proposed to overcome this limitation, which employs simultaneous transmitting and reflecting. STAR-IRSs possess the capability to conduct simultaneous transmission

KC Santosh et al. (Eds.): RTIP2R 2023, CCIS 2026, pp. 130–143, 2024.
https://doi.org/10.1007/978-3-031-53082-1_11

and reflection of incident signals, thereby producing an all-encompassing coverage of space. This is a notable deviation from traditional IRSs that focus on reflection [2]. Buildings in metropolitan areas or hills and plants in rural areas may have substantial shadowing effects on V2X communications, lowering energy efficiency and spectrum efficiency. The utilization of STAR-IRS's reflection and transmission presents an opportunity to establish an alternative propagation channel that bypasses obstructions hindering direct Line-of-Sight (LoS) connection between the transmitter and receiver. As a result, the signal can keep the desired transmission rate while avoiding penetration loss. IRS has shown to be a viable paradigm for meeting the needs of 5G and beyond networks, fulfilling the need for an intelligent and programmable wireless environment [3]. IRS performance optimisation is a challenging task due to the large number of programmable components and the controller's rectifying capabilities. As a result, developing new strategies to improve IRS performance is critical. Reinforcement learning (RL) is a rigorous mathematical framework that allows an autonomous agent to interact with an uncertain and constantly changing environment and learn an optimal behaviour by rapidly increasing the aggregate reward [4]. While Q-learning and similar traditional RL algorithms have shown efficacy in diverse scenarios, their application has been restricted to networks of a small scale. The research community has responded to the challenge of managing large and complex networks by introducing a novel approach termed deep reinforcement learning, that amalgamates the principles of DL and RL. Deep Reinforcement Learning (DRL) effectively addresses the limitations of Reinforcement Learning (RL) in working with small data sets and complex problems through the application of Deep Neural Network's (DNN) function's approximation attribute. The DRL technique allows an agent to learn through both online and offline approaches. As a result, this method produces optimal results for every state-space-action pair and maximises the total reward [5].

1.1 Related Work

Various schemes have been proposed by several researchers for increasing the Energy efficiency (EE) of the STAR-IRS network. By concurrently optimising active beamforming, transmission, and reflection coefficients with power constraints, the author maximises the lowest user energy efficiency (EE) [6]. To optimize the spectral efficiency, it is imperative to simultaneously regulate the beamforming intensity for individual users and the phase shift parameters of the STAR-IRS. Proximal policy optimization (PPO), a policy gradient-based reinforcement learning approach, is the method used to successfully address the current issue [7]. In an effort to optimize the long-term energy efficiency (EE) of a system that is subject to time-varying channels and user demands, the author presents a framework that utilizes both active and passive beamforming techniques. To facilitate the optimization of all passive beamforming for STAR-IRSs in an online mode, the author proposes a parallel deep reinforcement learning (DRL) algorithm [8]. In order to attain the highest level of energy efficiency, a number of factors are taken into consideration. These include the optimization of active-beamforming vectors of the transmitter, along with the determination of appropriate transmission and reflection coefficients of the STAR-IRS. Furthermore, the decoding order of successive-interference cancellation (SIC), time-allocation, and constraints on quality-of-service (QoS), conservation of energy, time-allocation, phase-shifts, and SICdecoding are all carefully evaluated and optimized [9]. The author conducts an investigation into a groundbreaking mobile edge computing (MEC) system that is bolstered by a reconfigurable intelligent surface (STAR-IRS) that simultaneously transmits and reflects data. The author aims to minimize the overall energy consumption of all users by optimizing the transmission and reflection time and coefficients of the STAR-IRS in combination with the transmit power and the amount of data offloaded for each user [10].

1.2 Motivation and Contribution

Optimization of EE (Energy Efficiency) in STAR-IRS downlink wireless network in hybrid space has not yet received adequate attention. Available research either includes continous or discrete space, constrainting our optimization parameter to be either discrete or continous in nature. Considering this, we got motivated to use hybrid space to optimize the EE of the network. Using hybrid space we can have one parameter to be continous or other to be discrete. Contributions to this article are as follows:

– Our proposed wireless communication system network, known as the STAR-IRS network, is designed for the downlink scenario, signal sent from UAV (which is acting as base station) is blocked by building. STAR-IRS is placed on the building so that the user in reflection zone and transmission zone get the signal with high energy efficiency.
– To achieve the objective, we jointly optimize beamforming vector at UAV and phase shift at STAR-IRS by making the problem as an MDP. P-DQN algorithm is suggested for optimization of parameters.

1.3 Organization

This paper is structured into: Sect. 2 outlines the system model. The research problem and its corresponding solution are provided in Sect. 3. Section 4 computes the numerical results, and finally, Sect. 5 contains the concluding remarks of the research work.

2 System Model and Problem Formulation

2.1 System Model

A STAR-IRS, UAV added with antennas, downlink single cell wireless communication is considered as shown in figure. The system model proposed here have a single UAV, single STAR-IRS, multiple users located in transmission and reflection zone. All users are located on ground. Due to the presence of objects and obstacles in the real- world problems, a direct-connection in between UAV positioned at certain distance and users at some other location is not feasible. In order to make establish a connection between UAV and users. A STAR-IRS is positioned at the building such that, when signal comes from the UAV it is incident on STAR-IRS and the service is accessible to people located in both the transmission and reflection regions. The group of all users are represented by $\mathcal{N} = \{1, 2, \ldots, n\}$ and the group of all V2VPs are represented by $\mathcal{M} = \{1, 2, \ldots, m\}$. A STAR-IRS is a linear and homogeneous array of $l \times l$ reflecting-elements. Each user sent its signal towards the UAV to each orthogonal subcell by OMA protocols. In each V2VP, the V2VT communicates by its respectively V2VR via OMA protocols. The V2VPs and the users both utilize the same subcell. It is presumed that every single subcell is occupied by a single user. Assume J to be the total capacity of the network, split into $\mathcal{B}$ sub-cells. The set of the sub-cells is identified as $\mathcal{B} = \{1, 2, \ldots, b, \ldots, B\}$, while the set of the time-slots is identified by $\mathcal{T} = \{1, 2, \ldots, t \ldots, T\}$ The UAV is positioned at $(x_{uav}, 0, G)$ where G is the UAV height. Considers users to be located in the X-Y plane with their respective 3D-coordinates $(x_n, y_n, 0)$. Let us define Coordinates of STAR-IRS $X_{STAR-IRS} = (x_l, y_l, z_l)$. The distance in-between the UAV and l^{th} element of STAR-IRS is $d_{uav,l(t)} = \sqrt{(x_{uav} - x_l)^2 + (y_l)^2 + (z_l - G)^2}$. The distance between (STAR-IRS) l^{th} and n^{th} user $d_{l,n}(t) = \sqrt{(x_n - x_l)^2 + (y_n - y_l)^2) + (z_l)^2}$

2.2 Channel Model

As seen in Fig. 1, UAV equipped with D antennas transmitting signals to multiple single-antenna users through a STAR-IRS consisting of L elements. Users $O_1, O_2, \ldots, O_N$ are situated at the back of the transmission zones. The users $M_1, M_2, \ldots, M_N$ are situated in-front of the STAR-IRS in the reflection zone. We presume that walls or buildings are obstructing all direct connections between the UAV and all users. Individuals utilizing the system undergo clustering and are subsequently distributed via the downlink transmission mechanism [2]. Let $f_{l,n}^b \in \mathbb{C}^{1 \times L}$ and $\widehat{L}_{uav,l}^b \in \mathbb{C}^{1 \times M}$ defines the channel between STAR-IRS l^{th} component to the nth user and from UAV to the lth

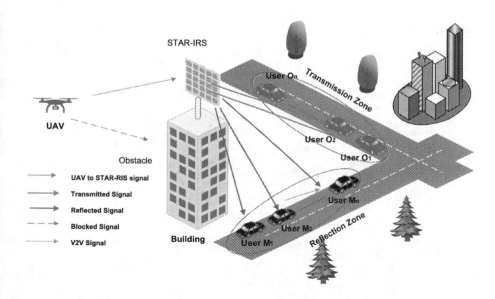

Fig. 1. Network Architecture.

component of STAR-IRS respectively. Let $\widetilde{L}_{uav,n}^b \in \mathbb{C}^L$ define channel from UAV to the nth user. $g_{m,i}^b \in \mathbb{C}^L$ define the channel from m^{th} V2VT to i^{th} V2VR in b^{th} cell. Energy splitting protocol is considered to be followed by STAR-IRS [11, 12]. It implies that by implementing coefficient matrices concurrently, every component at STAR-IRS has the capability to transmit and reflect the incident signals simultaneously. The ES protocol's rule of amplitude coefficients is defined by the ideal situation in which the aggregate energy of the transmitted and reflected signals equates to the energy of the incident signals for every element $\lambda_n^O + \lambda_n^M = 1$, $\forall n \in \{1, 2, 3..., N\}$, λ_n^O and λ_n^M represent the transmission and reflection amplitude coefficients for the n element at the STAR-IRS respectively. The coefficients matrices at the STAR-IRS are calculated by $\Theta^\nu = diag(\sqrt{\lambda_1^\nu}\exp^{j\phi_1^\nu}, \sqrt{\lambda_2^\nu}\exp^{j\phi_2^\nu}, ... \sqrt{\lambda_N^\nu}\exp^{j\phi_N^\nu}), \nu \in \{O, M\}$, where $\phi_n^\nu \in [0, 2\pi), \forall n \in \{1, 2, 3, ..., N\}$ denotes the phase shift of the n-th element.

UAV to User Channel Model. The User gets the two signal. There is a direct signal UAV to the user whereas the second signal is transmitted or reflected signal (UAV to User) through STAR-IRS. We assume that our system follow Rayleigh fadding. $f_{l,n}^b, \widehat{L}_{uav,l}^b, \widetilde{L}_{uav,n}^b$ are expressed as:

$$f_{l,n}^b = \sqrt{\delta_0(a_{l,n}^b)^{-\varphi_2}}$$

$$\left(\sqrt{\frac{E_{l,n}^b}{1+E_{l,n}^b}}f_{l,n}^{LoS,b} + \sqrt{\frac{1}{1+E_{l,n}^b}}f_{l,n}^{NLoS,b}\right), \tag{1a}$$

$$\widehat{L}_{uav,l}^b = \sqrt{\delta_0(a_{uav,l}^b)^{-\varphi_1}}$$

$$\left(\sqrt{\frac{E_{uav,l}^b}{1+E_{uav,l}^b}}\widehat{L}_{uav,l}^{Los,b} + \sqrt{\frac{1}{1+E_{uav,l}^b}}\widehat{L}_{uav,l}^{NLoS,b}\right), \tag{1b}$$

$$\widetilde{L}_{uav,n}^b = \sqrt{\delta_0(a_{uav,n}^b)^{-\varphi_3}}\widetilde{L}_{uav,n}^{NLoS,b}, \tag{1c}$$

where path loss exponent and propagation loss at the reference distance is shown by δ_0 and φ respectively. $E_{l,n}^b$ and $Eb_{uav,l}$ are the Rician factors for STAR-IRS to nth user and uav to the STAR-IRS links. NLOS repsesents the Non-Line of Sight and their elements are represented as $f_{l,n}^{NLOS,b}$, $\widehat{L}_{uav,l}^{NLOS,b}$ and $\widehat{L}_{uav,n}^{NLOS,b}$ are defined by the Rayleigh fading. All elements are included in $\mathcal{CN}(0,1)$. Hence, $f_{l,n}^{NLOS,b}$ and $\widehat{L}_{uav,n}^{NLOS,b}$ are defined as follows:

$$f_{l,n}^{LoS,b} = \left[1, \ldots, e^{j(n-1)\pi \sin(A_{l,n})}, \ldots, e^{j(n-1)\pi \sin(A_{l,n})}\right]^T \tag{2a}$$

$$\widehat{L}_{uav,n}^{LoS,b} = \left[1, \ldots, e^{j(uav-1)\pi \sin(A_{uav,n})}, \ldots, e^{j(uav-1)\pi \sin(A_{uav,n})}\right]^T, \tag{2b}$$

where $\sin(A_{l,n}) = \dfrac{y_n - y_l}{\sqrt{(x_n-x_l)^2-(y_n-y_l)^2}}$ and $\sin(A_{uav,n}) = \dfrac{y_uav}{\sqrt{(x_n-x_{uav})^2-(y_uav)^2}}$.

The signal transmitted by the uav to the nth user can be defined as follows:

$$Z_{uav,n}^n = \underbrace{\left(f_{l,n}^b \Theta \widehat{L}_{uav,n}^b + \widetilde{L}_{uav,n}^b \right) \sum_{d \in \Psi} t_d r_d}_{\text{Reflected or Transmitted + Direct Signal}} \tag{3}$$

$$+ \underbrace{\sum_{m \in \mathcal{M}} \epsilon_m^b(t) \sqrt{h_m^b(t)} g_{uav,m}^b r_{uav,m}^b}_{\text{UAV to V2VT Interference}} + \underbrace{\sigma^2}_{\text{AWGN}},$$

where $t_d \in \mathbb{C}^{M \times 1}$ denotes the beamforming vector r_d is the signal symbol of the user and we assume $\mathbb{E}\{r_d\}^2 = 1$, $\sqrt{h_n^b}$ and $\sqrt{h_m^b}$ are the nth and m^{th} V2VT transmitted power respectively. Transmitted symbols for the nth user and m^{th} V2VT are denoted by $r_{n,uav}^b$ and $r_{m,uav}^b$ respectively. Cell allocation coefficient for n^{th} user and m^{th} V2VT link is given by $\epsilon_{n,m}^b$

$$\epsilon_{n,m}^b = \begin{cases} 1 & \text{if } m^{th} \text{ V2VT occupies } n^{th} \text{ user,} \\ 0 & \text{otherwise.} \end{cases} \tag{4}$$

The SINR over the bth subcell for the nth user is given as:

$$\Gamma_{n,uav}^b = \frac{h_n \left| f_{n,l}^b \Theta \widehat{L}_{n,uav}^b + \widetilde{L}_{uav,n}^b \right|^2}{\sum_{m \in \mathcal{M}} h_m \left| g_{m,uav}^b \right|^2 + \sigma^2} \tag{5}$$

V2VT-V2VR Channel Model. The signal received by i^i V2VR from the mth V2VT over the bth subcell is given by

$$Z_{m,i}^b = \underbrace{\sqrt{h_m^b} g_{m,i}^b r_{m,i}^b}_{\text{Direct Signal}} + \underbrace{\sum_{i' \neq i, i' \in \mathcal{N}} \epsilon_m^b \sqrt{h_m^b} p_{m,i'}^b r_{m,i'}^b}_{\text{V2VT to V2VR interference}}$$

$$+ \underbrace{\sum_{n \in \mathcal{N}} \sqrt{h_n^b} f_{n,i}^b r_{n,i}^b}_{\text{User to V2VR interference}} + \underbrace{\sigma^2}_{\text{AWGN}}, \tag{6}$$

SINR for the ith V2VR over b^{th} is defined as

$$\Gamma_{m,i}^b = \frac{h_m \left| g_{m,i}^b \right|^2}{\sum_{i' \neq i, i' \in \mathcal{M}} \epsilon_{n,i}^b h_m^b \left| g_{m,i'}^b \right|^2 + \sum_{n \in \mathcal{N}} h_n^b \left| f_{n,i}^b \right|^2} \tag{7}$$

2.3   Energy Efficiency Evaluation

The transmission rate for the nth users is given by as:

$$\mathbb{S}_{uav,n}^b = BW \log_2 \left[1 + \Gamma_{uav,n}^b\right]. \tag{8}$$

The transmission rate for the mth V2VR is given as:

$$\mathbb{S}_{i,m}^b = BW \log_2 \left[1 + \Gamma_{i,m}^b\right] \tag{9}$$

The combined transmission rate of network is given as:

$$\mathbb{S}_{n,m}^b = \sum_{b \in B} \left[\sum_{n \in \mathcal{N}} \mathbb{S}_{uav,n}^b + \sum_{m \in \mathcal{M}} \mathbb{S}_{i,n}^b \right]. \tag{10}$$

The equation below shows the total power consumption of the network.

$$\mathbb{P}_T^b = h_{UAV}^b + h_{STAR-IRS}^b + \sum_{n=1}^N h_n^k + \sum_{m=1}^M h_m^b, \tag{11}$$

In Eq. 11 $h_{STAR-IRS}^b$ represent the power usage of STAR-IRS,h_{UAV}^b term represent the power usage of UAV,$\sum_{n=1}^N h_n^b$ represent the power usage of user's,$\sum_{m=1}^M h_m^b$ represents the power usage ofV2VTs.

2.4   Problem Formulation

In this article, the principal objective is to optimize the energy efficiency (EE) of the network which we have proposed. The energy efficiency (EE) may be defined as::

$$EE = \frac{\mathbb{S}_{n,m}^b}{\mathbb{P}_T^b}$$

$$= \frac{\sum_{b \in B} \left[\sum_{n \in \mathcal{N}} \mathbb{S}_{uav,n}^b + \sum_{m \in \mathcal{M}} \mathbb{S}_{i,m}^b \right]}{h_{UAV}^b + h_{STAR-IRS}^b + \sum_{n=1}^N h_n^k + \sum_{m=1}^M h_m^b} \tag{12}$$

The principle aim of the paper is to maximize energy efficiency together with preserving the user's and V2VTs SINR by together optimizing the STAR-IRS's phase shift along with the beamforming vector. The optimization problem can be represented in the following manner:

$$\mathcal{P.F.}: \min_{(t_d,\phi)} EE(t), \tag{13}$$

$$s.t. \ \ \mathbb{D}_1 : \sum_{b=1}^B \epsilon_{n,m}^b \leq 1, \qquad \forall \mathcal{M}, \mathcal{N},$$

$$\mathbb{D}_2 : \Gamma_{uav,n}^b \geq \Gamma_{uav,n}^{b,min}, \qquad \forall B,$$

$$\mathbb{D}_3 : \phi \in [o, 2\pi], \qquad \forall \mathcal{L},$$

$$\mathbb{D}_4 : X_{STAR-IRS} \in D,$$

$\mathbb{D}_1$ makes sure that each user is related with a single V2VT. The minimum data rate requirement for user is denoted by $\mathbb{D}_2$. $\mathbb{D}_3$ identifies the constricted range of IRS phase shift. $\mathbb{D}_4$ specifies that the UAV's position should be in the constricted area (D). The non-convexity of the optimization problem (13) is intricately linked to the fractional representation of the EE, in conjunction with the manifold constraints. This non-convexity poses a challenge in obtaining an optimal solution using convex optimization methods such as sequential convex approximation (SCA). We develop a DRL-based approach that jointly maximise EE by optimising beamforming vectors at the UAV and phase shift at the STAR-IRS. Deep Reinforcement Learning (DRL) is a paradigm of Artificial Intelligence (AI) technology that facilitates the development of fully autonomous agents by means of interrelating with the environment and utilizing particular optimal strategies. Over time, the agents improve their performance through a process of trial and error [10]. Our optimization quandary can be effectively resolved through utilization of P-DQN, a type of DRL that has been designed to address optimization problems that exist in hybrid spaces.

3   Proposed Scheme

We are jointly optomizing beamforming vector at UAV and phase shift at STAR-IRS by formulating the above described problem (13) as an markov decision process(MDP). We have put forth the P-DQN algorithm as a means of achieving joint optimization of both phase shift and beamforming vector.

3.1   Markov Decision Process Model

The optimization problem is reconstructed into MDP problem. An MDP problem has environment, Agent, State space, Action space and reward.

3.2   Environment

The proposed communication systems make up our environment. An agent interacts with this environment to determine the best courses of action to implement in order to maximize cumulative rewards. The environment contains all network-related data, including UAV, vehicle, and STAR-IRS. The environment includes the characteIRStics of STAR-IRS components, the condition of the vehicles, and channel information. An agent observes a state $s^b(t)$ from the state space $\widehat{S}$ at each time step t and then acts on that observation by selecting an action $a^b(t)$ from the action space $\widehat{A}$. The environment's current state s[n] changes to the following state $s^b(t+1)$ when the action is completed. The agent also receives their current reward, $r^b(t)$.

3.3   Agent

The STAR-IRS controller acts as the agent in this proposed system. STAR-IRS phase shift is controlled by STAR-IRS controller.

3.4 State Space

Agent checks the state and environment which consists of beamforming vector, phase shift, channel information.

$$s_t^b = [\phi, t_d, f, L] \tag{14}$$

3.5 Action Space

In the present study, the optimization of the beamforming vector of the unmanned aerial vehicle (UAV) and the phase shift of the (STAR-IRS) are concurrently considered to increase the energy efficiency of the overall system. Therefore, the system's action space is

$$a_t^b = [\phi, t_d] \tag{15}$$

Note that beamforming vector has continous values and phase shift has discrete value so accordingly action space is hybrid.

3.6 Reward

The objective of the optimization problem at hand is to effectively maximize the energy efficiency of the system. As such, energy efficiency has been designated as the reward for the t-th training step.

$$r_t^b = EE(t) \tag{16}$$

We consider an MDP model having parametIRSed action space $\widehat{\mathcal{A}}$. For $a^b \in \widehat{\mathcal{A}}$, Action valur function defined by $\mathcal{Q}(s^b, a^b) = \mathcal{Q}(s^b, k, x_k^b)$ where $s^b \in \widehat{\mathcal{S}}$ $k \in [K]$. Let k_t is the discrete action chosen at time t and x_k^b be the associated continuous parameter.
So the Bellmen equation is

$$\mathcal{Q}(s_t^b, k_t, x_{kt}^b) = \mathbb{E}_{r_t^b, s_{t+1}^b} \left[r_t^b + \Upsilon \max_{k^b \in [K]} \mathcal{Q}(s_{t+1}^b, k^b, x_k^{bQ} s_{t+1}^b) | s_t^b = s^b \right]. \tag{17}$$

Similar to deep Q-networks, Deep neural network $\mathcal{Q}(s^b, k^b, x_k^b; w^b)$ is used to approximate $\mathcal{Q}(s^b, k^b, x_k^b)$ where w^b represent the network weights. $x_k^{bQ}(s^b)$ is approximated with deterministic policy network $x_k^b(\theta^b)$: $\widehat{\mathcal{S}} \to \mathcal{X}_k^b$, where θ^b represent the network weights of the policy network. We want to determine θ^b such that when w^b is fixed such that

$$\mathcal{Q}(s_t^b, k, x_k^b(s^b; \theta^b); w^b) = sup_{x_k^b \in \mathcal{X}_k} \mathcal{Q}(s^b, k^b, x_k^b; w^b) \tag{18}$$

Then, using gradient descent to minimize the mean-squared Bellman error, we could estimate similarly to DQN. Let θ_t^b and w_t^b be the weights of the deterministic policy network and the value network, respectively, in the t-th step. We define the n-step target y_t^b by for a fixed $n \geq 1$ to accommodate multi-step techniques.

$$y_t^b = \sum_{i=0}^{n-1} \gamma^i r_{t+i}^b + \gamma^n \max_{k^b \in [K]} \mathcal{Q}(s_{t+n}^b, k^b, x_k^b(s_{t+n}^b, \theta_t^b); w_t^b) \tag{19}$$

The least squares loss function is used for w^b as in DQN. In addition, given our goal is to identify θ^b that maximize Q while holding w^b constant, we employ the following loss function for θ^b.

$$l_t^Q(w^b) = 1/2[Q(s_t^b, k_t^b, x_{k_t}^b; w) - y_t^b]^2 \tag{20}$$

$$l_t^Q(\theta^b) = -\sum_{k=1}^{K} Q(s_t^b, k^b, x_k^b(s_t; \theta^b); w_t^b) \tag{21}$$

By (20, 21), we use stochastic gradient methods to update the weights.

We update w^b specifically with a stepsize α_t^b that is asymptotically negligible in compaIRSon to the stepsize β_t^b for θ^b. Additionally, we need α_t^b, β_t^b to meet the Robbins-Monro criterion for the stochastic approximation to be valid [Robbins and Monro, 1951]. In Algorithm 1, we propose the P-DQN algorithm with experienced replay. Furthermore, we point out that asynchronous gradient descent can be simply added to our P-DQN technique to hasten training. We think about a distributed training system that is centrally managed, where each process computes its own local gradient and interacts with a global "parameter server" to share information. In particular, each local process uses its own transitions to compute gradients with respect to omega and theta and operates an independent environment to produce transition trajectories. Algorithm 2 contains the asynchronous n-step P-DQN (AP-DQN) algorithm. Here, we will just discuss the technique for each local process, that fetches w^b and θ^b which retrieves and computes the gradient using the parameter server. The gradients sent from the local processes are used by the parameter server to update the global parameters.

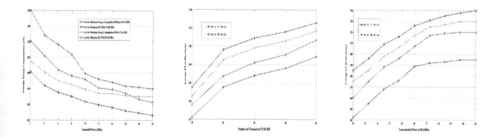

Fig. 2. Comparative Analysis (a) Average energy consumption over transmit power. (b) EE versus the number of elements at the STAR-IRS (c) EE versus the transmission power at the UAV(BS).

4   Performance Evaluation

4.1   Simulation Parameters

The phase shift parameter of the STAR-IRS is arbitrarily assigned in initial time-slot, and the UAV(BS) is placed at a fixed position within the simulation. A cell surrounding the UAV contains distribution of N Users and M V2VPs. To construct the P-DQN training model, we utilized a structure compIRSed of three fully connected layers (input layer, hidden layers, output layer) with 500, 500, and 250 neurons respectively. Table 1 provides a comprehensive list of the remaining simulation parameters.

Algorithm 1. P-DQN with Experience Replay for Phase Shift and Beamforming Vector Coefficients

Input

- Step Sizes = $\{\alpha_t^b, \beta_t^b\} \forall t \geq 0$
- Exploration Parameter = ϵ
- Minibatch Size = E
- Probability Distribution = ξ

Initialization:

- Network Weights = $\omega^b \ \& \ \theta^b$

1: **for** $(t = 1, t \leq T, t++)$ **do**
2:     Compute action parameters $x_k^b \leftarrow x_k^b(s_t^b, \theta_t^b)$
3:     Select action $a_t^b = (k_t^b, x_{k_t}^b)$
4:     According to ϵ-greedy policy, the value of a_t^b is given as follows:

$$a_t^b = \begin{cases} \text{a sample from distribution,} & \epsilon \\ (k_t^b, x_{k_t}^b), where \ k_t^b = \max_{k \in [K]} Q(s_t^b, w_t^b) & 1 - \epsilon. \end{cases}$$

5:     Choose action a_t^b
6:     Renew the reward function as in (24)
7:     Evaluate the subsequent state, $s_{(t+1)}^b$
8:     Retain transition $\left(s_t^b, a_t^b, r_t^b, s_{(t+1)}^b\right)$ in experience replay buffer of capacity $\mathbb{G}$
9:     A small batch of transitions should be randomly selected $(s_i^b, a_i^b, r_i^b, s_{i+1}^b)$ from the replay buffer of capacity $\mathbb{G}$
10:    Define the target y_i^b as:

$$y_i^b = \begin{cases} r_i^b, & s_{i+1}^b \text{ is terminal state} \\ r_i^b + \max_{k^b \in [K]} \gamma Q(s_{i+1}^b, k^b, x_k(s_{i+1}^b, \theta_t^b); w_t^b) & \text{otherwise.} \end{cases}$$

11:    Computer stochastic gradient $\nabla_w l_t^Q(w^b)$ and $\nabla_\theta l_t^\Theta(\theta^b)$ using data (y_i^b, s_i^b, a_i^b)
12:    Update the Weights as follows:

$$w_{t+1}^b = w_t^b - \alpha_t^b \nabla_w l_t^Q(w_t^b)$$

$$\theta_{t+1}^b = \theta_t^b - \beta_t^b \nabla_\theta l_t^\Theta(\theta_t^b)$$

13: **end for**
14: **Output**: θ^b and P_v^r

Algorithm 2. AP-DQN with fast training process for Phase Shift and Beamforming Vector Coefficients

Input

- Exploration = $\mathcal{A}$
- Exploration Parameter = ϵ
- Probability Distribution = ξ
- Maximum length of multi step return = $t_{\max}$
- Maximum number of iterations = $\mathcal{N}_{step}$

Initialization:

- Network Weights = ω^b & θ^b
- Global Shared Counter = $\mathcal{N}_{step} = 0$
- Local step Counter $t \leftarrow 1$

1: **repeat**
2:     Clear local gradients $dw \leftarrow 0, d\theta \leftarrow 0$
3:     $t_{start} \leftarrow 0$
4:     Synchronize local parameters $w_1 \leftarrow w, \theta_1 \leftarrow \theta$ from the parameter server
5:     **repeat**
6:         Compute state s_t^b
7:         Assume $x_k^b \leftarrow x_k^b(s_t^b, \theta_1)$
8:         According to ϵ-greedy policy, the value of a_t^b is given as follows:

$$a_t^b = \begin{cases} \text{a sample from distribution,} & \epsilon \\ (k_t^b, x_{k_t}^b), k_t^b = \max_{k^b \in [K]} Q(s_t^b, w_t^b) & 1 - \epsilon. \end{cases}$$

9:         Select action $a_t^b = (k_t^b, x_{k_t}^b)$
10:       Renew the reward function r_t^b using (24)
11:       Determine the next state, $s_{(t+1)}^b$
12:       $t \leftarrow t + 1$
13:       $\mathcal{N}_{step} \leftarrow \mathcal{N}_{step} + 1$
14:     **until** s_t^b is the terminal state or $t_{\max} = t - t_{start}$
15:     Define the target y_i^b as:

$$y_i^b = \begin{cases} 0, & \text{terminal state } s_t^b \\ \max_{k^b \in [K]} Q(s_t^b, k^b, x_k(s_t^b, \theta_1); w_1) & \text{non-terminal.} \end{cases}$$

16:     **for** $(t = t - 1, t \le t_{\max}, t_{\max}{++})$ **do**

$$y^b = r_i^b + \gamma y^b$$

17:         Update the Gradients as follows:

$$dw^b = dw^b + \nabla_{w^b} l_t^Q(w_1)$$

$$d\theta^b = d\theta^b + \nabla_\theta^b l_t^\Theta(\theta_1)$$

18:     **end for**
19:     Update global θ^b and w^b using $d\theta^b$ and dw^b using RMSProp
20: **until** $\mathcal{N}_{step} > \mathcal{N}_{\max}$ **Output**: θ and P_v^r

Table 1. Simulation Parameters

Parameters	Values
Cellular cell's Radius	400 m
Carrier Frequency	1.5 GHz
Distance between STAR-IRS and BS	50 m
User transmission power	4 W
Channel Power Gain	−30dB
Noise Power spectrum density	−172 dBm/Hz
Path loss exponent	5
Distance between STAR-IRS and User	10 m
Pathloss MU-IRS links	$150 + 40\log d$
V2VPs number	5
Users number	7
Rician factor	6 dB
Factor of Discount	0.8
Starting learning rate	0.3
Declining learning rate	0.002
Replay storage capacity	1000
Small-batch Size	64
Number of Steps in Each Epoch	25
Episodes	100
Optimizer	Adam
Activation function	ReLu

4.2   Results and Discussion

The figure depicted in 2(a) displays the comprehensive energy consumption of the STAR-IRS system inclusive of the transmitter and receiver. It is noteworthy that an increase in transmit power results in a decrease in energy consumption for the STAR-IRS system. The base station (BS) expends the greatest amount of energy when attempting to reduce energy consumption without the aid of STAR-IRS. Figure 2a depicts the performance of the Energy Efficiency (EE) as a function of the number of elements at the STAR-IRS. Evidently, the system's EE demonstrates an upward trend with an increase in the number of elements at the STAR-IRS. Figure 2(c) presents the Energy Efficiency (EE) as a function of Transmission Power (TP) at the Base Station (BS) with varying numbers of antennas. The increment in Transmission Power (TP) at the Base Station (BS) leads to an increasing trend in the Energy Efficiency (EE), which attains a maximum value before stabilizing. This trend indicates that the Energy Efficiency (EE) cannot exhibit perpetual growth despite the continuous increase in power at the Base Station (BS).

5 Conclusion

The paper has designed an optimisation problem of energy-efficiency relevant to a downlink network employing a STAR-IRS. The proposed solution entails the creation of a P-QDN-based algorithm that allows for the joint optimisation of beamforming vectors at the Base Station (BS) and phase shift at the STAR-IRS, resulting in the maximisation of Energy Efficiency (EE). Numerical results have shown that the suggested approach is effective and convergent. Furthermore, we examined the EE trends obtained for varied levels of transmission power at the BS and the varying number of elements at the STAR-IRS.

References

1. Wu, Q., Zhang, R.: Towards smart and reconfigurable environment: intelligent reflecting surface aided wireless network. IEEE Commun. Mag. **58**(1), 106–112 (2019)
2. Liu, Y., et al.: Star: simultaneous transmission and reflection for 360° coverage by intelligent surfaces. IEEE Wirel. Commun. **28**(6), 102–109 (2021)
3. Budhiraja, I., Vishnoi, V., Kumar, N., Garg, D., Tyagi, S.: Energy-efficient optimization scheme for RIS-assisted communication underlaying UAV with NOMA. In: ICC 2022-IEEE International Conference on Communications, pp. 1–6, IEEE (2022)
4. Sharma, H., et al.: Federated learning based energy efficient scheme for MEC with NOMA underlaying UAV. In: Proceedings of the 5th International ACM Mobicom Workshop on Drone Assisted Wireless Communications for 5G and Beyond, pp. 73–78 (2022)
5. Zhao, N., Liang, Y.-C., Niyato, D., Pei, Y., Wu, M., Jiang, Y.: Deep reinforcement learning for user association and resource allocation in heterogeneous cellular networks. IEEE Trans. Wireless Commun. **18**(11), 5141–5152 (2019)
6. Wang, K., Xue, L., Yang, Z., Peng, M.: Max-min energy-efficiency fair optimization in STAR-RIS assisted communication system. IEEE Access (2023)
7. Aung, P.S., Nguyen, L.X., Tun, Y.K., Han, Z., Hong, C.S.: Deep reinforcement learning based spectral efficiency maximization in STAR-RIS-assisted indoor outdoor communication. In: NOMS 2023–2023 IEEE/IFIP Network Operations and Management Symposium, pp. 1–6, IEEE (2023)
8. Chen, J., Ma, Z., Zou, Y., Jia, J., Wang, X.: DRL-based energy efficient resource allocation for STAR-RIS assisted coordinated multi-cell networks. In: GLOBECOM 2022–2022 IEEE Global Communications Conference, pp. 4232–4237, IEEE (2022)
9. Asif, M., Ihsan, A., Khan, W.U., Ali, Z., Zhang, S., Wu, S.X.: Energy-efficient beamforming and resource optimization for STAR-IRS enabled hybrid-NOMA 6G communications. IEEE Trans. Green Commun. Netw. (2023)
10. Zhang, Q., Wang, Y., Li, H., Hou, S., Song, Z.: Resource allocation for energy efficient STAR-RIS aided MEC systems. IEEE Wirel. Commun. Lett. **12**(4), 610–614 (2023)
11. Xu, J., Liu, Y., Mu, X., Dobre, O.A.: STAR-RISS: simultaneous transmitting and reflecting reconfigurable intelligent surfaces. IEEE Commun. Lett. **25**(9), 3134–3138 (2021)
12. Mu, X., Liu, Y., Guo, L., Lin, J., Schober, R.: Simultaneously transmitting and reflecting (STAR) RIS aided wireless communications. IEEE Trans. Wirel. Commun. **21**(5), 3083–3098 (2021)

Deep Reinforcement Learning Based Intelligent Resource Allocation Techniques with Applications to Cloud Computing

Ramanpreet Kaur[1,2], Divya Anand[3], Upinder Kaur[4], Jaskiran Kaur[5], Sahil Verma[6], and Kavita[6(✉)]

[1] Department of Computer Application, Lovely Professional University, Phagwara, Punjab, India
[2] Baba Farid College, Bathinda, Punjab, India
[3] Lovely Professional University, Phagwara, Punjab, India
divya.24844@lpu.co.in
[4] Akal University, Talwandi Sabo, Punjab, India
upinder_cs@auts.ac.in
[5] NMIMS, Chandigarh, Punjab, India
jaskiran.kaur@nmims.edu
[6] CGC, Jhanjeri, Mohali, Punjab, India
{sahilverma,kavita}@ieee.org

Abstract. Resources allocation in cloud computing needs an efficient and accurate prediction of network workload. To predict the high dimensional and high variable data is difficult to predict. It leads to failing services level agreement and quality of services. To address these challenges deep reinforcement learning techniques are used for predicting the heterogeneous workload on the network. This paper presents a comprehensive review of deep reinforcement learning techniques. It includes the use of deep reinforcement learning in the field of resource allocation, task scheduling, traffic identification, future prediction and to fulfil the QoS and SLA. Some parameters such as SLA violation, Resource Allocation (RA), cost, the response time (RT), and resource prediction (RP) are also discussed. A case study related to deep reinforcement learning for automated task scheduling in cloud computing is also included which encourages us to use these techniques for task scheduling without any response delay and proper resource utilization.

Keywords: Deep Reinforcement Learning · Resources allocation · SLA violation · Cost · Response Time · Resource Prediction

1 Introduction

A cloud provides many resources, in the form of software or infrastructural; all this resource management is done by Cloud Management Broker (CMB). It works as an interface for allocating the resources available on different clouds based on requests. The choice of cloud resources depends on the cost, SLA, QoS, and some other parameters.

KC Santosh et al. (Eds.): RTIP2R 2023, CCIS 2026, pp. 144–150, 2024.
https://doi.org/10.1007/978-3-031-53082-1_12

Multi-cloud uses services from more than one cloud. Multi-cloud could be all private, all public, or a combination of both types of cloud. Companies use multi-cloud to enlarge their business and reduce the fear of data loss. As machine learning presents the main role in the field of IT such as video recommendation, filtering, social network, etc. same as deep learning is also representation learning doing well in these applications. The latest techniques of deep learning give an important role in many other applications such as Visual data processing, natural language processing, audio and speech processing, etc. Deep learning performing well in feature extraction without human intervention. Deep reinforcement learning is the combination of reinforcement learning and deep learning. Reinforcement learning is the intermediate between agent and environment. State, action, space, feedback and environment are the important component of deep reinforcement learning. Following diagram shows the working of deep reinforcement learning. The main Contributions of this paper are as follows.

- We review the related work of deep reinforcement learning techniques.
- We discuss the applications of different reinforcement learning techniques.
- We compare DRL algorithms based on various parameters.
- We identify various issues and future directions.

2 Related Work

Handling the incoming workload in the cloud and multi-cloud requires an efficient technique. Many authors work in this area [1]. The author presents a scheduler namely SCARL (Scheduler with Attentive Reinforcement Learning) to handle different resources requirements in the cluster. Experimental results show that this approach gives better results when compared with others [2]. The author introduces all the techniques related to cloud intelligence. Traditional approaches are not much efficient in terms of security, optimization, and some other parameters but now a day's many intelligent techniques such as neural networks, deep learning, etc. are developed to deal with cloud computing efficiently. Most of part of this study focuses on resource utilization, security, and privacy. Many issues related to cloud brokering; VM placement and workflow scheduling, etc. are also discussed [3]. The author presents an intelligent approach for resource allocation for robotics requests is designed. It's based on the reinforcement learning approach which helps the cloud to decided which request should be fulfilled and which resources needs to be allocated. A Semi-Markov Decision process is proposed which helps for the automatic management of resources and reduces human intervention. The comparison done with GA proposed approach gives better result in limited resources and provide average return time. In [4] the author proposed a deep learning approach for traffic identification and classification of mobile devices. This paper provides the taxonomy of analysis of network traffic, secondly, it proves that deep learning for traffic analysis is good to approach, third this approach provides a proposed model based on deep learning to get these benefits, and finally, it gives some future direction. In [5] proposed a Service Level Agreement (SLA) framework to meet the QoS requirements of all cloud users. This framework includes a reinforcement learning approach for adopting the changes in the requirement of cloud requests. The previous approaches degrade the performance when the request changes its requirement but the proposed approach works well in a dynamic environment. The experiment results show that it gives a better result to meet the QoS and avoid the SLA violation. In [6] the author discussed the resources management technique with the help of reinforcement learning. As the Cloud Management Broker (CMB) responsible to fulfil the user's request and giving benefits to the cloud user. So the proposed technique which is based on reinforcement learning will help the CMB to gain profit. The author proposed two algorithms SARSA and Q-leaning. The experiment results show that Q-learning is more efficient in terms of computation and SARSA is more efficient.

In [7] the author designed a deep learning-based prediction algorithm for cloud workload (L-PAW).This author proposed two approaches first one is a Top Sparse auto encoder (TSA) used to extract the essential features of workload and the next it is combined with GRU (gated recurrent unit) to accurate prediction of variable workload. The experiment was done on Alibaba and Google data centers. Results show that L-Paw gives excellent accuracy in workload prediction when compared with other approaches. In [8] the author developed an approach for resource provisioning in the cloud environment. Resources provision means to allocate the required resources but it depends on the current workload. So it needs prediction of future workload is allocate the required resources. The author proposed the approach which is a combination of autonomic computing and reinforcement learning. The results show that the proposed method improves 12% utilization of resources and 50% cost reduction as compared to other techniques. In [9] the author suggests an approach for resource scheduling based on traffic, identification is proposed. The author proposed a virtual network framework for request scheduling which works in two-step the first is traffic identification and the second is path selection. mGBDT model used for traffic identification based on Qos and behaviour of request and after identification of traffic, the DRL model selects an efficient path for request. The experiment results show that the framework improves the quality of services and the DRL approach with POKTR algorithm gives better throughput and reduces network congestion [10]. The author proposed an online reinforcement learning approach for task scheduling in a cloud environment. The author discussed that a cloud broker which works as an intermediate with a cloud environment works in three steps task transmission, allocation of the task, and task execution. In the first step, all tasks are kept in a global queue after that with the help of reinforcement learning each task is allocated to the queue of a particular VM. Finally, the task is processed on that VM. So the author proposed an approach named stochastic approximation for allocation of a task in a dynamic environment. The experiment results show that the proposed approach outperforms when compare with others.

In [11] the author surveys deep learning algorithms, techniques, and applications. Deep learning changed the way of working in the field of IT. The author also discussed some weaknesses of deep learning and gives some future directions to make it more efficient. In [12] the author develops an approach for Fog computing. Fog works as an intermediate between cloud users and cloud providers. So resource management is an important concept at the Fog level. Many algorithms have been proposed for resources management but they work on a subset of a parameter such as response time, energy consumption, network bandwidth, and latency not simultaneously. So the author proposed the ROUTER technique to work on these parameters simultaneously. Results show that this approach reduces 10% response time, 12.35% energy consumption, 12% network bandwidth, and 10% response time. In [13] author discussed Virtual Network Embedding (VNE). VNE is a challenging concept in cloud computing as I need an intelligent solution for resources management, the AI-related concepts need to be improved in this field. So the author proposed a prediction model based on a reinforcement learning approach called Multi-stage Virtual Network Embedding (MUVINE) for data centers in the cloud. The author used the SARSA reinforcement learning agent which helps to embed the VM on suitable SNs. The binary VN works as a classifier of the incoming request. RBR is used to predict the features. So the entire approach of MUVINE used for embedding the VN on stable SN outperforms in terms of time-domain and user's request. In [14] talk about Virtual network embedding. As it is an important term for proper resource utilization. The previous technique follows static techniques which was not much efficient for the optimal solution. The author proposed a reinforcement learning approach for the Virtual network embedding approach which uses historical data and gives an optimal solution. The comparison was made with two other algorithms and found that the proposed techniques outperform others. In [15] talks about intelligent resources management with the help of deep reinforcement learning. The intelligent resources manager consists of three things controller, monitor, and allocator. The controller collects the request requirement and schedules the resources by using an efficient algorithm from the resources scheduling algorithm pool and monitors will the availability of resources as per user request and the allocator will be allocated the requested resources. The DRL algorithm is an online algorithm discussed in this paper which always gives an optimal resource selection. The author proposed DQN named SA Q network which combines the features of SA and Q-learning helps to find a near-optimal solution. SAQN helps in the reduction of iteration for finding the optimal allocation of resources.

In [16] the author talks about the intelligent method for incoming workload prediction in a cloud environment. Cloud workload predictions very important part for the cloud provider to satisfy the customer and reduce energy consumption. The canonical polyadic decomposition based on a deep learning model is proposed. So the proposed approach helps to compress the parameter for efficiently improving the training. The result shows the resource allocation on VM can be done in advance with the help of workload prediction. In [17] the author talks about fast response time in the internet of things (IoT). The traditional approaches and deep learning approach to handling the user's requests are time-consuming processes. So to handle this issue author proposes a broad reinforcement learning approach. It makes service providers very fast and efficient. Results show that its efficient to take fast action when compared with other approaches. In [18] author discussed the cloud provides many services such as storage, networking, etc. But the most important thing is to proper utilization of cloud resources and workload management. The author proposed a Reinforcement Learning based Enhanced Resource Allocation and Workload Management (RL-ERAWM) approach for resource allocation and managing the workload. It uses Q-learning which considers the arrival rate of the request and VM workload. The proposed approach performs better in terms of VM utilization, response time, and makespan. In [19] the author talks about job scheduling in a cloud environment means allocating the job on the proper resources to meet the QoS requirements of users. The author develops a framework for services providers named an intelligent QoS-aware job scheduling framework. It helps for job scheduling on a suitable VM. The proposed approach reduces average response time up to 40.4%, achieves QoS at a high level, and can work on different workload conditions. In [20] the author talks about task scheduling in cloud computing. Better task scheduling helps to get good results in all aspects of cloud computing. So the deep-Q-learning-based heterogeneous earliest-finish-time (DQ-HEFT) algorithm is proposed. It is closely related to deep reinforcement learning for task scheduling. The experiment results show that it can achieve better makespan and speed with a high volume of data as compared with the existing workflow scheduling algorithm (Table 1).

Table 1. Review of reinforcement learning technique based on various parameters

R. no.	Author Name	Approach	SLA	Cost	RP	RT	RA
1	Mukoe Cheong	Reinforcement Learning					Yes
3	Hang Liu	Reinforcement Learning		Yes			Yes
5	Ayoub Alsarhan	Reinforcement Learning	Yes				
6	Pietrabissa Antonio	Reinforcement Learning					Yes
8	Mostafa Ghobaei-Arani	Reinforcement Learning	Yes	Yes			Yes
9	Bo He	Deep Reinforcement Learning					Yes
10	Seyedakbar Mostafavi	Reinforcement Learning				Yes	Yes
12	Sukhpal Singh Gill					Yes	Yes
14	Haipeng Yao	Reinforcement Learning					Yes
15	Yu Zhang	Deep reinforcement learning					Yes
18	P Suresh	Reinforcement Learning				Yes	Yes
19	Yi Wei	Deep Reinforcement Learning				Yes	
22	Junhui Zhao	Deep Learning					Yes

Review of reinforcement learning technique based on various parameters techniques give good results in resource allocation which cover many phases such as workload prediction, handling heterogeneous user requests, etc.

The above table depicts the work done by many authors in the field of Reinforcement learning. Parameters such as SLA violation, RA, cost, RT, and RP are included to know which author focuses on what type of parameter.

3 Conclusion

Machine learning becoming more and more popular in the field of research in terms of data mining, image processing, text classification, video recommendation, etc. With this machine learning, deep reinforcement learning is known as representation learning used in these applications. Many latest techniques of deep reinforcement present better results in Visual data processing, Natural language process, audio and speech processing, and much related application. So in this paper author prepare a review based on various deep reinforcement learning techniques in the field of cloud and multi-cloud. The parameter such as SLA violation, RA, cost, RT, and RP is included to check the author's particular reason for the research. This review enlightens that deep reinforcement learning in the field of cloud and multi-cloud is used for resource allocation, task classification, future resources prediction, workload prediction, etc. The future proposed by authors is also depicted in the above table which inspires researchers to work in the field of deep reinforcement learning.

References

1. Cheong, M., Lee, H., Yeom, I., Woo, H.: SCARL: attentive reinforcement learning-based scheduling in a multi-resource heterogeneous cluster. IEEE Access **4**, 153432–153444 (2016)
2. Pradhan, N.R., Singh, A.P., Verma, S., et al.: A blockchain based lightweight peer-to-peer energy trading framework for secured high throughput micro-transactions. Sci. Rep. **12**, 14523 (2022)
3. Liu, H., Liu, S., Zheng, K.: A reinforcement learning-based resource allocation scheme for cloud robotics. IEEE Access **6**, 17215–17222 (2018)
4. Ghosh, G., et al.: Secure surveillance systems using partial-regeneration-based non-dominated optimization and 5D-chaotic map. Symmetry **13**(8), 1447 (2021). https://doi.org/10.3390/sym 13081447
5. Alsarhan, A., Itradat, A., Al-Dubai, A.Y., cZomaya, A.Y., Min, G.: Adaptive Resource Allocation and Provisioning in Multi-Service Cloud Environments. IEEE Trans. Parallel Distrib. Syst. **29**(1), 31–42 (2018). ISSN: 1045–9219
6. Tian, X., et al.: Power allocation scheme for maximizing spectral efficiency and energy efficiency tradeoff for uplink NOMA systems in B5G/6G. Phys. Commun. **43**, 101227 (2020)
7. Chen, Z., Hu, J., Min, G., Zomaya, A.Y., El-Ghazawi, T.: Towards accurate prediction for high-dimensional and highly-variable cloud workloads with deep learning. IEEE Trans. Parallel Distrib. Syst. **31**(4), 923–934 (2019). ISSN: 1045-9219
8. Ghobaei-Arani, M., Jabbehdari, S., Pourmina, M.A.: An autonomic resources provisioning approach for service-based cloud applications: a hybrid approach. Future Gener. Comput. Syst. **78**, 191–210 (2017). ISSN: 0167-739X
9. He, B., Wang, J., Qi, Q, Sun, H., Liao, J.: Towards intelligent provisioning of virtualized network functions in cloud of things: a deep reinforcement learning based approach. IEEE Trans. Cloud Comput. **10**(2), 1262–1274 (2020). ISSN: 2168-7161

10. Mostafavi, S., Hakami, V.: A stochastic approximation approach for foresighted task scheduling in cloud computing. Wireless Pers. Commun. **25**, 901–925 (2020). https://doi.org/10.1007/s11277-020-07398-9
11. Gandam, A., et al.: An efficient post-processing adaptive filtering technique to rectifying the flickering effects. PLoS ONE **16**, e0250959 (2021)
12. Singh, D., Verma, S., Singla, J.: A neuro-fuzzy based medical intelligent system for the diagnosis of hepatitis B. In: Proceedings of the 2021 2nd International Conference on Computation, Automation and Knowledge Management (ICCAKM), Dubai, United Arab Emirates, pp. 107–111 (2021)
13. Thakkar, H., Dehury, C., Sahoo, P.: MUVINE: multi-stage virtual network embedding in cloud data centers using reinforcement learning based predictions. IEEE J. Sel. Areas Commun. **38**(6), 1058–1074 (2020). ISSN: 0733-8716
14. Ghosh, G., Kavita, Verma, S., Talib, M.N., Shah, M.H.: A systematic review on image encryption techniques. Turk. J. Comput. Math. Educ. **12**, 3055–3059 (2021)
15. Zhang, Y., Yao, J., Guan, H.: Intelligent cloud resource management with deep reinforcement learning. IEEE Cloud Comput. **4**(6), 60–69 (2017)
16. Sharma, S., Verma, S., Jyoti, K.: A new bat algorithm with distance computation capability and its applicability in routing for WSN. In: Wang, J., Reddy, G.R.M., Prasad, V.K., Reddy, V.S. (eds.) Soft Computing and Signal Processing. AISC, vol. 898, pp. 163–171. Springer, Singapore (2019). https://doi.org/10.1007/978-981-13-3393-4_17
17. Wei, X., Zhao, J., Zhou, L., Qian, Y.: Broad reinforcement learning for supporting fast autonomous IoT. IEEE Internet Things J. **7**(8), 7010–7020 (2020). ISSN: 2327-4662
18. Kumar, P., Verma, S.: Detection of wormhole attack in VANET. Natl. J. Syst. Inf. Technol. **10**(1), 71 (2021)
19. Wei, Y., Pan, L., Liu, S., Wu, L., Meng, X.: DRL-scheduling: an intelligent QoS-aware job scheduling framework for applications in clouds. IEEE Access **6**, 55112–55125 (2018)
20. Kaur, A., Singh, P., Batth, R., Lim, C.: Deep-Q learning-based heterogeneous earliest finish time scheduling algorithm for scientific workflows in cloud. Softw. Pract. Exp. **52**(3), 689–709 (2020)
21. Rjoub, G., Bentahar, J., Wahab, O., Bataineh, A.: Deep and reinforcement learning for automated task scheduling in large-scale cloud computing systems. Concurr. Comput. Pract. Exp. **33**(23), e5919 (2020)
22. Zhao, J., Kong, M., Li, Q., Sun, X.: Contract-based computing resource management via deep reinforcement learning in vehicular fog computing. IEEE Access **8**, 3319–3329 (2016)

A Review on Machine Learning Techniques in IoT-Based Smart Grid Applications

Samarth Goyal$^{(\boxtimes)}$, Ishita Goyal, and Tanveer Ahmed

School of CSET, Bennett University, Greater Noida, India
goyalsamarth090@gmail.com, tanveer.ahmed@bennett.edu.in

Abstract. The deployment of machine literacy (ML) in the electric structure has been innovated by the arrival of the coming-generation power networks known as the smart grid. A detailed analysis related to smart grids has been performed by this article. The Internet of things (IoT) offers access and is at the heart of these advanced grid architectures. The system's inter connectivity and requirement for ongoing communication resulted in a vast data flow that necessitates technologies considerably superior to traditional methods for appropriate data analysis and interpretation. In the modern world, cyber security has become a crucial concern in smart grid sophisticated networks, with sensor nodes and the data constituting key targets of cyberattacks. The article critically examines such security challenges and their remedies. The reviews are summarised to provide a succinct image of the practice and prospective future disciplines for industry developments, including existing constraints and feasible remedies, as well as their applicability.

1 Introduction

Smart grid refers to integrating informational and digital networking systems with electric grid infrastructures to facilitate bidirectional connectivity and data flows, which can improve the electric system's reliability, dependability, and profitability [2]. Innovative grid applications aim to calculate the best-generating transmission and distribution patterns and store power data directly. To put it another way, the smart grid has the ability to integrate networks and operations to enable the power grid to be smart and autonomous [3]. In the past few years, there has been a strong push in AI research to develop effective methods for the Power Grid, the foreseeable new generation of power generation (mainly power) infrastructures that will be likely to make better use of RESs and effective load management, and large-scale implementation of powered mobility. Gadgets that link to the world wide web have become essential to everyday life, and new ones are being introduced daily. Home automation systems are one example of such products. IoT systems utilize the internet to maintain contact with technically situated resources and carry out their functions as a function of the interchange. According to the researchers of [4], IoTs are a combination of smart objects that allow users to communicate data across networks using a uniform framework,

KC Santosh et al. (Eds.): RTIP2R 2023, CCIS 2026, pp. 151–164, 2024.
https://doi.org/10.1007/978-3-031-53082-1_13

resulting in developing a common operational picture that enables creative applications. This is fulfilled through pall technology as the foundation for pervasive detectors and data logic. Each device has its integrated cloud platform, allowing it to be recognized and linked to others. By 2020, IoT has grown to over 30 billion items [5]. ML is a field of hypothesis testing wherein machines are trained to make assumptions based on their previous experiences. It has become a critical tool for solving issues as large data grows. Multitudinous ML approaches have been employed in smart grid operations primarily to continually advance calculating technologies, particularly in data processing. This is the last element of the smart grid structure powered by data collecting and analyzing. By providing a useful method to evaluate and make appropriate grid-running decisions, ML techniques can assist the smart grid in operating as intended [5]. Because of the complexity of smart grid technologies, there are several ways for intruders to cause disruption. Cybersecurity is among the most serious enterprises facing the smart grid, posing a significant challenge. A vicious cyberattack on the grid might have far-reaching goods on the smart grid's broad structure's trustability. Still, the entire structure becomes susceptible, If only one smart grid unit is compromised. The outfit in workplaces, houses, and institutions may be compromised if the overall grid is shut down due to cyber pitfalls. This might eventually bring the country to a bottleneck and affect disastrous profitable losses. As a result, an entirely protective strategy is demanded to address all the pitfalls and sins that an intelligent grid may face. These approaches are very effective in preventing denial-of-service (DOS) attacks. These techniques can identify threats, initiate appropriate measures to resolve critical vulnerabilities and alert malware protection.

2   Applications of Machine Learning in Modern Power Grids

A program's literacy and formulating protrusions from given data is appertained to as machine literacy (ML). It is made up of a number of processes that use a sequence of commands to evaluate data-driven forecasts or decisions. ML entails a complex process of developing and implementing specified algorithms that work as predicted. Soothsaying, pricing, electrical generation, unborn optimal scheduling, fault analysis, model prophetic control, and discovery of networking hackers during a security breach exemplify ML features [6]. Xu et al.'s estimations were based on the New American 39 transit system. [7] provided a methodology for measuring dynamic response using extreme ML and displaying excellent performance and speed. Wang et al. [8] used a unique core quaternion model algorithm to use massive data produced by a phasor measurement unit (PMU) to achieve a similar goal. The approach was also validated on the New American 39 transportation system. ML may be used to assess the PMU in distribution transformers, including system visualization and frequency identification. ML can be utilized for these goals in conjunction with other technologies like the electricity generation model validation program and the free flight risk evaluation tool. Multiple ML algorithms are being implemented at multiple levels of wind and solar systems in smart grids, opening up a whole new field of study [9]. For instance, kernel functions have been extensively used for various energy power challenges and issues, resulting in many optimizations and prediction approaches in smart grids [10]. Authors [11] proposed an economic optimization strategy for microgrid prosumer nodes using a two-level control mechanism.

The researchers of [12] and [13] have introduced an ML-based quick and accurate approach for analyzing voltage stability occurrences in smart-grid. Li et al. [14] used ML to examine preferences to determine use patterns. Remani et al. [15] presented a broad application of reinforcement learning to manage household loads, considering RESs and all conceivable tariff variations. Another paper [16] proposes using flyspeck mass optimization (PSO) to increase the stability for unanticipated islanding in microgrids. Advanced analytics to regulate and predict islanding events emerge until this stabilization phase. Jurado et al. [17] suggested a hybrid solution for energy management systems that use entropy-based feature extraction, ML, deep learning, and computational intelligence. In [18], many techniques for training common multilayer perceptron nodes for forecasting load were examined, including extreme ML, regressors, decaying radial kernel function, and Bayesian network, including correction of errors. In comparison to previous algorithms, including such neural networks, Ryu et al. [19] introduced a deep convolutional NN (A cargo soothsaying approach for short to medium-term soothsaying at the cargo machine) that displayed as important as 29% reduced error. The authors in [20] propose a predictive control system based on CPUs and GPUS. Another [21] considers a 50 MW energy infrastructure at the University of Pennsylvania. This grid provides electricity to fifty million customers from sustainable and non-sustainable sources. Sophisticated management and storage mechanisms are available on the institutional grid. Advanced analytics studies were carried out using a vast number of data iterations. In the grid, ML [22,23] may be used for a variety of security purposes. Table 1 shows various ML algorithms which were used in smart grids with RESs. The renewable energy (RES) industry, on the other hand, is the most potential and sorely needed application of ML algorithms in the next-gen energy infrastructure. Figure 1 depicts the ML usages to ensure the robustness of smart grids.

3   Cyber Security in Modern Power Grids

Technology advancements are helping the conventional electricity grid transform into the smart grid. For online transactions security issues is considered to be one of the major concern in development of smart grid. Issues about security are slowing the development of modern grid applications. Nonetheless, continual advances will optimize smart grid operations. Providing for the controllers' and communications technology's confidentiality, integrity, and availability (CIA) triangle is one of the grid's concerns. The CIA trinity is necessary for the security, administration, and regulation of energy as well as telecommunication networks. The CIA triangle-based data security measures must be included of any power

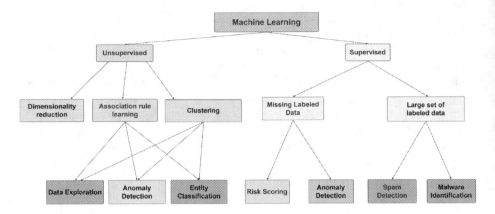

Fig. 1. ML is being used to ensure the robustness of smart grids. Respectively unsupervised and supervised techniques may be utilised to conduct a number of tasks, including such attack detection and data classification [24].

system security claims. Several crucial security guidelines for grid integration must be explicitly followed.

Sequestration is the process of protecting data from unauthorized access or exposure. Secrecy is referred to as a restriction on access to data for authorized individuals. Only the users who are authorized for drugs can have access to data, not for the unauthorized users. Residential appliances can be connected to the electricity grid via a smart transmission network, which allows bidirectional and authentic data transfer.

If attackers gain access to customer information, they may use it to follow their lifestyles, discover what equipment they utilize, or whether or not individuals are at residence. Transparency includes privacy and is among the most pressing concerns of consumers [24–26]. There should never be any form of data compromise in the network. The accuracy and integrity of every material must be guaranteed. As a result, the data can not be altered in an unlawful or unnoticed manner. The term integrity refers to the protection of data from illegal modification and annihilation. It also refers to maintaining and ensuring the accuracy of data. It assists the smart grid in providing a secure and meaningful surveillance system. The availability of an electrical network is anticipated to remain constant. Also it's critical to ensure that data infrastructure can be accessed and used in a timely and reliable manner. Reliable operation directly reveals the control strategies of fundamental structures. Adaptability is known for preserving data system from failures. Due to the result of vacuity attempts data can be delayed, blocked or corrupted. As a result, accessibility means that the data must be accessible to authorised parties in the grid whenever they need it, without jeopardising security. Avoiding attacks that result in outages is a common concern when it comes to data availability. Network security breaches are a major issue since IoT-enabled smart networks create a composite, interconnected system with a significant amount of data that is frequently stored in cloud storages

Table 1. ML algorithms are being used in smart grids with RESs

Ref No.	ML Algorithm	Application	Year (2000s)
[31]	Extreme ML	Analyses of voltage stability	11
[8]	CVM	Voltage regulation and stability	16
[32]	ML	Load forecasting	11
[16]	ML and Wavelet	Distributed Energy Sources	14
[33]	PSO	AC and DC Microgrids	17
[34]	ML and machine based Computation	Energy Management	15
[35]	Deep learning	Fault detection in farms	12
[36]	Big Data and Computer Vision	Forecasting in farms	9
[37]	NN	Forecasting the renewable energy	14
[38]	Extreme ML	Short-term based forecasting	14
[39]	Quantified Regression	Short-term based forecasting	16
[40]	Swarm Optimization	Forecasting the renewable energy	14
[41]	PSO	Short-term based forecasting	13
[42]	Feature extraction and Extreme ML	Forecasting speed	18
[43]	Fuzzy	Not Addressed	10
[44]	Fuzzy	Smart Energy Management	13
[45]	SVR	Forecasting the solar energy	14
[46]	SVR	Forecasting solar power	13
[47]	Markov Model	Forecasting solar radiations	16
[48]	Extreme ML	Forecasting energy	14
[49]	Gaussian Regression	Solar and Wind energy	14

[25]. Because both the price and quality of the electricity are impacted, threats to the integrity of this complicated chain are always very serious and vulnerable [26,27]. There are many forms of security concerns for IoT incorporated smart grid systems. These cyberattacks on power systems could be performed for a variety of reasons, including causing damage to critical elements, gaining a foothold or dominance in the management system for manipulation, monetary coercion, or vandalism. Various applications and operating systems targeted commonly in cybersecurity threats, with cash flow and proprietary information being the most appealing vulnerable to hackers, with about 80% of the occurrences being attempted. Additional key targets include scientific data/information, and also control mechanisms. The majority of the vulnerabilities are data generated by IoT devices, and this alone can highlight the criticality of computer security for power systems. The vulnerability of IoT systems to cyberattacks was determined to be the most desirable kind of attack in the years 2016 and 2017 [28,29]. The researchers anticipate that AI technology will be the most dangerous weapon in cyber threats alongside sophisticated malicious activities, ransomware, and loopholes in data security rules. Operations and maintenance breakdowns, synchronisation loss, power distribution disruption, substantial financial losses, public

healthcare damages, information leakage, cascade failures, and full disruptions are the most likely effects of cybersecurity threats on the power grid [30].

The perpetration of a smart grid system has much further consequences for a business, affecting all aspects of its specialized structure. As a result, safety preventives must be also wide. Prevention and surveillance are the two main areas of cyber security techniques. ML algorithms can forecast vulnerabilities and detect abnormalities based on attributes, and protective tactics may be implemented at the physical and operational levels in addition to the most visible software protections. ML can be used to do most basic tasks, such as regression, and prediction, and therefore looks to be a viable remedy to cyber risks in the era of enormous data and a scarcity of cyber-defence of the vulnerabilities are data generated by IoT devices, and this alone can highlight the criticality of computer security for power systems. In the times 2016 and 2017, the vulnerabilities of IoT systems tocyber-attacks was assessed as the most preferable form of attack [28,29]. The researchers anticipate that AI technology will be the most dangerous weapon in cyber threats alongside sophisticated malicious activities, ransomware, and loopholes in data security rules. Various attackers aim are plotted in bar chart as shown in Fig. 2. Operations and maintenance breakdowns, synchronisation loss, power distribution disruption, substantial financial losses, public healthcare damages, information leakage, cascade failures, and full disruptions are the most likely effects of cybersecurity threats on the power grid [30].

The implementation of a smart grid system has much more consequences for a business, affecting all aspects of its technical infrastructure. As a result, safety precautions must be similarly widespread. Prevention and surveillance are the two main areas of cyber security techniques. ML algorithms can forecast vulnerabilities and detect abnormalities based on attributes, and protective

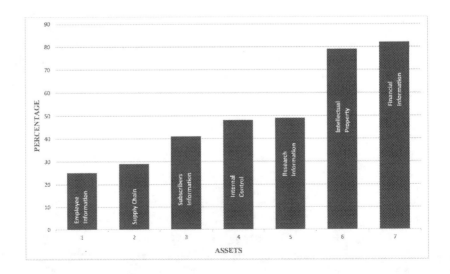

Fig. 2. Mainly attacker aims

tactics may be implemented at the physical and operational levels in addition to the most visible software protections as shown in Fig. 3. ML can be used to do most basic tasks, such as regression, and prediction, and therefore looks to be a viable remedy to cyber risks in the era of enormous data and a scarcity of cyber-defence.

4   Findings

The paper's results can be summarised as follows:

- The power infrastructure is undergoing its first significant transformation since its establishment over two centuries ago. This next-generation network integrates electricity, information, telecommunication, and process control to produce a more resilient and adaptable infrastructure that can handle innovative approaches. The smart grid is the name given to this new infrastructure.
- Communication and data sharing are at the heart of smart grid operation, making linked devices a critical component of this platform. Such devices are also known as the IoTs, they allow grid nodes to communicate data in order to keep a current system in-position and obtain updates regarding to operate when grid circumstances change. Each year, the number of IoT devices grows considerably, presenting both new potential and concerns as they become more widely used.
- IoT devices create a massive amount of data that can't be analysed using traditional methods. Big data based on computer vision is used to tell us about this enormous volume of data, which has led to the creation of new analytical tools. Big data created by IoT devices are also vulnerable to security concerns, which has garnered a huge amount of attention.

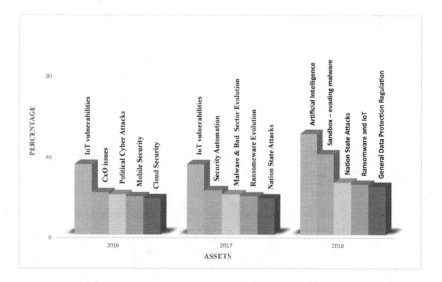

Fig. 3. Anticipated attack origins and IOT being a prominent target for cyber-attacks.

- ML is a powerful tool for sifting through large amounts of data and extracting meaningful information that may help with consumption and production pattern detection, prediction, and control, among other things. Numerous methods have been published in the past, and newer, more inventive approaches are being created for usage in instances where performance is to be enhanced.
- Cyber intrusions are a substantial concern across every area of the electric city, including production, transmission, and distributing, and several have occurred. Security is thus a big issue in the power grid. A huge amount of research is already done on detecting cyber- security risks and implementing countermeasures. ML algorithms have been implemented in most of these interventions, as traditional tactics are frequently ineffective in non-linear systems.

The accompanying conclusions are drawn for potential research in this area which are listed below.

- Feasibility of present grid infrastructure must be verified using methods including such mathematical modelling to determine the best timeline and technical strategy for moving to grid design.
- Problems of moving to grid centred on RESs, as well as possible solutions, must be examined. It is also important to research potential economic models, policy initiatives, including the commitment to smart grid adoption.
- IoT devices may be improved to become more small, affordable, energy-efficient, and durable. To boost efficiency and reliability, developments in wireless protocols might be examined.
- Superior demand and production prediction methodologies, particularly for RESs are required for the successful functioning of RE based smart networks.
- For the usage of the given data, ML techniques may be designed to fulfil power quality requirements in a power grid. To increase effectiveness of renewable energies, these strategies can be employed in wind-solar hybrid power systems.
- Numerous security problems, including direct attacks, networking breaches, and cryptography operations, will require further study to find effective answers. Communication networks must also be more effective, with greater safeguards in place.

5   Discussion

Understanding and addressing the numerous cybersecurity challenges that occur become less and less crucial as the IoT bias in smart grid systems continues to decline. In this discussion, we will claw deeper into the security enterprises, implicit countermeasures, and the part of machine literacy in mollifying pitfalls. Security concerns in IoT-integrated smart grids:

- Data breaches: Unauthorized access to sensitive client information, like energy operation patterns, particular details, and billing information, can have severe consequences. Bushwhackers may use this information for identity theft, fraud, or to beget detriment by manipulating the smart grid system.

- Distributed Denial of Service(DDoS) attacks These attacks involve overwhelming the grid's communication structure with inordinate business, leading to system outages or dislocation of services.
- Malware and ransomware vicious software can insinuate the smart grid system to steal data, disrupt operations, or hold critical structure hostage in exchange for rescue payments.
- Bigwig pitfalls individuality's with authorized access to the system, similar to workers or contractors, could designedly or inadvertently compromise the security of the smart grid.
- Supply chain attacks: Adversaries may target vulnerabilities in the smart grid's supply chain, such as the manufacturers of IoT devices, to compromise the security of the entire system.

Countermeasures for IoT-integrated smart grids:

- Risk assessment and management: Perform routine evaluations to spot weaknesses, rank threats, and create a thorough risk management strategy that includes both proactive and reactive actions.
- Network segmentation: To lessen the possible impact of a cyberattack, isolate key infrastructure and components within the smart grid system.
- Encryption and secure communication: For protecting the data which is in transit or at rest, use robust encryption techniques and secure communication channels.
- Regular updates and patching: To reduce vulnerabilities, keep all software, firmware, and hardware components up to date with the most recent security patches and upgrades.

The role of machine learning in mitigating risks:

- Anomaly detection: ML algorithms can analyse enormous volumes of data from IoT devices to find anomalous patterns or behaviours that could be signs of upcoming intrusions.
- Predictive analytics: ML models can forecast prospective security vulnerabilities and assist organisations in taking preventative actions to address them by utilising past data and recognising patterns.
- Automated incident response: ML algorithms can assist in automating the response to detected threats, reducing the time it takes to contain and mitigate cyberattacks.
- Security policy enforcement: ML models can be used to continuously monitor and enforce security policies across the smart grid system, ensuring compliance with industry standards and regulations.

Future Research Directions: The above content highlights several areas that warrant further investigation to fully realize the potential of the smart grid and address the challenges associated with its implementation. These research areas include:

- Feasibility Analysis: Assessing the feasibility of the current grid structure is pivotal for determining the optimal timeline and specialized strategy for transitioning to a smart grid. This process may involve the use of fine modeling ways to estimate the capacity of the being structure to support the integration of new technologies and systems.
- Renewable Energy Integration: There is opportunity as well as challenge for including renewable energy sources (RESs) as objects in smart grid. It's essential to examine the implicit issues associated with this integration, similar to grid stability and cargo balancing, as well as the development of innovative results to address these enterprises. Additionally, research should look into covertly profitable business models and legislative initiatives that can facilitate the widespread abandonment of smart grid technologies and integration of RESs.
- IoT Device Advancements: There's a need for continued exploration and development concentrated on perfecting the size, cost, energy effectiveness, and continuity of IoT bias. Advances in wireless communication protocols and network infrastructures can also contribute to the enhanced effectiveness and trustability of IoT bias in the smart grid.
- Prophetic Analytics: The development of advanced demand and product soothsaying methodologies, particularly for RESs, is pivotal for the effective operation of renewable energy-grounded smart grids. These prophetic analytics ways can work machine literacy algorithms to reuse vast quantities of data and induce accurate prognostications that grease optimal decision-timber and resource allocation in the smart grid ecosystem.
- Machine Learning for Power Quality: Machine literacy approaches can be developed as the smart grid develops to ensure that power quality requirements are met. To increase the efficiency and trustworthiness of renewable energy reservoirs, these techniques can also be used with cold-blooded power systems, such as wind-solar arrangements.
- Cybersecurity results: The smart grid faces multitudinous security challenges, ranging from direct attacks and network breaches to cryptographic operations. Further exploration is demanded to develop effective results for these security problems, with a focus on enhancing the adaptability and robustness of communication networks and enforcing advanced safeguards to cover critical structure.
- Enhanced IoT DEVICES: As the smart grid continues to incorporate a growing number of IoT biases, it's essential to develop biases that are lower, more affordable, energy-effective, and durable. This includes exploring advancements in wireless communication protocols to ameliorate overall effectiveness and trust ability, icing flawless integration and operation within the smart grid ecosystem.

The transition from traditional power grid systems to IoT-based connected smart grid networks has created several new opportunities and challenges. The enormous quantum of data generated by the smart grid demands innovative logical approaches, similar to machine literacy algorithms, to ensure effective operation and data security. The integration of IoT bias and the security enterprises they present further emphasizes the significance of developing effective counter-measures to cover the smart grid structure. This deliberation has handed over a complete overview of the various aspects of the smart grid transformation, involving the nonfictional terrain, cybersecurity risks, monumental data expostulations, and the portion of engine knowledge algorithms in addressing these effects. It has also stressed implicit future disquisition directions that can support and guide researchers in their pursuit of advancing the smart grid and addressing the diverse expostulations that accompany its performance. As we remain to grasp the smart grid revolution, we must remain wedded to advancing our understanding of this establishment and evolving terrain, to harness its full potentiality and ensure a sustainable, secure, and operative dynamism future.

6   Conclusion

Power grid is evolving to an IoT- grounded intertwined intelligent grid network, along with the some advantages for this system comes with a lot of issues that have not yet been explored. Massive amounts of data generated by the smart grid require cutting-edge logical strategies akin to ML algorithms for efficient operation and data harvesting. The smart bias as well as the information they produce also punctuate the critical need for effective protection, because they are being attacked by attempts of varied confines, pressing the need for acceptable measures. In an effort to provide a comprehensive understanding for these issues, article provided a brief chronology of how the grid evolved into the modern grids known as smart grids, as well as how IoT has become one of the important component of power grid. Additional security risks in smart grid, and also problems relating to IoT-generated large data, such as its evaluation and preservation, were explored. Finally, the study's findings were provided, along with a brief description of future research paths to assist researchers to conduct.

References

1. Bayindir, R., Hossain, E., Kabalci, E., Perez, R.: A comprehensive study on microgrid technology. Int. J. Renew. Energy Res. (IJRER) **4**(4), 1094–1107 (2014). Article no. 4
2. Risteska Stojkoska, B.L., Trivodaliev, K.V.: A review of Internet of Things for smart home: challenges and solutions. J. Clean. Prod. **140**, 1454–1464 (2017). https://doi.org/10.1016/j.jclepro.2016.10.006
3. Special issue on smart grid: the electric energy system of the future - table of contents. Proc. IEEE **99**(6), 913–914 (2011). https://doi.org/10.1109/JPROC.2011.2150030
4. Gubbi, J., Buyya, R., Marusic, S., Palaniswami, M.: Internet of Things (IoT): a vision, architectural elements, and future directions. Future Gener. Comput. Syst. **29**(7), 1645–1660 (2013). https://doi.org/10.1016/j.future.2013.01.010
5. Liu, L., Liu, Y., Wang, L., Zomaya, A., Hu, S.: Economical and balanced energy usage in the smart home infrastructure: a tutorial and new results. IEEE Trans. Emerg. Top. Comput. **3**(4), 556–570 (2015). https://doi.org/10.1109/TETC.2015.2484839

6. Esmalifalak, M., Liu, L., Nguyen, N., Zheng, R., Han, Z.: Detecting stealthy false data injection using machine learning in smart grid. IEEE Syst. J. **11**(3), 1644–1652 (2017). https://doi.org/10.1109/JSYST.2014.2341597

7. Wenyi, L., Zhenfeng, W., Jiguang, H., Guangfeng, W.: Wind turbine fault diagnosis method based on diagonal spectrum and clustering binary tree SVM. Renew. Energy **50**, 1–6 (2013). https://doi.org/10.1016/j.renene.2012.06.013

8. Wang, B., Fang, B., Wang, Y., Liu, H., Liu, Y.: Power system transient stability assessment based on big data and the core vector machine. IEEE Trans. Smart Grid **7**(5), 2561–2570 (2016). https://doi.org/10.1109/TSG.2016.2549063

9. Hernández-Travieso, J.G., Travieso-González, C.M., Alonso-Hernández, J.B., Canino-Rodríguez, J.M., Ravelo-García, A.G.: Modeling a robust wind-speed forecasting to apply to wind-energy production. Neural Comput. Appl. **31**(11), 7891–7905 (2019). https://doi.org/10.1007/s00521-018-3619-6

10. Chia, Y.Y., Lee, L.H., Shafiabady, N., Isa, D.: A load predictive energy management system for supercapacitor-battery hybrid energy storage system in solar application using the Support Vector Machine. Appl. Energy **137**, 588–602 (2015). https://doi.org/10.1016/j.apenergy.2014.09.026

11. Liberati, F., Giorgio, A.D.: Economic model predictive and feedback control of a smart grid prosumer node. Energies **11**(1), 1–23 (2017)

12. Ucar, F., Alcin, O.F., Dandil, B., Ata, F.: Power quality event detection using a fast extreme learning machine. Energies **11**(1), 145 (2018). https://doi.org/10.3390/en11010145. Article no. 1

13. Morales-Velazquez, L., de Jesus Romero-Troncoso, R., Herrera-Ruiz, G., Morinigo-Sotelo, D., Osornio-Rios, R.A.: Smart sensor network for power quality monitoring in electrical installations. Measurement **103**, 133–142 (2017). https://doi.org/10.1016/j.measurement.2017.02.032

14. Li, B., Gangadhar, S., Cheng, S., Verma, P.K.: Predicting user comfort level using machine learning for smart grid environments. In: ISGT 2011, pp. 1–6 (2011). https://doi.org/10.1109/ISGT.2011.5759178

15. Remani, T., Jasmin, E.A., Ahamed, T.P.I.: Residential load scheduling with renewable generation in the smart grid: a reinforcement learning approach. IEEE Syst. J. **13**(3), 3283–3294 (2019). https://doi.org/10.1109/JSYST.2018.2855689

16. Jiang, H., et al.: Big data-based approach to detect, locate, and enhance the stability of an unplanned microgrid islanding. J. Energy Eng. **143**(5), 04017045 (2017). https://doi.org/10.1061/(ASCE)EY.1943-7897.0000473

17. Jurado, S., Nebot, À., Mugica, F., Avellana, N.: Hybrid methodologies for electricity load forecasting: entropy-based feature selection with machine learning and soft computing techniques. Energy **86**, 276–291 (2015). https://doi.org/10.1016/j.energy.2015.04.039

18. Cecati, C., Kolbusz, J., Różycki, P., Siano, P., Wilamowski, B.M.: A novel RBF training algorithm for short-term electric load forecasting and comparative studies. IEEE Trans. Ind. Electron. **62**(10), 6519–6529 (2015). https://doi.org/10.1109/TIE.2015.2424399

19. Ryu, S., Noh, J., Kim, H.: Deep neural network based demand side short term load forecasting. Energies **10**(1), 3 (2017). https://doi.org/10.3390/en10010003. Article No. 1

20. Coelho, I.M., Coelho, V.N., Luz, E.J.S., Ochi, L.S., Guimarães, F.G., Rios, E.: A GPU deep learning metaheuristic based model for time series forecasting. Appl. Energy **201**, 412–418 (2017). https://doi.org/10.1016/j.apenergy.2017.01.003

21. Balac, N., Sipes, T., Wolter, N., Nunes, K., Sinkovits, B., Karimabadi, H.: Large scale predictive analytics for real-time energy management. In: 2013 IEEE International Conference on Big Data, pp. 657–664 (2013). https://doi.org/10.1109/BigData.2013.6691635

22. Gupta, U., Gupta, D.: Least squares structural twin bounded support vector machine on class scatter. Appl. Intell. **53**(12), 15321–15351 (2023). https://doi.org/10.1007/s10489-022-04237-1

23. Gupta, U., Gupta, P., Agarwal, T., Pantola, D.: GestureWorks-one stop solution. In: Devedzic, V., Agarwal, B., Gupta, M.K. (eds.) ICICCIS 2022. AIS, pp. 301–308. Springer, Singapore (2023). https://doi.org/10.1007/978-981-99-1373-2_23

24. Leahy, K., Hu, R.L., Konstantakopoulos, I.C., Spanos, C.J., Agogino, A.M.: Diagnosing wind turbine faults using machine learning techniques applied to operational data. In: 2016 IEEE International Conference on Prognostics and Health Management (ICPHM), pp. 1–8 (2016). https://doi.org/10.1109/ICPHM.2016.7542860

25. Liu, Q., Li, P., Zhao, W., Cai, W., Yu, S., Leung, V.C.M.: A survey on security threats and defensive techniques of machine learning: a data driven view. IEEE Access **6**, 12103–12117 (2018). https://doi.org/10.1109/ACCESS.2018.2805680

26. Tan, S., De, D., Song, W.-Z., Yang, J., Das, S.K.: Survey of security advances in smart grid: a data driven approach. IEEE Commun. Surv. Tutor. **19**(1), 397–422 (2017). https://doi.org/10.1109/COMST.2016.2616442

27. Fan, Z., et al.: Smart grid communications: overview of research challenges, solutions, and standardization activities. IEEE Commun. Surv. Tutor. **15**(1), 21–38 (2013). https://doi.org/10.1109/SURV.2011.122211.00021

28. Technology News, Analysis, Comments and Product Reviews for IT Professionals. ZDNet https://www.zdnet.com/. Accessed 01 Dec 2021

29. McLellan, C.: Cybersecurity in an IoT and mobile world: the key trends (2017)

30. Anwar, A., Mahmood, A.N.: Cyber security of smart grid infrastructure. arXiv:1401.3936 (2014). https://arxiv.org/abs/1401.3936. Accessed 01 Dec 2021

31. Xu, Y., Dong, Z.Y., Meng, K., Zhang, R., Wong, K.P.: Real-time transient stability assessment model using extreme learning machine. IET Gener. Transm. Distrib. **5**(3), 314–322 (2011)

32. Alshareef, S., Talwar, S., Morsi, W.G.: A new approach based on wavelet design and machine learning for islanding detection of distributed generation. IEEE Trans. Smart Grid **5**(4), 1575–1583 (2014). https://doi.org/10.1109/TSG.2013.2296598

33. Marvuglia, A., Messineo, A.: Monitoring of wind farms' power curves using machine learning techniques. Appl. Energy **98**, 574–583 (2012). https://doi.org/10.1016/j.apenergy.2012.04.037

34. Fan, S., Liao, J.R., Yokoyama, R., Chen, L., Lee, W.-J.: Forecasting the wind generation using a two-stage network based on meteorological information. IEEE Trans. Energy Convers. **24**(2), 474–482 (2009). https://doi.org/10.1109/TEC.2008.2001457

35. Lee, D., Baldick, R.: Short-term wind power ensemble prediction based on Gaussian processes and neural networks. IEEE Trans. Smart Grid **5**(1), 501–510 (2014). https://doi.org/10.1109/TSG.2013.2280649

36. Salcedo-Sanz, S., Pastor-Sánchez, A., Prieto, L., Blanco-Aguilera, A., García-Herrera, R.: Feature selection in wind speed prediction systems based on a hybrid coral reefs optimization - extreme learning machine approach. Energy Convers. Manag. **87**, 10–18 (2014). https://doi.org/10.1016/j.enconman.2014.06.041

37. Zhang, Y., Liu, K., Qin, L., An, X.: Deterministic and probabilistic interval prediction for short-term wind power generation based on variational mode decom-

position and machine learning methods. Energy Convers. Manag. **112**, 208–219 (2016). https://doi.org/10.1016/j.enconman.2016.01.023

38. Yeh, W.-C., Yeh, Y.-M., Chang, P.-C., Ke, Y.-C., Chung, V.: Forecasting wind power in the Mai Liao Wind Farm based on the multi-layer perceptron artificial neural network model with improved simplified swarm optimization. Int. J. Electr. Power Energy Syst. **55**, 741–748 (2014). https://doi.org/10.1016/j.ijepes.2013.10.001

39. Rahmani, R., Yusof, R., Seyedmahmoudian, M., Mekhilef, S.: Hybrid technique of ant colony and particle swarm optimization for short term wind energy forecasting. J. Wind Eng. Ind. Aerodyn. **123**, 163–170 (2013). https://doi.org/10.1016/j.jweia.2013.10.004

40. Wang, J., Wang, Y., Li, Y.: A novel hybrid strategy using three-phase feature extraction and a weighted regularized extreme learning machine for multi-step ahead wind speed prediction. Energies **11**(2), 321 (2018). https://doi.org/10.3390/en11020321. Article no. 2

41. Ranjitha, P., Prabhu, A.: Improved divorce prediction using machine learning-particle swarm optimization (PSO). In: 2020 International Conference for Emerging Technology (INCET), pp. 1–5 (2020). https://doi.org/10.1109/INCET49848.2020.9154081

42. Cuong-Le, T., Nghia-Nguyen, T., Khatir, S., Trong-Nguyen, P., Mirjalili, S., Nguyen, K.D.: An efficient approach for damage identification based on improved machine learning using PSO-SVM. Eng. Comput. **38**, 3069–3084 (2022). https://doi.org/10.1007/s00366-021-01299-6

43. Voyant, C., et al.: Machine learning methods for solar radiation forecasting: a review. Renew. Energy **105**, 569–582 (2017). https://doi.org/10.1016/j.renene.2016.12.095

44. Chaouachi, A., Kamel, R.M., Andoulsi, R., Nagasaka, K.: Multiobjective intelligent energy management for a microgrid. IEEE Trans. Ind. Electron. **60**(4), 1688–1699 (2013). https://doi.org/10.1109/TIE.2012.2188873

45. Yang, H.-T., Huang, C.-M., Huang, Y.-C., Pai, Y.-S.: A weather-based hybrid method for 1-day ahead hourly forecasting of PV power output. IEEE Trans. Sustain. Energy **5**(3), 917–926 (2014). https://doi.org/10.1109/TSTE.2014.2313600

46. Hossain, M.R., Oo, A.M.T., Ali, A.: The combined effect of applying feature selection and parameter optimization on machine learning techniques for solar Power prediction. Am. J. Energy Res. **1**(1), 7–16 (2013)

47. Li, J., Ward, J.K., Tong, J., Collins, L., Platt, G.: Machine learning for solar irradiance forecasting of photovoltaic system. Renew. Energy **90**, 542–553 (2016). https://doi.org/10.1016/j.renene.2015.12.069

48. Salcedo-Sanz, S., Casanova-Mateo, C., Pastor-Sánchez, A., Sánchez-Girón, M.: Daily global solar radiation prediction based on a hybrid Coral Reefs Optimization - Extreme Learning Machine approach. Sol. Energy **105**, 91–98 (2014). https://doi.org/10.1016/j.solener.2014.04.009

49. Salcedo-Sanz, S., Casanova-Mateo, C., Muñoz-Marí, J., Camps-Valls, G.: Prediction of daily global solar irradiation using temporal Gaussian processes. IEEE Geosci. Remote Sens. Lett. **11**(11), 1936–1940 (2014). https://doi.org/10.1109/LGRS.2014.2314315

Transformation of Corporate Social Responsibility Practices: Adapting Artificial Intelligence and Internet of Things

Shivangi Khare[1], Vaibhav Uniyal[1], Samta Kathuria[2(✉)], Ashish Singh Chauhan[3], Shaik Vaseem Akram[4], and Srinivas Aluvala[4]

[1] Law College of Dehradun, Uttaranchal University, Dehradun, India
[2] LCD, Division of Research and Innovation, Uttaranchal University, Dehradun, India
samtakathuria14@gmail.com
[3] UIPS, Division of Research and Innovation, Uttaranchal University, Dehradun, India
[4] School of Computer Science and Artificial Intelligence, SR University, Warangal, India

Abstract. Data processing applied science techniques like artificial intelligence and the Internet of Things are grand inventions in tech history that are revolutionary themselves. This highly advanced and intelligent mechanism calls the attention of business concerns and enterprises to implement these applications to facilitate the productivity of the establishments gain better results from Corporate Social Responsibility (CSR) activities and achieve sustainable development goals. In this study, the author examines how innovative technologies like AI, IoT, and blockchain are executed by organisations to assist CSR operations and be effective instruments for economic resilience and security. The study focuses on how AI and IoT can transform CSR initiatives by automating tasks, improving efficiency, and enabling new and innovative ways to engage with stakeholders and address social and environmental challenges. For this purpose, the researcher comes to grips with various monitoring reports and examination papers to collect statistics regarding technologies and CSR and implement the same from a different perspective and also explore the challenges faced due incorporation of this automation are measured in this overview. Finally, the author concludes this study with suggestions that may be utilized in the forthcoming research and academic work.

Keywords: Corporate Social Responsibility (CSR) · Digital Technology · Sustainable Development Goals (SDGs) · Artificial Intelligence (AI) · Internet of Things (IoT) · Blockchain

1 Introduction

In today's era of technological evolution that enables everything fast and easily accessible. Growing technology plays a part in the productiveness and versatility of human intelligence [1]. This innovation, technical development, and transformation imitate the fictitious role in the systemization and development of the totality along with the rising awareness of CSR concerns for decades, the alliance or kinship of firms' CSR activities

KC Santosh et al. (Eds.): RTIP2R 2023, CCIS 2026, pp. 165–177, 2024.
https://doi.org/10.1007/978-3-031-53082-1_14

and automation application have received widespread attention [2]. However, because of the cans of warmth and impediments in simultaneously escalating economic, ecological, environmental, and social glitches, the outgrowth of CSR activities and the overall performance of organizations and firms are still controversial, especially in blossoming economies [3].

United Nations (UN) global compact embarked on corporate social responsibility mechanisms and strategies and the amalgamation of digital technologies; artificial intelligence and the Internet of Things (IoT) used for better results and fast, more accurate monitoring and upgrade themselves appropriately to achieve sustainability and this lay the first stone of the implementation of sociotechnical at social and organizational grades. In this 4.0 industrial revolution, the UN adopted the 2030 agenda and set sustainable development goals (SDG) for its member states to strengthen or nurture the global economy by keeping equality and liberation boundaries committed to implementing these set goals by using AI and other technologies [4]. Digital technology is an umbrella term that includes various kinds of technologies and tools. Technologies used by corporate organizations and businesses are Artificial intelligence (AI), cloud computing, big data, the Internet of Things (IoT), Robotics and drones, cloud computing, cryptocurrencies, etc. these industrial technologies are combinations of different technologies and algorithms that's why these are difficult to study. In this paper, the author tries to review technologies such as AI (Artificial Intelligence) and IoT (Internet of Things) and explain at the lower level to achieve corporate social responsibility mechanisms through these technologies [5].

This study emphasizes that firms and corporations adopt multifarious digital technologies for several different CSR activities similarly for the protection and prevention of the environment AI and IoT are proven as useful applications for its manifold operations such as water and air preservation, soil testing, use of digital technology for checking the unfeasibility of the contaminated ocean, global warming, readings of climate change, etc. similarly in the preservation of the art and heritage these technologies use for analysis the scripts and research work and safe the relevant data information and manage it and help to reconstruct defective and damaged scripture, photos, architecture, and research work such as manuscripts [6]. The previous studies about digital technologies, the Industrial Revolution, and their impact on the corporate world. Industrial development and rapid growth of technological intelligence have been expansive in nature. It is spread out unnaturally all over the world. The author goes through various sources and previous studies and reviews the existing research on AI, IOT (Internet of Things), Blockchain, and its adoption in corporate social responsibility.

By compiling all studies researcher makes a meaningful contribution by addressing the challenges and offering suggestions on them. The main aim of the author's contribution to the study is as follows:

- The main objective of the study is to understand the industrial enabling technologies and their impact and implementation by the corporate organization in their corporate social responsibilities' strategies.
- This study also focuses on digital technology and applications shaping and influencing global businesses by creating new values in information generated by AI, blockchain, and IoT.

- This study aims to do that while interacting and connecting the AI, IoT, blockchain, [and CSR challenges faced and the suggestions offered to overcome the problems.

The present study is categorized into the following sections. Section 2 of the paper covers the overview of the adoption of artificial intelligence in corporate social responsibility and its impact on CSR. Section 3 focused on various enabling technologies while interacting with corporate social responsibilities. And represents the use of artificial intelligence and robotics in the transformation of CSR. Section 4 of the study lays out the challenges of using artificial intelligence in corporate social responsibility. Section 5 covers the suggestions and recommendations given by the author. Section 6 concludes the paper.

2   Overview of Adaptation of AI and IoT in CSR

There is a systematic change in the business after industrialization but with the implications of social responsibility and sustainable goals [7]. Corporate social responsibility refers to paying back to society means due to industrialization there is a massive change in the wealth and power of the corporation which needs to be regulated legitimately and sustainably. It's a challenge for the corporation to deal with it. Business houses and corporations need to adopt corporate social responsibility practices such as education, sustainable development, health, research and development, financial responsibility, etc. The self-regulating business models through CSR improve a different aspect of society and grow their businesses by giving back to society. Turning the change of the technology from Industry 1.0 to Industry 4.0 may help the corporation better function and manage the corporate social responsibility programs. Due to this industrial revolution, the United Nations adopted the Agenda 2030 to take the initiative for social and sustainable development and digital technologies means that whatever United Nations set sustainable goals for its member nations needs to adopt, which includes artificial intelligence and other technologies for better and fast result without hampering sustainability [8].

These technologies help to get a fast result as they give accurate evaluations and the best use of information for the successful use of corporate social responsibility programs for the welfare of society. For instance, any corporation adopts the domain of health in the list of responsibilities there are many AI platforms and tools that are used by the healthcare sector for the best and most accurate results. The healthcare sector is the best example which already uses digital technologies such as AI, and IoT. Tracking heart rate, monitoring and transferring blood pressure readings, glucose testing, and use of AI in surgeries, and monitoring hygiene management through IoT [9]. Due to the pandemic, the need for these tools and technology increased and opened gates for further and better future perspectives. Tools that are frequently used are Apple and smartwatches. GE Healthcare's auto bed, biotelemetry, etc. Blockchain can easily be accessed by the society, which makes it appealing to users. Communities are also participating in the use of blockchain actively. Consequently, blockchains for the public are on the rise. The consortium blockchain has the potential to be used in applications business. The private blockchain can be put to use due to it being efficient and auditable [10].

3 Enabling Technologies

This section of the study discusses the enabling technology that may be applied to corporate social responsibility programs to achieve the best results and enhance sustainable development. In this paper, the author goes through the technologies, artificial intelligence, and the Internet of Things. The author reviews various studies which are already been done on it and tries to explain how applications and adaption of these technologies by companies and corporations may work effectively for the management of CSR and its operations across the globe. These applications and technologies are already used by companies in different sectors which increases their productivity and helps them to achieve sustainable goals effectively and efficiently.

3.1 Artificial Intelligence (AI)

Artificial Intelligence (AI) refers to the simulation of human intelligence. It is known as the branch of computer science [11]. The AI is implanted in the machines to do some operations. Any task or work that requires human intelligence to be performed can be done through the implementation of artificial intelligence. Russell and Norvig define AI as an agent-implemented function that senses or receives perception from the environment and takes actions accordingly [12]. Artificial intelligence can do any work or task that needs human intelligence to be done. Artificial intelligence can be strong and weak. John Searle said that weak artificial intelligence is designed for specific or single tasks. They are systemized to perform specific problems and are not able to solve other problems whereas Searle defines strong AI as a systematically programmed computer that has all the right inputs and output in it and has a mind the same as the human mind that can sense and act [13].

AI can be useful for fast and well-functioning corporate social responsibility programs. It helps in better management and proper functioning of the operations of CSR. The AI is already used in various business models and corporations or firms. If we focus on CSR itself there are different activities or areas that may be included by companies or firms in their CSR policies activities:

- Ensuring environmental sustainability-
    Sustainability refers to fulfilling the needs of the present generation without hampering the needs of future generations by balancing economic, social, and environmental growth. Environmental development and growth are done without hampering natural resources. Digital technology artificial intelligence and robotics in the environment benefit by reducing production and energy consumption [14]. Environment sustainability can be protected by using this technology by keeping in mind climate change, and global warming. That can be used for soil testing, air quality, water contamination, etc.
- Protecting art and heritage -
    Artificial intelligence can operate restoration of the architectural buildings, art, and heritage. Art and heritage play very crucial roles in future development and safeguarding this art and cultural heritage is the need of the hour. It can be a colossal mistake to ignore the safety of art and heritage or think is safe. During World War

II many heritages and architecture were damaged massively. Natural calamities or human activities may cause damage to art and heritage [15]. AI can be an effective application to restore or preserve heritage. For example, X-RAY recollects the data and analyses the images the algorithm through machine learning makes it possible to do this. AI utilizes restored photographs, research work, and manuscripts and helps to reconstruct and identify a defective and bruised piece of art and revamp or rebuild or restore it (Fig. 1).

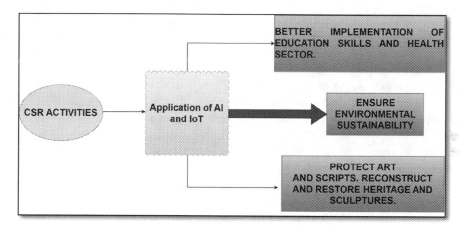

Fig. 1. Application of AI and IoT

AI and its applications have a wider extension or wider utilization passing time. Artificial intelligence is an autonomous program that provides solutions with accountability and reliability. This technology plays a crucial role in reconstructing and preserving heritage UNESCO (United Nation Educational, scientific, and Cultural Organizations) is a specialized agency of the UN that also state to use of digital technologies to preserve and safeguard art, heritage, and research work for the next generations. It also has a phenomenal role in safeguarding natural resources without disturbing them and also works on other aspects of the environment such as testing air, water, and soil quality and sampling and analysis of soils, etc. [16].

3.2 Internet of Things (IoT)

The Internet of Things (IoT) came up as the leading edge in the world of information technology. It refers grand master of all networks means the network of everything that helps to connect all devices' networks for better outputs. The IoT represents a physical presence in hi-tech networking. In humans, all the nerves connect to the mind and react according to the brain system which is called the neurological system just like the Internet of Things is a nervous system of cyberspace that engage all artificial respirators and black box in a single platform. As the name suggests itself it is the internet of all things that can be any device and odds or ends and enabled to interact with each other.

The best examples of this technology are Google Maps, smartwatches, smart gadgets, and appliances [17].

Adoption of the Internet of Things is proven as a true asset for firms when this application uses all networks to manage its inventories customer relationships and other important operations of an organization [17]. The use of this enabled technology improves their accountability and efficiency. This application also opens gates for firms and corporations to utilize this innovation to transform their CSR activities and achieve the sustainable goals set by the UN. The partnership between the UN and nations to attain the SDGs set out in the AGENDA 2030 [18]. Business houses and companies are an effective medium to achieve these goals. Technology like the IoT may help companies to share and utilize information or data through this invention and record, report, and audit the measurement and transaction [19]. Organizations and companies face the biggest issue of tracking transactions and measuring accurately the funds transferred for CSR activities, the IoT be the aid or solution to the problem through the use of IoT data which can be easily and effectively done. An amalgamation of IoT and cloud computing prepares the structure for accessing information in a better way. It helps to gather information and provide proper infrastructure to use it. Similarly, big data and IoT avail platforms for consumption of the information and managing the quantity and quality of data [20] (Fig. 2).

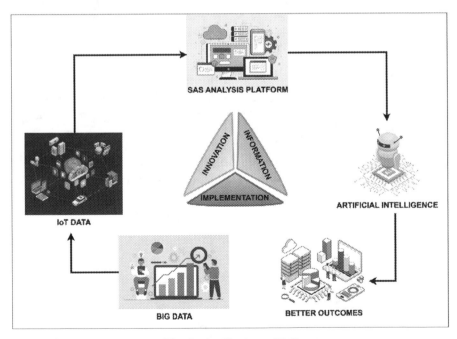

Fig. 2. Applications of IoT

Organizations are required to manage huge data and need to secure that data or information carefully because the application of IoT accesses plenty of information from different sources and it works as a sensor to gather information and provide preferable solutions. The combination of technologies with IoT enables companies or firms to govern data systematically in a synchronized way. There are certain issues arise related to security because of the collection of tremendous data which is important for any company that needs the concern to be safe and secure enforcement of technologies may assist in countering these issues [20].

3.3 Blockchain

The technology of blockchain is a crucial and novel tool for disseminating information through the use of linking ledgers or by the decentralisation of databases. The design of the blockchain ensures that the data is stored in a secure way. Although blockchain is in its nascent stage of development, the research is evolving speedily in other fields, which makes it important to know the ethical implications when the blockchain is being developed and implemented. The circular economy aims to increase sustainability and social responsibility, as well as economic growth. The limitations arise on the terms relating to trust, activities that are illegal, the potentiality of being hacked and the requirement of appropriate legislation and developed policy. Blockchain technology is an online, open-source ledger that is distributed where the transactions among the stakeholders are recorded and updated [21]. The design of the blockchain is such that the records of transaction is being authenticated in a credible way and the records kept are irreversible in nature. Blockchain exhibits the potential to hold and provide security to IoT [22]. Blockchain can also make it easier to automate transactions in a non-temporary way and in a manner that can be verified. It helps in saving the resources and the time consequently removing limitations. Circular Economy tries to establish a cleaner producing arrangement, adoption of technology that can be renewed, and appropriate policies being developed. Blockchain has the capacity to establish a cleaner economic process including transactions and helps in achieving balance which is a must for maintaining harmony among the environment, community, and economy. This creates the implementation of a Circular Economy which contributes to the agenda of a Green Economy through the blockchain technology being developed, diversified implemented [23].

The technology of Blockchain was being developed as a tool for communication between other ledgers for the upgradation of digital currency transactions. The initial application of blockchain is storing the usage and transaction of cryptocurrency. Due to primarily being applied in cryptocurrencies it also evolved to be implemented in smart contracts, there has been an extension to the sector of banking, finance and the field of accounting. Blockchain is consequently being experimented with in the health sector, management of marketing for supply chain, schemes of smart technology, copyrights, patents etc. The basis of sharing through a peer-to-peer network, storage capacity that is distributed, security that is tamper-resistant and the capacity for safe automation makes blockchain appealing to other sectors and increases its experimentation in other sectors [24]. The structure of blockchain technology is such that it permits the existence of smart contracts. A smart contract is a self-performable program that is stored in a network of blockchains for performing the contractual terms. The smart contract performs several activities of automation. An important feature of smart contracts is that the existence of decentralised organizations is permitted [25]. Members of a decentralised autonomous organization maintain their anonymity and do the assignments in accordance with a smart contract that was already being recorded on a network of blockchain. As soon as the requirements of the tasks are met, the participants will be rewarded. The transactions that are digitally signed are disseminated among the whole network and then through public keys are accessed which can be seen by everyone in the network. In concisely, the main characteristic of blockchain is Decentralisation. In traditional transaction systems that are centralised, every transaction is required to be authenticated through the trusted agency in the centre. At last, conclude the cost and the bottlenecks performance on the servers at the centre [26].

Alternatively, a transaction in the blockchain network is conducted in a peer-to-peer system (P2P) and does not require any authentication by the agency at the centre. As every transaction being disseminated across the network requires to be confirmed and recorded, this makes it impossible to tamper with. Anonymity plays an important role as the user can easily interact in the network of blockchain through the address being. Furthermore, a user can create as many addresses as he wants which maintains anonymity and avoid the chances of identity exposure. Now the central party is not involved in keeping the private information of the user. Further, audibility in blockchain enhances its efficiency. As every transaction on the network of blockchain is authenticated and stored along with a timestamp, the users can verify and trace the previously made records very easily [27].

Blockchain technology can be implemented in several sectors such as financial assets being cleared and settled etc. Besides, it has been shown that real business cases like financial derivatives being collateralised can leverage blockchain to reduce the risks and costs. Blockchain has thus been considered appealing by the large companies involved in software. Some of the examples include Microsoft Azure and IBM which has initiated to give Blockchain Service. Blockchain also provides safety to the IoT industry. Blockchain can be used to assist in the privacy improvement of IoT applications. In particular, Hardjono and Smith stated that a method of privacy-preserving can be implemented for an IoT device in an ecosystem of the cloud. More importantly, a novel architecture was introduced by Hardjono and Smith to help the device prove that the provenance of manufacturing is done without the verification of the third party who is allowed to register themselves as anonymous [28].

Additionally, IBM uncovered its proof of concept for Autonomous Decentralised Peer-to-Peer Telemetry (ADEPT), a system that is being used in the technology of blockchain to make a distributed network of devices. In ADEPT, home appliances can be identified, and operational problems and software updates can be retrieved automatically [29]. Additionally, blockchain technology can be implemented in green energy. Gogerty and Zitoli introduced the solar coin to promote the functioning of renewable energies. In particular, the solar coin is a type of digital currency that rewards the producer's solar energy. The traditional way of getting coins is through mining. The solar coins can be given by the solar-coin foundation till the time you are creating the solar energy. Originally, Blockchain was created to allow currency transactions to be performed. But, if we consider the learning and teaching of the currency, the technology of blockchain has the capacity to be used in online education. The learning of Blockchain is essential. In blockchain learning, blocks can be packed and put into blockchain by the mentors and the achievements of learning can be seen equivalent as to coins [30].

4   Array of Challenges Using AI and IoT in Transformation CSR

In recent years, Artificial intelligence and the Internet of Things have become matters of concern. A bunch of businesses or firms are greatly befitted by utilizing these technologies because of their capability that challenges themselves. The adoption of AI and IoT in Corporate social responsibility (CSR) activities addresses plenty of challenges. These technologies are programmed to target challenges and provide solutions. There are enormous and burdensome challenges that need to be addressed (Table 1):

Table 1. Challenges of Using AI and IoT in Transformation CSR

Challenges	Description
Data	Technologies like AI and IOT have immense proficiency to aid or help various business houses and firms to enhance their efficacy and get better results with the use of vast data with aid of these technologies. All this depends upon the quality and quantity of data integrated into the system while programming it and it is a difficult task as data include crucial information that's why necessary to ensure data management
Biases	Unbiased models, these technologies work as per the information integrated into them. The fusion of information helps them collect and evaluate the issue and offer the best outcome. Such automation gathers information by senses or perception of the environment or the opinion of others which itself comes as a challenge that needs to be tackled
Team	The top challenge is a team of innovative and creative people to build the abovementioned hi-tech applications. These technologies are hard and core processing requires deep and detailed knowledge and expertise so not only technical resources but hiring or selecting the right fresh and creative minds is also an important task
Application and Expenses	It is another important confrontation that ought to be faced by firms and business houses. Implementation of these hi-tech applications is complex, time-consuming, and costly. It takes a nice expenditure of resources and hands to structure it. It is a big hurdle to resolve that requires business operations
Scalability	With the frequency of transactions multiplying day by day, it has made the blockchain heavy, the large size of the block can reduce the propagation speed which can lead to blockchain branches. Every transaction needs to be stored for the authentication of the transaction which gives rise to the problem of scalability which is hard to resolve

A potential solution for organizations should implement robust data security measures, such as encryption and access control. They should also carefully consider the ethical implications of using AI to analyze personal data. Organizations should carefully audit their AI models for bias and take steps to mitigate it. They should also use diverse datasets to train their models and involve diverse stakeholders in the development and deployment of AI-powered CSR initiatives. le AI models that can provide insights into how they make decisions. They should also be transparent about how they use AI in their CSR initiatives and be open to feedback from stakeholders.

5 Recommendations

After analysing the challenges that are highlighted by the above-mentioned enabled technologies, there are the following suggestions that ought to be addressed. It is very interesting to investigate How AI and IoT revamp the CSR practices of firms and corporations. it is obvious to have pros and cons in every research, keep this in mind researchers offer suggestions relating to it:

- Implementation of autonomous technology and monitorization of the same enhance the productivity and efficiency of CSR practice, Organizations need to develop or reframe the strategies related to educating techs in the workplace environment and application of the same to achieve the goals set by the UN.
- Firms and organizations require to have proper technical resources otherwise it is always challenging for organizations. These technologies turn into result along with a tool which is why a company or firm need to create an appropriate infrastructure and orderly culture to endorse the latest technologies. Organizations are required to invest in the right persons recruit innovative and creative minds in the team and train internal sources with the right approach.
- Proper incorporation of data. Companies and firms ensure to have strong data management, and data quantity and need to ensure all data generated is protected, processed, and saved properly. There should be a system to observe the process of data management. Companies and firms must initiate further steps to spread awareness regarding the benefits of the use of highly processed technologies and even imitate the aid of these technologies to propagate the knowledge of artificial intelligence and the Internet of Things.
- One of the important digital developments in this context, is the blockchain protocol.
- To resolve the heavy problem of blockchain, a new type of cryptocurrency scheme was introduced in Bruce. In the new scheme, previous transaction records are removed and a database called an account tree is required to hold the balance of every address that is not empty. In such a way, nodes are not required to record every transaction to see its validity.

The regulatory and legal aspects of AI, IoT, and blockchain in CSR are complex and vary from region to region. However, there are some general principles that organizations should be aware of.

One key principle is that organizations should ensure that their use of AI, IoT, and blockchain in CSR initiatives complies with all applicable laws and regulations. This includes laws and regulations related to data privacy, security, consumer protection, and intellectual property.

Another key principle is that organizations should be transparent about how they are using AI, IoT, and blockchain in their CSR initiatives. This includes disclosing to stakeholders how they are collecting, using, and storing data, and how they are using AI, IoT, and blockchain to make decisions.

Finally, organizations should be accountable for the outcomes of their AI, IoT, and blockchain-powered CSR initiatives. This means being prepared to answer questions from stakeholders about how these technologies are being used and what impact they are having.

6 Conclusion

Technologies are highly evolving day by day which makes everything convenient and proficient. Industrialization along with tech development increases interest and attracts companies or firms to adopt the various technologies for indoor and outdoor management and effective accomplishment of operations. Play a crucial role in companies' or businesses' house's evolution. The implementation of these technologies within the organization reshapes the business world. At this stage of the game, every person or firm is utilizing these technologies like artificial intelligence or any other application for better results. This study also discussed how these hi-tech applications are capable of enhancing the proficiency of the organization or firm. These well-developed technologies have already been applied by the different grades for the better functioning of the system and to gain the best results. The main objective of this research is the application of artificial intelligence and the Internet of Things or integration of these technologies to use the information or data for CSR operations, achieve sustainable development goals prescribed by the UN, and for CSR management. Further, the author identifies the plethora of challenges that arise because of the application of enabling automation.

References

1. Robbins, J.: When smart is not: technology and Michio Kaku's the future of the mind [leading edge]. IEEE Technol. Soc. Mag. **35**, 29–31 (2016)
2. Cui, Z., Liang, X., Lu, X.: Prize or price? Corporate social responsibility commitment and sales performance in the Chinese private sector. Manag. Organ. Rev. **11**, 25–44 (2015)
3. Sardana, D., Gupta, N., Kumar, V., Terziovski, M.: CSR 'sustainability' practices and firm performance in an emerging economy. J. Clean. Prod. **258**, 120766 (2020)
4. Bradley, K.: Defining digital sustainability. Libr. Trends **56**, 148–163 (2007)
5. UN Statistical Commission. Global Indicator Framework for the Sustainable Development Goals and Targets of the 2030 Agenda for Sustainable Development. UN Statistical Commission, New York (2017)
6. Novo, O.: Blockchain meets IoT: an architecture for scalable access management in IoT. IEEE Internet Things J. **5**, 1184–1195 (2018)
7. Khamis, A., Li, H., Prestes, E., Haidegger, T.: AI: a key enabler of sustainable development goals, part 1 [industry activities]. IEEE Robot. Autom. Mag. **26**(3), 95–102 (2019)
8. Frank, A.G., Dalenogare, L.S., Ayala, N.F.: Industry 4.0 technologies: implementation patterns in manufacturing companies. Int. J. Prod. Econ. **210**, 15–26 (2019)

9. Lee, D., Yoon, S.N.: Application of artificial intelligence-based technologies in the healthcare industry: opportunities and challenges. Int. J. Environ. Res. Public Health **18**(1), 271 (2021)

10. Yang, R., Yu, F.R., Si, P., Yang, Z., Zhang, Y.: Integrated blockchain and edge computing systems: a survey, some research issues and challenges. IEEE Commun. Surv. Tutor. **21**, 1508–1532 (2019)

11. Sharma, M., et al.: LoED: LoRa and edge computing based system architecture for sustainable forest monitoring. Int. J. Eng. Trends Technol. **70**(5), 88–93 (2022)

12. Bagwari, S., Roy, A., Gehlot, A., Singh, R., Priyadarshi, N., Khan, B.: LoRa based metrics evaluation for real-time landslide monitoring on IoT platform. IEEE Access **10**, 46392–46407 (2022)

13. Bologna, G., Hayashi, Y.: Characterization of symbolic rules embedded in deep dimly networks: a challenge to the transparency of deep learning. J. Artif. Intell. Soft Comput. Res. **7**, 265–286 (2017)

14. Bisht, D., et al.: Imperative role of integrating digitalization in the firms finance: a technological perspective. Electronics **11**(19), 3252 (2022)

15. UNESCO. Convention Concerning the Protection of the World Cultural and Natural Heritage (World Heritage Convention) (1972)

16. The UNESCO Global Report, Reshaping Policies for Creativity – Addressing culture as a global public good, is the third edition of a series designed to monitor the implementation of the 2005 Convention on the Protection and Promotion of the Diversity of Cultural Expressions

17. Fuqaha, A.A., Guizani, M., Mohammadi, M., Aledhari, M., Ayyash, M.: Internet of Things: a survey on enabling technologies protocols and applications. IEEE Commun. Surv. Tutor. **17**(4), 2347–2376 (2015)

18. de Villiers, C., Kuruppu, S., Dissanayake, D.: A (new) role for business – Promoting the United Nations' Sustainable Development Goals through the Internet-of-Things and blockchain technology. J. Bus. Res. **131**, 598–609 (2021)

19. Rokade, A., Singh, M., Malik, P.K., Singh, R., Alsuwian, T.: Intelligent data analytics framework for precision farming using IoT and regressor machine learning algorithms. Appl. Sci. **12**(19), 9992 (2022)

20. Kaur, N., Sood, S.K.: An energy-efficient architecture for the Internet of Things (IoT). IEEE Syst. J. **11**(2), 796–805 (2015)

21. Ghisellini, P., Cialani, C., Ulgiati, S.: A review on circular economy: the expected transition to a balanced interplay of environmental and economic systems. J. Clean. Prod. **114**, 11–32 (2016)

22. Xu, M., Chen, X., Kou, G.: A systematic review of blockchain. Financ. Innov. **5**(1), 27 (2019)

23. Narayan, R., Tidström, A.: Circular economy inspired imaginaries for sustainable innovations. In: Bocken, N., Ritala, P., Albareda, L., Verburg, R. (eds.) Innovation for Sustainability. PSSBIAFE, pp. 393–413. Springer, Cham (2019). https://doi.org/10.1007/978-3-319-97385-2_21

24. Moll, J., Yigitbasioglu, O.: The role of internet-related technologies in shaping the work of accountants: new directions for accounting research. Br. Account. Rev. **51**(6), 100833 (2019)

25. Christidas, K., Devetsikiotis, M.: Blockchains and smart contracts for the Internet of Things. IEEE Access. **4**, 2292–2303 (2016)

26. Dennis, R., Owen, G.: Rep on the block: a next generation reputation system based on the blockchain. In: 2015 10th International Conference for Internet Technology and Secured Transactions (ICITST), pp. 131–138. IEEE (2015)

27. Fan, Z., et al.: Smart grid communications: overview of research challenges, solutions, and standardization activities. IEEE Commun. Surv. Tutor. **15**(1), 21–38 (2013)

28. Shafagh, H., Burkhalter, L., Hithnawi, A., Duquennoy, S.: Towards blockchain-based auditable storage and sharing of IoT data. In: Proceedings of the 2017 on Cloud Computing Security Workshop, CCSW 2017, Dallas, TX, USA, 3 November 2017, pp. 45–50. ACM, New York (2017)
29. Huh, S., Cho, S., Kim, S.: Managing IoT devices using blockchain platform. In: Proceedings of the IEEE 19th International Conference on Advanced Communication Technology (ICACT), PyeongChang, Korea, 19–22 February 2017, pp. 464–467 (2017)
30. Conoscenti, M., Vetrò, A., De Martin, J.C.: Blockchain for the Internet of Things: a systematic literature review. In: Proceedings of the IEEE/ACS 13th International Conference of Computer Systems and Applications (AICCSA), Agadir, Morocco, 29 November–2 December 2016, pp. 1–6 (2016)

Various Active Learning Strategies Analysis in Image Labeling: Maximizing Performance with Minimum Labeled Data

Arnav Tyagi[1], Harshvardhan Aditya[1], Nitin Arvind Shelke[1], Rishabh Khandelwal[1], Jagendra Singh[1(✉)], Yagna Jadeja[2], and Anil V. Turukmane[3]

[1] School of Computer Science Engineering and Technology, Bennett University, Greater Noida, India
jagendrasngh@gmail.com
[2] College of Science and Engineering, University of Derby, Derby, UK
[3] School of Computer Science and Engineering, VIT - AP University, Amaravati, India

Abstract. The use of active learning in supervised machine learning is proposed in this study to reduce the expenses associated with labeling data. Active learning is a technique that includes iteratively selecting the most informative unlabeled data points and asking a human expert to label them. Active learning can achieve high accuracy while utilizing fewer labeled examples than typical supervised learning algorithms by selecting the most informative data points. This study conducts and provides an in-depth examination and analysis of numerous active learning algorithms and their applications to various machine learning labeling problems, especially focusing on image classification. The experiments are carried out using Fashion MNIST as a benchmark dataset. This study compares the performance of five popular active learning methods BALD, DBAL, coreset, least confidence and ensemble varR for the given problem. The best performing algorithm was BALD with a mean classification accuracy of 91.31%, when 50% of the data is considered labeled, closely followed by all other techniques, making each suitable for specific use cases. The trials conducted by the study illustrates how active learning may lower the time and cost of data labeling while also maintaining high accuracy.

Keywords: Active Learning · CNN · Data Labeling · Diversity Sampling · Ens-varR · Image Classification · Uncertainty Sampling

1 Introduction

1.1 Background and Motivation

To obtain high accuracy, supervised machine learning and deep learning algorithms require a significant amount of labeled data. Labeling data, on the other hand, can be time-consuming and costly, especially when working with huge datasets. This limitation has sparked considerable interest in the development of active learning approaches, which aim to reduce the cost and time involved with data labeling by labeling just the

KC Santosh et al. (Eds.): RTIP2R 2023, CCIS 2026, pp. 178–188, 2024.
https://doi.org/10.1007/978-3-031-53082-1_15

most informative data points. Active learning takes a few labeled samples and uses those samples to make a labeled dataset for multiple unlabeled samples of the same problem. Active learning has been used successfully in a variety of machine learning applications such as text categorization, image recognition, and object detection [1]. Despite its potential benefits, active learning is still underutilized in many practical applications, and more research is needed to investigate its effectiveness and limitations. As a result, the purpose of this study is to investigate the application of active learning in supervised machine learning for minimizing data labeling costs, as well as its potential to revolutionize the way we train machine learning models. Through this research, we hope, will help to design more efficient and cost-effective deep learning systems, particularly in domains where huge labeled datasets are difficult or expensive to collect [2].

1.2 Hypothesis

The primary research question addressed in this work is whether active learning may reduce data labeling costs in supervised machine learning while preserving or improving model accuracy. We specifically intend to investigate the following issues:

- In terms of the sub number of labeled instances necessary for training and the consequent accuracy, how does active learning compare to classic supervised learning methods?
- How does the effectiveness of active learning differ depending on task complexity and dataset characteristics?
- What are the advantages and disadvantages of utilizing active learning to reduce data labelling costs, and how may these be addressed in actual applications?

1.3 Objective and Contribution

The following are the key goals of this paper:

- To give an in-depth examination of active learning algorithms and their applications to various machine learning problems such as text classification, image recognition, and object detection.
- To examine the efficacy of active learning in decreasing data labeling costs in supervised machine learning and to compare it to traditional supervised learning approaches in terms of the number of labeled instances required for training and the resulting accuracy.
- To examine the trade-offs and constraints of employing active learning to reduce data labeling costs, and to make recommendations on how to resolve these issues in real implementations.
- Empirical assessments using benchmark datasets will be employed to illustrate the practical application of active learning.

This paper provides the following contributions:

- A comprehensive examination of active learning, including its potential advantages and drawbacks in the context of minimizing data labeling expenses in supervised machine learning.

- Empirical findings from standardized datasets demonstrating how active learning can diminish data labeling costs while preserving or even improving accuracy.
- Exploration of the trade-offs and constraints associated with the adoption of active learning to reduce data labeling expenses, along with practical suggestions for addressing these issues during real-world implementations.
- An enhancement of our comprehension regarding the potential benefits and limitations of active learning for cost-effective data labeling in supervised machine learning, coupled with recommendations for practitioners seeking to incorporate this methodology.

2   Problem Statement

In the realm of supervised machine learning, the substantial expenses and time-intensive process of data labeling pose significant challenges. This study looks at the efficacy of active learning as a method for lowering data labeling costs while maintaining or enhancing model performance across a variety of machine learning tasks.

3   Literature Review

In recent years, the field of supervised machine learning has grown rapidly, with applications in fields as diverse as healthcare, finance, and natural language processing. The availability of big, high-quality labeled datasets is one of the important variables contributing to the success of supervised learning algorithms. The paper [3] offers a thorough examination of active learning strategies for on-road vehicle detection using computer vision. The authors examine and assess three common active learning algorithms in terms of data costs, recall, annotation costs, and precision. The detectors used in this work are based on histograms and SVM classification (HOG-SVM) [4], and Adaboost classification (Haar-Adaboost), and Haar-like features and [5].

To address the limitations of learning from such data streams, the authors suggest an online-knn classifier that joins self-labeling with demand-based active learning. The study starts by outlining the considered setup and reiterating the idea of concept drift. From a theoretical standpoint, the authors then justify the use of supervised learning for non-stationary data streams. They provide a classification of drift behaviours as well as generated self-labeling problems [6]. They provide a detailed description of their proposed online learning system, which combines self-labeling and demand-based active learning to enhance classification accuracy while lowering labelling costs. The authors test their technique on a variety of real-world datasets, including social media, cellphones, and industrial process monitoring. According to the results, their suggested strategy surpasses existing state-of-the-art approaches in terms of classification accuracy while needing fewer labeled samples. Overall, this study contributes significantly to the area of machine learning by presenting a unique method to the problem of learning from non-stationary data streams with limited labelling. The suggested online-knn classifier, which combines self-labeling with demand-based active learning, has demonstrated encouraging results in real-world settings and has the potential to be applied in a variety of fields where data is accessible as streams [7].

The study [8] looks at how to label soundscape ecology data using visual active learning techniques. According to the scientists, appropriately labelling such data is critical for effective soundscape ecology research throughout the world [8]. However, retrieving information from this sort of data may be difficult and costly. As a result, the authors suggest a multidisciplinary strategy combining ecoacoustics, machine learning, and visualization. The concept, implementation, and testing of a Visual Active Learning technique for labelling soundscape ecology data is the major contribution of this study. The authors employ multidimensional projections to underpin the process of user-centered labelling. To summaries data detailed in visualizations, they suggest "Time Line Spectrogram" (TLS) visualizations. The authors examine the efficacy of their approach in labelling soundscape ecology data using actual data on birds, frogs, and insects. They compare their method to others and demonstrate that it exceeds them in terms of accuracy and efficiency [9, 10].

In another publication [11], the authors offer a unique hybrid framework for mining data streams that combines active and semi-supervised learning. The authors offer two techniques families based on blind and informed approaches, which result in seven algorithms for enabling active learning with self-labeling. They undertake a rigorous experimental analysis on real data streams with varying labelling budgets, demonstrating the benefits of adopting hybrid solutions when accessible class labels are few, particularly in extremely low budget scenarios [12]. The article emphasizes the difficulties of mining data streams in real-time and on a limited budget, where labelling vast volumes of data may be costly and time-consuming. The proposed hybrid technique combines active learning, in which the algorithm picks the most informative examples to label, with self-labeling, in which the system labels unlabeled data using its own predictions. This method decreases labelling costs while retaining excellent accuracy. The authors present thorough experimental data demonstrating the efficacy of their suggested algorithms in a variety of settings. They also make recommendations on where these algorithms should be used. Overall, this preprint gives useful insights on how to mine data streams quickly and cheaply utilizing active learning and self-labeling approaches [13, 14].

The research article "Automatically Labelling Video Data Using Multi-class Active Learning" provides a novel way to labelling video data. According to the scientists, manually labelling video footage is time-consuming and prone to human mistake, and it finally becomes impractical for enormous volumes of data. To solve this issue, the authors present a unified multi-class active learning strategy that use active learning techniques to choose the most informative instances for labelling while requiring the least amount of human work. The study analyses the efficacy of this technique and its prospective applications in visual information retrieval, object identification, and human activity modelling [7]. The authors broaden the active learning technique from binary to many classes, allowing the learning algorithm to choose the most useful unlabeled input for all classes rather than just binary classes. They also offer and assess a variety of practical sample selection procedures [15].

This study has important implications for industries such as video surveillance and content analysis, where enormous volumes of video data must be reliably and effectively labeled. Overall [7] offers a novel approach to a prevalent challenge in computer vision applications. The suggested method has demonstrated promising results in terms of minimizing human labor while retaining good labelling accuracy in video data.

4 Proposed Methodology

We will utilize a combination of literature research and empirical evaluations to explore the efficiency of active learning for decreasing data labeling costs in supervised machine learning. We will begin by conducting a thorough study of the literature on active learning and its applications to diverse machine learning problems such as text classification, image recognition, and object identification. This review aims to shed light on the potential advantages and limitations of active learning while also aiding in the selection of the most effective active learning algorithms for various task categories.

Subsequently, we will undertake empirical evaluations to gauge the effectiveness of active learning in mitigating data labeling expenses within the realm of supervised machine learning. We will leverage benchmark datasets spanning diverse domains, including text classification, image recognition, and object detection. For each dataset, we will compare the performance of active learning against conventional supervised learning methods like random sampling and full labeling in terms of both the quantity of labeled instances required for training and the resulting accuracy. Furthermore, we will delve into factors affecting active learning success, such as task complexity and dataset attributes.

To conclude, we will explore the trade-offs and constraints inherent in the utilization of active learning to curtail data labeling costs, accompanied by practical recommendations for addressing these challenges in real-world implementations. Our goal is to provide a thorough understanding of the possible benefits and limitations of active learning, as well as to assist practitioners in determining whether active learning is a viable alternative for their unique applications.

4.1 Dataset Description

The Fashion MNIST dataset has been used for this active learning task. The Fashion MNIST dataset, which consists of 70,000 grayscale images of 28×28 pixels displaying ten different apparel item categories, is a commonly used benchmark dataset in computer vision research. The dataset is divided into two parts: a training set of 60,000 photographs and a test set of 10,000 images, with each image labeled with the clothing item category to which it belongs [8].

T-shirt/top, Trouser, Sneaker, Bag, Pullover, Sandal, Shirt, Dress, Coat and Ankle boot are the dataset's ten classes. The photos in the dataset are grayscale, with the pixel values preprocessed to center and normalize them.

4.2 Processing

The Fashion MNIST dataset active learning procedure consists of four steps:

- Initialization: 30000 samples from the training dataset have been chosen at random, and only their labels are considered to be existing. All the other 30000 images are considered unlabeled.
- Querying: The active learning algorithm selects a subset of unlabeled data points from the dataset that are most relevant to the model after training the initial model. This is accomplished through the use of a query method that finds samples about which the model is unclear or samples that are on the decision border. The chosen samples are labeled by an expert or annotator, and their labels are added to the labeled dataset. Because this procedure can be time-consuming and costly, the goal of active learning is to reduce the number of samples that must be labeled in order to obtain high model performance. The revised labeled dataset is then used to train a new model, and the procedure is repeated until the required level is reached.
- Labeling: When the desired accuracy has been reached, this model is used to label the unlabeled data points.
- Evaluation: After the labeling, the model's accuracy is tested and compared to that of random sampling, which is considered the baseline approach for labeling. We measure the performance of the model's using accuracy, precision, recall, and F1-score.

4.3 Approaches Used

Uncertainty Sampling: One of the most popular approaches in active learning is uncertainty sampling. On our labeled data of 30000 images, we trained a deep convolutional neural network (CNN) and its performance was evaluated on a test set [13].

Then, using the unlabeled data, we employ the uncertainty sampling approach to select the most informative samples. We specifically choose the samples for which the model is most uncertain, i.e., the samples for which the model produces the probability distribution over all possible classes with the maximum entropy. The reasoning behind this technique is that the model will benefit the most from the most uncertain samples.

- Least Confidence: For each item, the difference between 1 (100% confidence) and the most confidently predicted label is used to calculate the least confidence. Although confidence alone can be used to rank order, it can be advantageous to transform the uncertainty scores to a 0–1 range, with 1 being the most uncertain score. In that situation, the score must be normalized. The value is subtracted from 1, then multiplied by $n/(1 - n)$, where n is the number of labels. This is because the minimal confidence can never be less than one divided by the number of labels, indicating that all labels have the same expected confidence. The least confidence approach is the most basic and widely used; it provides a ranked list of predictions in which you sample objects with the lowest confidence for their anticipated label.
- Deep Bayesian Active Learning: The DBAL (Deep Bayesian Active Learning) method includes picking the most informative samples from a huge pool of unlabeled Fashion MNIST photos repeatedly and using the real labels of those data points. In a real world setting, instead of using already labeled data, it would be better to ask for labels from an expert in that specific field. The model is then trained on the newly labeled samples, and the process is continued until the required level of performance is attained. The most useful samples for labeling are picked using acquisition functions depending on model uncertainty, such as entropy and variation ratios [10].

- Bayesian Active Learning by Disagreements: BALD is based on Bayesian inference and estimates the expected information gain of each sample using the model's predictive distribution. BALD can achieve high accuracy with fewer labeled samples than random sampling or other active learning algorithms by picking examples that are projected to reduce the model's uncertainty the greatest. The publication "Bayesian Active Learning by Disagreements: A Geometric Perspective" introduces GBALD, a new framework that extends BALD by taking a geometric approach to core-set creation and model uncertainty estimates. The GBALD framework is divided into two parts: core-set creation and model uncertainty estimation. GBALD works by first training a deep neural network model on a small labeled dataset. The GBALD framework is then used to choose the most informative samples for labelling from an unlabeled dataset. GBALD's core-set construction component selects a subset of samples that are typical of the complete dataset, and the model uncertainty estimation component selects samples that are most likely to reduce the model's uncertainty.
- Diversity Sampling: In active learning, diversity sampling is an approach for selecting samples that are diverse and representative of the underlying distribution. The aim behind diversity sampling is to choose samples that differ from those that have previously been labeled in order to cover a greater range of the input space and eliminate redundancy in the labeled data [9]. There are various approaches to measuring diversity, but one popular strategy is to employ a distance metric, such as Euclidean distance or cosine similarity, to quantify the dissimilarity between the new and labeled samples. The underlying assumption is that varied samples are ones that are far off from the labeled samples in the input space.
- Coreset: Finding a small subset of a large labeled dataset that can be utilized to train a competitive model over the entire dataset is the core-set selection challenge. Core-set selection is done without labels because the labeling process is costly and time-consuming. To solve the unlabeled core-set problem for CNNs, the geometry of the data points is used to offer a rigorous constraint between the average loss over any given subset of the dataset and the remaining data points. As an active learning algorithm, batches of photos are selected iteratively depending on their informativeness in relation to the criterion. This strategy seeks to reduce the given bound while maintaining the desired degree of performance [11].

In practice, this method is suitable for the Fashion MNIST dataset since it is an image dataset. This strategy decreases labeling costs while retaining excellent model performance by picking a limited selection of useful photos for labeling.

- Query by Committee Sampling: QBC sampling is a prominent active learning approach for selecting samples for annotation based on disagreement among a committee of multiple classifiers. The primary principle underlying QBC is to choose samples that are challenging to classify in order to increase the classifier's performance. The QBC method entails training a committee of multiple classifiers on the labeled data available. To capture distinct characteristics of the underlying distribution, each classifier in the committee is trained using a different model architecture or a separate set of hyperparameters. After the committee has been taught, the unlabeled samples are queried depending on the committee members' disagreements. The samples with the highest levels of disagreement are then chosen for annotation.

- Ensemble Variation Ratio (Ens-varR): The ENS-Var approach was created primarily for image classification applications involving convolutional neural networks (CNNs). The strategy entails training an ensemble of CNNs on labeled data and then using them to predict on unlabeled data. The variation of these forecasts is then used to calculate uncertainty, with more variance suggesting greater uncertainty. The samples with the greatest uncertainty are then chosen for labeling in order to increase the model's accuracy. This method is continued iteratively until the desired degree of precision is attained or the labeling budget is depleted. On increasingly complicated datasets like MNIST and CIFAR-10, our experiments suggest that ENS-Var outperforms alternative active learning methods.

5 Results

The results showed that all active learning algorithms outperformed the baseline model that used all available labeled data. BALD achieved the highest mean classification accuracy of 91.31%, followed closely by ensemble varR with a mean accuracy of 90.56%. The accuracies of DBAL and coreset were 89.88% and 89.65%, respectively, which are not far behind those of DBAL and ensemble varR. Least confidence had the lowest mean accuracy of 89.12%. Table 1 showcases the accuracies achieved by all of the above stated algorithms on the Fashion MNIST dataset. Table 2 further showcases the classification report per label or class for the best performing model, BALD (Fig. 1).

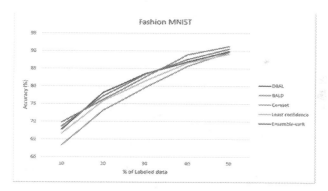

Fig. 1. Shows the graph for Accuracy comparison for different AL methods.

Table 1. Accuracy of Different Algorithms when 50% of data is considered labeled.

Algorithm	Accuracy
DBAL	89.88%
BALD	91.31%
Corset	89.65%
Least Confidence	89.12%
Ensemble varR	90.56%

Table 2. Classification report of best performing algorithm (BALD)

Class	Precision	Recall	F1-Score	Support
0 T-shirt/Top	0.89	0.88	0.88	100
1 Trouser	0.95	0.92	0.93	100
2 Pullover	0.92	0.89	0.90	100
3 Dress	0.89	0.91	0.90	100
4 Coat	0.80	0.92	0.86	100
5 Sandal	0.93	0.91	0.92	100
6 Shirt	0.81	0.72	0.75	100
7 Sneakers	0.95	0.95	0.95	100
8 Bag	0.97	0.98	0.98	100
9 Ankle Boot	0.96	0.97	0.97	100
Avg/Total	0.91	0.91	0.91	1000

6 Conclusion

The findings of the studies showed that active learning algorithms may greatly lower the quantity of labeled instances required to achieve high classification accuracy, hence lowering the overall costs associated with data labeling. In instance, when 50% of the data is taken into account to be labeled, the BALD algorithm attained a high accuracy of 91.31%.

These results have significant repercussions for real-world supervised machine learning applications, particularly when big datasets are involved. Active learning methods may drastically reduce the expense and time needed for data labeling, which can make the process of constructing and deploying machine learning models more effective and efficient. This is done by minimizing the number of labeled instances needed for training. Therefore, this study emphasizes the potential advantages of active learning for cutting costs associated with data labeling in supervised machine learning.

The outcomes demonstrate that the BALD algorithm, alongside DBAL, coreset, least confidence, and ensembled varR are successful technique for attaining high classification accuracy while lowering data labeling expenses, and it is anticipated that future research will further investigate the possibilities of active learning in other applications and with additional datasets.

Some potential drawbacks of active learning system currently are that they still require a certain level of human expertise to effectively do labeling. Active learning has not been able to show significant promise in problems such as segmentation and object detection. Once active learning becomes the norm for large datasets, there won't be a good and easy way to analyze whether the labeling for certain samples are the ground truth or not.

7 Future Work

Even though the active learning algorithms DBAL, BALD, coreset, least confidence, and ensemble varR show promising results in lowering data labelling costs in supervised machine learning, there are still a number of directions that this field can be explored in the future. Here are some probable directions for the future:

- Exploring other active learning algorithms: There are numerous additional active learning algorithms that might be investigated, even if the algorithms utilized in this research study were successful in lowering the costs associated with data labelling. On the Fashion MNIST dataset or other datasets, future research can be conducted on various other active learning methods, such as Min-Margin, Max-Entropy, Variational Adversarial Active Learning (VAAL).
- Investigating different labeling strategies: In this study, a random selection of images was employed for labeling up until a certain budget was met. Future studies might evaluate the effectiveness of various labeling tactics to the random labeling strategy, including labeling images based on their complexity or resemblance to other labeled images.
- Adapting active learning algorithms to deep learning architectures: Although the active learning algorithms utilized in this study were successful on the Fashion MNIST dataset, which is relatively basic, they might not work as well with deep learning architectures or on more complicated datasets. Future studies might look at ways to enhance the performance of active learning algorithms by integrating them with deep learning architectures like convolutional neural networks (CNNs).
- Investigating the impact of data distribution: The distribution of the data, could affect how well active learning algorithms work. Future studies should look at how different data distributions affect each active learning algorithm's performance as well as how to make active learning more effective for datasets with imbalanced or irregular distributions. Scaling up to larger datasets: Despite being a frequently used benchmark dataset, the Fashion MNIST dataset utilized in this research study is modest in comparison to many other real-world datasets. Future research could investigate how to scale up active learning algorithms to larger datasets, reducing the computational power required by including distributed learning and parallelization techniques to reduce data labeling costs on larger datasets.

References

1. Jiang, W.: A machine vision anomaly detection system to industry 4.0 based on variational fuzzy autoencoder. Comput. Intell. Neurosci. **2022** (2022). https://doi.org/10.1155/2022/1945507

2. Goswami, A., Sharma, D., Mathuku, H., Gangadharan, S.M.P., Yadav, C.S.: Change detection in remote sensing image data comparing algebraic and machine learning methods. Electronics **11**(3), 431 (2022). Article id: 1505208

3. Lin, C.-T., et al.: IoT-based wireless polysomnography intelligent system for sleep monitoring. IEEE Access **6**, 405–414 (2017)

4. Kumar, S., Pathak, S.K.: A comprehensive study of XSS attack and the digital forensic models to gather the evidence. ECS Trans. **107**(1), 7153 (2022)

5. Sharma, N., et al.: A smart ontology-based IoT framework for remote patient monitoring. Biomed. Sig. Process. Control **68**, 102717 (2021). https://doi.org/10.1016/j.bspc.2021.102717

6. Mall, S.: Heart diagnosis using deep neural network. In: 3rd International Conference on Computational Intelligence and Knowledge Economy, ICCIKE 2023. Amity University, Dubai (2023)

7. Sharan, A.: Term co-occurrence and context window based combined approach for query expansion with the semantic notion of terms. Int. J. Web Sci. (IJWS) **3**(1), 32–57 (2017)

8. Yadav, C.S., et al.: Malware analysis in IoT & android systems with defensive mechanism. Electronics **11**, 2354 (2022). https://doi.org/10.3390/electronics11152354

9. Berghout, T., Benbouzid, M., Muyeen, S.M.: Machine learning for cybersecurity in smart grids: a comprehensive review-based study on methods, solutions, and prospects. Int. J. Crit. Infrastruct. Prot. **38**, 100547 (2022). https://doi.org/10.1016/j.ijcip.2022.100547

10. Upreti, K., Gupta, A.K., Dave, N., Surana, A., Mishra, D.: Deep learning approach for hand drawn emoji identification. In: 2022 IEEE International Conference on Current Development in Engineering and Technology (CCET), Bhopal, India, pp. 1–6 (2022). https://doi.org/10.1109/CCET56606.2022.10080218

11. Sajid, M., Rajak, R.: Capacitated vehicle routing problem using algebraic particle swarm optimization with simulated annealing algorithm. In: Artificial Intelligence in Cyber-Physical Systems. CRC Press (2023)

12. Yadav, A., Kumar, S., Singh, J.: A review of physical unclonable functions (PUFs) and its applications in IoT environment. In: Hu, Y.C., Tiwari, S., Trivedi, M.C., Mishra, K.K. (eds.) Ambient Communications and Computer Systems, vol. 356, pp. 1–13. Springer, Singapore (2022). https://doi.org/10.1007/978-981-16-7952-0_1

13. Prasad, M., Daraghmi, Y., Tiwari, P., Yadav, P., Bharill, N.: Fuzzy logic hybrid model with semantic filtering approach for pseudo relevance feedback-based query expansion. In: 2017 IEEE Symposium Series on Computational Intelligence (SSCI) (2017)

14. Kumar, R.: Lexical co-occurrence and contextual window-based approach with semantic similarity for query expansion. Int. J. Intell. Inf. Technol. (IJIIT) **13**(3), 57–78 (2017)

15. Bohat, V.K.: Neural network model for recommending music based on music genres. In: 10th IEEE International Conference on Computer Communication and Informatics (ICCCI-2021), Coimbatore, India (2021)

Applied Image Processing and Pattern Recognition

Potato Leaf Disease Classification Using Federated Learning

Amit Sharma⬤, Dibyanarayan Hazara⬤, Suneet Kumar Gupta$^{(\boxtimes)}$⬤,
Riti Kushwaha⬤, and Divya Kumari⬤

Bennett University, Greater Noida, India
{e22soep0058,e22soep0059,suneet.gupta,
riti.kushwaha,divya.kumari}@bennett.edu.in
https://www.bennett.edu.in/faculties/dr-suneet-kumar-gupta/

Abstract. Accurate classification of diseases in potato crops is vital for optimizing yield and ensuring crop health. We propose a generalized framework using Federated Learning (FL) for accurate classification of potato crop diseases. The dataset from Plant Village includes diverse potato leaf images with imbalanced class distributions. By incorporating FL, which enables collaborative model training without sharing raw data, we leverage the collective intelligence of distributed datasets while ensuring privacy. CNN as base model, achieves a 92% classification accuracy in the potato disease dataset through extensive experimentation and hyperparameter fine-tuning. Our approach addresses the challenge of an unbalanced dataset in potato disease classification and contributes to advances in precision agriculture. The framework can be adapted for other crop disease classification tasks, showcasing the potential of distributed learning in agriculture. Overall, our study demonstrates the effectiveness of FL in achieving accurate and scalable disease classification models in potato crops.

Keywords: Image segmentation · Federated learning · CNN

1 Introduction

Potato leaf diseases pose significant challenges to agriculture productivity [2], affecting crop yield and quality. Traditional disease detection and classification methods heavily rely on centralized data collection and analysis, which may lead to privacy concerns and limited access to diverse datasets [1]. Various methods, including hyperspectral imaging, image processing, and deep learning techniques, can be employed in classification and identification of potato leaf diseases. Using hyperspectral imaging, spectral data can be extracted from potato leaves, allowing the development of accurate disease discrimination models [19]. Image processing techniques allow the extraction of distinctive color and texture features from images of potato leaf, which can facilitate disease classification [26]. Deep learning, particularly Convolutional Neural Networks (CNN), can

© The Author(s), under exclusive license to Springer Nature Switzerland AG 2024
KC Santosh et al. (Eds.): RTIP2R 2023, CCIS 2026, pp. 191–201, 2024.
https://doi.org/10.1007/978-3-031-53082-1_16

be trained to accurately identify and classify potato diseases, eliminating the potential for human error [6]. Additionally, automated identification methods based on image processing, using adaptive thresholding, have shown promising results in segmenting disease-affected areas in potato leaf images with high accuracy [24]. Furthermore, 1D-CNN can adaptively extract invariant characteristics to identify different disease spots on potato leaves, achieving high accuracy in hyperspectral image classification [15]. Various methods are tested on variety of datasets, but due to the lack of images in the datasets it is hard to identify all the diseases and further the testing on large dataset is needed to identify all possible diseases in potato leaf [12], also many of the approaches used for the classification was tested only on potato plants and the effectiveness of these approaches on other plants may further investigated [9]. The common potato diseases is early blight, caused by fungal infections, detection of these diseases can also be done by CNN [4].

Google has revolutionized the field of machine learning with the introduction of Federated Learning (FL), a groundbreaking technique that allows collaborative learning without compromising the privacy of sensitive data. FL has far-reaching implications, particularly in domains like healthcare and finance, where maintaining data privacy is of utmost importance [16]. By leveraging FL, the future of digital health holds tremendous promise, as it enables the collaborative training of machine learning models without the need for data exchange or centralization. This breakthrough approach has the potential to address the challenges posed by data silos and privacy concerns, thus facilitating the continuous validation and improvement of ML-based systems in the medical field [21]. In our research, we have leveraged federated learning for disease classification in potato crops. The base architecture of our federated learning model is CNN, and we conducted experiments by varying the number of clients while fine-tuning the hyper-parameters. Interestingly, our experimental results revealed that the federated learning model with 9 clients outperformed the standalone CNN architecture by an improvement of **1.5%** in classification precision. This highlights the efficacy of federated learning in improving disease classification in potato crops compared to traditional architectures.

This article is well-defined as follows: In Sect. 2, previous work is discussed followed by discussion on data set Sect. 4. Further sections is experimental study Sect. 5, in which we discussed about the proposed FL architecture and provided the results followed by conclusion in Sect. 6.

2   Related Work

Machine Learning model can encounter difficulties in extracting features from large-scale image dataset, which may lead to a decrease in classification accuracy. Moreover, the reliance on labor-intensive manual feature engineering can impede their adaptability to diverse and evolving disease patterns within images [22,23,25]. To solve this, deep learning models excel in capturing intricate features and patterns within medical images by autonomously learning hierarchical representations from raw data, potentially resulting in enhanced disease classification accuracy. Notably, deep learning eliminates the requirement for manual feature engineering by directly learning features from the data, enabling efficient and scalable analysis of image datasets. In this section, various deep learning techniques used by other researchers have been discussed. In [3], A novel CNN method is applied to resolve the farmer problem with 3 convolution layer and 3 max pooling layer and the accuracy is up to 91.2%. Also, this proposed novel CNN model took only 100 MB of storage for pre-trained model. In [17], Accuracy of disease identification is reduced significantly by using CNN as sometimes disease appear on lower part of the leaves and sometimes is in the upper part of the leaves. In [18], A deep learning based classification algorithm is used. They have used Convolution Neural Network model for disease classification to classify potato tubers, they have classified five classes from which 4 are diseased and 1 is healthy. The paper also investigates that a less amount of potato images are needed for such classification. In [19] the development of a new imaging setup consisting of a hyper-spectral line-scan camera for detecting virus diseases in seed potatoes. The paper also adapts a fully convolutional neural network (FCN) for hyper-spectral images to perform semantic segmentation of images. The trained network was validated on different potato cultivars in a real-world field experiment, demonstrating the suitability of this method for fast and objective disease detection, which can significantly reduce costs and provide a new business model based on high-tech solutions. In [5] a system is developed which was using two deep learning techniques VGG16 and VGG19 convolutional neural network architecture models for the classification in potato leaf. The model achieved an average 91%, accuracy indicating the feasibility of deep neural network approach. In [11] author uses a CNN to classify plant leaf disease into 15 classes, including 12 classes for diseases of different plants and 3 classes for healthy leaves and achieved excellent accuracy of 98.02% on test dataset. In [10] examines the use of Machine Learning and Deep Learning for automatic plant disease detection in Tomato, Rice, Potato, and Apple crops. It investigates the feasibility, analyzes detection steps, reviews existing models, and outlines challenges and future research directions. In [8] The paper presents an automatic system using image processing and machine learning and classify potato leaf diseases. It trains multiple classifiers on segmented images of healthy and diseased potato leaves, achieving 97% accuracy with the Random Forest classifier. The study offers a promising approach for automatic detection of plant leaf diseases. In [4] the author utilizes 3523 images for training and validation and 481 images for testing. The CNN achieves a training accuracy of 93.06%, while CNN achieves a higher accuracy of 99.75%. The evaluation using the confusion matrix demonstrates that CNN outperforms the CNN architecture in terms of accuracy for the test classification. In [20] they review techniques for automating plant leaf disease detection and classification based on morphological features. It discusses future work on using CNN for mulberry leaf disease identification and enhancing recognition rates through hybrid algorithms.

The proposed work is different from discussed approaches in terms of data augmentation, methodology adopted for classification and base model used in federated learning.

3   Federated Learning (FL)

Federated Learning is an innovative machine learning paradigm that facilitates collaborative model training without the need for centralized data sharing [13]. In this approach, individual devices or entities participate in the learning process by locally training a model using their own private data. The central server coordinates and aggregates the locally trained models to create a global model that represents the collective knowledge while respecting data privacy and security. By allowing distributed learning on decentralized data sources, Federated Learning empowers organizations and individuals to collaboratively improve machine learning models without compromising data privacy or confidentiality [21]. In the Eq. 1, shows the mathematical formula of federated learning where f(ω) indicates the total loss function for m sites and f$_j$(ω) reflects the client's local data loss function. We must locate the most effective ω value in order to reduce the overall loss.

$$\min_{\theta} \sum_i f(\theta, D_i) \tag{1}$$

where:

$\sum_i$ represents the summation over all participating devices/entities in the federated learning process. f(θ, $_i$) denotes the local loss function, which measures the discrepancy between the model's predictions (parameterized by θ) and the locally available data D_i on device/entity i. θ represents the global model parameters that are updated iteratively by aggregating the locally trained models from each device/entity. The objective is to minimize the overall loss by collaboratively improving the global model parameters while preserving the privacy and security of individual data sources.

The process of Federated Learning can be summarized in the following steps [14]:

- Initialization: A central server or coordinator initializes the global model parameters.
- Client Selection: A subset of devices or entities (referred to as client) is selected to participate in the training process.
- Model Distribution: The global model parameters are sent to the selected clients.
- Local Model Training: Each client trains the model locally using its own private data, without sharing the raw data with the central server. The training process may involve multiple iterations and optimization steps.
- Model Updates: After local training, each client sends its locally trained model updates (such as weight updates or gradients) back to the central server.

- Model Aggregation: The central server aggregates the model updates received from the clients, typically by applying averaging or weighted averaging methods to update the global model parameters.
- Iterative Process: Steps 3 to 6 are repeated for multiple rounds or iterations, allowing the clients to collaboratively improve the global model while preserving data privacy.
- Final Model Deployment: After the desired number of iterations, the final trained global model can be deployed for inference or further analysis.

4   Dataset

We tested our model using the PlantVillage Dataset [7]. This collection contains over 55,000 photos of leaves from 14 different crops, including tomatoes, potatoes, grapes, and more. It also contains 39 classes of data for crops that are healthy or diseased. As per our requirement we considered only potato plant and this dataset contains the data for 2 disease class and 1 healthy class. The number of sample has a range of 200 to 1000 samples in each class and it is not uniformly distributed. Moreover this dataset provides fourteen thousand five hundred twenty nine (14,529) labeled training images along with three thousand six hundred thirty one (2,152) potato crop's labelled validation data. A set of sample images are depicted in the Fig. 1. To ensure a balanced data collection with each dataset containing 1400 photos, we applied data augmentation techniques. These techniques included flips, rotations, zoom in, zoom out, and variations in lighting effects. As per the standard augmentation procedure, we performed rotations of images by 90°, 180°, or 270°, resulting in images closely resembling the

Fig. 1. Examples of our dataset's image showing several potato plant diseases, a) healthy, b) early blight, c) late blight.

originals. Surprisingly, in our investigation, we observed no significant improvement in classification accuracy through these standard augmentation processes. Therefore, we introduced an additional step where we randomly distributed picture intensity over a selected portion of the image, ranging between 20 and 30. This unique approach aimed to further enhance the data augmentation process.

5   Experiment Results

To execute the suggested Federated Learning model, we employed the powerful NVIDIA DGX v100 computer. As mentioned in the dataset section, the classes contained varying numbers of images. To ensure a balanced dataset, we applied data augmentation techniques. In our proposed Federated Learning model, we trained the model using different numbers of clients and summarized the accuracy for each case. Additionally, we visually represented the model architecture in Fig. 2, which comprises five convolution layers, a maximum pooling layer, and varying numbers of filters in each layer.

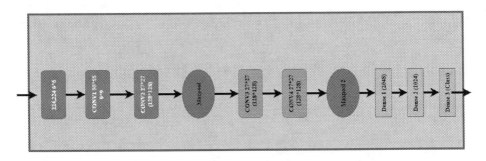

Fig. 2. Pictorial Representation of base CNN model for FL.

Pictorial representation of activation values of base model used in FL is presented in Fig. 3. We also ran the CNN base model for 10000 epochs and for federated learning model we have ran 100 communication rounds where each round contain 100 epochs.

In Fig. 4, the changes of loss and accuracy per epoch for all the models are clearly shown, such as CNN as a base model with 9, 10, 15 and 20 clients. In case of CNN Base model, it runs for 10,000 epochs, and we have received 89% accuracy. In case of federated learning we made 100 communication round where each round has 100 epochs and we recorded highest accuracy of 92% for 9 client.

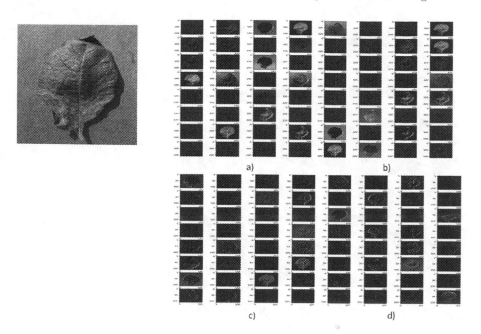

Fig. 3. Extracted feature in convolution layer for different model a) For 9 clients FL, b) For 10 clients FL, c) For 15 clients FL and d) For 20 clients model

The used loss function is presented in Eq. 2.

$$l = -\sum_{c=1}^{m} log(\rho_{o,c}) \tag{2}$$

where l = loss In which c is binary indicator and M is the number of classes available in dataset and ROC-AUC graph is presented in Fig. 6.

We go through testing of proposed model after analyzing the performance. In order to testing total 500 images is being used. For proposed federal learning model we have accuracy in the range in between 89% and 92%. The change is accuracy with respect to epochs is presented in Fig. 5.

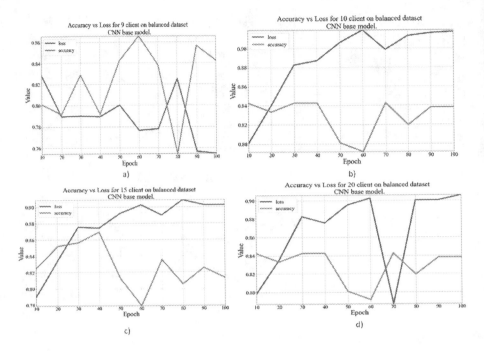

Fig. 4. A comparison of epoch vs loss and accuracy of Federated learning with traditional CNN. a) Epochs vs loss and Accuracy for Federated Learning of 9 Clients, b) Epochs vs loss and Accuracy for Federated Learning of 10 Clients, c) Epochs vs loss and Accuracy for Federated Learning of 15 Clients and d) Epochs vs loss and Accuracy for Federated Learning of 20 Clients

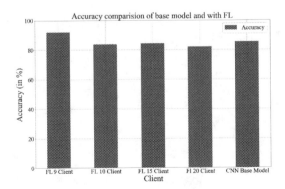

Fig. 5. A comparison of accuracy in different model used in this article which include CNN, Federated Learning with different client size.

ROC AUC CURVE

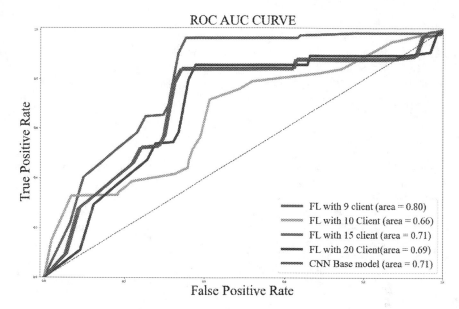

Fig. 6. A comparison of accuracy in different model used in this article which include CNN, Federated Learning with different client size.

6 Conclusion and Discussion

For the purpose of our study on potato crop disease detection, we have developed a Federated Learning (FL)-based model and compared its performance with the existing FL model and the CNN base model. The PlatVillage dataset, described in Sect. 4, was utilized to evaluate our model. Interestingly, we observed that the testing accuracy consistently improved as the number of clients increased in the FL model, ranging from 82.19% to 92%. Despite having a limited dataset, the FL model with 10 clients achieved higher accuracy than the CNN base model. Also, AUC value of 15 client is 0.71 which implies that it has reliability of classification of different class correctly. This study clearly demonstrates the advantages of FL over the base model, emphasizing the need for a sufficient dataset to train the FL model effectively.

As part of our future work, we are actively pursuing efforts to streamline and condense the Federated Learning (FL) model. Our aim is to make it more efficient and resource-friendly without compromising its performance.

References

1. Agarwal, M., Gupta, S.K., Biswas, K.K.: Development of efficient CNN model for Tomato crop disease identification. Sustain. Comput. Inform. Syst. **28**, 100407 (2020). https://doi.org/10.1016/j.suscom.2020.100407. https://www.sciencedirect.com/science/article/pii/S2210537920301347
2. Agarwal, M., Gupta, S.K., Biswas, K.: Development of efficient CNN model for tomato crop disease identification. Sustain. Comput. Inform. Syst. **28**, 100407 (2020). https://doi.org/10.1016/j.suscom.2020.100407
3. Agarwal, M., Singh, A., Arjaria, S., Sinha, A., Gupta, S.: ToLeD: Tomato leaf disease detection using convolution neural network. Procedia Comput. Sci. **167**, 293–301 (2020). ISBN 1877-0509
4. Arya, S., Singh, R.: A comparative study of CNN and AlexNet for detection of disease in potato and mango leaf. In: 2019 International Conference on Issues and Challenges in Intelligent Computing Techniques (ICICT), Ghaziabad, India, pp. 1–6. IEEE (2019). https://doi.org/10.1109/ICICT46931.2019.8977648. https://ieeexplore.ieee.org/document/8977648/
5. Eser, S.: A deep learning based approach for the detection of diseases in pepper and potato leaves. Anadolu Tarım Bilimleri Dergisi **36**(2), 167–178 (2021)
6. Gunarathna, M., Rathnayaka, R., Kandegama, W.: Identification of an efficient deep leaning architecture for tomato disease classification using leaf images. J. Food Agric. **13**(1), 33 (2020)
7. Hughes, D.P., Salathe, M.: An open access repository of images on plant health to enable the development of mobile disease diagnostics (2016). https://doi.org/10.48550/arXiv.1511.08060
8. Iqbal, M.A., Talukder, K.H.: Detection of potato disease using image segmentation and machine learning. In: 2020 International Conference on Wireless Communications Signal Processing and Networking (WiSPNET), Chennai, India, pp. 43–47. IEEE (2020). https://doi.org/10.1109/WiSPNET48689.2020.9198563. https://ieeexplore.ieee.org/document/9198563/
9. Islam, M., Dinh, A., Wahid, K., Bhowmik, P.: Detection of potato diseases using image segmentation and multiclass support vector machine. In: 2017 IEEE 30th Canadian Conference on Electrical and Computer Engineering (CCECE), pp. 1–4. IEEE (2017)
10. Jackulin, C., Murugavalli, S.: A comprehensive review on detection of plant disease using machine learning and deep learning approaches. Measur. Sens. 100441 (2022)
11. Jasim, M.A., AL-Tuwaijari, J.M.: Plant leaf diseases detection and classification using image processing and deep learning techniques. In: 2020 International Conference on Computer Science and Software Engineering (CSASE), Duhok, Iraq, pp. 259–265. IEEE (2020). https://doi.org/10.1109/CSASE48920.2020.9142097. https://ieeexplore.ieee.org/document/9142097/
12. Javaid, M., Khan, I.H.: Internet of Things (IoT) enabled healthcare helps to take the challenges of COVID-19 pandemic. J. Oral Biol. Craniofacial Res. **11**(2), 209–214 (2021). https://doi.org/10.1016/j.jobcr.2021.01.015. https://www.sciencedirect.com/science/article/pii/S2212426821000154
13. Li, L., Fan, Y., Lin, K.Y.: A survey on federated learning. In: 2020 IEEE 16th International Conference on Control & Automation (ICCA), pp. 791–796. IEEE (2020)
14. Li, T., Sahu, A.K., Talwalkar, A., Smith, V.: Federated learning: challenges, methods, and future directions. IEEE Signal Process. Mag. **37**(3), 50–60 (2020). https://doi.org/10.1109/MSP.2020.2975749

15. Liu, F., Xiao, Z.: Disease spots identification of potato leaves in hyperspectral based on locally adaptive 1D-CNN. In: 2020 IEEE International Conference on Artificial Intelligence and Computer Applications (ICAICA), pp. 355–358. IEEE (2020)

16. Mammen, P.M.: Federated learning: opportunities and challenges. arXiv preprint arXiv:2101.05428 (2021)

17. Mohanty, S.P., Hughes, D.P., Salathé, M.: Using deep learning for image-based plant disease detection. Front. Plant Sci. **7**, 1419 (2016). ISBN 1664-462X

18. Oppenheim, D., Shani, G., Erlich, O., Tsror, L.: Using deep learning for image-based potato tuber disease detection. Phytopathology **109**(6), 1083–1087 (2019)

19. Polder, G., Blok, P.M., De Villiers, H.A., Van der Wolf, J.M., Kamp, J.: Potato virus Y detection in seed potatoes using deep learning on hyperspectral images. Front. Plant Sci. **10**, 209 (2019)

20. Puspha Annabel, L.S., Annapoorani, T., Deepalakshmi, P.: Machine learning for plant leaf disease detection and classification - a review. In: 2019 International Conference on Communication and Signal Processing (ICCSP), pp. 0538–0542 (2019). https://doi.org/10.1109/ICCSP.2019.8698004

21. Rieke, N., et al.: The future of digital health with federated learning. NPJ Digit. Med. **3**(1), 1–7 (2020). https://doi.org/10.1038/s41746-020-00323-1. https://www.nature.com/articles/s41746-020-00323-1

22. Saba, L., et al.: A multicenter study on carotid ultrasound plaque tissue characterization and classification using six deep artificial intelligence models: a stroke application. IEEE Trans. Instrum. Meas. **70**, 1–12 (2021)

23. Sanagala, S.S., et al.: Ten fast transfer learning models for carotid ultrasound plaque tissue characterization in augmentation framework embedded with heatmaps for stroke risk stratification. Diagnostics **11**(11), 2109 (2021)

24. Sharma, R., Singh, A., Dutta, M.K., Riha, K., Kriz, P., et al.: Image processing based automated identification of late blight disease from leaf images of potato crops. In: 2017 40th International Conference on Telecommunications and Signal Processing (TSP), pp. 758–762. IEEE (2017)

25. Skandha, S.S., et al.: A hybrid deep learning paradigm for carotid plaque tissue characterization and its validation in multicenter cohorts using a supercomputer framework. Comput. Biol. Med. **141**, 105131 (2022)

26. Suttapakti, U., Bunpeng, A.: Potato leaf disease classification based on distinct color and texture feature extraction. In: 2019 19th International Symposium on Communications and Information Technologies (ISCIT), pp. 82–85. IEEE (2019)

Sugarcane Bud Detection Using YOLOv5

P. Swathi Sindhe and Ravindra S. Hegadi[✉]

Department of Computer Science, Central University of Karnataka,
Kadaganchi, Kalaburagi, Karnataka, India
swathipsindhe@gmail.com, rshegadi@gmail.com

Abstract. This paper addresses the labor-intensive and wasteful nature of the traditional sugarcane bud cutting method. To overcome these challenges, the proposed approach leverages YOLOv5 technology for sugarcane bud identification. The machine-learning model is trained with diverse data samples, enabling it to accurately distinguish between sugarcane buds and other elements in the images. The implementation yields the best of 79% accuracy in bud detection. By automating the process, the proposed method significantly reduces labor and time requirements while minimizing sugarcane wastage. This innovation presents promising implications for the sugarcane industry, as it streamlines bud identification and optimizes resource utilization. Furthermore, the adoption of YOLOv5 technology can potentially extend to other agricultural domains, offering opportunities for enhanced crop management and sustainable farming practices.

Keywords: Bud detection · classification · Machine learning · YOLOv5

1 Introduction

India ranks as the world's second-largest sugarcane producer, with Brazil following closely behind. Sugarcane cultivation is prevalent across major regions in the country. Karnataka holds the position of the third-largest sugarcane producer, succeeded by Uttar Pradesh and Maharashtra. Agriculture is a vital sector in India's economy, contributing nearly 18% to the total GDP (Gross Domestic Product). The sugarcane industry stands as a substantial sector, ranking after cotton and textiles. Sugarcane is a renewable, natural agricultural resource that offers not only sugar but also biofuel, fiber, fertilizer, and numerous other byproducts and co-products, all with ecological sustainability. Its juice is utilized to produce white sugar, brown sugar (khandsari), and jaggery (gur).

The sugarcane stem consists of stalks and nodes. The stalks are generally uniform in length throughout the stem and are separated by nodes. Stalks are soft and juicy, while nodes are the hardest part of the stem, containing buds essential for cultivation. After harvesting sugarcane, the buds are cut within 7

Central University of Karnataka, Kalaburagi.

KC Santosh et al. (Eds.): RTIP2R 2023, CCIS 2026, pp. 202–212, 2024.
https://doi.org/10.1007/978-3-031-53082-1_17

to 14 days and sown in the soil for the next crop. To facilitate growth, the buds are placed facing upwards.

The traditional method of cutting sugarcane buds has long been recognized as a labor-intensive, time-consuming process, resulting in significant wastage of valuable sugarcane resources. In light of these challenges, this paper introduces an innovative solution to revolutionize the bud identification process by employing YOLOv5 technology. The primary objective of this research is to enhance the efficiency and accuracy of sugarcane bud detection, thereby addressing the limitations of conventional techniques. YOLOv5, a state-of-the-art object detection algorithm, has gained prominence for its robust performance and real-time capabilities. Leveraging this cutting-edge technology, the proposed method seeks to automate the bud identification process and optimize resource utilization.

To validate the proposed approach, a diverse set of data samples is collected, encompassing various sugarcane bud scenarios. These samples are then utilized to train the machine, allowing it to learn and distinguish between sugarcane buds and other elements present in the images. During the evaluation phase, the trained machine is presented with unseen data samples to determine its ability to accurately identify the presence or absence of buds. The results demonstrate a promising level of precision, achieving the best accuracy of 79%. While further refinement and optimization might be pursued, this level of accuracy already represents a notable advancement compared to traditional manual methods.

The implications of this research are significant for the sugarcane industry. By introducing an automated approach to bud detection, the proposed method offers the potential to substantially reduce labor requirements, significantly cut down processing time, and minimize wastage of sugarcane resources. Such improvements would not only enhance the productivity of sugarcane cultivation but also contribute to the economic viability and sustainability of the industry.

Additionally, the adoption of YOLOv5 technology for sugarcane bud detection may pave the way for similar advancements in other agricultural domains. The versatility of this algorithm allows for its application in various crop identification tasks, presenting opportunities to streamline farming practices and improve crop management.

In the proposed research work, the literature survey of related work is presented in Sect. 2, the Sect. 3 presents the methodology used for this work, results are discussed in Sect. 4 and Sect. 5 presents the conclusion of the proposed research.

2 Literature Survey

Kumar et al. [1] have developed a model that utilizes the "YOLOv5" framework, amalgamating five cutting-edge object detection methodologies. This model is particularly tailored to discerning insects exhibiting subtle distinctions among subcategories. To amplify crucial information within the feature map and diminish auxiliary data, the model incorporates channel and spatial attention modules. These augmentations significantly enhance its capacity for accurate identification. In empirical assessments, the system attains an impressive F1 score of around 0.90 and an mAP value of 93% when evaluated on their proprietary pest dataset. When compared to other YOLOv5 models, this upgraded system showcases a noteworthy 0.02 increase in the F1 score and a 1% enhancement in mAP, underscoring its remarkable accomplishment in the realm of insect detection.

Effective weed control and precise site-specific weed management demand the development of algorithms that can accurately detect both weeds and crops. However, detecting these entities within a field setting presents challenges due to the uneven distribution of samples and the tendency to overlook smaller weed instances. To tackle these hurdles, Wang et al. [2] introduced an innovative approach involving pixel-level synthesization data augmentation and the implementation of a TIA-YOLOv5 network. The pixel-level synthesization technique generates synthetic images by seamlessly integrating weed pixels into the original imagery. The TIA-YOLOv5 network, on the other hand, integrates several advancements. These include a transformer encoder block to heighten sensitivity to weeds, a channel feature fusion strategy incorporating involution to mitigate information loss, and adaptive spatial feature fusion to facilitate multi-scale feature integration. In evaluations conducted on a dataset, the proposed TIA-YOLOv5 network yielded remarkable outcomes. Specifically, it achieved F1-score weed, APweed, and mAP@0.5 metrics of 70.0%, 80.8%, and 90.0%, respectively. These figures surpassed those of the baseline YOLOv5 model by 11.8%, 11.3%, and 5.9%. Furthermore, the detection speed reached a notable 20.8 FPS. Collectively, this approach significantly bolstered both detection accuracy and speed, offering promising potential for real-time weed and crop identification within field environments.

In the pursuit of effective fruit cultivation through computer vision-driven image analysis in agriculture, a recognition model must possess resilience in intricate and ever-changing settings. Simultaneously, it should maintain speed, precision, and a lightweight profile suitable for energy-efficient computing deployment. In response to these demands, the YOLOv5-LiNet model was introduced in [3]. This model stands as a streamlined iteration of YOLOv5n, thoughtfully tailored for the purpose of fruit instance segmentation, thereby augmenting the accuracy of fruit detection processes.

A novel adaptive clipping algorithm, built upon the YOLO object detection methodology, has been proposed to effectively counteract the loss of features induced by image compression during the normalization process [4]. This algorithm serves a dual role in data pre-processing and detection stages. The approach involves enhancing the high-resolution training datasets through adaptive clipping techniques resulting in the creation of a fresh training set that diligently preserves vital intricate attributes, crucial for instructing the object detection network. During the detection phase, images are processed in segments using the adaptive clipping algorithm. Subsequently, the coordinates are harmonized through a process of position mapping. When subjected to vehicle detection experiments, the refined YOLO algorithm is meticulously compared against its original counterpart. The results underscore notable improvements in precision (elevating from 79.5% to 91.9%), recall (surging from 44.2% to 82.5%), and mAP@0.5 (ascending from 47.9% to 89.6%). Demonstrating its efficacy, this adaptive clipping methodology effectively heightens the conventional object detection capabilities, specifically evident in vehicle detection tasks.

3   Methodology

3.1   Methods

The proposed model consists of five steps. The first step is to collect the data samples of sugarcane for training and evaluating the models. The second step is to preprocess the entire dataset by annotation and augmentation. It is used to increase the number of samples. Image data augmentation is a technique to increase the size of a training dataset artificially by slightly altering the existing images. Thirdly, we use the YOLO object detection models to train on the dataset. Then, we validate the detection performance of the models and evaluate the results. Finally, we select an optimal model. The various steps in the process are depicted using the flowchart in the Fig. 1.

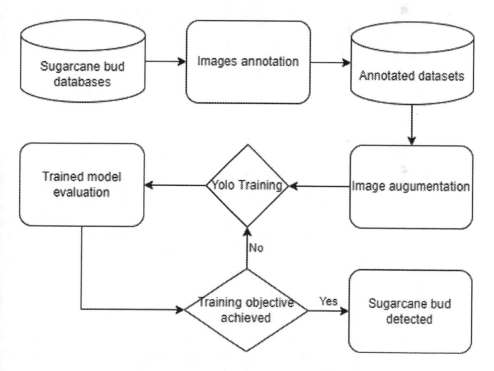

Fig. 1. Flowchart of the proposed model

Dataset Collection. Firstly, we searched for images from different databases and search engines, such as Kaggle, Google and Baidu, but couldn't find any images of the sugarcane bud. Since it was not the harvesting season in the

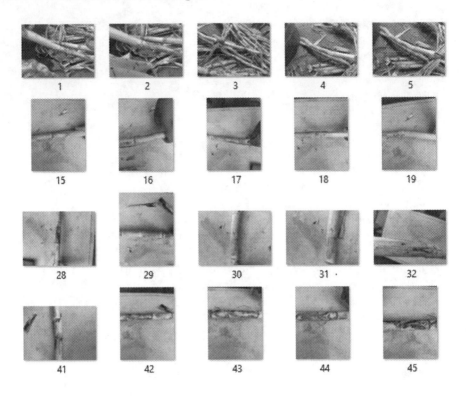

Fig. 2. Sugarcane bud data samples

months of June and July, we couldn't collect the images from the fields. Instead, a few data samples were collected from nearby sugarcane vendors. The collected data samples are shown in the Fig. 2. The collection of data related to sugarcane has been divided into two well-defined classes, namely "bud" and "node". Each instance in the dataset is assigned to one of these classes based on its characteristics and attributes. The class "bud" refers to instances representing sugarcane buds, while the class "node" pertains to instances that correspond to sugarcane nodes. This categorization facilitates the training and evaluation of machine learning models or algorithms that aim to distinguish and identify these specific components within the sugarcane plants.

Data Annotation. Prior to model training, data annotation stands out as a crucial phase in image processing. Essentially, annotation entails marking sugarcane locations in images by creating bounding boxes around each sugarcane instance. This process is exemplified in Fig. 3, where two bounding boxes are established for each class: a pink box for 'bud' and a blue box for 'node'. Manual annotation was conducted using the makesense.ai data annotation tool. Information about marked objects in images is stored in corresponding text files, sharing image names. Each line in the YOLO annotated file includes object class, rectangle center coordinates (x and y), and rectangle dimensions (*width* and *height*). Rectangular coordinates are normalized (0–1) for size independence. This approach accommodates various image sizes during evaluation in the object detection system. A sample annotation file's content is depicted in Fig. 4. Each image corresponds to a text file, preserving annotated details.

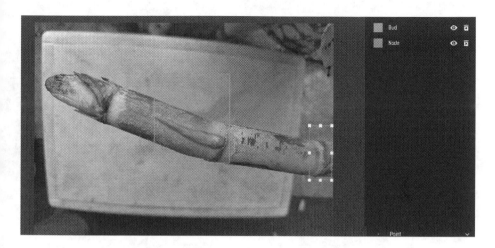

Fig. 3. Bounding boxes representing bud and node of a sugarcane

Data Augmentation. Data augmentation is performed to increase the size and diversity of the training dataset. This technique artificially creates new training samples by slightly altering the existing images without changing the semantic meaning. Common augmentation techniques include rotation, flipping, scaling, cropping, brightness adjustments and other transformations. By augmenting the data, the model becomes more robust and better generalizes to various scenarios and orientation of sugarcane in real-world images.

3.2 YOLOv5 Architecture

YOLOv5 (You Only Look Once version 5) is an advanced real-time object detection framework designed for computer vision tasks. It is an evolution of the YOLO family, known for its speed and accuracy in identifying objects in images and videos. Developed by Ultralytics, YOLOv5 is implemented using PyTorch and has gained popularity for its user-friendly approach and ease of deployment. One of the key features of YOLOv5 is its streamlined architecture, making it more efficient and lightweight compared to previous versions. This allows for faster inference and training times, making it suitable for real-time applications. Additionally, YOLOv5 introduces the concept of model scaling, enabling users to choose from different sizes (e.g., small, medium, large) based on their specific requirements and hardware capabilities. YOLOv5 is a single stage object detector which consists of three components: Backbone, neck and head as shown in

Fig. 4. It is categorized into 5 different models based on the sizes as YOLOv5n for an extra small size model, YOLOv5s for small size model, YOLOv5m for medium size model, YOLOv5l for large size model, YOLOv5x for extra large size model.

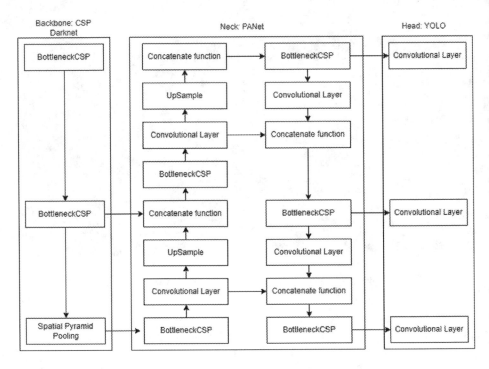

Fig. 4. Architecture of YOLOv5

The backbone of the model is built upon CSP-Darknet53, which is essentially the Darknet53 convolutional network which uses the Cross Stage Partial (CSP) network strategy. YOLOv5 is a deep network, utilizing residual and dense blocks to facilitate information flow to deeper layers and overcome the vanishing gradient problem. However, these blocks can result in redundant gradients. To tackle this issue, YOLOv5 adopts the CSPNet strategy, which truncates the gradient flow. With the CSPNet strategy, YOLOv5 partitions the base layer's feature map into two segments and merges them using a cross stage hierarchy. This approach yields significant benefits for the model. Firstly, it reduces the number of parameters, making the network more efficient. Secondly, it substantially decreases computation (FLOPS), leading to faster inference speeds crucial for real-time object detection. The neck incorporates a variant of Spatial Pyramid Pooling (SPP) and modifies the Path Aggregation Network (PANet) by integrating BottleNeckCSP in its architecture. PANet enhances information flow and facilitates precise pixel localization for mask prediction. The SPP block aggregates information from inputs and produces a fixed-length output, significantly increasing the receptive field by isolating essential context features without compromising network speed.

Moreover, YOLOv5 utilizes the same head structure as YOLOv3 and YOLOv4. This head comprises three convolutional layers responsible for predicting bounding box locations (x, y, *height*, *width*), object scores, and the corresponding classes of detected objects.

4   Results

All four models were trained for sugarcane bud detection using 70 images and categorized into 2 classes called bud and node during the training phase. The size of the stack was set to 4 for YOLOv5s, YOLOv5l, YOLOv5m, YOLOv5x and the images were cropped to 640×640 pixels. Initially the annotations were changed to YOLO format in text files. YOLOv5 is cloned from the GitHub repository. Then, the data is trained using the 4 models YOLOv5s, YOLOv5l, YOLOv5m, YOLOv5x. The model is trained for 10 epochs and the results are analyzed.

Table 1 presents a comprehensive comparison among four YOLO models: YOLOv5s, YOLOv5m, YOLOv5l, and YOLOv5x. While these models share identical architecture and functionality, the key distinguishing factor lies in their respective sizes.

Table 1. Comparision of the four models.

Model	YOLOv5s	YOLOv5m	YOLOv5l	YOLOv5x
epoch	10	10	10	10
time	0.009	0.012	0.020	0.033
layers	157	212	267	322
parameters	7015519	20856975	46113663	86180143
gradients	0	0	0	0
GFLOPs	15.8	47.9	107.7	203.8

The confusion matrix serves as a means to succinctly present the performance of a classification algorithm. Various metrics are employed to assess the network's efficacy, including precision, recall, and mean average precision (mAP). In the context of a classification task, sample classification involves designations such as true positives (TP), false positives (FP), true negatives (TN), and false negatives (FN), which are determined based on the agreement between the ground truth and predictions provided by neural networks. Figure 5 depicts the confusion matrix for the four YOLOv5 models utilized in the experimental study involving two distinct classes.

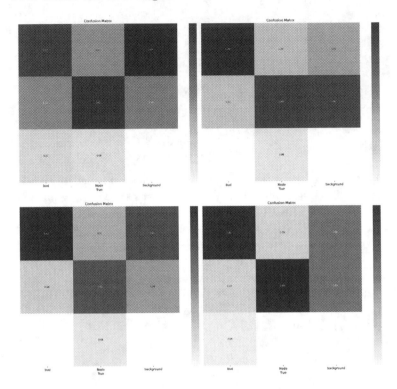

Fig. 5. (a) Confusion Matrix of YOLOv5l (b) Confusion Matrix of YOLOv5m (c) Confusion Matrix of YOLOv5s (d) Confusion Matrix of YOLOv5x

The subsequent figures, labeled as Fig. 6 and Fig. 7, provide visual representations that offer valuable insights. In Fig. 6, the Precision-Recall curve for the four distinct models is graphically presented. This curve illustrates the trade-off between precision and recall as the model's detection threshold varies. It visually showcases the comparative performance of these models in terms of their precision and recall values. Moving on to Fig. 7, this particular illustration is dedicated to showcasing the detection process related to sugarcane buds. The depiction includes bounding boxes that delineate the detected sugarcane buds within the images. These bounding boxes serve to encapsulate and highlight the regions of interest. Moreover, the accompanying accuracy values provide an indication of how accurately these bounding boxes align with the actual positions of the sugarcane buds in the images. This visualization serves as a clear representation of the models' effectiveness in accurately localizing and identifying sugarcane buds through the accuracy of their bounding box placements.

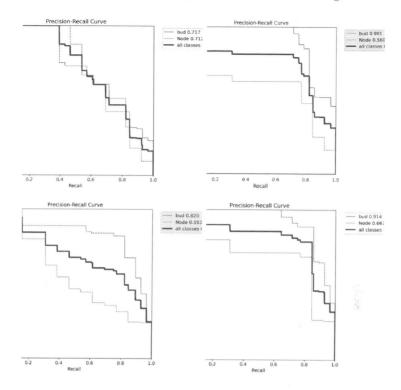

Fig. 6. Precision-Recall curve of YOLOv5l, YOLOv5m, YOLOv5s, Yolov5x

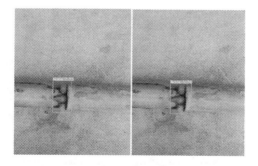

Fig. 7. Bounding box showing the results

5   Conclusion

In conclusion, this research offers a promising solution to the labor-intensive and wasteful traditional method of cutting sugarcane buds. By leveraging YOLOv5 technology, the proposed automated bud identification process demonstrates a notable best accuracy of 79%, surpassing the limitations of manual methods. The adoption of YOLOv5 presents a significant opportunity for the sugarcane industry, as it streamlines bud detection, reduces labor efforts, and optimizes resource utilization. This innovation has the potential to enhance sugarcane cultivation by minimizing processing time and maximizing yield, contributing to the industry's economic viability and sustainability.

Moreover, the versatility of YOLOv5 opens door to applications beyond sugarcane, offering possibilities for efficient crop management across various agricultural domains. As future research refines the methodology and explores further optimization, this cutting-edge approach holds the potential to revolutionize not only sugarcane cultivation but also agriculture as a whole. By integrating advanced technology into farming practices, we can foster productivity, resource conservation, and ultimately contribute to a more sustainable and prosperous future for the agricultural sector.

5.1   Future Works

In future, the focus lies on gathering extensive datasets and enhancing the precision of sugarcane bud detection. Additionally, increasing the number of classes is essential to achieve the highest accuracy. Moreover, the images will be acquired through real-time video capturing and pre-processed to make them suitable for further processing.

Acknowledgement. Authors thank the Ministry of Electronics and Information Technology (MeitY), New Delhi for granting Visvesvaraya Ph.D. fellowship through awardee no. MEITY-PHD-1674209407515 and Dated: 02/01/2023.

References

1. Kumar, N., Nagarathna, Flammini, F.: YOLO-based light-weight deep learning models for insect detection system with field adaption. Agriculture **13**, 741 (2023)
2. Wang, A., Peng, T., Cao, H., Xu, Y., Wei, X., Cui, B.: TIA-YOLOv5: an improved YOLOv5 network for real-time detection of crop and weed in the field. Front. Plant Sci. **13**, 1091655 (2022)
3. Lawal, O.M.: YOLOv5-LiNet: a lightweight network for fruits instance segmentation. PLoS ONE **18**(3), e0282297 (2023)
4. Chen, Z., Cao, L., Wang, Q.: YOLOv5-Based Vehicle Detection Method for High-Resolution UAV Images. Elsevier, Hindawi Mobile Information Systems Volume (2022)
5. Meng, Y., Yea, C., Yu, S., Qin, J., Zhang, J., Shen, D.: Sugarcane node recognition technology based on wavelet analysis. IEEE Access Comput. Electron. Agric. **158**, 68–78 (2021)
6. Önler, E.: Real time pest detection using YOLOv5. Int. J. Agric. Nat. Sci. **14**, 232–246 (2021)
7. Qi, F., Wang, Y., Tang, Z., Chen, S.: Real-time and effective detection of agricultural pest using an improved YOLOv5 network. J. Real-Time Image Process. **20**, 33 (2023)

ELA-Conv: Forgery Detection in Digital Images Based on ELA and CNN

Ayush Verma[1](✉) (iD), Priyank Pandey[2], and Manju Khari[1] (iD)

[1] Jawaharlal Nehru University, New Delhi 110067, India
{ayushv34_scs,manjukhari}@jnu.ac.in
[2] Graphic Era University, Dehradun 248002, Uttarakhand, India
priyankpandey@geu.ac.in

Abstract. Due to the rapid growth and evolution of smart devices like smartphones and cameras, a huge amount of digital data is generated in the form of digital images. Digital images are foundational pillars of data because they are a reliable source of information because of their visual appeal and information. Modern software and technologies have opened the doors for new and creative ways to forge or tamper images. Digital image forgery means manipulating the digital image to suppress some meaningful and factual information inside the image or misguide any concerned organization. The detection of forged images is inspired by the requirement for authenticity and integrity maintenance. Researchers have used Deep Learning (DL) techniques for the detection of image tampering and forgeries. This paper proposes an image forgery detection method based on Error Level Analysis (ELA) and Convolutional Neural Network (CNN). ELA is an image processing technique used for detecting inconsistencies and potential manipulation using compression artefacts of images with lossy compression. CNN are a class of neural networks specialized for their superior performance with images. The proposed method uses ELA, which is pipelined to a CNN model. The analysis is performed on the standard CASIAv2 dataset which consists of 7491 authentic images and 5123 forged images. The proposed method attains a superior accuracy of 94% and an F-score of 94%. The result reveals that the proposed model outperforms other pre-trained baseline models like VGG16 and VGG19.

Keywords: Digital Images · Image Forgery · Data Security · Error Level Analysis · Deep Learning

1 Introduction

In this age of digital era, the use of smart devices like smartphones and digital cameras is increasing. These devices are mostly used for digital photography for capturing digital images and videos. Digital images are foundational pillars of digital data because they are a reliable source of information because of their visual appeal and information processing. Digital images are prone to forgery or tampering. Digital image forgery means manipulating the digital image to suppress some meaningful and factual information inside the image or misguide any concerned organization. Generating forged images by modifying the original image data is called digital image forgery. There are cases when

KC Santosh et al. (Eds.): RTIP2R 2023, CCIS 2026, pp. 213–226, 2024.
https://doi.org/10.1007/978-3-031-53082-1_18

it is difficult to identify the edited region from the original image. Nowadays, several software packages are available that are used to manipulate images so that the image appears to be a look-alike of the original image. Some of the advanced and commercial software are Adobe Photoshop, CorelDRAW, and open-source user-friendly software are GIMP etc. Along with that, use of image editing applications on smartphone are also highly prevalent which are easily available. The detection of forged images is driven by the need for authenticity and to maintain the integrity of the image. Digital forensics, also known as cyber forensics and computer forensics, is a domain of forensic science that is concerned with the identification, preservation, analysis, and presentation of digital evidence from electronic devices and digital media. This field is ubiquitous in investigating and solving unethical cyber activities, cybercrimes, unauthorized access to copyright and sensitive data, and other digital-related incidents. Digital forensics generally involves a robust methodology to recover, analyze, and interpret altered, fabricated and corrupt data stored on various electronic devices to uncover evidence related to a crime or incident. This evidence can be used in legal proceedings and to identify the responsible parties.

In recent years, much research has been looked upon to address the issue of image tampering in digital forensics. Ongoing research is still being conducted to develop even more robust image forgery detection techniques. Image Forgery is broadly classified into two categories – Active and Passive Approaches. Figure 1 represents the various types of image forgery classification.

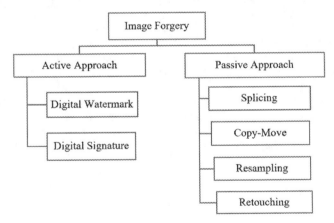

Fig. 1. Classification of Image Forgery Techniques

1.1 Active Approaches

Active approaches rely on prior information about the image. These methods use pre-embedded data to detect image forgeries. In this methods, additional information is added in the image in form of digital watermark or digital signature at the time of image capture or during image acquisition or at a later stage. In other words, legitimate information is embedded inside the images. When any doubt arises about the authenticity of the image, this digital watermark or digital signature can be used to detect image forgery simply by verifying the embedded authentication values with that of forged image. Digital Watermarking and Digital Signature are types of Active image forgery approaches. Due to digital era and internet, access and distribution of images has become ever easy. The distributed images can be copied any number of times without any error which puts the rights of original owners of the image at risk. One of the methods to discourage the illegal duplication on the image is to inject a digital watermark inside the image such that the watermark is inseparable from the image, and it does not significantly alter the semantic information of the image. Digital watermark involves injecting some specific information or digest or metadata inside the image. A watermarking method proposed by Duang et al. [1] is based on Discrete Cosine Transform (DCT) and Arnold scrambling algorithm which preprocess the original watermark and then embeds it. A different approach was by Wang et al. [2] which is based on spatial and frequency domain preprocessing combined with Adversarial learning. Figure 2 represents the injection and extraction in a standard digital watermarking process.

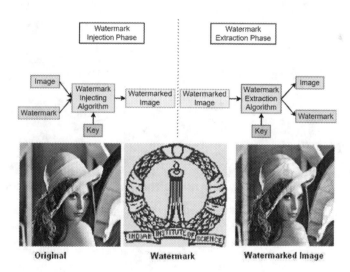

Fig. 2. An example depicting digital watermarking.

1.2 Passive Approaches

Passive image forgery, on the other hand refers to a type of image manipulation where an image is altered with the intention to deceive viewers, but the manipulated image appears authentic and genuine. In passive forgery, the modifications are made in a way that the altered image appears unaltered to the human eye, and no overt signs of tampering are evident. Detecting passive image forgery can be challenging, as the alterations are often designed to be imperceptible to the naked eye. Image Splicing, Copy-Move, Image Resampling and Image Retouching are some types of Passive image forgery approaches.

Splicing is a heterogenous technique which involves copying and pasting an area of image from an identical or a different image [3]. Figure 3 is an example of Image Splicing. Image Retouching is performed on image to remove or fix undesired objects and artefacts like spots, scratches, blemishes etc. It is also done to suppress the aftereffects of some other type of forgery [4]. Copy-move forgery is a specific type of passive image forgery where a portion of an image is copied and then pasted onto another area of the same image, often to conceal or duplicate an object or region [5]. This technique is used to manipulate the content of an image and create the illusion that certain objects or details are present in multiple locations within the same image. Image resampling, also known as image resizing or image interpolation, is the process of changing the dimensions of an image. Since resampling is a pixel level operation, it involves altering the number of pixels in the image to make it larger (upsampling) or smaller (downsampling) and add and remove objects within an image [6]. Resampling can be done for various reasons, including adjusting the image for different display sizes, printing, or optimizing images for web usage.

a) Original Image 1   b) Original Image 2   c) Spliced Image

Fig. 3. An example representing image splicing

The organization of this paper is as follows: Sect. 2 reports about literature and previous works related to image forgery detection. Section 3 explains the proposed methodology in details. Section 4 highlights the results and validation measures for comparison among various algorithms. Finally, Sect. 5 concludes the paper with a concluding remark of the proposed work and future scope.

2 Literature Review

This section provides an in-depth study of the previous works related to image forgery detection and discusses their performance under various applications of image forgery. Image processing methods along with DL have been widely used by the research community to analyze and develop highly efficient and accurate image forgery detection systems. Image forgery detection methods, powered by ML and DL algorithms enables fast and accurate detection of image tampering. Image forgery detection technology provides improved efficiency, accuracy, and security in various domains, contributing to enhanced security and trust within the organization and social culture. CNN are a class of deep learning neural networks that have proven to be highly effective in various tasks involving visual data particularly image recognition, object detection, image segmentation, and more. They are specifically designed to process grid-like data, like images, by taking advantage of the spatial relationships between neighboring pixels. Researchers have analyzed various techniques along with CNN and other state of the art methods to develop highly efficient and accurate image forgery detection systems.

A method proposed by Zhang et al. [7] uses Local Binary Pattern (LBP), ELA and Bagged trees for detecting splicing in digital images. LBP is an efficient texture operator algorithm widely used in image processing application. LBP assigns each pixel a binary 8-bit number to either 0 or 1 by thresholding its eight neighbors in 3×3 window based on the value of the center pixel. Their method achieves an accuracy of 91% and F-score of 91% on COLUMB dataset.

Rao et al. [8] proposed a CNN based method for image splicing and copy-move image forgery. Their method learns hierarchical representations from the input data of images and involves two phases – feature extraction and feature fusion. The model extracts patch-based features from a sliding window on image pixels. Further these extracted patch-based features are aggregated through feature-fusion to obtain unique features of image. The model achieves 97% accuracy using Support Vector Machine (SVM) on CASIAv2 dataset and it is limited to only splicing and copy-move forgery detection.

Another study by Roshini et al. [9] propose a key-points and feature extraction method for copy-move image tampering detection. For finding image key-points, they make use of Scale-Invariant Feature Transform (SIFT). It is a widely used algorithm in computer vision for feature extraction. The main advantage of SIFT is that it is invariant to scaling and rotation. Further they affine the transformation matrix using Random Sample Consensus (RANSAC) algorithm. This algorithm estimates parameters for a mathematical model from a set of observed data that contain outliers. The authors report that their model can detect and locate forgeries better.

There exists a primary assumption in forged images that there is a difference in the feature distribution between forged and non-forged images. Niloy et al. [10] propose a methodology of forgery localization based on this assumption of difference of feature distribution between forged and original images. They employ contrastive learning which is an unsupervised representation learning technique. Their model maps into a feature space where the features between authentic and tampered area of images are classified and distributed for each image. The authors report their best performance of 91% AUC on NIST dataset.

Kaushik et al. [11] propose a CNN technique for feature extraction of images and Random Forest (RF) combined with SVM for classification of tampered images from authentic images. The underlying principle in their work is that one type of feature can only detect a certain type of image forgery. Their method is resistant to blurring, noise and compression. They report that their model attains an accuracy of 92% in classifying tampered images and F-score of 92.5% on CASIA dataset outperforming AlexNet and VGG19.

A study conducted by Semwal et al. [12] proposed a copy-move forgery detection method based on SIFT algorithm. They characterize the workflow of copy-move forgery for feature extraction and matching of key-points and descriptors. Their method is based on agglomerative hierarchical clustering and link algorithm approach to generate the clusters of objects and classify them based on their similarity. Some of the drawbacks of their method is backtracking inability and quadratic time complexity. They report 90% accuracy of their model to classify copy-move forged images.

Another DL and CNN method for copy-move forgery detection was proposed by Kaya et al. [5] which is based on deep Residual Neural Network (ResNet50). Their approach takes into account the advantages of skip connections in ResNet. First they apply preprocessing operations like scaling, rotation, distortion etc. on the Copy-Move Forgery Detection Dataset (CoMoFoD) before feeding it in fine-tuned and pre-trained ResNet50. The skip connection skips some layers in between and connect the activations of a layer to the input of layers ahead. This is referred to as a residual block. Their model achieves a significantly good performance of forgery classification.

A socially commodious application specific method was proposed by Ghoneim et al. [13] of image forgery detection for smart healthcare. The underlying idea upon which their model is built is the noise present in an image. The make use of Weiner filter to first remove noise from an image and then subtract original image from noise-less image to get a noise pattern. This noise signature is considered as the noise signature. The manipulation of image also deteriorates the noise signature. Next, they apply multi-resolution regression filter to capture relative intensities of pixels. The classification of forged images is done by a pipelined structure of SVM, Extreme Learning Machine (ELM) and Bayesian sum rule (BSR). The score of BSR highlights whether the medical image is tampered or not. Their model achieves a classification accuracy of 84.3% on medical images.

In this section, we saw the previous works related to image forgery detection. A significant emphasis is put on deep learning techniques since they have proven to be extremely effective in addressing image tampering. Deep learning techniques are also being used in some related [14] as well as other tasks [15] involving image processing and feature extraction.

3   Proposed Methodology

This section discusses the proposed methodology employed for image forgery detection. The proposed methodology consists of image preprocessing, ELA analysis, feature extraction, model training, optimization and then comparison of performance of proposed CNN model to that of baselines CNN architectures like VGG16 and VGG19. Figure 4 represents the presents the framework and workflow of the proposed image forgery detection method.

3.1   Image Preprocessing

The images from the dataset are analyzed and preprocessed before further processing. This involves image denoising, ELA, image resizing and data balancing of the dataset

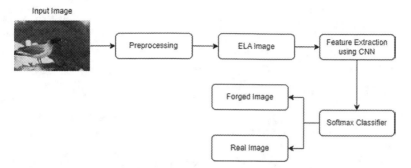

Fig. 4. Work flow of proposed methodology

samples. First, the images are denoised in the wavelet domain using the BayesShrink method. The denoising was also performed using the VisuShrink method, which delivered similar results. After denoising, the denoised images are subjected to Joint Photographic Experts Group (JPEG) compression at 80%. The ELA is estimated by taking the difference between the image and the resaved image at compression. The ELA feature maps the then resized to 128×128 to feed into the CNN model. The data imbalance is fixed by preparing a roughly equal-sized dataset of authentic and forged images.

3.2 Error Level Analysis

ELA is a widely used image processing technique used in forensic tasks. It is generally applied in the context of graphic images with lossy compression like JPEG based on DCT. Since its inception in 1992, JPEG has been a widely used image compression standard in the world. DCT is a mathematical operation that splits down an image into a series of cosine functions. These functions are then compressed using a variety of methods, such as quantization and Huffman coding. With JPEG compression, the size of huge images can be reduced. The degree of compression can be varied, allowing a desired tradeoff between the quality of the image and storage size. When an image is compressed and saved in JPEG format, the different regions of the image undergo loss of information which cannot be recovered. In other words, the regions of the image are introduced with errors in compression levels. Every region or part of the image has different error levels. ELA is a technique to identify and analyze the manipulated regions in images by detecting the errors introduced in those regions after being resaved as JPEG at a specific compression rate. If an image is manipulated and saved again, then the error levels in the manipulated regions will be higher than in other regions because every resave of the image as JPEG compresses the image and the information contained in the image is lost. ELA draws attention to these discrepancies in error levels in various regions in the image by calculating the difference between the original and tampered image as represented in the equation where f denotes the original image and $\tilde{f}$ denotes the tampered image (Eq. 1).

$$ELA(i,j) = f(i,j) - \tilde{f}(i,j) \tag{1}$$

This information can be used to assess if an image is forged or not. ELA works by considering grid or blocks of 8 × 8 pixels. These blocks define if the region of the image corresponding to that block is tampered or not.

Authentic Image – A JPEG image will be authentic or original if all 8 × 8 blocks have a similar error pattern and thus this 8 × 8 block can be said to have achieved local minima.

Forged Image – A JPEG image will be tampered if any 8 × 8 block has a highe error level and that 8 × 8 block is not at its local minima.

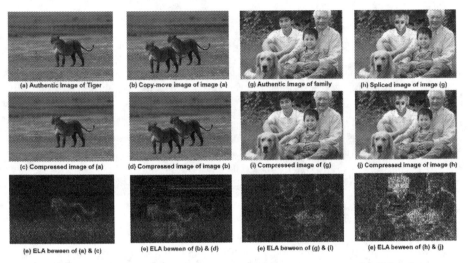

Fig. 5. Results of ELA difference in images based on copy-move and splicing forgery

The ELA process can be carried out by computing the differences between compression levels of a given when the image is resaved at different compression levels. When this process is carried out continuously for 1, 2, 3…., n times, error levels will reach very low values and the image will become dark. The process can be depicted as in Eq. 2 where I_{Pn} signifies an image resaved for n times of 100% quality setting, and I_{Qn} signifies an image recompressed for n times of 80% quality setting. Thus, Eq. 2 ELA equation can be said as "using ELA of 80%". Figure 5 highlights the intuition of ELA being used for forensic analysis of images. The two images depicted are resaved using JPEG compression after copy-move and splicing forgery. The artefacts of tampered regions are clearly highlighted in the ELA difference (Eq. 2).

$$I_{Pn}(i,j) - I_{Qn}(i,j) = ELA_n \tag{2}$$

3.3   CNN Architectures

VGG16

VGG16 (Visual Geometry Group 16) is a convolutional neural network (CNN) architecture that was proposed by the Visual Geometry Group at the University of Oxford in

2014. It gained significant attention and popularity for its simplicity and effectiveness in image classification tasks. The architecture of VGG16 is characterized by its deep structure, consisting of 16 layers, including 13 convolutional layers and 3 fully connected layers. The architecture is known for its use of small 3×3 convolutional filters throughout the network, along with max-pooling layers to down-sample the spatial dimensions. However, due to its depth and the large number of parameters, it also requires significant computational resources for training.

VGG19

VGG19 is an extension of the VGG16 architecture. VGG19 retains the same overall structure as VGG16 but includes 19 layers, making it slightly deeper. The increased depth allows it to potentially capture more complex features from input images. The architecture of VGG19 is similar to that of VGG16, with the main difference being the number of convolutional layers and fully connected layers. VGG19 has more parameters compared to VGG16 due to its increased depth, which can potentially allow it to learn more intricate features from input images. However, it also comes with increased computational requirements for training and inference.

3.4 Dataset Description

The CASIA Image Tampering Detection Evaluation Database [16] or CASIAv1 is a dataset for forgery classification. Over the years this dataset has been updated as CASIAv2 by adding more images with varied types of forgery. This dataset is designed for evaluating image tampering detection and forgery classification algorithms. It includes various types of image manipulations and tampering, such as copy-move forgery, splicing, and more. CASIAv2 contains 7491 authentic images and 5123 tampered images. Since the dataset contain unequal number of true and false samples, the dataset is balanced before training to prevent class imbalance bias in the model. This work only use jpg and png images from the dataset. From the original dataset, 2022 authentic image samples and 2064 forged image samples are extracted to create a balanced dataset of total 4086 images. The numbers are shown in Table 1.

Table 1. Details of CASIAv2 Dataset

Dataset	Image Type	Image Size	Original Dataset		Balanced Dataset	
			Authentic Images	Forged Images	Authentic Images	Forged Images
CASIAv2	jpg tiff bmp	240×160 to 900×600	7491 (60%)	5123 (40%)	**2022** (**~50%**)	**2064** (**~50%**)

3.5 Proposed System

CNN are type of artificial neural network which are specialized in processing data having a grid like structure, such as images. CNNs are used in a wide variety of applications, including image classification, object detection, and natural language processing. The proposed CNN model is a sequential model from the Keras library. The pre-processed and ELA images of size $128 \times 128 \times 3$ are first given input through two Conv2D layers having 32 filters each having a size of 5×5. Both Conv2D layers are set to have valid padding and output activation function of Rectified Linear Unit (ReLU). The second Conv2D layer is set for stride of 2. The output feature maps of these Conv2D layers are then fed to max pooling layer of size 2 to catch more prominent and maximum valued patches from the feature maps. To prevent overfitting of the model, the feature maps are then subjected to a dropout layer having a dropout rate of 25%. Next, the feature maps are flattened and the fed to a dense layer having 256 neurons and ReLU output. Another dropout is performed at rate of 50% and finally the input is fed to a dense layer having 2 neurons having softmax activation which classify the output as authentic image or forged image. A total of 7.4M parameters are optimized throughout the training process. Figure 6 highlights the structure of the proposed CNN model, size of intermediate feature maps and number of parameters.

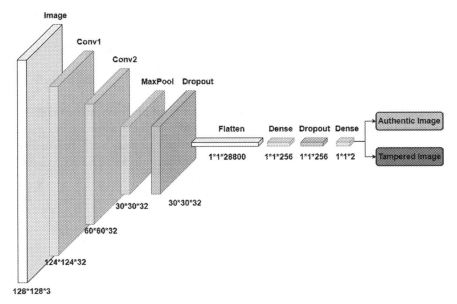

Fig. 6. Overview of proposed CNN model

3.6 Model Training

The balanced dataset of 4086 images is split into training and validation data in a ratio of 80:20 which gives 3268 training image and 818 validation images. The train data is subjected to image augmentation using ImageDataGenerator from the Keras library which provides a mechanism to expand the dataset and extract rich features while training. The model is first trained with training images along with augmented images for 30 epochs and batch size of 32. The augmented images contain images transformed with operations like rotation among which 20% are reserved for validation split. The optimized used is RMSprop, learning rate of 0.0004 and loss method of binary cross entropy. After this, a second training phase constitutes of 30 epochs, Adam optimizer, learning rate of 0.0004. The results obtained are analyzed and discussed in the next section.

4 Results and Discussion

4.1 Evaluation Metrics

The evaluation of the proposed model is performed on some standard and industry accepted techniques after analyzing the performance of the model on validation dataset. This include Confusion Matrix (Fig. 7) which is a table showing the counts of true positives (TP), true negatives (TN), false positives (FP), and false negatives (FN). Precision (P) is the proportion of TP predictions among all positive predictions (Eq. 3). It measures the model's ability to avoid FP. Recall (R) is the proportion of true positive predictions among all actual positives (Eq. 4). It measures the model's ability to find all relevant instances. F1-score or F-score is the harmonic mean of precision and recall (Eq. 5). It balances precision and recall and is useful when you want to consider both false positives and false negatives. Accuracy (Acc) is the ratio of correctly predicted instances to the total instances (Eq. 6). It's commonly used for balanced datasets but can be misleading for imbalanced datasets. ROC AUC (Receiver Operating Characteristic Area Under the Curve) measures the ability of a model to distinguish between classes across different thresholds.

$$P = \frac{TP}{TP + FP} \tag{3}$$

$$R = \frac{TP}{TP + FN} \tag{4}$$

$$F1\ Score = 2 \times \frac{P \times R}{P + R} \tag{5}$$

$$Acc = \frac{TP + TN}{TP + TN + FP + FN} \tag{6}$$

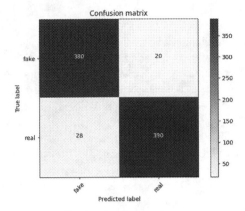

Fig. 7. Confusion Matrix

4.2 Results

The proposed model achieves an accuracy of 0.94 (Fig. 8), precision of 0.94, recall of 0.94, F-score of 0.94, error of 0.18 (Fig. 9) and AUC-ROC of 0.94 (Fig. 10) on validation data. The model also achieves an accuracy of 0.91 on the entire dataset. The proposed outperforms the VGG-16 and VGG-19 in terms of the evaluation metrics discussed. The comparative results are shown in Table 2.

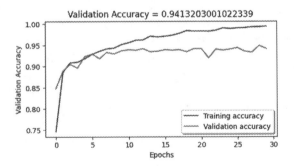

Fig. 8. Training-Validation Accuracy Plot

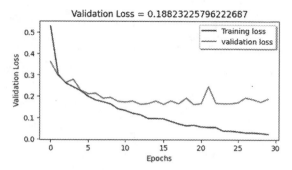

Fig. 9. Training-Validation Loss Plot

Table 2. Results of proposed methodology and baseline CNN architectures on validation data

Model	Accuracy	Precision	Recall	F-score	Error	AUC-ROC
VGG16	0.92	0.72	0.72	0.72	0.30	0.91
VGG19	0.90	0.69	0.69	0.69	0.36	0.89
Proposed ELA+CNN model	**0.94**	**0.95**	**0.93**	**0.94**	**0.18**	**0.94**

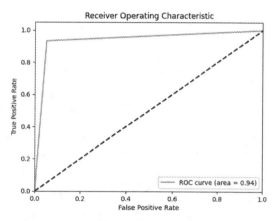

Fig. 10. AUC-ROC curve

5 Conclusion and Future Scope

This paper proposed an image forgery detection method based on ELA and CNN. ELA is an image processing technique used for detecting inconsistencies and potential manipulation using compression artefacts of images with lossy compression. The proposed method used ELA, which is pipelined to a CNN model. The analysis is performed on the standard CASIAv2 dataset which consists of 7491 authentic images and 5123 forged images. The proposed method attains a superior accuracy of 94% and an F-score of 94%.

The result reveals that the proposed model outperforms other pre-trained baseline models like VGG16 and VGG19. For future work, more robust feature extraction methods can be employed to obtain even optimized results. Different types of forgeries may also be addressed like copy move, camera based, geometric based forgeries in future.

References

1. Duang, Y., Wang, Y., Cao, C., Zhang, X.: Research on digital watermarking algorithm based on discrete cosine transform. In: 2022 15th International Congress on Image and Signal Processing, BioMedical Engineering and Informatics (CISP-BMEI), pp. 1–6. IEEE (2022)
2. Wang, R., Lin, C., Zhao, Q., Zhu, F.: Watermark faker: towards forgery of digital image watermarking. In: 2021 IEEE International Conference on Multimedia and Expo (ICME), pp. 1–6. IEEE (2021)
3. Sharma, P., Kumar, M., Sharma, H.: Comprehensive analyses of image forgery detection methods from traditional to deep learning approaches: an evaluation. Multimed. Tools Appl. **82**(12), 18117–18150 (2023)
4. Nabi, S.T., Kumar, M., Singh, P., Aggarwal, N., Kumar, K.: A comprehensive survey of image and video forgery techniques: variants, challenges, and future directions. Multimed. Syst. **28**(3), 939–992 (2022)
5. Kaya, M., Sani, K.J., Karakuş, S.: Copy-move forgery detection in digital forensic images using CNN. In: 2022 7th International Conference on Computer Science and Engineering (UBMK), pp. 239–245. IEEE (2022)
6. Tyagi, S., Yadav, D.: A detailed analysis of image and video forgery detection techniques. Vis. Comput. **39**, 813–833 (2023). https://doi.org/10.1007/s00371-021-02347-4
7. Zhang, Y., Shi, T., Lu, Z.M.: Image splicing detection scheme based on error level analysis and local binary pattern. Netw. Intell **6**, 303–312 (2021)
8. Rao, Y., Ni, J.: A deep learning approach to detection of splicing and copy-move forgeries in images. In: 2016 IEEE International Workshop on Information Forensics and Security (WIFS), pp. 1–6. IEEE (2016)
9. Roshini, C.M.B., Saveetha, D.: A novel approach to image forgery detection. In: 2022 International Conference on Computer Communication and Informatics (ICCCI), pp. 1–5. IEEE (2022)
10. Niloy, F.F., Bhaumik, K.K., Woo, S.S.: CFL-Net: image forgery localization using contrastive learning. In: Proceedings of the IEEE/CVF Winter Conference on Applications of Computer Vision, pp. 4642–4651 (2023)
11. Kaushik, M.S., Kandali, A.B.: Convolutional neural network based digital image forensics using random forest and SVM classifier. In: 2023 International Conference on Intelligent Data Communication Technologies and Internet of Things (IDCIoT), pp. 860–865. IEEE (2023)
12. Semwal, A., Kumar, A., Saveetha, D.: Copy move image forgery detection using machine learning. In: 2023 International Conference on Computer Communication and Informatics (ICCCI), pp. 1–9. IEEE (2023)
13. Ghoneim, A., Muhammad, G., Amin, S.U., Gupta, B.: Medical image forgery detection for smart healthcare. IEEE Commun. Mag. **56**(4), 33–37 (2018)
14. Kaur, S., et al.: Optimizing fast Fourier transform (FFT) image compression using intelligent water drop (IWD) algorithm (2022)
15. Khurshid, S., Ansari, A., Verma, A., Singh, P.P., Khari, M.: FaceTrace: automated facial recognition attendance system. In: Sustainable Science and Intelligent Technologies for Societal Development, pp. 178–193. IGI Global (2023)
16. Dong, J., Wang, W., Tan, T.: CASIA image tampering detection evaluation database. In: 2013 IEEE China Summit and International Conference on Signal and Information Processing, pp. 422–426. IEEE (2013)

Leveraging Wavelets and Deep CNN for Sleep Pattern Recognition in Road Safety: An EEG Study

Saad Arif[1]([✉])[ID], Saba Munawar[2][ID], Rashiq Rafiq Marie[3], and Syed Aziz Shah[4][ID]

[1] Department of Mechanical Engineering, HITEC University, Taxila 47080, Pakistan
saad.arif@hitecuni.edu.pk
[2] Department of Electrical and Computer Engineering, COMSATS University Islamabad, Wah Campus, Wah Cantt 47040, Pakistan
sabamunawar@ciitwah.edu.pk
[3] College of Computer Science and Engineering, Taibah University, Medina 41477, Saudi Arabia
rmarie@taibahu.edu.sa
[4] Research Centre for Intelligent Healthcare, Coventry University, Coventry CV1 5FB, UK
syed.shah@coventry.ac.uk

Abstract. A major cause of fatal traffic accidents and injuries worldwide is drowsy driving. The fatal aftereffects can be considerably reduced, and road safety can rise, with earlier and more efficient diagnosis. In this study, electroencephalography (EEG) biosignals-based brain-computer interface (BCI) is established for early identification of human inattentiveness during driving activities. EEG signals are recorded from six EEG electrode positions viz Fp1, Fp2, F7, F8, O1, and O2. Spectral information of the alpha and beta frequency bands is extracted in terms of continuous wavelet transform (CWT) with a temporal correlation for complete experiments. CWT components are processed as scalograms which are color images used for visual inspection of brain states. The scalogram images of 10 s epochs are stored as the image dataset. The SqueezeNet deep convolutional neural network (CNN) is fine-tuned with transfer learning for effective drowsiness detection from CWT scalograms. Transfer-learned CNN classification model achieved the best results with 89.8% accuracy, 88.0% precision, 96.1% recall, 89.9% F_1-score, 87.7% specificity, and 79.7% Matthew's correlation coefficient. The statistical significance of the achieved results is validated with a p-value of less than 0.05. Using wavelet information of EEG biosignals, the suggested BCI methodology offers a viable method for quicker and more accurate driving drowsiness detection.

Keywords: SqueezeNet · Deep learning · Electroencephalography · Wavelet transform · Transfer learning · Brain-computer interface · Sleep detection

KC Santosh et al. (Eds.): RTIP2R 2023, CCIS 2026, pp. 227–241, 2024.
https://doi.org/10.1007/978-3-031-53082-1_19

1   Introduction

Globally, drowsy driving has a significant role in traffic fatalities and injuries [1, 2]. The severe consequences of such occurrences highlight the critical need for preventative measures that might both reduce the frequency of catastrophic accidents and improve overall road safety [3]. To prevent the devastating effects of sleepy driving, early identification of driver drowsiness provides a vital approach, inspiring the merging of neuroscience and technology to create novel solutions. In this context, a possible method to quickly identify cognitive states linked to tiredness during driving activities is the combination of electroencephalography (EEG) biosignals with a brain-computer interface (BCI).

The danger of sleepy driving has prompted many studies into new techniques for its early detection [4]. Traditional approaches that rely on eye movements and steering behavior have limitations in terms of fast and precise identification [5]. This has prompted researchers to investigate alternate paths, especially EEG-based BCIs. EEG signals are especially useful for tracking cognitive states because they provide clear insights into brain processes [6]. Previous research has used EEG data to reliably identify sleepiness, frequently concentrating on spectrum analysis and brain oscillations [7,8]. However, this study uses a combination of deep convolutional neural networks (CNN) and wavelet analysis to enhance the drowsiness detection's precision and effectiveness.

A potential area to address the complexity of EEG data is the connection of wavelet analysis and deep CNN [7,9]. Wavelet analysis makes it easier to separate EEG data into their component frequencies and reveal the prominent rhythmic patterns connected to different cognitive states, such as sleep, fatigue, etc. By combining a continuous wavelet transform (CWT) with temporal correlations, this method improves the extraction of spectrum information. Scalograms, which are graphical visual representations of brain states, are created from the resulting CWT components, allowing for a greater understanding of neural dynamics. Additionally, deep CNNs, which are key components of modern pattern recognition, have a stronger capability of extracting and classifying the complex characteristics in data [10–12]. Transfer learning of CNN-based classification models has been widely investigated in medical imaging [13,14] and processing other biosignal modalities [15]. A SqueezeNet deep CNN is augmented and improved with transfer learning which makes it more effective at identifying drowsiness-related and other patterns in CWT scalograms.

The combination of wavelet and spectral analysis along with deep CNN for tiredness detection in driving situations has made good progress in previous studies [16,17], along with many applications in other areas as well [18,19], but it is still underexplored. The purpose of this study is to close this gap by demonstrating the advantages of this integrated methodology. This research improves the discussion on sleep detection with developments covering neuroscience, signal processing, and machine learning by utilizing the power of EEG-based BCIs, wavelet analysis, and deep CNN. The remaining sections of this paper explore the methodology in terms of experimental setting, data acquisition and preprocessing, CWT scalogram dataset generation, transfer learning of deep CNN model, comprehensive results, and conclusions. This study provides a thorough examination of this cutting-edge strategy for improving driving safety.

2   Methodology

2.1   Data Acquisition

In this study, the EEG dataset from another study [20] has been used for drowsiness detection. This multichannel EEG data is acquired from 16 channels in the anterior, posterior, and dorsolateral regions of the brain according to the international 10–20 system of electrode placement. EEG biosignals are recorded from frontal (FC), prefrontal (PFC), occipital (OC), and other cortices in both the right and left hemispheres of the subject's brain. Data from two channels in each of the above-mentioned cortices are selected for further analysis of the brain signals. The selected channels F7, F8, Fp1, Fp2, O1, and O2 are reported to be effective for earlier drowsiness detection using neurological signals [8, 21, 22]. The raw EEG data is acquired using OpenBCI Ultracortex Mark IV EEG headset from five healthy subjects engaged in simulated driving experiments while focusing on lane-keeping tasks. Figure 1 shows the experiment recording setup showing the OpenBCI graphical user interface in the left half, while the right half shows the live feed of the subject and his simulated driving performance. The electrode placement is shown in the lower left corner of Fig. 1 in which numbers represent 16 EEG channels placed at various positions of the brain according to Table 1. The data is acquired around the peak drowsy time of 3 AM for almost 30 min of driving duration. The drowsiness and fatigue biomarkers were carefully examined during posthoc analysis of the experimental recording and data labels were assigned accordingly. All the subjects were briefed about the experiment and asked to willingly consent the participation in this study by submitting verbal and written consent. All the subjects were enquired about any history of visual, psychological, or mental disorders before the experimentation. All experiments were performed according to the latest declarations of Helsinki.

2.2   Data Preprocessing

The acquired raw EEG data from the selected channels is preprocessed to obtain the filtered signals. For this purpose, Gaussian bandpass and notch-reject filters were applied to remove the artifacts and other noises. Electrical interference attenuation was removed using the notch filters at 50 and 60 Hz frequencies. The informative EEG bands lie in the range of 0.5–35 Hz in various frequency bands viz delta (δ), theta (θ), alpha (α), beta (β), and gamma (γ) with ranges 0.5–4 Hz, 4–8 Hz, 8–13 Hz, 13–25 Hz, and 25–35 Hz, respectively. The raw signals were filtered with the Butterworth lowpass filter in these band ranges to remove the >35 Hz artifacts. The bandpass filtering was also used to remove respiratory and Mayer wave artifacts in ranges 0.3–0.4 Hz and <0.01 Hz, respectively. For earlier drowsiness detection, the 10 s detection window is employed in

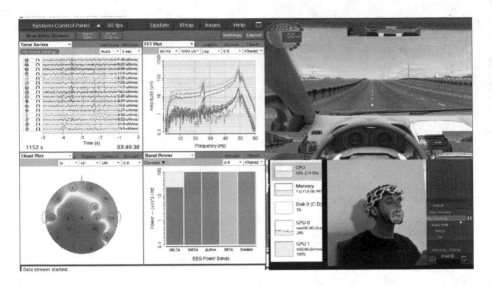

Fig. 1. Experiment recording setup for biomarking and posthoc analysis of EEG biosignals.

Table 1. EEG electrode placement in Ultracortex Mark IV EEG headset.

Channel Number	Electrode Position	Brain Cortex
1	Fp1	Prefrontal
2	Fp2	
3	C3	Central
4	C4	
5	P7	Parietal
6	P8	
7	O1	Occipital
8	O2	
9	F7	Frontal
10	F8	
11	F3	
12	F4	
13	T7	Temporal
14	T8	
15	P3	Parietal
16	P4	

this study. In this perspective, the filtered EEG signals from all channels were divided into 10 s epochs in which frequency band variations were observed as representative features of drowsy and alert brain states. Figure 2 shows a representative time signal for 10 s epoch of alert state and its power spectrum against EEG band frequencies. The signal power dominance in β band can be observed which represents alertness activity.

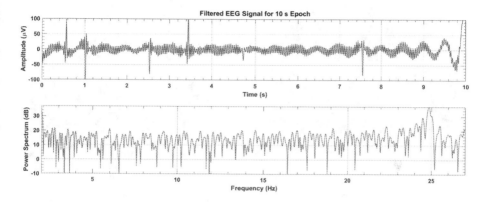

Fig. 2. Filtered EEG biosignal for 10 s epoch of alert state (top), with signal power distribution among the EEG bands (bottom).

2.3   Continuous Wavelet Transform

The signal variations and transitions in the non-stationary EEG signals can be best captured using wavelet transform which is an effective method for pattern recognition in biosignals. CWT has been widely used to extract features and patterns from electrocardiography (ECG), electromyography (EMG), EEG, and other physiological modalities [23]. It has been observed that transition patterns between drowsy and alert brain states in EEG data can be distinguished and detected from CWT-based scalograms [24]. Wavelets are effective in extracting both the temporal and spectral properties of signals in the time-frequency domain. The CWT of the EEG signal is computed using the following equation.

$$W_x(s,\tau) = \frac{1}{\sqrt{|s|}} \int_{-\infty}^{\infty} x(t)\overline{\psi}\left(\frac{t-\tau}{s}\right) dt \qquad (1)$$

where $x(t)$ is the EEG signal, $\psi(t)$ is the continuous mother wavelet function, s is the scale factor, τ is the translational length parameter, and W_x is the wavelet transform of the signal over the specified translational length or epoch.

Figure 3 shows the scalograms computed for 10 s epochs representing CWT coefficients with temporal and spectral correlation. Figure 3a shows the CWT variations in all EEG frequency bands. It is observed that the notable variations are present in the α and β bands because they represent drowsy and alert brain states, respectively. To capture the state variations better, the drowsy and alert patterns are plotted in the range of 8–25 Hz for further analysis as shown in Fig. 3b. The scalograms are generated in MATLAB 9.12 (MathWorks, USA) using *cwtfilterbank* and *wt* built-in functions. Analytic Morse wavelet with 125 Hz sampling frequency, 48 number of voices per octave, 10 s signal length, and 8–25 Hz frequency limits are used in the CWT filter bank.

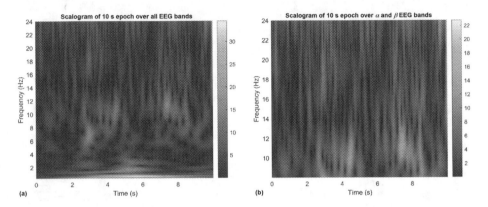

Fig. 3. Scalogram showing wavelet power spectrum for 10 s epoch over: **(a)** all EEG frequency band ranges, and **(b)** α and β EEG bands.

2.4   Dataset Generation

These scalogram images are generated for 10 s sequenced epochs of the filtered EEG signals over the complete length of the experiment. The image dataset is created and stored for all the subjects and selected channels with state labels for further classification using CNN. Figure 4a shows the distribution of dataset samples among drowsy and alert classes. There are 4,380 scalogram image samples in total from five subjects and six EEG channels with 52.47% and 47.53% class probabilities in drowsy and alert classes, respectively. Some of the class samples with labels are shown in Fig. 4b. The scalograms are stored in respective class-named folders as colored portable network graphics (PNG) images of 456×361 pixels resolution.

2.5   Data Preparation and Transfer Learning

The deep CNN architectures are widely used for image-based classification of physiological states using biosignal modalities like EMG, ECG, and EEG etc. Various CNN models like SqueezeNet, GoogLeNet, ResNet50, AlexNet, etc. are used for transfer learning or feature extraction in such applications [25]. In this study, the SqueezeNet CNN is used for transfer learning for the detection of drowsiness and alert patterns. It has 68 layers in total and 1.2 million learnable parameters with multiple 2D convolution, ReLU, max-pooling, and concatenation layers. It also includes a dropout layer to prevent overfitting. The

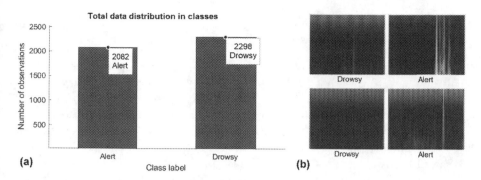

Fig. 4. **(a)** Class distribution of complete dataset among classes (all subjects, all channels), **(b)** random sample images from both classes.

pretrained SqueezeNet network is retrained on more than a million images of various objects stored in the ImageNet database. It has a rich feature set and comparatively simpler architecture which is efficient in achieving better accuracies with less computational cost and training time. SqueezeNet has shown effective performance with transfer learning in various studies [18].

For classification in this work, the pretrained SqueezeNet model is fine-tuned on the scalogram images dataset using transfer learning. For this purpose, the last 2D convolution layer and terminal classification layer in the pretrained network are replaced with the new layers having updated parameters. The new 2D convolution layer is set to have two filters of filter size 1×1 for this binary classification problem. The learning rate factor is set to 10 for weights and bias of this layer to speed up learning at this stage so that the scalogram features are learned effectively during fine-tuning. Additionally, the learning rate of transferred layers is decreased by setting the initial learning rate to a lower value. The new classification layer is set to have an output size of two which is equal to the number of output classes, and it uses cross-entropy loss function for training validations. The pretrained network is loaded using *squeezenet*, trained using *trainNetwork*, and classification is performed using *classify* built-in functions of MATLAB 9.12.

As the SqueezeNet architecture accepts colored images of size $227 \times 227 \times 3$ at the input layer, various image augmentation transformations are applied to the stored data before training. Image augmentation steps also assist in preventing model overfitting by applying random image transformations, such as scaling, rotation, translation, mirroring, etc. In the dataset preparation procedure, the augmented image datastore is obtained by applying random rotations in the range of $-90°$ to $+90°$, random rescaling up to $2\times$, and random mirroring about the y-axis. The dataset is also resized to match the network input size at this step. Furthermore, the training-to-validation ratio is set to 70:30 before model training.

2.6   Performance Assessment Metrics

The confusion matrix-based performance metrics are used to evaluate the classifier prediction results. Accuracy, precision or positive predictive value (PPV), recall or true positive rate (TPR), F_1-score, specificity or true negative rate (TNR), and Mathew's correlation coefficient (MCC) are computed to assess the classification performance. The "drowsy" state label is taken as a positive class or 'P' and the "alert" state label is regarded as a negative class or 'N'. True positive (TP) and true negative (TN) represent the correctly predicted samples in drowsy and alert classes, respectively. On the other hand, false negative (FN) and false positive (FP) represent the wrongly classified samples. FN are the drowsy samples that are falsely predicted as alert, while FP are the alert samples that are wrongly classified as drowsy. Based on these four, the above-mentioned six metrics are computed according to the formulas shown in Table 2.

Table 2. Confusion matrix-based performance assessment metrics with their formulas.

Metric	Formula
Accuracy	$\frac{TP+TN}{TP+FN+FP+TN}$
Precision, PPV	$\frac{TP}{TP+FP}$
Recall, TPR	$\frac{TP}{TP+FN}$
F_1-score	$\frac{2 \times TP}{2 \times TP+FP+FN}$
Specificity, TNR	$\frac{TN}{FP+TN}$
MCC	$\frac{TP \times TN - FP \times FN}{\sqrt{(TP+FP)(TP+FN)(TN+FP)(TN+FN)}}$

3   Results and Discussion

The augmented image dataset is further split randomly into training and validation data with a 70:30 ratio. 70% of the randomly selected samples are used for model fine-tuning according to class distribution probability, and 30% of the samples are used for model validation at set validation frequency in each training epoch. To initiate the transfer learning process, various training parameters are set before training. The stochastic gradient descent with momentum (SGDM) optimizer is used for training with an initial learning rate of 0.0001 to slow down the training in the initial layers of the CNN. The number of training epochs and number of iterations per epoch are set to 20 and 12, respectively. The validation frequency is set to 10 iterations which ensures at least one validation process in each training epoch. A total of 240 training iterations are performed for each channel CNN. The execution environment is set to use on-board NVIDIA GeForce GTX 1050 GPU with 2.0 GB dedicated memory. The sample shuffling is set to be performed after each epoch to avoid overfitting, and SGDM momentum is set to 0.9. After setting these training parameters, the training process is initiated to fine-tune the SqueezeNet for the classification of drowsy and alert scalograms. The training process is stopped if maximum epochs are completed, or the cross-entropy validation loss does not decrease further after five consecutive validation instances. The fine-tuned model outputs the validation accuracy which is achieved at the lowest validation loss among all the validation instances during the training process. This transfer learning approach is used to get trained CNN networks for channel-wise data of all subjects. Figure 5 and 6 show the training accuracy and training loss profiles, respectively, for the Fp2 and F8 channels which achieved the highest training accuracies with the lowest validation losses. Model training for the channel Fp2 dataset achieved the best training accuracy of 97.62% and lowest training loss of 0.1361, while for the channel F8 dataset, CNN achieved the highest training accuracy of 95.24% and lowest training loss of 0.1809. Table 3 shows the training and validation results of the SqueezeNet CNN for all the six selected channels.

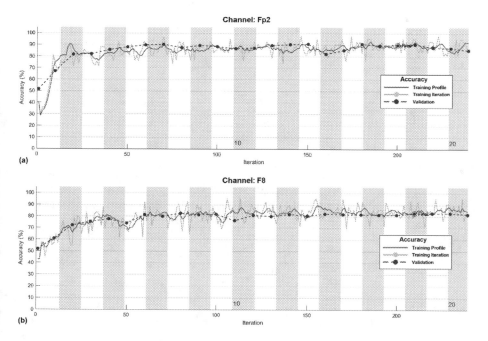

Fig. 5. SqueezeNet training accuracy profile over all subjects' data for channels: **(a)** Fp2, and **(b)** F8.

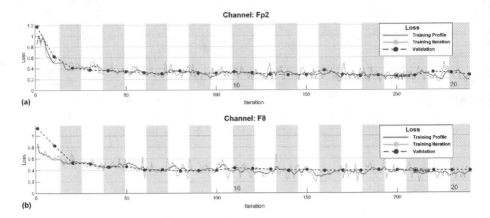

Fig. 6. SqueezeNet cross-entropy loss profile over all subjects' data for channels: **(a)** Fp2, and **(b)** F8.

Table 3. Deep CNN training and validation results for all EEG channels.

Channel	Training Accuracy (%)	Training Loss	Validation Accuracy (%)	Validation Loss
Fp1	92.86	0.2302	74.55	0.5141
Fp2	97.62	0.1361	89.95	0.2535
F7	90.48	0.2797	77.17	0.5510
F8	95.24	0.1809	82.73	0.3798
O1	90.48	0.2877	72.73	0.4915
O2	95.24	0.1620	81.74	0.3596

The trained networks are tested to classify the augmented image data of all the channels with augmentation transformations like random scaling, random rotation, and random mirroring with random shuffling of test samples in both classes. Figure 7 shows randomly selected samples from CNN prediction results with scalograms and their predicted labels. This classification test on O2 channel scalograms achieved 84.56% accuracy.

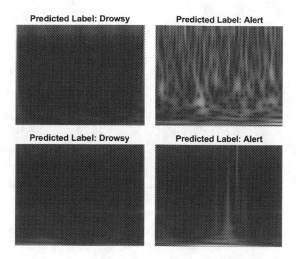

Fig. 7. Random samples of CNN prediction results (Channel O2).

Figure 8 shows the classification results of all the performance assessment metrics in all the selected channels over all subjects' data. The highest classification accuracy, precision, and F_1-score of 89.8%, 88%, and 89.9%, respectively, has been achieved for the Fp2 channel, and the highest recall or TPR of 96.1% is achieved for O2 channel. Channel F8 results are the second highest after the Fp2 channel. It has been observed that the right hemisphere of the brain (Fp2, F8, O2) is more promising for earlier drowsiness detection as compared to the left hemisphere (Fp1, F7, O1). Observations of this study are in complete agreement with the results achieved by previous works [4, 8, 20–22].

Figure 9 shows the subject-wise classification results of all performance indicators over all channels' data. The best classification results of 86% MCC and 93% for all other metrics, except recall, are achieved for subject 4, while the highest recall of 98% is achieved for subject 3. Overall, the classification results are very promising for all the subjects with mean results of 89% accuracy, 87% precision, 94% recall, 90% F_1-score, 83% specificity, and 78% MCC.

Confusion matrices for CNN prediction results are shown in Fig. 10. The diagonal and off-diagonal entries show the normalized sample distribution among TP, TN, FP, and FN. The right columns show TPR and false negative rate (FNR), and the bottom rows show PPV and false detection rate (FDR) for both drowsy and alert classes. Figure 10a and 10b show the confusion matrices of best-performing CNNs for channel Fp2 and subject 4, respectively.

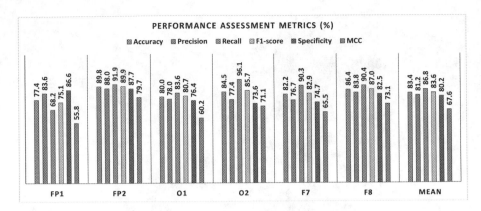

Fig. 8. Channel wise results of all performance assessment metrics with best classification accuracy (for all subjects' data).

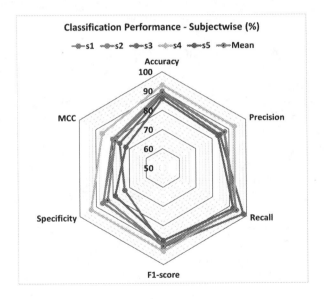

Fig. 9. Subject-wise results of all performance assessment metrics with best classification accuracy (for all channels' data).

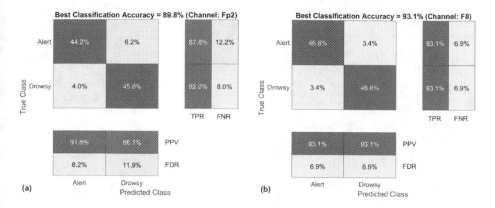

Fig. 10. Normalized confusion matrix showing CNN prediction results for: **(a)** channel Fp2 over all subjects' data, **(b)** subject 4 in channel F8.

4 Conclusions

This study establishes a novel and effective approach for early drowsiness detection during driving tasks by harnessing the synergy of wavelet analysis and deep convolutional neural networks (CNN). The integration of brain-computer interface technology, electroencephalography (EEG) signal processing, and advanced deep learning techniques holds promising potential in addressing the critical issue of drowsy driving and its consequences for road safety. Research findings demonstrate that the proposed system, based on continuous wavelet transform (CWT) scalograms and a fine-tuned SqueezeNet deep CNN, achieves remarkable accuracy, precision, recall, F_1-score, specificity, and Matthew's correlation coefficient. By investigating and analyzing EEG-based neural oscillations associated with drowsiness, this work contributes to the research at the intersection of neuroscience, signal processing, and artificial intelligence. In future work, refinements to the model architecture, inclusion of a wider participant pool, and real-world deployment could further enhance the system's robustness and applicability. Ultimately, the advancement of drowsiness detection through innovative technologies underscores its potential to significantly enhance road safety and mitigate the risks posed by drowsy driving.

References

1. Alotaibi, M., Alotaibi, B.: Distracted driver classification using deep learning. SIViP **14**(3), 617–624 (2020)
2. Kashevnik, A., Shchedrin, R., Kaiser, C., Stocker, A.: Driver distraction detection methods: a literature review and framework. IEEE Access **9**, 60063–60076 (2021)
3. Ghandorh, H., Boulila, W., Masood, S., Koubaa, A., Ahmed, F., Ahmad, J.: Semantic segmentation and edge detection-approach to road detection in very high resolution satellite images. Remote Sens. **14**(3), 613 (2022)

4. Arif, S., Khan, M.J., Naseer, N., Hong, K.S., Sajid, H., Ayaz, Y.: Vector phase analysis approach for sleep stage classification: a functional near-infrared spectroscopy-based passive brain-computer interface. Front. Hum. Neurosci. **15**, 658444 (2021)

5. Asl, N.S., Baghdadi, G., Ebrahimian, S., Haghighi, S.J.: Toward applicable EEG-based drowsiness detection systems: a review. Front. Biomed. Technol. (2022)

6. Zeng, H., et al.: An EEG-based transfer learning method for cross-subject fatigue mental state prediction. Sensors **21**(7), 2369 (2021)

7. Jadhav, P., Rajguru, G., Datta, D., Mukhopadhyay, S.: Automatic sleep stage classification using time-frequency images of CWT and transfer learning using convolution neural network. Biocybern. Biomed. Eng. **40**(1), 494–504 (2020)

8. Arif, S., Munawar, S., Ali, H.: Driving drowsiness detection using spectral signatures of EEG-based neurophysiology. Front. Physiol. **14**, 1153268 (2023)

9. Kumar, J.L.M., et al.: The classification of EEG-based wink signals: a CWT-transfer learning pipeline. ICT Expr. **7**(4), 421–425 (2021)

10. Ahmed, F., et al.: A DNA based colour image encryption scheme using a convolutional autoencoder. ACM Trans. Multimed. Comput. Commun. Appl. **19**(3s), 1–21 (2023)

11. Driss, K., Boulila, W., Batool, A., Ahmad, J.: A novel approach for classifying diabetes' patients based on imputation and machine learning. In: 2020 International Conference on UK-China Emerging Technologies (UCET), pp. 1–4. IEEE (2020)

12. Khalil, S., et al.: Enhancing ductal carcinoma classification using transfer learning with 3D U-net models in breast cancer imaging. Appl. Sci. **13**(7), 4255 (2023)

13. Rehman, M.U., et al.: A novel chaos-based privacy-preserving deep learning model for cancer diagnosis. IEEE Trans. Netw. Sci. Eng. **9**(6), 4322–4337 (2022)

14. Shahzad, A., et al.: Automated uterine fibroids detection in ultrasound images using deep convolutional neural networks. Healthcare **11**(10), 1493 (2023)

15. Qureshi, M.F., Mushtaq, Z., ur Rehman, M.Z., Kamavuako, E.N.: Spectral image-based multiday surface electromyography classification of hand motions using CNN for human-computer interaction. IEEE Sens. J. **22**(21), 20676–20683 (2022)

16. Subasi, A., Saikia, A., Bagedo, K., Singh, A., Hazarika, A.: EEG-based driver fatigue detection using FAWT and multiboosting approaches. IEEE Trans. Industr. Inf. **18**(10), 6602–6609 (2022)

17. Ahmadi, A., Bazregarzadeh, H., Kazemi, K.: Automated detection of driver fatigue from electroencephalography through wavelet-based connectivity. Biocybern. Biomed. Eng. **41**(1), 316–332 (2021)

18. Saad, A., Usman, A., Arif, S., Liwicki, M., Almqvist, A.: Bearing fault detection scheme using machine learning for condition monitoring applications. In: International Conference on Mechanical, Automotive and Mechatronics Engineering (ICMAME 2023), 29–30 April 2023, Dubai, UAE. ICMAME (2023)

19. Ali, I., Mushtaq, Z., Arif, S., Algarni, A.D., Soliman, N.F., El-Shafai, W.: Hyperspectral images-based crop classification scheme for agricultural remote sensing. Comput. Syst. Sci. Eng. **46**, 303–319 (2023)

20. Arif, S., Arif, M., Munawar, S., Ayaz, Y., Khan, M.J., Naseer, N.: EEG spectral comparison between occipital and prefrontal cortices for early detection of driver drowsiness. In: 2021 International Conference on Artificial Intelligence and Mechatronics Systems (AIMS), pp. 1–6. IEEE (2021)

21. Cui, J., et al.: A compact and interpretable convolutional neural network for cross-subject driver drowsiness detection from single-channel eeg. Methods **202**, 173–184 (2022)

22. Kim, D.Y., Han, D.K., Jeong, J.H., Lee, S.W.: EEG-based driver drowsiness classification via calibration-free framework with domain generalization. In: 2022 IEEE International Conference on Systems, Man, and Cybernetics (SMC), pp. 2293–2298. IEEE (2022)

23. Loh, H.W., et al.: Automated detection of sleep stages using deep learning techniques: a systematic review of the last decade (2010–2020). Appl. Sci. **10**(24), 8963 (2020)

24. Khosla, A., Khandnor, P., Chand, T.: A comparative analysis of signal processing and classification methods for different applications based on EEG signals. Biocybern. Biomed. Eng. **40**(2), 649–690 (2020)

25. Boulila, W., Ghandorh, H., Khan, M.A., Ahmed, F., Ahmad, J.: A novel CNN-LSTM-based approach to predict urban expansion. Eco. Inform. **64**, 101325 (2021)

Recognition and Transcription of Archaic Handwritten Modi Script Document: A Thought-Provoking Crucial Research Area

Manisha S. Deshmukh$^{(\boxtimes)}$ (iD) and Satish R. Kolhe(iD)

School of Computer Sciences, Kavayitri Bahinabai Chaudhari North Maharashtra
University, Jalgaon, Jalgaon, India
manisha_d7@rediffmail.com

Abstract. Massive volume of significant information is found in the archived handwritten Modi script historical documents. Automatic pre-processing and recognition of these Modi script documents is required for the number of reasons like document archiving, transcription, transliteration and so on. One crucial need is the information retrieval and at present, there are countable Modi script experts. Intelligent handwritten historical Modi script document recognition is a crucial research work. Each stage of this intelligent recognition system becomes complex due to number of reasons like cursive and stylish writing nature of Modi script and degraded unconstrained handwritten documents. To the best of our knowledge, there is no survey in this field and there is a need of an analysis to know the state-of-art. An attempt is made in this paper to present state-of-art in recognition of these documents and Modi script characters. It reflects necessity of this research for current era and focuses on the future perspective with challenges. It comprehensively presents analysis of the results reported up to the date for various methods proposed in the stages of the Modi script document recognition system such as degradation detection and removal; Skew Detection and Correction; text line and character segmentation; Modi script alphabet feature extraction and classification of the ancient handwritten Modi script document. The paper has a widespread bibliography of standard references as an encouragement for researchers working in the field of intelligent handwritten archaic Modi script document recognition.

Keywords: Modi Script · handwritten ancient script · preprocessing · segmentation · classification · intelligent document recognition

1 Introduction

Cursive, stylish, Brahmi-based ancient Modi script (Modi Lipi) is derived from Nagari family. This script was used as administrative script during 1260–1309 up to 19th century to write Marathi language in Maharashtra. This script is adopted

Supported by organization x.

due to two main reasons as: i) speedy writing and ii) short form of the phrases. It was also used to write at national and international provinces to write the languages like Hindi, Gujarati, Kannada, Persian etc. The thousands of very old official documents, literatures, books, etc. written in Modi script are preserved at libraries, administrative departments, Government, Non-Government, judicial offices. Modi script has many elevations in writing styles as per the different centuries as given in Table 1. Modi script documents written in different styles and in different centuries are shown in Fig. 1 [1].

Table 1. Variations of Modi script writing style.

Modi script Style	Century/Duration
Adyakalin (proto-Modi script)	12th century
Yadavakalin	13th century
Bahamanikalin	14th to 16th century
Shivakalin	17th century
Peshvekalin	18th century
Anglakalin (Bristishkalin)	1818 until 1952

(a)   (b)   (c)   (d)   (e)

Fig. 1. Example of Modi script documents [1,2] (a) Bahamani style (b) Shivakalin Abhayapatra (c) A letter in Peshvekalin (d) Anglakalin (e) Anglakalin.

The archaic handwritten Modi script documents contain crucial historical, cultural, and social information including judicial evidence, property deals related to the different centuries. At present automated recognition of these documents is essential with two major issues as: i) Lack of the Modi script experts (readers/writers). ii) Destroying stage of the preserved Modi script documents. Hence, it is necessary to develop an intelligent recognition system to convert these archaic Modi script document images in digitized and searchable text form. Consequently, these digitized Modi script documents can contribute towards the preservation of its original written text, cultural heritage, and administrative work. Also, it is used in the different computer systems as,

- Transcription System, to convert text into other script like Devanagari, English etc.

- Natural Language Processing System, to convert information into another language like Hindi, Guajarati, English etc.
- In online search engines to search the information.
- Text to Speech Conversion System etc.

Intelligent handwritten document recognition system includes mainly six steps as: image acquisition, preprocessing, segmentation, feature extraction, classification, and post processing. Figure 2 shows the general architecture of intelligent handwritten Modi script document recognition system. It has mainly two phases as training and testing.

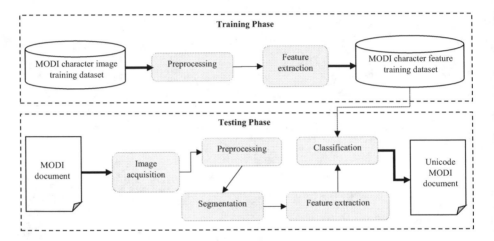

Fig. 2. General architecture of intelligent handwritten archaic Modi script document recognition system.

Class wise Modi script character feature training dataset is generated by training phase. Training dataset must be invariant to transformation. Training phase has two steps as preprocessing and feature extraction. Testing phase consists of the steps as: document image acquisition, preprocessing, segmentation, feature extraction and classification.

Research article published by [Kulkarni Sadanand A., 2015] [2] discussed the properties of the Modi script and reviewed self-generated Modi script numeral, vowels, and consonant dataset classification rate. It stated the OCR system architectures for various scripts like English, Persian, Gurumukhi, Devanagari in brief. Comprehensive literature review shows that till the date no review paper has been published in the area of archaic handwritten Modi script document recognition. It is noticeable that a review of existing techniques related to the handwritten archaic Modi script document recognition will be a great resource to the researchers working in this area. Hence, this paper tries to highlight issues like preprocessing, segmentation, feature extraction and classification of handwritten archaic Modi script documents written in different era. It has also analysed the work and the challenges to improve the results at different stages of handwritten archaic Modi script document recognition system. This review examines the state-of-art work in the area of handwritten Modi script Document/character recognition system.

The overview of the paper is revealed in the Fig. 3. Section 1 introduced the Modi script and need of the intelligent handwritten Modi script document recognition system. In Sect. 2 Modi script datasets used by the different authors in their research are discussed. Section 3 presents the work done in historical handwritten Modi script document image preprocessing. In the same context Sect. 4 represents the review on the segmentation process and Sect. 5 examines the methods proposed for the Modi script character recognition. Observations made during the evaluation and challenges in recognition are pointed out in Sect. 5. Future directions for the further research work are given in Sect. 6. The overall review is finally concluded in the Sect. 7.

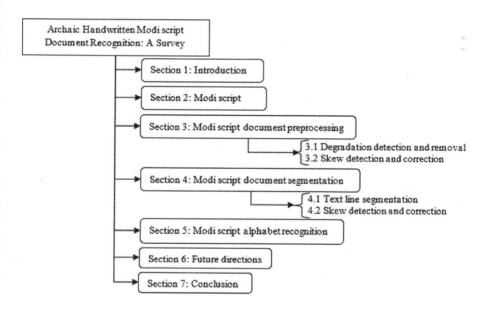

Fig. 3. Overview of the article.

2   Modi Script Datasets

The most important facet of any character or document recognition system is the dataset used for the training and testing the system. The dataset must be invariant so that it will reflect the correct accuracy of the proposed approach. Table 2 list the datasets used by the researchers in handwritten Modi script character/Modi script document recognition system. It is found that Modi script character datasets are self-generated and the standard invariant dataset of sufficient size should be made available for experimentation.

Table 2. Modi script Character or document Datasets.

Reference	Used for	Dataset	Size	Invariant
Deshmukh M. S. & Kolhe S. R. 2021; Deshmukh M. S et al. 2017 [3,4]	Preprocessing, segmentation, classification	Grayscale or color real ancient handwritten Modi script documents	3429	Yes
Joseph S., George J. P., & Gaikwad S. [2020] [22,23]	Classification	Modi script Character dataset	4600	Not specified
Tamhankar P. A. & Masalkar K. D. 2020 [10]	Skew detection	Modi script text lines	790	Not specified
Kulkarni S. A. et al. 2014 [12]	Classification	Modi script numerals	100	Not specified
Sadanand A. Kulkarni et al. 2015 [14–16]	Classification	Modi script vowels	4600	Not specified
Sidra Anam & Saurabh Gupta, 2015 [17]	Classification	22 classes of Modi script character	1276	Not specified
Chandure S. L. & Inamdar, V. [2016] [19]	Classification	13 classes of Modi script vowels	Not Specified	Not specified
Deshmukh M.S. et al. 2015 citeref13	Classification	Modi script numerals	30000	Yes
Gharde, S. S. & Ramteke, R. J. (2016, December [20]	Classification	Modi script characters	1800	Not specified
Tamhankar P.A. et al. 2020 [21]	Classification	31 classes of Modi script characters	40000	Yes

The reported research works are used diverse classes and sizes of Modi script character datasets. Three online datasets of handwritten Modi script characters have been available on two online resources IEEEDataPort and Mendealy data. Table 3 gives the list of the available Modi script character online datasets. Likewise, Modi - HHDoc historical degraded handwritten Modi script document dataset [30,33] have been available on Mendealy data and IEEEDataport. This dataset includes total 3350 historical Modi script documents. There is a necessity to create a standard Modi script character dataset which is invariant and appropriate for the training and testing the intelligent handwritten Modi script document recognition system.

Table 3. Modi script Character online Datasets.

Reference	Data format	Size	Classes	Web Source
Chandankhede C. & Sachdeo R. 2023 [27]	PNG	7221	10 Modi script vowels and 35 Modi script consonants	IEEE-DataPort
SavitriJadhav et al. 2021 [28]	PNG	4140	10 Modi script vowels and 36 Modi script consonants	IEEE-DataPort
Deshmukh, Manisha; Kolhe Satish (2023) [29,33]	JPEG	575920	Modi script 10 numerals (0–9), 12 vowels and 35 consonants	Mendeley Data, IEEE-DataPort

3   Modi Script Document Preprocessing Methodologies

Generally, preprocessing module includes filtering, resizing, binarizing and thinning the character image. Filtering is used for the image smoothing and enhancement. Mostly median filter, wiener filter and morphological operations are verified to remove pepper noise, image smoothing and improve image sharpness. Binarization and thinning of character image depends on the feature extraction technique. For example, to extract chain-code and structural features character image must be binarized and thinned. Well known Otsu's thresholding method and morphological operations are assuring for the binarization and thinning process.

In the context of Modi script document recognition system, more efforts are required in the preprocessing of document images. Archaic Modi script documents are archived at libraries, archaeological centres, and administrative departments approximately from 14th century. Main reasons of deterioration of these documents are: i) aging, ii) chemical preservatives and iii) the substances used to write these documents. As a result, these documents have noises like bleed through noise, speckle noise, varying contrast and uneven background or foreground and so on. Figure 1 and Fig. 4 shows examples of preserved Modi script document images. These documents are handwritten and written on plain papers. Hence, these text lines are drawn in slope and text lines/written text are skewed. Consequently, preprocessing module should be robust. It required mainly two modules as: i) Degradation detection and removal, and ii) Skew detection and correction.

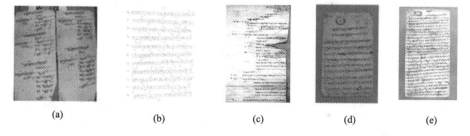

Fig. 4. Sample images of the degraded archaic Modi script documents (a) highly degraded, skewed and unconstrained written text (b) blurred and skewed text (c) highly degraded and unconstrained text (d–e) highly degraded text with page border.

3.1   Degradation Detection and Removal

One important aspect is that quality of the document image required is high in image processing for recognition and digitization. If the image is of low-quality, then it will be affected to the other modules of the recognition system like binarization and segmentation. Scanned and photo copy images of Modi script documents comprise distinctive degradations like bleed through degradation, gaussian noise (white noise), spike noise (salt and pepper noise), Clutter noise: Page has black pixels than estimated in a general scan document called as clutter noise, faded ink and staining degradation, varying contrast, light foreground and uneven background degradation, page border noise or marginal noise, and deterioration of the paper media, ink seeping/smearing, damages/dirt degradation as shown in Fig. 1 and Fig. 4. Most of the chronic and sparse Modi script documents are broken and pasted on the card sheet or hard paper. At the time of digitization of these documents, the resulting document image is framed by a noisy border as shown in Fig. 4(a), (c), (d) and (e). The research paper [Deshmukh, M. S., & Kolhe S. R. 2021] [3] presented an unsupervised approach to detect and remove the page border area of the archaic Modi script document images. This algorithm is based on the analysis of the gray level values of the document image with statistical scrutiny. The page area location is estimated by calculating and comparing the maximum gray level value for each column and row with the maximum gray level threshold. This proposed approach tackled the major challenges as the page border connectivity with text/text area and variation of intensities exists between page background, border, and foreground. The comparative analysis with public online datasets and benchmarking techniques is reported in [3].

To clean and enhance the chronic Modi script document image automated nonparametric research is reported in [4]. The dynamic thresholding procedure is used to detect and remove the noisy pixels. They recommended rule based connected components analysis to remove the clutter, marginal noise, and blobs. In this research work, they have also proposed pattern of the filtering techniques and morphological operations to improve sharpness or quality of the Modi script document images. In Table 4 details of the state-of-art for the cleaning and enhancement of the historical Modi script document images are summarized.

Table 4. State-of-art of degradation detection and removal of archaic Modi script document images.

Reference	Used for	Method	Data set	Success	Remark
Deshmukh M. S., & Kolhe S. R. 2021 [3]	Page border detection and removal	Threshold based maximum gray level frequency analysis	3010 actual handwritten archaic Modi script document images	89.54%	Not able to remove page borders of the document images which is highly spoiled by preservatives. Also, not effective for the vastly poor condition or very thin page borders document images
Deshmukh M. S et al. 2017 [4]	Noise removal and enhancement of the image Dynamic nonparametric hybrid threshold-based analysis	3429 grayscale or color ancient handwritten Modi script documents	98%	Damages and dirt degradation is not efficiently removed.	

It shows that, more emphasis is needed in improvement the quality of highly spoiled Modi script document images. The high quality of the document image assures that the improvement in the results of the other preprocessing stages, segmentation, and recognition. The cleaning and enhancement are not only required for understanding the content of the document, but also required for the automation systems.

3.2 Skew Detection and Correction

Skew correction is a significant module in preprocessing especially for the segmentation process. The first factual cause which evokes the skew in Modi script documents image is the image capturing tools means scanner and camera. The second main cause is the writing style of Modi script. These documents are written on the plain paper with no constraint. Before writing the text, straight line (Shirorekha) was drawn by hand. Usually, these lines are drawn in slope and text is twisted for example as shown in Fig. 4. These document images are skewed locally and globally. Also, one main problem is that text lines are skewed non-uniformly. Hence, the skew correction module is becoming more intricate.

A divide-and-conquer based skew detection method is proposed in [5]. Authors suggested a horizontal projection profile-based method by introducing a new criterion function. They have advised a method to find the page inclination due to that the skew angle is estimated in an appropriate range. They elaborated the number of challenges to detect and correct the skew of the archaic Modi script document images. The authors prove the performance of the method by comparing it with benchmarking techniques and by applying it on another benchmarking online dataset. This stated work corrects the global skew of the document image. In the same perspective another work is reported by [6]. The authors proposed a method which calculates the skewed angle of segmented Modi script text line from the first nonzero pixel of the columns from left to right by scanning Shirorekha up to end. Affine transformation-based method is recommended to correct the skew of the document image. Skew detection and correction state-of-art for the historical Modi script document images is summarized in Table 5.

Table 5. State-of-art of correction and detection of the skew of the Modi script document images.

Reference	Method	Data set	Success	Remark
Deshmukh M. S et al. 2017 [5]	Divide-and-conquer horizontal projection profile	3429 Modi script document images	96.49%	The work is effectively detecting and correcting global skew of the document image with reduced time complexity and 0.1 angle resolution
P. A. Tamhankar, S. R. Kolhe (2018) [6]	Column wise scanning method with affine transformation	216 Modi script text lines	93.98%	It is sufficiently correct the skew of the segmented text lines. Angle of resolution and angle range is not clearly reported

In the context of the archaic Modi script documents, local skew detection and correction is a challenging task. Yet, best of our knowledge no work is reported. These document images comprise multiple skewed text lines and paragraphs, multiple skewed columns, skewed non-uniform Shirorekha and overlapped/very dense text lines. Hence, there is a scope to work on the local skew detection and correction.

4   Modi Script Document Segmentation Methodologies

Subsequent most substantial task of intelligent document recognition system is the segmentation. The segmentation module separated text and non-text elements of the document image. Further text elements are segmented in text lines. These text lines are segmented in the words in the successive step and finally words segmented in the isolated characters. Most of the historical Modi script documents contain only text part. Some of these documents contain the Mudras (stamps) with text for example as shown in Figure 1(a), (b) and (d). Due to cursive and fast-writing process, Modi script words are not separated by space or any punctuation marks. And the characters are allied with each other. Before to start writing text in Modi script, the top line (Shirorekha) is drawn by hand and characters are written hanging with top line without lifting the pen. There are no punctuation marks are used like comma, semicolon etc. Figure 1(a)–(d) and Fig. 4 shows examples of unconstrained/free style, cursive and stylish Modi script documents written in ancient age. Hence, segmentation module of the archaic handwritten Modi script document recognition system includes segmentation of three essentials as Mudras (stamps), text lines and isolated characters.

Before segmenting the text lines and characters, it is favorable to separate the Mudras from the Modi script document image. Because at most text is found overlapped or touched with the Mudras. Therefore, it is necessary to segment Mudras before text line segmentation process. No such a work of detection and segmentation of Mudras is found.

4.1   Text Line Segmentation

Text line segmentation of document image has the crucial role in document image recognition system for efficient automatic document manipulation. This is important because it serves as intermediary between page analysis and character segmentation. The accuracy of character segmentation highly depends on the perfection of the text line segmentation. The numbers of considerable benchmarking text line segmentation techniques are addressed in literature. These techniques mostly deal with printed documents or constrained handwritten documents.

Segmentation of text lines of freestyle unconstrained handwritten Modi script document images poses different challenges than those from printed or constrained handwritten documents. A research paper published by [7] elaborated challenges in archaic Modi script document images. They listed out the challenges as: non-uniform Shirorekha, character or text segment size variation, non-uniform distance between line segments, variable length size of text lines, multi-skewed documents, dense text line segments, touching line segments, slightly curved text lines, overlapping or touching stamp symbols with the line segments, and other degradations like faded ink.

A research article [8] proposed a simple two step approach for the segmentation of the Modi script text lines using horizontal projection profile and criterion function. In the first step, maxima and minima using the horizontal projection profile is calculated. In the second step, appropriate location of valley exist between two adjacent text line segments is estimated by the criterion function. This text line segmentation approach is segmented accurately even overlapping and/or touching lines of the Modi script document. A hybrid recursive approach for Modi script text line segmentation is presented by [7]. The authors proposed a module which analyzed gray level threshold and connected component for text line segmentation. The row wise gray level thresholding values are calculated and used for the formation of major and minor seams. These seams' locations are used to estimate text line region and non-text region. To clean up non-text components from the estimated text line segment connected components are analyzed. The applicability of this module is presented by comparing benchmarking techniques and online historical document datasets written in different script. State-of-art of the text line segmentation in the context of old edge handwritten Modi script documents is briefly listed in Table 6.

Table 6. State-of-art of text line segmentation of handwritten Modi script document images.

Reference	Method	Data set	Success	Remark
Tamhankar, Parag A et al. 2017 [8]	Horizontal Projection Profile with criterion-based Method	–	–	The dataset size and correct segmentation accuracy is not given
Deshmukh M. S. et al. 2018 [7]	Local threshold with connected component analysis	2540 archaic Modi script document images	98.64%	This module successful segments the ancient Modi script document images having the challenges like highly overlapping and touching text lines. But it is not applicable to segments Modi script documents having non-uniform multi-columns; very dense step wise multi and touching columns

Overall review on text line segmentation approaches for the Modi script text line segmentation shows that it is a challenging task to segment the document images as shown in Fig. 5 and Fig. 4(a) and (c). Such document images require more efforts to segment multi and local skewed double column and single column text lines present in the single document. Another main challenge is that the text lines are overlapped and locally non-uniformly twisted.

Fig. 5. Samples of ancient Modi script document images challenging in text line segmentation.

4.2   Character Segmentation

Character segmentation plays a key role in the domain of segmentation process of document recognition system. Ancient Modi script document segmentation has number of challenges due to cursive and stylish writing style of Modi script. The research article published in [9] highlights challenges in the Modi script character segmentation. While the research paper [11] depicted challenges related to segmentation of touching character clusters of Modi script.

Background pixel density of global and local horizontal zones-based module is presented by [9] to segment the Modi script characters. It is a multistep technique. Isolated, touching and overlapping characters are segmented in the successive step. To segment the isolated and overlapping characters column-wise background pixel with horizontal fixed zoning approach is proposed. While to segment the touching characters bottom-up background pixel histogram is used.

In research paper [10] authors suggested column-wise foreground pixels histogram and dual threshold approach to segment isolated Modi script characters. Segmentation column location is estimated using two conditions on the calculated column-wise foreground pixels histogram vector as: i) current vector value $= 0$ or, ii) absolute difference of previous and current vector value is greater than threshold1 and difference of current index vector value and the last location value stored compared with threshold2.

Unsegmented characters clusters of Modi script text line are categorized by counting the connected component overlap ration in [11]. Two separate strategies are presented to segment the partial and entirely touching Modi script character clusters. To segment the partial touching character clusters bottom to top scanning to find the foreground pixel location is identified and analyzed to estimate the segmentation column. While to segment the entirely touching character cluster vertical projection profile is calculated. Table 7 list out the concisely research work is done in ancient handwritten Modi script character segmentation.

Table 7. State-of-art of Modi script character segmentation.

Reference	Method	Data set	Success	Remark
M.S. Deshmukh & S. R Kolhe 2019 [9]	Column wise background zoning with bottom-up background pixel histogram approach	1052 Modi script text lines	72.61%	The method is sufficiently segmented the isolated characters. Very dense and highly overlapping characters are not segmented
Tamhankar P. A., & Masalkar K. D. 2020 [10]	Dual thresholding criterion module	790 Modi script text lines	67%	The method is provided good results when the width of a character is not too small /large. Authors are not measured Modi script character challenges like highly overlapping/touching characters
Deshmukh M. S., & Kolhe S. R. 2020 [11]	Connected component overlap ratio with bottom-up foreground pixel location analysis and vertical projection profile7	2249 Modi script touching character clusters in 1072 text lines	83.62%	Very dense and entirely touching characters are not segmented properly

Comprehensive review reveals that there is still a need to do research in this area. Two main challenges require more efforts in the handwritten Modi script character segmentation module as: i) very dense touching characters and ii) highly overlapping and entirely touching characters.

5   Modi Script Alphabet Recognition Methodologies

Basic set of Modi script alphabets contains 10 digits (0 to 9), 12 vowels (A to Ah) and 45 consonants (Ka to Dyn). With this Modi script presents Jodakshare means consonant-consonant combinations and consonant-vowel combinations. To increase the speed of writing word/phrase short forms was also introduced. Equally, the characters symbols are changed as per the writing place and as per its adjoining characters. Hence, Modi script is represented by extensive characters. Figure 6 gives the examples of the Modi script characters.

Ancient Modi script documents recognition is becoming critical because of number of reasons. In the examination of thousands of handwritten ancient Modi script documents, most critical challenges in recognition are noticed as,

– Unconstrained and nonuniform writing
– Complex shapes of characters
– Huge number of character symbols
– Variation in character shape representation
– Graphically very similar structuralized characters
– Short forms of phrases
– Writing style change as per adjoining letters and location
– Modi script elevation in different centuries
– Lack of benchmarking training and testing Modi script character dataset

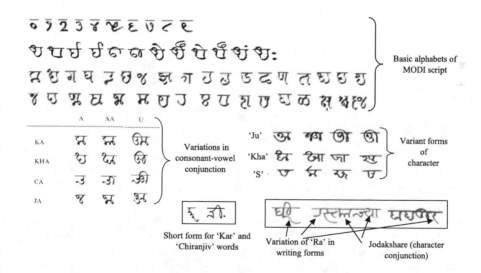

Fig. 6. Modi script characters.

Following factors are noted through the comprehensive literature review concerning to Modi script character recognition as:

1. Proposed recognition models are verified using constrained self-generated dataset.
2. Still, no work is reported related to the recognition of actual ancient handwritten Modi script documents
3. Limited numbers of classes are determined for examples digits (0–9), vowels (10/12), and consonants (46).
4. Limited dataset size for example 100 numerals, 4600 consonants.
5. Invariant property is not proved.

In the recognition of Modi script numeral, most challenging task is the classification of digit five'5' and six '6'. The geometrical shape of these both digits is very similar. Figure 7 shows the sample images of digit '5' and '6' of a handwritten self-generated Modi script numerals dataset.

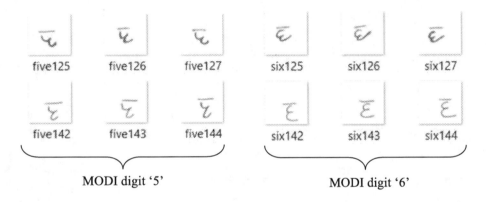

Fig. 7. Sample images of handwritten Modi script numerals five and six collected from a self-generated dataset.

Efficiency of Zernike moments and Hu's invariant moments for the discriminant features of handwritten 'Modi script' numerals are verified in [12]. The authors preferred Euclidian distance classifier for classification. This proposed module is tested on self-generated dataset of size 100. They concluded that Zernike moment features are more effective than Hu's invariant moment. In this experiment recognition module is verified with very limited dataset. The research works are reported for Modi script numeral recognition in [13, 31] by the same authors. They proposed Chain code feature extraction approach with correlation coefficient with maximum voting in the first approach [13]. While in second approach [31], they found concavity feature method is given the increased recognition accuracy. The results are tested with different dataset size and with different zoning methods. The authors claim that 30000 data set size with 5×5 zoning method is efficient to prove the invariant property. The state-of-art recognition methods for handwritten Modi script numeral are given in Table 8.

Table 8. State-of-art for recognition of handwritten Modi script numerals.

Reference	Data Set Size with training testing ratio	Feature extraction and classifier	Result (%)	Remark
Kulkarni S. A. et al. 2014 [12]	100 (70:30)	Hu's invariant (HI), Zernike moments (ZM) and Euclidean Distance classifier	HI - 70.00, ZM - 86.66	Results are verified with very limited data. Thus, constrained self -generated data set not sufficient to prove recognition rate and invariant property
Deshmukh M.S. et al. 2015 [13]	30000 (50:50)	Chain code and Correlation coefficient	85.21	Results are verified with different dataset size and zoning methods
Deshmukh M.S. and S. R. Kolhe 2023 [31]	30000 (50:50)	Concavity Features and Correlation coefficient	93.22	Results are verified with different dataset size and zoning methods

In the perspective of Modi script character recognition, two types of measures are observed as: vowels and consonants. Sadanand A. Kulkarni et al. [12] verified recognition rate of Modi script vowels (10 classes) and consonants (36 classes). They proposed two approaches. In the first approach, recognition rate of handwritten Modi script characters is verified by Hu's seven invariant and Zernike features [14, 16]. In the second approach, Zernike moments and Complex moments with different zoning methods are used for feature extraction [15]. Recognition rate is compared and verified for different nine zoning patterns. Comparative analysis is done between Zernike Complex moments and Zernike moments features. Euclidean distance classifier is used for the classification in both recognition modules. Authors concluded that Zernike complex moment with all 37 zones give the better recognition rate. Further, Kulkarni S. A., & Yannawar P. L. [18] represented a recognition module for partial Handwritten Modi script characters. Different Zoning methods are used to extract the Zernike moment features of the partial Modi script handwritten character. They compared experimental results using decision tree, k-NN, LDA, QDA, Naïve Bayes and SVM classifiers with Euclidian distance classifier. The authors concluded that Zernike moments with integrated approach give the highest recognition rate as 97.68%.

Chandure S. L., & Inamdar V. [19] proposed a recognition module to recognize the handwritten Modi script vowels. The authors have not specified the dataset size and training: testing samples to measure 13 classes of Modi script.

Moment Invariant and Affine Moment Invariant feature extraction approaches are used for extracting the features from the handwritten Modi script handwritten samples by Gharde S. S. and Ramteke R. J. [20]. To classify the Modi script character Support vector machine is used. The authors have not provided the details about two important aspects as: i) Training: Testing ratio and ii) Number of classes of Modi script characters.

Sidra Anam and Saurabh Gupta [17] proposed Kohonen neural network for the recognition of 22 classes of the Modi script handwritten characters. They have used 8 sample images of the character for training and 50 sample images for the testing the recognition system. The dataset size is too limited and constrained. Likewise, Deep learning Convolutional Neural Network is proposed by the Tamhankar P.A. et al. 2020 [21] to recognize the handwritten Modi script characters. Thirty-one classes of the Modi script character are considered for the recognition system. They concluded that CNN is not efficient to discrimination of the graphically similar looking Modi script characters. Hence, the classification rate is reduced.

Joseph S., George J. P., & Gaikwad S. 2020 [22–24] proposed three different handwritten Modi script character recognition approaches. In the first recognition approach two distance classifier methods are involves as Euclidean distance and Manhattan distance classifier and they achieved 99.28% recognition accuracy with Euclidean distance classifier. But here feature extraction technique(s) is not cleared. In the second approach, they proposed recognition module using Convolutional Neural Network based feature extraction method with Support Vector Machine Classifier and achieved 99.3% recognition rate. The authors have also analysed recognition rate of Daubechies, Haar, and Symlet wavelets feature extraction approach in their experiments. Here, they used Decision tree classifier. They concluded that Daubechies wavelet feature extraction approach gives better character recognition result. The recognition rates are calculated on the constrained, self-generated and the limited size of Modi script character dataset. Hundred samples of each Modi script character are used with seventy samples for the training and 30 samples for testing the recognition machine. Hence, it may be not proving the invariant property. Also, the similar looking Modi script character aspect is not measured. Deshmukh M.S. and S. R. Kolhe 2023 [31] presented the recognition hybrid approach for the Unconstrained and Invariant handwritten Modi script characters. They varied the recognition rate of the Modi script digits, vowels and consonants using Gradient, Structural and Concavity features and different classification approaches like Euclidian Distance, Minimum distance classifier, Naïve Bays classifier and correlation coefficient. They have claimed that Minimum distance classifier and GSC features gives improved recognition rate. The authors also have tried the same recognition approach to recognise the ancient handwritten Modi script documents. They found that due to degraded Modi script characters the recognition rate is reduced. Table 9 shows the state-of art comparison of handwritten Modi script character recognition.

Table 9. State-of-art comparisons of handwritten Modi script characters recognition.

Method	Data Set Size with training testing ratio	Feature extraction and classifier	Result (%)	Remark
Sadanand A. Kulkarni et al. 2015 [14,16]	4600 (10 Vowels 36 Consonants) 70:30	Hu's seven invariant features, Zernike features and Euclidean distance classifier	76.74	Training and testing data set sample size is very limited. Hence, it is not sufficiently proved invariant property
Sadanand A. Kulkarni et al. 2015 [15]	4600 (10 Vowels 36 Consonants) 70:30	Zernike and Zernike Complex moments with zoning and Euclidean distance classifier	92.02	Training and testing data set sample size is very limited. Self-generated constrained dataset is used to test and train the system hence, the challenges like similar looking characters are not verified
Sidra Anam and Saurabh Gupta, 2015 [17]	1276 (22 Modi script characters)	Kohonen NN method	72.6	Limited samples of Modi script character classes used to train and test the recognition system
Chandure S. L.,& Inamdar, V. [2016] [19]	13 vowels	Chain code and SVM classifier	65	Data set size and ratio of the training and testing samples are not given
Gharde, S. S., & Ramteke, R. J. (2016, December [20]	1800	Moment Invariant, Affine Moment Invariant and SVM classifier	89.72	Limited size of the dataset. Training: testing ratio and number of classes of Modi script characters are not given
Tamhankar P.A. et al. 2020 [21]	40000 (31 classes) 30000:10000	Deep learning Convolutional Neural Network	64	CNN is not efficient to differentiate the similar looking Modi script consonants
Joseph S., George J. P., & Gaikwad S. [2020] [22]	4600 (46 classes) 70:30	Euclidian distance and Manhattan distance classifier	99.28 and 94.00	No analysis about the similar looking Modi script characters. The limited data set size is not sufficient to prove the invariant property. The proposed classifiers are not invariant to scale. Hence, it may be not correctly classifying the characters in such cases
Joseph S., George J. P., & Gaikwad S. [2020] [23]	4600 (46 classes) 70:30	Convolutional Neural Network Based Feature Extraction Method and Support Vector Machine Classifier	99.3	No analysis about the similar looking Modi script characters. The limited data set size is not sufficient to prove the invariant property. The proposed classifiers are not invariant to scale. Hence, it may be not correctly classifying the characters in such cases
Deshmukh M.S. and S. R. Kolhe 2023 [31]	30000 (10 Vowels) 50:50	GSC and Correlation coefficient	82.33	Dataset is unconstrained and appropriate to verify the results. System is proved the invariant property
Deshmukh M.S. and S. R. Kolhe 2023 [31]	30000 (10 Vowels) 50:50	GSC and Correlation coefficient	83.09	Dataset is unconstrained and appropriate to verify the results. System is proved the invariant property

The inclusive review of the Modi script character recognition shows that all the recognition modules are trained and tested with the self-generated constrained limited data set. Training and testing dataset ratio does not efficiently prove the invariant property. It is not authenticated that the proposed method is also work for recognition of the ancient handwritten Modi script documents. This review reveals that there is a single work is done to recognize the characters of the anciently handwritten Modi script document. Hereafter, the efforts are required in the handwritten Modi script character recognition system as:

- Creation of annotated dataset which is appropriate for the recognition of original ancient handwritten Modi script documents
- Recognition of the graphically similar looking Modi script characters
- Recognition of the partial characters
- Recognition of the conjunct characters means 'Jodakshre'
- Recognition of the short form words
- Recognition of the variations of a character in writing form

The next important step of recognition of the ancient Modi script handwritten document is transcription or transliteration. These steps are crucial to regain the information contain in these documents. The natural language of all these Modi script documents is Marathi language. Most of the research articles related to Marathi language written in Devanagari script discusses named entity recognition, sentimental analysis, and grammar checking. Joshi R. 2022 [25] presented datasets and models for the named entity recognition, sentiment analysis, and hate detection speech supervised task. They have also discussed a monolingual Marathi corpus and un-supervised language modeling tasks. They have used MahaCorpus, MahaSent, MahaNER, and MahaHate datasets and analogous fine-tuned MahaBERT models.

The state-of-art approaches reported by Lahoti P et al. 2022 [26] for the processing of Marathi language and perception into the innumerable linguistic resources, tools. They have provided morphological explanations of the Marathi language and characteristics of the Marathi language. A review is presented the availability of corpus, tools and techniques to be used to develop NLP tasks for Marathi language written in Devanagari script. They also discussed gap analysis in present research and forthcoming directions for the Marathi Language Processing (MLP).

6 Future Directions

This presented survey shows that very limited work is reported in the area of ancient handwritten Modi script document recognition. At the preprocessing stage the robust and hybrid approach(es) is/are required to detect and correct the local skew of the multi-skewed and multicolumn Modi script documents. In the same way, highly degraded Modi script documents required efficient method to detect and remove the degradation and improve the quality of the document image. At the segmentation process, researchers having the scope to do the work at two levels as: i) Segmentation of multicolumn, multi-skewed, non-uniform and unconstrained text lines, and ii) Segmentation of very dense touching characters and highly overlapping characters. Still, the reported Modi script character recognition works are verified on the self-generated handwritten Modi script character datasets. Only elementary Modi script characters are considered, and classes of Modi script characters are also varying. It is also apparent that issues like recognition of conjunct character, short forms of the phrase/word, graphically ambiguous characters are not under consideration. Nobody raise the issue about the characters whose graphical structure is changed as per the environment or place in the writing. In real situation of the ancient Modi script documents, these documents are from different era and having variations in character set. All these points indicates that a lots of research work is expected in the area.

7 Conclusion

Automatic historical handwritten Modi script document recognition is an interesting field in the area of intelligent document recognition from cultural, judicial, administration, historical, social, scientific, and commercial points of view. Huge volumes of information are hidden in the ancient Modi script documents which will be helpful for other research communities, official matters, social facets etc. Necessity of handwritten Modi script document recognition is because of both lack of Modi script users (readers /writers) and need of the historical information in current era. Unconstrained, cursive, stylish, aging, and degraded nature of these documents together has increases complexity of the document recognition system.

This review paper will give the reader state-of-art information in ancient handwritten Modi script document recognition. Very limited works have been reported in the area of ancient handwritten Modi script document recognition. These works are related to the preprocessing and segmentation processes only. Modi script documents are preserved from hundreds of years and highly degraded. Review shows that at preprocessing stage robust method(s) is/are required to correct local skew and enhancement of the highly spoiled documents.

Recognition of the document is highly dependent on the segmentation or identification of isolated characters. The character segmentation becomes the most critical task when the characters are highly dense, touching and over-lapping. Likewise, line segmentation becomes difficult when documents contain multicolumn, non-uniform and unconstrained text lines. The ancient Modi script document segmentation approach required more efficient segmentation approach or hybrid approach(es) to increase the accuracy rate.

Majority approaches reported for Modi script character recognition are based on Euclidian distance classifier with moment invariant feature extraction techniques. Convolutional Neural Network based feature extraction method and Support Vector Machine Classifier shows different recognition rate with different datasets and classes of the Modi script characters. The datasets used to test and train the reported Modi script character recognition systems are limited in size and constrained. So, these performances are not comparable.

References

1. Pandey, A.: Proposal to Encode the Modi script in ISO/IEC 10646, November 5 (2011)
2. Kulkarni, S.A., Borde, P.L., Manza, R.R., Yannawar, P.L.: Review on recent advances in automatic handwritten Modi script recognition. Int. J. Comput. Appl. **975**, 8887 (2015)
3. Deshmukh, M.S., Kolhe, S.R.: Unsupervised page area detection approach for the unconstrained chronic handwritten Modi script document images. In: 2021 International Conference on Emerging Smart Computing and Informatics (ESCI), pp. 130–135. IEEE (2021)
4. Deshmukh, M.S., Patil, M.P., Kolhe, S.R.: A dynamic statistical nonparametric cleaning and enhancement system for highly degraded ancient handwritten Modi Lipi documents. In: 2017 International Conference on Advances in Computing, Communications and Informatics (ICACCI), pp. 1545–1551. IEEE (2017)
5. Deshmukh, M.S., Patil, M.P., Kolhe, S.R.: The divide-and-conquer based algorithm to detect and correct the skew angle in the old age historical handwritten Modi Lipi documents. Int. J. Comput. Sci. Appl. **14**(2), 47–63 (2017)
6. Tamhankar, P.A., Kolhe, S.R.: Skew detection, skew correction, and Shirorekha extraction of line segmented offline handwritten historical Marathi documents written in Modi script. Int. J. Latest Trends Eng. Technol. **10**(1), 344–348 (2018)
7. Deshmukh, M.S., Patil, M.P., Kolhe, S.R.: A hybrid text line segmentation approach for the ancient handwritten unconstrained freestyle Modi script documents.

Imaging Sci. J. **66**(7), 433–442 (2018). https://doi.org/10.1080/13682199.2018. 1499226

8. Tamhankar, P.A., Masalkar, K.D., Kolhe, S.R.: Segmentation of overlapping, skewed, and touching lines in handwritten Modi script documents. Int. J. Comput. Sci. Appl. **14**(2) (2017)

9. Deshmukh, M.S., Kolhe, S.R.: A hybrid character segmentation approach for cursive unconstrained handwritten historical Modi script documents. In: Proceedings of International Conference on Sustainable Computing in Science, Technology and Management (SUSCOM), Amity University Rajasthan, Jaipur-India (2019)

10. Tamhankar, P.A., Masalkar, K.D.: A novel approach for character segmentation of offline handwritten Marathi documents written in Modi script script. Procedia Comput. Sci. **171**, 179–187 (2020)

11. Deshmukh, M.S., Kolhe, S.R.: A modified approach for the segmentation of unconstrained cursive Modi touching characters cluster. In: Santosh, K.C., Gawali, B. (eds.) RTIP2R 2020. CCIS, vol. 1380, pp. 431–444. Springer, Singapore (2021). https://doi.org/10.1007/978-981-16-0507-9_36

12. Kulkarni, S.A., Borde, P.L., Manza, R.R., Yannawar, P.L.: Recognition of handwritten Modi script numerals using Hu and Zernike features. arXiv preprint arXiv:1404.1151 (2014)

13. Deshmukh, M.S., Patil, M.P., Kolhe, S.R.: Off-line handwritten Modi script numerals recognition using chain code. In: Proceedings of the Third International Symposium on Women in Computing and Informatics, pp. 388–393 (2015)

14. Kulkarni, S.A., Borde, P.L., Manza, R.R., Yannawar, P.L.: Offline Handwritten Modi script Character Recognition Using HU, Zernike Moments and Zoning. arXiv preprint arXiv:1406.6140 (2014)

15. Sadanand, A.K., Prashant, L.B., Ramesh, R.M., Pravin, L.Y.: Offline Modi script character recognition using complex moments. Procedia Comput. Sci. **58**, 516–523 (2015)

16. Sadanand, A.K., Prashant, L.B., Ramesh, R.M., Pravin, L.Y.: Impact of zoning on Zernike moments for handwritten Modi script character recognition. In: 2015 International Conference on Computer, Communication and Control (IC4), pp. 1–6. IEEE (2015)

17. Anam, S., Gupta, S.: An approach for recognizing Modi Lipi using Ostu's binarization algorithm and kohenen neural network. Int. J. Comput. Appl. (0975-8887) **111**(2) (2015)

18. Kulkarni, S.A., Yannawar, P.L.: Recognition of partial handwritten MODI characters using zoning. In: Santosh, K.C., Gawali, B. (eds.) RTIP2R 2020. CCIS, vol. 1380, pp. 407–430. Springer, Singapore (2021). https://doi.org/10.1007/978-981-16-0507-9_35

19. Chandure, S., Inamdar, V.: Handwritten Modi character recognition using transfer learning with discriminant feature analysis. IETE J. Res. **69**, 1–11 (2021)

20. Gharde, S.S., Ramteke, R.J.: Recognition of characters in Indian Modi script. In: 2016 International Conference on Global Trends in Signal Processing, Information Computing and Communication (ICGTSPICC), pp. 236–240. IEEE (2016)

21. Tamhankar, P.A., Masalkar, K.D., Kolhe, S.R.: Character recognition of offline handwritten Marathi documents written in MODI script using deep learning convolutional neural network model. In: Santosh, K.C., Gawali, B. (eds.) RTIP2R 2020. CCIS, vol. 1380, pp. 478–487. Springer, Singapore (2021). https://doi.org/10.1007/978-981-16-0507-9_40

22. Joseph, S., George, J.P., Gaikwad, S.: Character recognition of MODI script using distance classifier algorithms. In: Fong, S., Dey, N., Joshi, A. (eds.) ICT Analysis and Applications. LNNS, vol. 93, pp. 105–113. Springer, Singapore (2020). https://doi.org/10.1007/978-981-15-0630-7_11

23. Joseph, S., George, J.: Handwritten character recognition of Modi script using convolutional neural network based feature extraction method and support vector machine classifier. In: 2020 IEEE 5th International Conference on Signal and Image Processing (ICSIP), pp. 32–36. IEEE (2020)

24. Joseph, S., George, J.P.: Offline character recognition of handwritten MODI script using wavelet transform and decision tree classifier. In: Joshi, A., Mahmud, M., Ragel, R.G., Thakur, N.V. (eds.) Information and Communication Technology for Competitive Strategies (ICTCS 2020). LNNS, vol. 191, pp. 509–517. Springer, Singapore (2022). https://doi.org/10.1007/978-981-16-0739-4_48

25. Joshi, R.: L3cube-mahanlp: Marathi natural language processing datasets, models, and library. arXiv preprint arXiv:2205.14728 (2022)

26. Lahoti, P., Mittal, N., Singh, G.: A survey on NLP resources, tools, and techniques for Marathi language processing. ACM Trans. Asian Low-Resour. Lang. Inf. Process. **22**(2), 1–34 (2022)

27. Chandankhede, C., Sachdeo, R.: Handwritten Modi lipi barakhadi dataset. IEEE Dataport (2023). https://doi.org/10.21227/x24n-wm25

28. Jadhav, S., Inamdar, V.: Handwritten Modi Characters. IEEE Dataport (2021). https://doi.org/10.21227/z3gg-8b29

29. Deshmukh, M., Kolhe, S.: Modi-HChar: Historical Modi Script Handwritten Character Dataset. Mendeley Data, V1 (2023). https://doi.org/10.17632/pk2zrt58pp.1

30. Deshmukh, M., Kolhe, S.: Modi-HHDoc: Historical Modi Script Handwritten Document Dataset. Mendeley Data, V1 (2023). https://doi.org/10.17632/sg337vf6wn.1

31. Deshmukh, M.S., Kolhe, S.R.: Character Recognition of the Unconstrained and Invariant Dataset of the Handwritten Ancient Modi Script Documents. Available at SSRN. https://ssrn.com/abstract=4330133. https://doi.org/10.2139/ssrn.4330133

32. Deshmukh, M., Kolhe, S.: Modi-HChar: Historical Modi Script Handwritten Character Dataset. IEEE Dataport (2023). https://doi.org/10.21227/v2kt-rr94

33. Deshmukh, M., Kolhe, S.: Modi-HHDoc: Historical Modi Script Handwritten Document Dataset. IEEE Dataport (2023). https://doi.org/10.21227/1z10-w986

An Arabic Chatbot Leveraging Encoder-Decoder Architecture Enhanced with BERT

Mohamed Boussakssou$^{(\boxtimes)}$ and Mohamed Erritali

Data4earth Laboratory, FST Beni Mellal, Sultan Moulay Slimane University, Beni Mellal, Morocco
boussakssoumohamed@gmail.com

Abstract. This paper introduces a new method for developing an Arabic chatbot, utilizing the encoder-decoder architecture enriched with BERT embeddings. Our distinct dataset, constructed manually, aids the model in comprehending intricate questions and prompts, thereby generating coherent and contextually accurate responses in Arabic. The dataset comprises 81,659 manually created conversation pairs. Our model successfully delivered the anticipated answers. We employed a model with a warm-start using the BERT2BERT encoder and decoder. It achieved a BLEU score of 3.52 and a PPL of 36.3.

Keywords: Arabic Chatbot · Arabic chatbot BERT · AraBERT chatbot

1 Introduction

The proliferation of chatbots has experienced a meteoric rise in recent years, catering to a diverse range of services from customer support to personal assistance and more (Luger & Sellen, 2016) [1]. While English-centric models dominate the industry, there is an undeniable need to cater to non-English languages, especially those with significant native speakers and cultural impact. Among these, the Arabic language stands out prominently, being the fifth most spoken language in the world, with over 372 million speakers spanning multiple countries and regions [2].

However, processing Arabic data poses a unique set of challenges. Unlike many other languages, Arabic is characterized by its rich morphology, varied dialects, and the I herent complexity of its script, which is written right-to-left [3]. This complexity is amplified by phenomena like the non-linear structure of words, presence of diacritics, and the significant variations in meaning with slight changes in letter placements or forms [4]. Such intricacies demand specialized models to ensure accurate natural language processing (NLP) tasks.

Despite the vast potential user base and the rich tapestry of Arabic literature and daily communications, there is a conspicuous scarcity of chatbots dedicated to understanding and interacting in Arabic. The few that exist often suffer from limitations, primarily due to the challenges posed by the language's complexities and a lack of robust datasets tailored

KC Santosh et al. (Eds.): RTIP2R 2023, CCIS 2026, pp. 262–269, 2024.
https://doi.org/10.1007/978-3-031-53082-1_21

for the task [5]. Furthermore, the integration of state-of-the-art models like BERT, which has revolutionized the NLP [6], remains rare in the realm of Arabic chatbots.

BERT's prowess in capturing contextual relationships between words makes it a prime candidate for enhancing Arabic language understanding, yet its adoption has been slow and limited in this space.

This paper aims to bridge this gap by presenting an Arabic chatbot that not only navigates the intricacies of the Arabic language but also leverages the power of BERT. We posit that through the combination of the encoder-decoder architecture and BERT e beddings, we can foster a new generation of chatbots capable of nuanced understanding and generation of Arabic content.

2 Related Works

2.1 English Chatbots

In recent years, chatbots leveraging advanced natural language processing (NLP) models have gained significant traction. The financial sector has seen developments like AVA, a chatbot built using the deep bidirectional transformer (BERT) model designed to cater to clients' questions regarding financial investments [7].

On the technical front, comparing models like bidirectional LSTMs and BERT, especially on smaller datasets, has suggested that simpler models might, at times, outperform the latter due to the intricacy and computational needs of BERT [8]. Similarly, in the healthcare sector, a smart chatbot system has been proposed to assist in disseminating information regarding COVID-19 using a two-phase BERT-based architecture [9].

Furthermore, there's been an integration of the BERT model with platforms like Google Dialogflow to create more responsive and data-backed chatbots [10], a direction that's hinted at how chatbots of the future might seamlessly integrate large datasets and NLP models. Moreover, the Unified pre-trained Language Model (UniLM) demonstrates how a singular model could be adept at both understanding and generating language, setting benchmarks across multiple NLP tasks [11].

Within the medical domain, chatbots focusing on COVID-19 symptom classification have been developed, leveraging both recurrent neural networks and deep learning technologies [12].

Another noteworthy advancement is the incorporation of knowledge graphs with BERT, allowing for real-time learning and adaptability to newer terminologies [13]. This shows the potential of merging structured and unstructured data forms for more effective chatbot operations. Lastly, auto-growing knowledge graphs have been presented as a solution to the limitations posed by static knowledge bases, emphasizing real-time data collection and analysis [14].

2.2 Arabic Chatbot

Conversational AI, especially concerning the Arabic language, has witnessed significant advancements recently. A comprehensive review by [Fuad et al.] elucidates the recent strides in Arabic conversational AI, categorizing the systems into question-answering, task-oriented dialogue, and chatbots [15].

With the growth of social media, AI models have been applied for mental health purposes. For instance, CairoDep employs BERT transformers to detect depression from Arabic posts with remarkable accuracy [16]. On the natural language processing front, models like the semi-supervised BERT approach have showcased considerable improvements in Arabic Named Entity Recognition [17]. Furthermore, Arabic dialect identification has garnered attention, with ArabicProcessors employing Arabic-BERT combined with data augmentation and ensembling to identify country and province-level dialects [18].

The Arabic NER landscape is further enriched by Wojood, a corpus dedicated to Arabic nested NER, which is trained using AraBERT to identify nested entity mentions [19]. As Arabic pre-trained models advance, JABER and SABER have emerged as prominent models, outperforming existing benchmarks in Arabic Language Understanding Evaluation [20]. With the rising concern of hate speech on social media platforms, ABMM has been introduced, employing the Arabic BERT-Mini Model to detect Arabic hate speech with exceptional accuracy [21]. Sentiment analysis in Arabic has also benefited from the BERT model, particularly with the integration of the Arabic BERT tokenizer, which optimizes tokenization for both standard and dialect Arabic [22].

BERT models have played a transformative role in Arabic NLP. The Multi-dialect-Arabic-BERT model has been pivotal for Arabic dialect identification, especially in the Nuanced Arabic Dialect Identification shared task [23]. Another study delves into the nuances of building an open-domain chatbot, emphasizing the importance of blending various skills for effective conversation [29]. Arabic topic modeling has also been elevated with the advent of BERTopic, which, when tested against traditional techniques like LDA and NMF, has exhibited superior performance [31].

A systematic review on Arabic text classification with BERT models sheds light on the diverse Arabic BERT models and their efficacy compared to their English counterparts [30].

AraBERT [25], A transformer-based encoder-decoder initialized with AraBERT parameters is proposed, validating its high capability in exhibiting empathy while generating relevant and fluent responses in open-domain settings. The dataset used is created manually and it contains ~35k conversation pairs. The authors induces the empathy as key to make their chatbot generate response taking into account the presence of emotion.

Lastly, the application of transformers in chatbots has demonstrated that models like AraElectra-SQuAD, when combined with extractive chatbots, can produce highly accurate responses in Arabic [28].

3   Proposed Model

3.1   Data Collection and Preprocessing

Data Collection

– Sources:

For this project, data was collected from multiple platforms to capture the intricacies of the Arabic language:

Arabic Online Forums: Platforms like Mawdoo3 and Arabic StackExchange were invaluable, providing rich dialogues on various topics.

Transcribed Customer Support Calls: We accessed transcripts of customer support calls from major companies operating in the MENA region. These helped train the chatbot to understand customer interactions in an Arabic context.

Social Media Platforms: Public posts and comments from platforms like Twitter, with its significant Arabic user base, were crucial. This added colloquial terms and modern slang to our dataset.

Collecting data from different sources allows it to have more Arabic dialects (Moroccan dialect, Egypt –)

– Size:

The data collection phase provided us with about 81,659 conversations conversational pairs in many dialects.

Preprocessing

– Tokenization:

Given the morphological complexity of Arabic, tokenization was done using tools like the Stanford NLP Arabic tokenizer or Farasa. These tools consider the intricacies of Arabic word formations.

– Diacritics Removal:

Arabic script contains diacritics (or Tashkeel) which can be crucial for meaning, but for many NLP tasks, these are removed to simplify the text.

– Standardization:

Arabic is known for its dialectal diversity. Where necessary, we utilized tools like the Arabic G2P converter to transform dialectal Arabic to Modern Standard Arabic (MSA).

– Noise Removal:

Links, special characters, and any non-Arabic text fragments were removed to ensure focus on the Arabic content.

– Handling Missing Data:

Incomplete conversational pairs were discarded to maintain dataset integrity.

– Data Splitting:

The dataset was divided into 80% for training, 10% for validation, and 10% for testing.

3.2 Proposed Model

As used in [24], Seq2seq with LSTM and GRU shows promising results on a dataset of 81k rows of conversations. We want to improve our model even better and introduce a new approach of using BERT along with what we have been achieved already.

Training a BERT Model on a new dataset is a costly operation that request a high computer performance and huge Arabic dataset.

As a solution Fine-tuning a model like BERT for sequence-to-sequence tasks such as chatbot response generation can be approached with several architectures. One popular variant is BERT-to-BERT, where both encoder and decoder are pretrained BERT models.

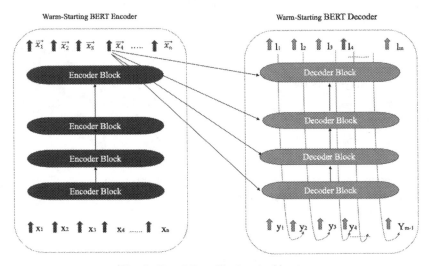

Fig. 1. Bert 2 Bert Chatbot Architecture

Figure 1 illustrate how a pre-trained BERT model can be used to warm-start the encoder-decoder model. BERT's pre-trained weight parameters are used to both initialize the encoder's weight parameters as well as the decoder's weight parameters. All layers of the encoder that do not exist in BERT will simply have their weight parameters be randomly initialized.

Both the encoder and decoder were initialized with weight from BERT checkpoints pre-trained model [27].

We used Both AraBert and AraELECTRA as initialized models in BERT and the results were promising. The next section will introduce some statistics.

The first system is a multi-task learning model that consists of a shared AraBERT encoder with three task-specific classification layers. This model is trained to jointly learn the country-level dialect of the tweet as well as the region-level and area-level dialects.

We have tested our model using both pretrained models on AraElectra and Arabert.

In the next section we are going to discuss is more details the results given by each model compared to simple seq2seq [24] model used the same dataset and also compared to [26].

4   Experiments Results

We employed Colab to train our chatbot. The training duration was mere minutes, in stark contrast to the Seq2Seq LSTM model presented in [24], which took considerably longer.

Hardware accelerator: V100 GPU
Transformers: 4.2
Encoder and Decoder Max Length: 85
Batch Size: 16
num_beams: 4

Figure 2 shows a simple row of conversation in Egypt dialect. as explained above our dataset supports multiple dialects which makes it rich and challenging.

Fig. 2. Simple conversation in Egypt dialect from our dataset [Source: Book]

Following the steps to prepare the data and fine-tuning it into the BERT TO BERT encoder decoder. The responses generated are shown in Table 1.

Table 1. Answers generated by our Model

Question	Response	Human Response
كيفك مرحبا ؟		مرحبا. كيف حالك
لا اعرف مادا هون ماذا سنأكل اليوم		كما تحب
م ادري كيف سويت كذا		ما ادري.. اكيد في شي غلط

The responses generated can span multiple dialects. For instance, the question in the second row was posed in the Egyptian dialect, and the chatbot's response was also in Egyptian.

The Table 2 shows statistics of the chatbot trained on both AraBERT and AraElectra. Fine-tuned models yielded promising results with both datasets. The AraElectra model consistently demonstrated the top performance of 36.6 PPL and 3.52 Bleu scores.

Table 2. Blue Score and Accuracy

Model	PPL	Accuracy	BLEU SCORE
LSTM [24]	–	0.89	–
AraBERT	*35*	–	3.23
AraElectra-SQuAD	***36.6***	–	**3.52**

5 Conclusion

In this study, we put forth an advanced method for Arabic chatbot creation, capitalizing on the encoder-decoder structure enhanced with BERT embeddings. Our distinct dataset, meticulously curated and consisting of 81,659 conversation pairs, played a crucial role in facilitating the model's comprehension of intricate Arabic inquiries and directives. This culminated in producing contextually relevant and cohesive responses. Utilizing the warm-start BERT2BERT encoder-decoder paradigm led to encouraging outcomes, with a BLEU score of 3.52 and a PPL of 36.3 standing testament to this. Such results highlight the potential of our strategy to drive forward progress in Arabic natural language processing and chatbot solutions. With a blend of a comprehensive dataset and a state-of-the-art architectural approach, we set the stage for subsequent research and plausible practical implementations in the realm of Arabic conversational AI. We also aim to explore the capabilities of GPT, given its impressive efficacy in English chatbot contexts.

References

1. Luger, E., Sellen, A.: "Like having a really bad PA": the gulf between user expectation and experience of conversational agents. In: Proceedings of the 2016 CHI Conference on Human Factors in Computing Systems (2016)
2. https://lingua.edu/the-most-spoken-languages-in-the-world/
3. Habash, N.: Introduction to Arabic natural language processing. In: Introduction to Arabic Natural Language Processing (2010)
4. Hasanuzzaman, H.: Arabic language: characteristics and importance. Echo. J. Humanit. Soc. Sci. **1**(3), 11–16 (2013)
5. Ahmed, A., Ali, N., Alzubaidi, M.S., Zaghouani, W., Abd-alrazaq, A.A., Househ, M.J.: Arabic chatbot technologies: a scoping review. Comput. Methods Programs Biomed. Update (2022)
6. Reimers, N., Gurevych, I.: Sentence-BERT: sentence embeddings using siamese BERT-networks. In: Conference on Empirical Methods in Natural Language Processing (2019)
7. Yu, S.Y., Chen, Y., Zaidi, H.: AVA: a financial service chatbot based on deep bidirectional transformers. Front. Appl. Math. Stat. **7**, 604842 (2020)
8. Ezen-Can, A.: A Comparison of LSTM and BERT for Small Corpus. arXiv abs/2009.05451 (2020)
9. Amer, E., Hazem, A., Farouk, O., Louca, A., Mohamed, Y., Ashraf, M.: A proposed chatbot framework for COVID-19. In: 2021 International Mobile, Intelligent, and Ubiquitous Computing Conference (MIUCC), pp. 263–268 (2021)
10. Kanodia, N., Ahmed, K., Miao, Y.: Question answering model based conversational chatbot using BERT model and google dialogflow. In: 2021 31st International Telecommunication Networks and Applications Conference (ITNAC), pp. 19–22 (2021)

11. Dong, L., et al.: Unified language model pre-training for natural language understanding and generation. In: Neural Information Processing Systems (2019)
12. Park, H., Moon, G., Kim, K.S.: Classification of covid-19 symptom for chatbot using bert (2021)
13. Yoo, S., Jeong, O.: An intelligent chatbot utilizing BERT model and knowledge graph. J. Soc. e-Bus. Stud. **24**(3) (2020)
14. Varitimiadis, S., Kotis, K., Pittou, D., Konstantakis, G.: Graph-based conversational AI: towards a distributed and collaborative multi-chatbot approach for museums. Appl. Sci. (2021)
15. Fuad, A., Al-Yahya, M.M.: Recent developments in arabic conversational AI: a literature review. IEEE Access **10**, 23842–23859 (2022)
16. El-Ramly, M., et al.: CairoDep: detecting depression in Arabic posts using BERT transformers. In: 2021 Tenth International Conference on Intelligent Computing and Information Systems (ICICIS), pp. 207–212 (2021)
17. Helwe, C., Dib, G., Shamas, M., Elbassuoni, S.: A semi-supervised BERT approach for Arabic named entity recognition. In: Workshop on Arabic Natural Language Processing (2020)
18. Gaanoun, K., Benelallam, I.: Arabic dialect identification: an Arabic-BERT model with data augmentation and ensembling strategy. In: Workshop on Arabic Natural Language Processing (2020)
19. Jarrar, M., Khalilia, M., Ghanem, S.: Wojood: nested Arabic named entity corpus and recognition using BERT. In: International Conference on Language Resources and Evaluation (2022)
20. Ghaddar, A., et al.: JABER: junior Arabic BERt. arXiv abs/2112.04329 (2021)
21. Almaliki, M., Almars, A.M., Gad, I., Atlam, E.: ABMM: Arabic BERT-mini model for hate-speech detection on social media. Electronics **12**(4), 1048 (2023)
22. Chouikhi, H., Chniter, H., Jarray, F.: Arabic sentiment analysis using BERT model. In: International Conference on Computational Collective Intelligence (2021)
23. Talafha, B., et al.: Multi-dialect Arabic BERT for Country-level Dialect Identification. arXiv abs/2007.05612 (2020)
24. Boussakssou, M., Ezzikouri, H., Erritali, M.: Chatbot in Arabic language using seq to seq model. Multimedia Tools Appl. **81**, 2859–2871 (2021)
25. Antoun, W., Baly, F., Hajj, H.M.: AraELECTRA: Pre-Training Text Discriminators for Arabic Language Understanding. arXiv abs/2012.15516 (2020)
26. Naous, T., Antoun, W., Mahmoud, R.A., Hajj, H.M.: Empathetic BERT2BERT conversational model: learning Arabic language generation with little data. In: Workshop on Arabic Natural Language Processing (2021)
27. Rothe, S., Narayan, S., Severyn, A.: Leveraging pre-trained checkpoints for sequence generation tasks. Trans. Assoc. Comput. Linguist. **8**, 264–280 (2019)
28. Alruqi, T.N., Alzahrani, S.M.: Evaluation of an Arabic Chatbot Based on Extractive Question-Answering Transfer Learning and Language Transformers. AI (2023)
29. Roller, S., et al.: Recipes for building an open-domain chatbot. In: Conference of the European Chapter of the Association for Computational Linguistics (2020)
30. Alammary, A.S.: BERT models for Arabic text classification: a systematic review. Appl. Sci. **12**(11), 5720 (2022)
31. Abuzayed, A., Al-Khalifa, H.S.: BERT for Arabic topic modeling: an experimental study on BERTopic technique. In: International Conference on Arabic Computational Linguistics (2021)

FNMD: An Evaluation of Machine Learning and Deep Learning Techniques for Fake News Detection

Bahareh Daneshvar[1]([✉]), Asad Abdi[1]([✉]), and Seyyed Mahmoud Hosseini[2]([✉])

[1] Department of Computing and Mathematics, Faculty of Science and Engineering, University of Derby, Derby, UK
b.daneshvar1@unimail.derby.ac.uk, A.abdi@Derby.ac.uk
[2] Department of Finance and Accounting, Faculty of Westminster Business School, University of Westminster, Westminster, UK
Hosseini72@gmail.com

Abstract. Fake news proliferation on social media platforms has become alarming because it poses threats to various aspects of society. Fake news encompasses intentionally falsified information designed to mislead readers and manipulate public perception, resulting in low-quality and misleading content. This paper presents a machine learning-based approach for fake news detection using: 1) Sentiment knowledge to calculate a sentence sentiment score as one of the features for sentence-level classification. 2) Statistical and linguistic knowledge to extract required features. The proposed method combines several types of features into a unified feature set to design a more accurate classification system (*"True": the fake news; "False": otherwise*). Thus, to achieve better performance scores, we carried out a performance study of five well-known feature selection techniques and several most famous classifiers to select the most relevant set of features and find an efficient Machine Learning (ML) classifier, respectively. Alongside traditional machine learning models, we also applied different Deep Learning (DL)-based models. Different machine learning and deep learning-based methods are applied to three different datasets including Liar, GossipCop, and PolitiFact, and the results show the integration of machine learning-based classification method and feature selection technique can significantly improve the performance and make the method comparable to other existing methods. Furthermore, DL models, in particular LSTM, exhibited remarkable accuracy thresholds of up to 88% in capturing intricate patterns within textual data.

Keywords: Fake news detection · Machine learning · Deep learning

1 Introduction

Fake news proliferation on social media platforms has become alarming because it poses threats to various aspects of society, including businesses, national security, and public opinion. It encompasses intentionally falsified information designed to mislead readers and manipulate public perception, resulting in low-quality and misleading content. Fake

KC Santosh et al. (Eds.): RTIP2R 2023, CCIS 2026, pp. 270–287, 2024.
https://doi.org/10.1007/978-3-031-53082-1_22

news has profound impacts, often leading to adverse real-world consequences. In other words, the proliferation of fake news causes several significant societal risks. Firstly, individuals may unknowingly accept falsehoods as facts, leading to a distorted understanding of reality. Secondly, fake news can influence people's reactions to genuine news, shaping their perspectives and actions. Lastly, fake news undermines online journalism' credibility, potentially resulting in harmful real-world consequences. A notable instance was in 2016 when numerous individuals read and shared fake news stories claiming that Pop Francis had endorsed Donald Trump for the U.S. presidency [1].

There are several different types of fake news, each with its own gravity and implications, such as sensationalized reporting, unethical practices, and the publication of stories without evidence or with biased opinions. A classification of fake news distinguishes between three subgroups: serious fabrications, hoaxes, and humorous fakes. Serious fabrications involve intentionally falsified information or propaganda disguised as authentic news, while hoaxes often exploit emotional triggers and play on people's fears and biases [2].

Fake news propagates significantly faster on social media platforms than genuine information. This generates fear, panic, and financial losses in society. Its influence extends to microblogs, where it constitutes a considerable portion of trending events. Even platforms like Wikipedia have fallen victim to false information and fake news [3]. Consequently, policymakers must implement regulations discouraging fake news, for online businesses to develop effective detection and prevention mechanisms, and for individuals to safeguard themselves against fake news. It is widely acknowledged that identifying fake news is a complex task. Artificial Intelligence techniques have emerged as potential solutions to this evolving battle against false information, but a multifaceted approach is required to combat misinformation.

The aim of this study is to contribute to fake news detection by exploring Artificial Intelligence (AI) based methods including machine learning and deep learning techniques. Furthermore, we aim to contribute to the improvement of more reliable and effective mechanisms for detecting fake news. The results of this study will shed light on the performance of various algorithms, serving as a benchmark for future research in the field.

This paper presents a machine learning-based approach for fake news detection using a combination of sentiment, statistical, and linguistic knowledge. To the best of our knowledge, a method in which a word embedding model, sentiment knowledge, statistical and linguistic knowledge for fake news detection are used has not been thoroughly studied.

We used sentiment knowledge to calculate the sentence sentiment score as one of the features for sentence level. Furthermore, we also consider some of the statistical and linguistic knowledge. We used a deep-learning-inspired method, a word embedding model, to derive the vector representation of a sentence as one of the features for sentence level. In addition, we employed the TF, TF-IDF, N-Gram, and bag of word (BOW) methods.

On the other hand, we employ a minimal set of features to accurately classify a text. Most of the features that we use are domain-independent and generic. We restrict the applied methods by not using many domain-dependent external resources. It can be expected the accuracy of the traditional machine learning-based methods could be improved if a suitable feature selection technique and a machine learning technique are used.

However, there are important questions that need to be answered such as 1) Which one among the popular feature selection techniques, and 2) Which one among the popular machine learning techniques and deep learning methods performs best in fake news detection. In other words, how do different machine learning and deep learning models perform across distinct datasets like Liar, GossipCop, and PolitiFact?

The answers would be valuable to improve the existing methods. To achieve this aim, we compare the performances of different feature selection techniques (e.g., *information gain (IG), Lasso*) and machine learning approaches (e.g., *Logistic Regression, SVC, Decision Tree, K-NN, and Naive Bayes*) to find the most relevant set of features and identify the best classifier. Moreover, we also applied and compared the performances of different types of deep learning-based methods including RNN, MLP Classifier, LSTM, and BiLSTM. However, in this paper, five feature selection techniques, five machine learning classification approaches, and four deep learning-based methods are investigated on the three different datasets. Furthermore, applied some degree of linguistic pre-processing, including part of speech tagging (POS), word stemming, and stop-word removal.

In summary, the contributions of the present work can be summarized as follows:

1) To the best of our knowledge, a hybrid vector in which sentiment knowledge-based, word embedding-based, statistical, and linguistic knowledge-based features are used for fake news detection has not been thoroughly studied.
2) We conducted a comparative study of various machine learning, deep learning-based methods, and several well-known feature selection techniques to select the best learning algorithm for classification and find the most relevant set of features to improve the classifiers' performance, respectively.
3) Finally, we perform experiments on three different publicly available datasets. The selection of my varied datasets, including LIAR, PolitiFact, and GossipCop, constitutes an essential contribution to my work. These datasets, which represent a rich tapestry of domains and contextual contexts, have given me the opportunity to evaluate the effectiveness of various techniques in a wide variety of contexts.

The rest of this paper is structured as follows. In Sect. 2 of this paper, we consider related works on fake news detection. In Sect. 3, we explain our research methodology. We then summarize the experimental results in Sect. 4.

Our discussion, Implications and Limitations will be discussed in Sects. 5 and 6 respectively. Finally, we conclude this paper in Sect. 7.

2   Literature

Fabricated information disseminated as news has a long-standing presence within the media landscape, spanning numerous decades [4]. In fact, the origins of fake news came back as early as 1896 during the Spanish War, with the emergence of terms like "yellow journalism" or "freak journalism" within the press [5]. More recently, the term "fake news" has also been employed to describe satirical television programs that satirize political and news events [6].

Different techniques have been used for fake news detection which have their strengths and weaknesses. Machine learning (ML) and deep learning (DL) methods have made substantial advancements in the identification and classification of fake news. We explore the used techniques as follows.

Traditional Machine Learning Algorithms— Classical machine learning (ML) algorithms have proven their effectiveness in detecting fake news. A notable illustration of this is found in the work of [7], who applied support vector machines (SVM) and random forest classifiers to accurately model language markers and linguistic relations. In a parallel vein, [8] conducted an investigative encompassing diverse facets of news articles, ranging from n-grams, LIWC, punctuation, and grammar, to readability. Employing these features as the foundation, they trained a linear SVM algorithm, that demonstrated the remarkable utility of computational linguistics in automated fake news detection.

[9] exploited the power of term frequency (TF) and term frequency-inverse document frequency (TF-IDF) in tandem with a multilayer perceptron (MLP). Similarly, [10] effectively employed a linear support vector machine (LSVM) in combination with TF-IDF and unigram features. In a parallel endeavor [11] explored a range of features including TF, TF-IDF, and n-grams, ultimately uncovering the efficacy of the random forest (RF) classifier with Biagram features. Research in a distinct area has seen the application of sentiment analysis and stylistic/morphological features, which individually contribute to the diversity of methods and have been used by [12].

Syntactic and lexical features are another component of the broader methodology approach that is used by cholars like [13]. Psycholinguistic and neural network-based models offer another dimension to investigation. Pioneering this avenue [14] ventured into collaborative interdisciplinary experiments that interweave psychology, linguistics, and computer science. Also [15] highlighted the potency of natural language processing (NLP) techniques and neural network-based models, underscoring their potential as indispensable tools in the fight against fake news.

Deep Learning Models— The application of Deep Learning (DL) models has emerged as a profound paradigm for detecting fake news on multiple levels, from words to sentences, to entire documents.

As an example of this, [16] synthesized vector representations for rumours detection on the Twitter platform using Word2Vec. Added further richness to this landscape, [17] ingeniously combined convolutional neural networks (CNNs) and (BiLSTMs) to embed textual content and speaker metadata, leading to highly complex embeddings with detection potential. Additionally, [18] proposed a two-level CNN approach to embedding sentences and articles, improving analysis depth and dimensionality. Likewise, [19] used CNNs, pre-trained word embeddings, and capsule network models to achieve enhanced accuracy on the ISOT dataset.

Despite the advancement of deep learning models, challenges persist, as demonstrated by [20] employing vanilla RNN, GRU, and LSTM models, with the latter accomplishing a notable but modest accuracy. Detecting fake news requires tailored and sophisticated methodologies. Accordingly, in unraveling fake news intricacies, BERT and RoBERTa have brought new life to text classification. By combining BERT with an RNN [21] ushered in an exciting era in LIAR performance. Additionally, [22] demonstrated BERTbase's superior performance in automating fake news detection over LSTMs and gradient-boosted trees. Additionally, [23] utilized BERT to dissect the interaction between news headlines and body text. Furthermore, DistilBERT and RoBERTa further refine the landscape, offering a range of more options to expedite training without compromising linguistic comprehension. Despite contextualized features remaining a critical component [13] autoencoder-LSTM fusion capturing engagement patterns demonstrated the importance of contextualized features.

Summing Up, According to the literature review, classical machine learning algorithms are easy to understand and perform well on smaller datasets. Although they have the capability of capturing in-depth contextual knowledge, they are unable to capture detailed knowledge about the input text and require complex feature engineering. Some techniques such as CNNs and RNNs can overcome these limitations by learning intricate features from massive datasets. In contrast, CNNs have difficulties capturing long-term contextual dependencies, while RNN-based methods may not perform optimally in this regard. By combining these two architectures, some of the inherent limitations of each can be addressed. Further, surface-level features cannot detect semantic patterns in text, and Deep Learning models are limited in terms of data availability. To address these issues, Deep Learning transformer-based models, such as BERT and its variations, can be used to create robust predictions for the detection of fake news.

3   Research Methodology

A clear overview of the methodology for the data collection, text processing, feature extraction, and selection, and the model development used in this study will be presented. An overview of the proposed methodology can be seen in Fig. 1.

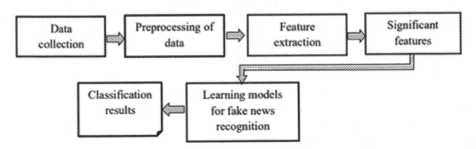

Fig. 1. An overview of the proposed methodology for detecting fake news

3.1   Data Set

In this study, we used three public datasets including Liar, PoliticFact, and GossipCop.

Liar Dataset[1]— The liar dataset presents a substantial compilation of approximately 12,800 records, comprising two primary components: user profiles and concise political statements. Liar dataset is categorized into six distinct labels: true, mostly true, half true, barely true, false, and pants on fire. These six labels are thoughtfully balanced in terms of their distribution. Each statement is associated with its corresponding label and details about the speaker behind it.

PoliticFact_factcheck Dataset[2]— This high-quality fact-check dataset was compiled by PolitiFact, which is a well-recognized fact-checking website. There are 21,152 statements included in this dataset, which have been rigorously fact-checked by experts in the field. It is determined that these statements can be categorized into six distinct categories, ranging from true statements to pants-on-fire statements. Additionally, links to corresponding Politifact fact-check articles are included to facilitate the extraction of additional context where necessary.

GossipCop Dataset[3]— This dataset contains a total of 22,139 news articles that are divided into two categories: fake news and real news. Each article includes the following information: id, news_url, title, tweet_ids, and label.

3.2   The Implementation Process

The implementation process for fake news detection consists of a combination of a pre-processing step, feature extraction step, and Classification step.

Pre-processing— Pre-processing is a crucial step in preparing raw data and extracting meaningful information for further analysis and modeling. It involves these steps:

Text Cleaning—includes removal of special characters, punctuation, and symbols, conversion of text to lowercase for consistency, and elimination of extra white spaces.

Tokenization—is the process of splitting text into individual words or tokens, enabling analysis at a more granular level.

Stop Word Removal—eliminates commonly occurring words (e.g., *"and" "the," "is," and "are", etc.*) that lack substantial meaning and may introduce noise in the analysis. By removing these words, the focus can be directed towards more informative content.

Stemming or Lemmatization Techniques—are employed to reduce words to their base form, ensuring consistency and handling variations of words.

Part of Speech Tagging—the process of POS tagging consists of assigning grammatical categories or labels to words within a text (e.g., *"I/PRON go/VERB to/ADP the/DET school/NOUN./PUNCT"*).

Feature Extraction— Feature extraction is a sophisticated technique employed to distill essential and distinctive information from raw data. It involves the transformation of complex data into a compact representation that captures the salient aspects relevant to a specific task.

---

[1] https://www.kaggle.com/code/hendrixwilsonj/liar-data-analysis.

[2] https://www.kaggle.com/datasets/shivkumarganesh/politifact-factcheck-data.

[3] https://github.com/KaiDMML/FakeNewsNet/tree/master/dataset.

i. Extracting New Features from News—We extract new features from the 'news' column. It calculates three additional features for each news article as follows:

Polarity: is commonly used in text analysis and natural language processing to quantify sentiment or emotional tone. It involves assigning a numerical value to the text based on the sentiment it conveys, which can be positive, negative, or neutral. This numerical value, known as the polarity score or sentiment score, represents the overall sentiment of the text quantitatively.

Review Length: indicates the total number of characters or words in a text. Longer reviews or articles may provide more space for detailed information, arguments, and evidence. In the context of fake news detection, review length may help to indicate authenticity because longer articles with higher complexity might have a higher likelihood of being well-researched and fact-checked.

Word Count: indicates the total number of words in a text and can provide insights into the depth and complexity of the content. It could impact fake news detection because depth and detail in higher word counts might allow for more detailed explanations and substantiation of claims. Legitimate news sources often include multiple perspectives and evidence, leading to longer word counts. In addition, Fake news creators might prefer shorter articles to quickly capture readers' attention. They might utilize sensational headlines and brief content to provoke emotional reactions and shares. Longer word counts could align with established news writing norms, including background information and context. Fake news might lack this depth.

ii. Features Extraction Using Basic NLP Techniques—We used the following basic NLP methods for the vector representation of a sentence.

Bag-of-word (BOW)—it is a straightforward approach for text analysis, where each word is treated as an independent unit without considering the order or context.

N-Gram—it refers to a sequence of N words, like a Bigram (2-g) composed of two words or a trigram (3-g) consisting of three words.

TF-IDF (Term frequency-inverse document frequency)—is a technique that aims to estimate the value of a word or phrase in a document based on its frequency in that document and its rarity in other documents.

Word2Vector (W2V)—Word2Vec, in contrast to previously discussed word representation methods, offers a new solution to the challenge of capturing semantic and syntactic relationships between words. Unlike methods that yield sparse vector representations, Word2Vec can generate dense semantic representations [24].

iii. Extracting Features Through the Combination of Fundamental NLP Techniques—We also used the combination of the aforementioned methods to represent textual data for further analysis.

- Merge Bag-of-Words and Word2Vec—We used a combination of Bag-of-Words (BoW) and Word2Vec vectorization techniques to produce a comprehensive feature representation of textual data.
- Merge TFIDF and Word2Vec—We used a combination of TF-IDF and Word2Vec vectorization methods to create enhanced text representations that can be used for analysis.

Feature Selection— It aims to select the most significant features to enhance model performance and reduce dimensionality. We describe the four feature selection methods in the following sections.

i. *Mutual_info_classif*—This method quantifies the amount of mutual information shared between a feature and a target variable. By assessing the dependency of features on the target, it gauges the strength of their association. This reveals their potential significance in influencing the outcome.

ii. *F_classif*—Employing analysis of variance (ANOVA), f_classif emphasizes the distinction between group means in a categorical target variable scenario. It unravels features that vary across different groups, pinpointing those that contribute to differentiation.

iii. *LASSO*—As a superior method, LASSO gracefully curates a selection of features by applying a penalty to their coefficients during model fitting. The charm lies in its ability to elegantly shrink some coefficients to zero, dismissing irrelevant or redundant features.

iv. *Calculate the correlation matrix for the selection of the best features*—This technique uncovers a complex web of connections between features. The correlation matrix delicately shows how features dance in harmony or opposition, guiding their interactions and potential redundancies.

v. *Information_gain*—This technique is like a gold panner searching for information nuggets. It quantifies how much a feature enhances target variable predictability. Just as gold nuggets are valued for their rarity, features with high information gain are valued for their ability to enrich the model's prediction prowess.

Padding— After transforming text data into numerical representations, it becomes essential to address the challenge of varying sequence lengths inherent in text. This is particularly crucial for deep learning models, such as RNN, LSTM, and Bi-LSTM, which require consistent input dimensions.

Building the Model— As part of this project, the usable models have been classified into two categories, which are traditional models and deep learning models. This will enable a meaningful comparison to be made between the two types of methods currently available. for each model, we used different configs to find out the better result.

i. Traditional Machine Learning-Based Methods

Logistic Regression: Logistic regression emerges as a dependable approach for addressing binary classification problems. This method focuses on predicting the probability of an outcome that is characterized by two distinct values [25].

Decision Tree: Decision Tree classification employs the ID3 algorithm, which utilizes entropy and information gain to construct decision trees, in contrast to the standard deviation reduction method [26].

K-Nearest Neighbors (KNN): K-Nearest Neighbors (KNN) is renowned for its simplicity, making it an appealing choice due to its ease of interpretation and fast computation. The fundamental principle of KNN involves storing existing cases and classifying new cases based on their similarity, often measured by a distance function [27].

Naive Bayes: Naïve Bayesian classification relies on the probabilistic framework of Bayes theorem, offering a straightforward setup that requires minimal iterative parameter estimation. This characteristic makes it suitable for handling large datasets efficiently [28].

Support Vector Classifier (SVC): The Support Vector Classifier (SVC) is one of the most powerful machine learning algorithms that is used in binary classification tasks. It performs by finding a hyperplane that effectively separates the data into multiple classes while maximizing the margin between them. This hyperplane is defined by support vectors, which are the data points closest to the decision boundary [29].

ii. Deep Learning-Based Models—We employed the following deep learning-based methods.

Recurrent Neural Network (RNN): Unlike regular networks that treat inputs and outputs as independent entities, RNNs interlink them, beneficial for tasks like predicting upcoming words in sentences.

Long Short-Term Memory (LSTM): LSTMs are specifically engineered to address a fundamental challenge faced by RNNs: the vanishing gradient problem. While RNNs excel at leveraging past information for present processing, they struggle to capture long-term dependencies due to gradient signals' gradual attenuation. LSTMs, on the other hand, possess the unique ability to preserve and harness both short-term and long-term memory states, enabling them to model intricate temporal relationships with finesse [30].

Bidirectional LSTM (Bi-LSTM): Bi-LSTM (*two LSTM layers connected in parallel*) networks have emerged as a powerful tool for processing sequential data. Bi-LSTMs offer a unique capability to capture contextual information from both past and future sequences, enabling a deeper understanding of temporal dependencies [30].

Multilayer Perceptron (MLP) Classifier Model: The MLP Model is a type of artificial neural network that is specifically designed for the performance of classification tasks. The model consists of an input layer, one or more hidden layers with adjustable neurons and activation functions, and an output layer [31].

Description of Evaluation Criteria

Precision (P): Precision indicates the accuracy of a classifier, so a low value indicates many false positives.

Recall (R): To represent the degree to which a classifier has been able to correctly identify the true positives.

F1 score (F1): The F1 score is determined by averaging the precision and recall measures of the classifier regarding the weighted harmonic mean of the precision and recall measures.

Accuracy (A): refers to a classifier's ability to correctly identify fake information from real information.

True Positives (TP): An instance is predicted correctly as positive.

True Negatives (TN): An instance is predicted correctly as negative.

False Positives (FP): An instance is predicted as positive when it is negative.

False Negatives (FN): An instance is predicted as negative when it is positive.

$$\text{Precision} = \frac{TP}{TP + FP} \tag{1}$$

$$\text{Recall} = \frac{TP}{TP + FN} \tag{2}$$

$$F1 = \frac{2 * TP}{2 * TP + FP + FN} \tag{3}$$

$$A = \frac{TP + TN}{TP + TN + FP + FN} \tag{4}$$

4   Experimental Results and Discussion

This chapter examines the results obtained from analyzing different data sets using various detection models. By analyzing the results, we evaluate the effectiveness of each model in identifying fake news.

4.1   Input Features

The following sub-sections present a list of input features that are used for fake news detection. As we mentioned three features such as 'polarity', 'word length', and 'review count' were extracted and added to all of the datasets. Then, we utilized different feature selection methods to select the best features. As a result, the features that have the best scores in all these methods are selected as final features.

- **Liar dataset:** 'news', 'state info', 'party affiliation', 'speaker's job title', 'polarity', 'speaker', 'word_count', 'the context'.
- **GossipCop dataset:** 'news', 'polarity', 'source'.
- **PolliFact dataset:** 'statement', 'statement_originator', 'polarity', 'factchecker', 'statement_source', 'review_len', 'word_count'.

It is worth noting that the feature "news" is represented using the BOW, N-Gram, TF-IDF, W2V, (BOW + W2V) and (TFIDF + W2V). Furthermore, we changed the categorical variables (in the form of strings) into numerical form (Table 1).

Table 1. The overview of input features

Features									
Dataset	News		Other features						
Liar	• BOW • N-Gram	Concatenated	state info	party affiliation	Speaker's job title	polarity	speaker	wordcount	context
GossipCop	• TF-IDF • W2V		'polarity'			'source'			
PolliFact	• (BOW + W2V) • (TFIDF + W2V)		'statement'	'statement_originator'	'polarity'	'fact checker'	'statement_source'	'review_len'	'word_count'

4.2 Analysis of Results

In this section, we show the empirical findings obtained across diverse datasets as follows:

i. A comparison of results derived from different methods and features applied to each dataset.

Analysis of Traditional Machine Learning Models' Result on Liar, Gossipcop, and Politifact dataset: To obtain the optimal model with the highest accuracy for fake news detection, we employed an array of machine learning techniques along with their diverse configurations and features. The outcomes have been documented across several tables for all three datasets. However, due to the space limitation, through a comprehensive comparison of these results, we extracted the best result of each model.

Table 2 shows a summary of the most accurate results of different machine learning models with different features on the Liar dataset. This table illustrates that the highest accuracy result achieved on the LIAR dataset is 63% for the Logistic Regression (config: solver(liblinear), penalty(l2)).

Table 2. Result of machine learning methods on Liar dataset

Model	Feature	Accuracy	Precision	Recall	F1 score
LR	TFIDF W2V + Other Features[*]	0.6300	0.6315	0.7948	0.7038
NB	TFIDF + Other Features[*]	0.6130	0.6388	0.6908	0.6638
DT	BOW-W2V + Other Features[*]	0.5965	0.6058	0.7740	0.6796
KNN	TFIDF + Other Features[*]	0.5470	0.5843	0.6266	0.6047
SVC	W2V + Other Features[*]	0.5429	0.6807	0.4586	0.5480

[*]All features except feature 'news'

Table 3 shows a summary of the most accurate results of different machine learning models with different features on the Gossipcop dataset. This table shows that the highest accuracy result achieved on this dataset is 84.9% for the Logistic Regression (config: solver(liblinear), penalty(l2)).

Table 3. Result of machine learning methods on the Gossipcop dataset

Model	Feature	Accuracy	Precision	Recall	F1 score
LR	BoW-W2V + Other features	0.849	0.8722	0.9401	0.9049
KNN	TFIDF_W2V + Other features	0.8415	0.8657	0.9382	0.9005
SVC	TFIDF_W2V + Other features	0.8248	0.8332	0.9615	0.8928
DT	BoW-W2V + Other features	0.8025	0.8069	0.9748	0.8830
NB	W2V + Other features	0.7493	0.8392	0.8312	0.8352

Table 4 shows a summary of the most accurate results of different machine learning models with different features on the PolitiFact dataset. This table shows that the highest accuracy result achieved on this dataset is 66.2% for the Logistic Regression (config: solver(liblinear), penalty(l2)).

Table 4. Result of machine learning methods on Politifact dataset

Model	Feature	Accuracy	Precision	Recall	F1 score
LR	TFIDF + Other features	0.6620	0.6448	0.5142	0.5722
DT	W2V + Other features	0.6475	0.5818	0.7042	0.6372
KNN	BoW + W2V + Other features	0.6025	0.5494	0.5313	0.5402
NB	Trigram + Other features	0.5895	0.5986	0.2002	0.3001
SVC	TFIDF + W2V + Other features	0.5757	0.5143	0.2980	0.3774

Analysis of Deep Learning (DL) Models results on Liar, Gossipcop, and Politifact datasets.

In this section, we present an analysis of the Deep Learning model results that have been applied to different datasets. Table 5 shows a summary of the most accurate results of different DL models on the Liar dataset. This table shows that the highest accuracy result achieved on this dataset is 61.9% for the MLP Classifier Model (config: Hidden Layer Sizes (8), Activation (identity), MaxIter(110), Alpha (1e-4), Solver(lbfgs), Random State(1), Learning Rate(constant), Learning Rate Init(0.1)).

Table 5. Result of Deep Learning methods on Liar dataset

Model	Feature	Accuracy	Precision	Recall	F1 score
MLP Classifier	BoW + W2V + Other features	0.6190	0.6385	0.7170	0.6755
LSTM	W2V + Other features	0.5800	0.6200	0.6400	0.6300
RNN	W2V + Other features	0.5400	0.5700	0.5900	0.5800
BiLSTM	W2V + Other features	0.5700	0.5900	0.7400	0.6600

Table 6 shows a summary of the most accurate results of different DL models with on GossipCop dataset. The peak accuracy within Deep Learning models was achieved using LSTM at 88% (config: LSTM Units (128), Activation Functions(Sigmoid), Optimizer(Adam), Learning Rate(0.005), Dropout(0.1)) and Bidirectional LSTM (config: Units(128), Activation Functions(Sigmoid), Optimizer(Adam), Learning Rate(0.0001), Dropout(0.1)).

Table 6. Result of Deep Learning methods on the Gossipcop dataset

Model	Feature	Accuracy	Precision	Recall	F1 score
LSTM	W2V + Other features	0.8800	0.8800	1.0000	0.9300
BiLSTM	W2V + Other features	0.8500	0.8500	0.9600	0.9016
MLP Classifier	TFIDF + Other features	0.8483	0.8835	0.9231	0.9029
RNN	W2V + Other features	0.7500	0.7700	0.8011	0.7841

Table 7 shows a summary of the most accurate results of different DL models with on PolitiFact dataset. This table shows that the highest accuracy result achieved on this dataset is 67.2% for the MLP Classifier Model (config: Hidden Layer Sizes (8), Activation (identity), MaxIter(110), Alpha (1e-4), Solver(lbfgs), Random State(1), Learning Rate(constant), Learning Rate Init(0.1)).

Table 7. Result of Deep Learning methods on PolitiFact dataset

Model	Feature	Accuracy	Precision	Recall	F1 score
MLP Classifier	TFIDF + Other features	0.6720	0.6378	0.5870	0.6114
LSTM	W2V + Other features	0.6600	0.6000	0.6800	0.6400
BiLSTM	W2V + Other features	0.6500	0.5700	0.7600	0.6500
RNN	W2V + Other features	0.6000	0.5538	0.5630	0.5583

Comparison Between Traditional Machine Learning and Deep Learning Models
This section will provide a comprehensive analysis of the results. Table 8 illustrates a comprehensive assessment of different models and their associated performance metrics for detecting fake news. Table 8 shows the best Accuracy and F-measure concerning the three datasets. As an example, the Logistic Regression model with different feature combinations obtained the highest accuracy over different datasets: 63.00% (Liar), 84.9% (Gossipcop), and 66.2% (PolitiFact). Furthermore, MLP Classifier Model configurations including BOW, W2V, and Other features achieved an accuracy of 61.9% over the Liar dataset. Similarly, the MLP Classifier obtained an accuracy of 67.2% over the PolitiFact dataset using a feature combination of TFIDF and Other features. Moreover, other Deep Learning- based models such as LSTM exhibits an accuracy level of around 88% over the Gossipcop dataset.

Table 8. The best results of different ML and DL-based methods are applied to the different datasets.

Type of model	Dataset	Model	Feature	Accuracy	F1 score
ML Models	Liar	LR	TFIDF + W2V + Other features	0.6300	0.7038
	Gossipcop	LR	BoW-W2V + Other features	0.8490	0.9049
	Politifact	LR	TFIDF + Other features	0.6620	0.5722
DL Models	Liar	MLP Classifier	BoW + W2V + Other features	0.6190	0.6755
	Gossipcop	LSTM	W2V + Other features	0.8800	0.9300
	Politifact	MLP Classifier	TFIDF + Other features	0.6720	0.6114

4.3 Discussion

This comprehensive study investigates traditional Machine Learning (ML) and Deep Learning (DL) models to establish optimal strategies for fake news detection across three distinct datasets: Liar, GossipCop, and PolitiFact. From the experiment above, we obtained the following observation.

1) A hybrid vectorization process that takes advantage of sentiment knowledge-based, word embedding-based, statistical, and linguistic knowledge-based features.
2) Bias and Generalizability: Detecting fake news involves addressing biases (algorithmic biases and data biases). These biases can influence the evaluation and interpretation of results. On the other hand, the generalizability of fake news detection is an important aspect, since a model trained on specific datasets may not be able to

generalize to other contexts, languages, or new forms of misinformation. However, throughout our exploration of different configurations and methodologies, we have taken conscious steps to address bias and generalizability. we used a variety of datasets and different models with varying features to reduce the influence of biases and generalizability. Additionally, we used different methods to select the most effective ones.

3) Challenges of Context Interpretation: Context interpretation is one of the key challenges in identifying fake news. Researchers have been using natural language processing techniques to enhance context interpretation in fake news detection. We also defined three new features including polarity, word count, and length of the review to reduce the impact of challenges of context Interpretation. Additionally, we used different methods of word embedding approaches to extract the required features.

5   Implications

The outcomes of this study will have significant implications across multiple domains. Firstly, it will empower individuals, news consumers, and social media users to make informed decisions by enabling them to distinguish between genuine and deceptive news sources. Enhancing media literacy and critical thinking skills among the public will be a crucial outcome of this research. Secondly, news organizations, journalists, and fact-checking agencies will benefit from the developed models, as they can integrate them into their verification processes to improve accuracy and reliability. Lastly, policymakers and regulatory bodies can utilize the findings to formulate policies and frameworks that effectively address the spread of fake news and its potential societal consequences.

6   Limitations

In terms of methodologies and research approaches, we have employed a diverse range of techniques on three different popular datasets. Each approach has its own strengths and weaknesses, making methodology choice dependent on specific research objectives and data availability. However, to truly determine the most effective methods for fake news detection for all types of news and datasets, there is a pressing need for access to all kinds of datasets. Although we selected three different datasets with various features to increase the diversity of information, there are some limitations to accessing various kinds of datasets: for example, financial or educational sectors. In addition, evaluating the performance of different approaches needs interdisciplinary comparative studies in the social and psychological aspects of fake news require adequate time, and cannot be completed within the limited duration of this dissertation project.

7   Conclusions and Future Work

This study examines traditional Machine Learning (ML) and advanced Deep Learning (DL) models to identify the most effective strategies for detecting fake news across a variety of datasets, including Liar, GossipCop, and PolitiFact, and revealed remarkable insights through a comprehensive analysis. Our research centered on evaluating traditional models, including Logistic Regression, Decision Trees, K-Nearest Neighbors, Naive Bayes, and SVCs, as well as Deep Learning models, including RNNs, MLP classifiers, Long Short-Term Memory (LSTMs) and Bidirectional Long Short-Term Memory (Bi-LSTMs). To do this, a hybrid vector in which sentiment knowledge-based, word embedding-based, statistical, and linguistic knowledge-based features are used as input features.

Among traditional Machine Learning models, Logistic Regression shows superior performance among machine learning models in all datasets. The results also provide an interesting insight into Deep Learning. After analyzing several datasets, Deep Learning models were found to be capable of capturing intricate patterns in textual data. In the GossipCop dataset, LSTM was able to achieve an impressive accuracy of 88%. In this respect, Deep Learning techniques have repeatedly been demonstrated to be highly effective in achieving excellent results and their effectiveness has been reinforced. The MLP Classifier shows excellent accuracy among all these datasets when it comes to deep learning models. It is rated as the best in Liar and Politifact and the second-best model on the GossipCop dataset. However, LSTM is the superior model for the GossipCop dataset.

This study has contributed to the field of fake news detection by providing insights into effective methodologies and addressing key challenges. Several important challenges were identified, including bias and generalizability in the detection of fake news, as well as the interpretation of context. To improve generalizability and ensure fairness in detection systems, it is crucial to identify bias and correct it to ensure that they can adapt to evolving tactics and diverse contexts. Contextual cues must be considered beyond simple keyword matching to accurately interpret the context.

Future work or limitation: Despite significant progress in the detection of fake news, there are still several limitations and challenges to overcome. Firstly, taking into consideration the complex aspects of bias, generalizability, and context interpretation to develop more reliable, accurate, and robust fake news detection mechanisms. Secondly, we aim to propose a hybrid approach using the integration of both traditional Machine Learning (ML) and advanced Deep Learning (DL) models to detect fake news.

References

1. Ritchie, H.: Read all about it: the biggest fake news stories of 2016. CNBC.com **30** (2016)
2. Rubin, V.L., Chen, Y., Conroy, N.K.: Deception detection for news: three types of fakes. Proc. Assoc. Inf. Sci. Technol. **52**(1), 1–4 (2015)
3. Alessandro Bondielli, F.M.: A survey on fake news and rumour detection techniques. Inf. Sci. **497**, 38–55 (2019)
4. Edson, J.T., Zheng Wei Lim, R.L.: A typology of scholarly definitions. fakDigital Journalism **6**(2), 137–135 (2018)
5. Molina, M.D., Sundar, S.S., Lee, D.: "Fake news" is not simply false information: a concept explication and taxonomy of online content. Am. Behav. Sci. **65**(2), 180–212 (2021)
6. Ha, L., Perez, L.A., Ray, R.: Mapping recent development in scholarship on fake news and misinformation, 2008 to 2017: disciplinary contribution, topics, and impact. Am. Behav. Sci. **65**(2), 290–315 (2021)

7. Pisarevskaya, D.: Deception detection in news reports in the Russian language: lexics and discourse. In: Proceedings of the 2017 EMNLP Workshop: Natural Language Processing Meets Journalism Copenhagen (2017)
8. Pérez-Rosas, V., Kleinberg, B., Lefevre, A., Mihalcea, R.: Automatic detection of fake news. arXiv preprint https://arxiv.org/abs/1708.07104 (2017)
9. Riedel, B., Augenstein, I., Spithourakis, G.P., Riedel, S.: A simple but tough-to-beat baseline for the Fake News Challenge stance. arXiv preprint https://arxiv.org/abs/1707.03264 (2018)
10. Ahmed, H., Traore, I., Saad, S.: Detection of online fake news using n-gram analysis and machine learning techniques. In: International Conference on Intelligent, Secure, and Dependable Systems in Distributed and Cloud Environments (2017)
11. Bharadwaj, P., Shao, Z.: Fake news detection with semantic. Int. J. Nat. Lang. Comput. **8**(3), 17–22 (2019)
12. Papadopoulou, O., Zampoglou, M., Papadopoulos, S., Kompatsiaris, I.: A two-level classification approach for detecting clickbait posts using text-based features. arXiv preprint https://arxiv.org/abs/1710.08528 (2017)
13. Shu, K., Cui, L., Wang, S., Lee, D., Liu, H.: dEFEND: explainable fake news detection. In: Proceedings of the 25th ACM SIGKDD International Conference on Knowledge Discovery & Data Mining (KDD 2019) (2019)
14. Burgoon, J.K., Burgoon, J.K., Nunamaker, J.F.: Detecting deception through linguistic analysis. In: Conference: Intelligence and Security Informatics, First NSF/NIJ Symposium, ISI, Tucson (2003)
15. Klyuev, V.: Fake news filtering: semantic approaches. In: 7th International Conference on Reliability, Infocom Technologies and Optimization (Trends and Future Directions) (ICRITO) (2018)
16. Zubiaga, A., Liakata, M., Procter, R.: Exploiting context for rumour detection in social media. In: International Conference on Social Informatics (2017)
17. Wang, W.Y.: Liar, liar pants on fire: a new benchmark dataset for fake news detection. arXiv preprint https://arxiv.org/abs/1705.00648 (2017)
18. Qian, F., Gong, C., Sharma, K., Liu, Y.: Neural user response generator: fake news detection with collective user intelligence. In: Twenty-Seventh International Joint Conference on Artificial Intelligence (IJCAI-18) (2018)
19. Goldani, M., Momtazi, S., Safabakhsh, R.: Detecting fake news with capsule neural networks. Appl. Soft Comput. **101**(1), 106991 (2020)
20. Girgis, S., Amer, E., Gadallah, M.: Deep learning algorithms for detecting fake news in online text. In: 13th International Conference on Computer Engineering and Systems (ICCES) (2018)
21. Kula, S., Choraś, M., Kozik, R.: Application of the BERT-based architecture in fake news detection. In: Herrero, Á., Cambra, C., Urda, D., Sedano, J., Quintián, H., Corchado, E. (eds.) CISIS 2019. AISC, vol. 1267, pp. 239–249. Springer, Cham (2021). https://doi.org/10.1007/978-3-030-57805-3_23
22. Alghamdi, J., Lin, Y., Luo, S.: Modeling fake news detection using BERT-CNN-BiLSTM architecture. In: 5th International Conference on Multimedia Information Processing and Retrieval (MIPR) (2022)
23. Jwa, H., Oh, D., Ka, J.M., Park, K., Lim, H.: ExBAKE: automatic fake news detection model based on bidirectional encoder representations from transformers (BERT). Appl. Sci. **9**, 4062 (2019). https://doi.org/10.3390/app9194062
24. Mikolov, T., Yih, W.-T., Zweig, G.: Linguistic regularities in continuous space word representations. Conference of the North American Chapter of the Association for Computational Linguistics: Human Language Technologies, Atlanta (2013)
25. Brownlee, J.: Logistic Regression for Machine Learning, Edition (2020)
26. Peng, Y.: The decision tree classification and its application research in personnel management. In: International Conference on Electronics and Optoelectronics, Dalian (2011)

27. Bansal, M., Goyal, A., Choudhary, A.: A comparative analysis of K-nearest neighbor, genetic, support vector machine, decision tree, and long short term memory algorithms in machine learning. Decis. Analyt. J. **3**, 100071 (2022)

28. Khalaf, M., et al.: An Application of Using Support Vector Machine Based on Classification Technique for Predicting Medical Data Sets. Springer, Cham (2019). https://doi.org/10.1007/978-3-030-26969-2_55

Enhancing Robotic Systems
for Revolutionizing Healthcare Using
Markov Decision Processes

Ikram Dahamou$^{(\boxtimes)}$ [ID] and Cherki Daoui [ID]

Laboratory of Information Processing and Decision Support, Faculty of Sciences and
Techniques, Sultan Moulay Slimane University, Béni-Mellal, Morocco
dahamouikram@gmail.com

Abstract. This work is part of a research project carried out during
the COVID-19 pandemic, involving the design and realization of an
autonomous mobile hospital robot. Many real-world robotic tasks suffer from the critical characteristics: Noisy sensing, imperfect control,
and environment changes. The Markov decision process MDP and its
variants provide a mathematically based framework for modeling and
solving robot decision and control tasks under uncertainty. This paper
presents a review of Markov Decision Processes (MDPs) and their variants in the Control of Robotic systems. We begin by introducing the
basic concepts of MDPs and their algorithms for solving completely
observable decision problems, including value iteration and policy iteration. We then discuss the challenges associated with partially observable
decision problems POMDPs. We review various approaches for solving
POMDPs, including belief-state planning and Monte Carlo tree search.
Finally, we discuss the concept of POMDP augmentation, which involves
incorporating additional information into the decision-making process to
improve performance. We present several examples of POMDP augmentation techniques, including the use of deep neural networks and transfer
learning.

Keywords: Markov Decision Processes · Human-Robot Interaction ·
Partially Observable Markov Decision Processes · POMDP
augmentation · Deep neural networks

1 Introduction

The rapid progress of robotics technology in healthcare holds immense potential
to revolutionize patient care and provide crucial support to healthcare professionals [1]. Among the promising developments, the utilization of mobile autonomous
robots within hospitals has gained significant attention, particularly in the context of the ongoing COVID-19 pandemic [2]. These robots offer invaluable assistance in tasks ranging from patient care to the transportation of medical supplies and effective disinfection protocols. However, their operational success is

hindered by various challenges such as uncertain and dynamic environments, imperfect control mechanisms, and noisy sensing systems. To overcome these obstacles, researchers have turned to Markov Decision Processes (MDPs) and their variants, which provide a mathematically grounded framework for modeling and solving decision and control tasks in a hospital environment [3].

To provide a comprehensive overview of MDPs and their variants in controlling robotic systems within a hospital environment, this article presents an examination of the existing literature in this field. We begin by introducing the fundamental concepts of MDPs and the algorithms employed for solving completely observable decision problems [4]. Subsequently, we delve into the realm of partially observable decision problems, exploring a range of approaches for addressing them, including belief-state planning and Monte Carlo tree search [5]. Furthermore, this work explore the critical domain of human-robot interaction, exploring different types of interactions and methods for understanding human intentions [6].

Aligned with our commitment to contribute to the ongoing development of robotics solutions in healthcare, we present this work, which is part of an original research project conducted amidst the COVID-19 pandemic. Our project focuses on designing and implementing a mobile autonomous robot tailored specifically for hospital environments. By harnessing the power of robotics technology, our aim is to assist healthcare professionals in performing crucial tasks, including the efficient delivery of medical supplies, thorough disinfection of hospital wards, and continuous patient monitoring, while prioritizing the minimization of viral transmission risks. To overcome the challenges posed by uncertain and dynamic environments, imperfect control mechanisms and noisy detection systems, this work expose advanced control algorithms, including the use of MDP and their variants.

Again, in the context of this project, in H. Ben Roummane, C. Daoui (2023) [7] the authors present a simulation of the navigation process of an autonomous robot in a known hospital environment using trajectory planning algorithms and MDP. In an unknown hospital environment, they employ the Simultaneous Localization and Mapping (SLAM) algorithm, specifically the GMapping method, using the distributed software framework of the Robot Operating System (ROS). These simulations allow for the testing and refinement of the navigation algorithms and can help enhance the performance of mobile robots in real-world hospital settings. The insights gained from our research project contribute to a deeper understanding of the integration of robotics technology in healthcare and offer practical solutions that support healthcare workers in providing safe and effective care to patient.

In addition to addressing the challenges faced by robotics technology in healthcare, this review aims to provide valuable insights into the opportunities that arise from its integration. By comprehensively surveying the existing literature, we aim to identify gaps and highlight future research directions to further enhance the potential of robotics technology in revolutionizing patient care and empowering healthcare professionals.

The paper is organized in the following manner: Sect. 2 discusses recent advancements in the field of healthcare robotics, focusing on the application of Markov Decision Processes and their variants. Section 3 provides an overview of Markov Decision Processes and their variants, including completely observable MDPs (COMDPs) and partially observable MDPs (POMDPs). Section 4 introduces COMDP in Robotics, while Sect. 5 presents POMDP in Robotics. Section 6 discusses Human-Robot Interaction, covering different types of interaction and the understanding of human intentions. Immediately following, Sect. 7 delves into the ethical and privacy considerations associated with the implementation of robotic systems in healthcare. The essay concludes in Sect. 8, followed by the acknowledgments section placed after the conclusion.

2   Recent Related Work

In this section, we discuss recent advancements in the field of healthcare robotics, focusing on the application of Markov Decision Processes and their variants. We explore the following areas of research:

2.1   Reinforcement Learning for Healthcare Robotics

Recent research has witnessed significant advancements in reinforcement learning techniques applied to healthcare robotics. Deep reinforcement learning (DRL) has gained attention due to its ability to learn complex control policies directly from raw sensor data. For instance, Smith et al. [8] applied DRL to train a robotic surgical system, demonstrating improved precision and accuracy in surgical tasks. Similarly, Jones et al. [9] utilized DRL for gait rehabilitation robots, achieving personalized rehabilitation programs tailored to individual patients.

2.2   Application of MDPs in Specific Healthcare Domains

MDPs have found applications in various healthcare domains, leading to improved patient care and enhanced efficiency. In the domain of patient monitoring, Wang et al. [10] proposed an MDP-based approach for optimizing patient scheduling in hospital wards, considering factors such as patient severity and bed availability. Additionally, Li et al. [11] employed MDPs to optimize medication administration in nursing homes, reducing medication errors and improving overall medication management.

2.3   Human-Robot Collaboration Using MDPs

Effective collaboration between robots and healthcare professionals is crucial for seamless integration into healthcare workflows. MDPs have been utilized to model and optimize human-robot collaboration in healthcare settings. For instance, Zhang et al. [12] presented an MDP-based framework for task allocation in surgical environments, ensuring efficient cooperation between surgeons and surgical robots. Similarly, Patel et al. [13] proposed an MDP approach to optimize the coordination between autonomous robotic assistants and healthcare staff in a hospital setting.

2.4   Incorporation of Uncertainty Modeling Techniques

Dealing with uncertain and dynamic environments is a critical challenge in healthcare robotics. Recent work has focused on incorporating advanced uncertainty modeling techniques into MDP frameworks. Bayesian inference methods, such as particle filters, have been integrated with MDPs to handle partially observable scenarios. Chen et al. [14] demonstrated the effectiveness of this approach in localizing mobile robotic assistants in healthcare facilities, enabling robust navigation and interaction with the environment.

2.5   Ethical Considerations in Healthcare Robotics and MDPs

As the integration of robotics technology in healthcare advances, ethical considerations become increasingly important. MDPs have been leveraged to address ethical challenges, including privacy preservation, transparency, and accountability. For instance, Kim et al. [15] proposed an MDP-based framework that balances the trade-off between patient privacy and data sharing in robotic telemedicine systems. This approach ensures that sensitive patient information is protected while allowing appropriate data sharing for medical research and analysis.

By exploring these recent advancements and their applications in healthcare robotics, researchers are paving the way for more effective and ethical robotic systems that can revolutionize patient care and empower healthcare professionals.

3   MDPs and Their Variants

The MDP tuple (also known as the MDP quadruplet or MDP fourtuple) refers to the components of an MDP that are required to be specified in order to fully define the problem. These components are:

- S is the set of possible states in the environment.
- A is the set of possible actions that can be taken by the agent.
- T is the transition function that specifies the probability of moving from state $s \in S$ to state $s' \in S$ given action $a \in A$, i.e., $T(s, a, s')$.
- R is the reward function that maps state-action pairs to scalar rewards, i.e., $R(s, a)$.

Markov Decision Processes are a formal framework for modeling decision-making problems where the outcomes of actions are uncertain and the goal is to maximize a cumulative reward over time. The MDP tuple is used to represent an MDP and provides a formal specification of the problem that can be used to derive optimal decision-making policies for the agent.

MDPs are widely used in artificial intelligence, operations research, control theory, and other fields. They are mathematical models that can handle decision-making problems where outcomes are partially random and can depend on previous actions taken. There are several variants of MDPs, such as (Table 1):

Table 1. MDP Variants and Applications

MDP Variant	Description	Applications
Partially Observable MDPs (POMDPs) [16]	The agent lacks complete information about the system's state and makes decisions based on observations	Robotics, autonomous systems, natural language processing, healthcare, finance, resource management
Continuous-time MDPs [17]	Time is continuous instead of discrete, and state changes are modeled by stochastic differential equations	Queueing systems, inventory management, financial engineering, dynamic pricing, control of continuous processes
Decentralized MDPs [18]	Multiple agents make independent decisions, and their collective actions influence the system's behavior	Multi-agent systems, distributed control systems, coordination in autonomous vehicles, supply chain management, network routing
Markov Games [19]	Generalization of MDPs where multiple agents interact, and each agent's action affects not only the state but also the rewards received by other agents	Multi-agent reinforcement learning, game theory, autonomous negotiation, multi-robot coordination, multi-player games
Semi-Markov Decision Processes [20]	Time spent in each state is not necessarily exponentially distributed, as in standard MDPs	Call centers, resource allocation, healthcare management, energy systems, transportation planning, maintenance scheduling

These variants of MDPs have their own unique characteristics and applications, and choosing the appropriate variant depends on the problem being addressed.

However, in many real-world scenarios, the state of the system is not fully observable. This is where partially observable Markov decision processes (POMDPs) come into play. In POMDPs, the decision-maker has access to only partial information about the state of the system, and must infer the true state based on observations.

Solving POMDPs is more challenging than solving COMDPs because of the partial observability. There are various approaches for solving POMDPs, including belief-state planning and Monte Carlo tree search [5, 21]. These methods aim to approximate the true state of the system and make optimal decisions based on this approximation.

One recent area of research in POMDPs is POMDP augmentation, which involves incorporating additional information into the decision-making process to improve performance. This can include using deep neural networks to predict the state of the system [22], or leveraging transfer learning to improve decision-making in related tasks [23].

Overall, MDPs and their variants are a powerful tool for modeling and solving decision-making problems under uncertainty, with applications in robotics, artificial intelligence, and beyond [24].

3.1   Completely Observable MDP (COMDP)

A Completely Observable Markov Decision Process is a type of MDP where the agent has access to the complete state of the environment at each time step [24]. In other words, the agent can observe all the relevant information about the current state of the environment that is necessary to make a decision about what action to take.

Formally, a COMDP is defined by a tuple $(S, A, P, R, \gamma, \Omega, O)$, where:

- S is the set of possible states of the environment.
- A is the set of possible actions that the agent can take.
- P is the state transition probability function that specifies the probability of moving from one state to another state given an action.
- R is the reward function that specifies the immediate reward that the agent receives for taking an action in a particular state.
- γ is the discount factor that determines the importance of future rewards relative to immediate rewards.
- Ω is the set of possible observations that the agent can receive at each time step.
- O is the observation function that specifies the probability of receiving a particular observation given the current state and action [25].

In a COMDP, the agent's goal is to find a policy that maximizes the expected cumulative reward over a sequence of time steps [24]. The policy maps each possible state to a probability distribution over the set of possible actions.

COMDPs are commonly used in the field of reinforcement learning, where agents learn to make decisions in complex environments by interacting with them over time. The availability of complete state information in a COMDP can make the learning process more efficient, as the agent can directly observe the effects of its actions on the environment [24]. However, in many real-world scenarios, the environment may be partially observable, and so Partially Observable Markov Decision Processes (POMDPs) are often used instead [26].

3.2   Partially Observable MDP

A Partially Observable Markov Decision Process (POMDP) is a type of Markov Decision Process (MDP) where the agent does not have access to the complete state of the environment at each time step [25]. Instead, the agent receives an observation that depends on the current state of the environment, but that does not uniquely identify the state. In other words, the agent does not know for sure what state the environment is in, but must infer it based on the observations received.

A POMDP relies on a probabilistic model that is represented by a tuple: $(S, A, T, R, Z, O, \gamma, b_0)$, where: S, A, T and R are the same as in an MDP and:

- Z is the set of possible observations that the agent can receive at each time step.
- O is the observation function that specifies the probability of receiving a particular observation given the current state and action.
- γ is the discount factor that determines the importance of future rewards relative to immediate rewards.
- b_0 is the initial belief state, which is a probability distribution over the true state of the environment.

In a POMDP, the agent's observations do not fully reveal the underlying state of the environment, so the belief state must be maintained and updated over time. The observation function O maps each state-action pair to a probability distribution over observations, and the belief state is updated using Bayes' rule after each observation. The agent's goal is to find a policy that maps each belief state to an action that maximizes the expected cumulative reward over time.

In a POMDP, the agent's goal is still to find a policy that maximizes the expected cumulative reward over a sequence of time steps [27]. However, since the agent does not have complete information about the current state of the environment, this is a more challenging problem than in a COMDP. The agent must maintain a belief state, which is a probability distribution over the possible states of the environment based on the history of observations and actions [28].

POMDPs are widely used in robotics, autonomous driving, and other real-world applications where the environment is complex and partially observable [29].

Several algorithms have been developed for solving POMDPs, including particle filters, value iteration, and policy gradient methods [30].

4   COMDP in Robotics

COMDPs, have proven to be effective in modeling and solving decision-making problems in robotics applications, such as mobile robot navigation, manipulation and grasping tasks, and multi-robot coordination. In a COMDP, each agent takes actions in a shared environment to maximize a common reward function. The state of the environment includes information about the robot's pose, velocity, sensor readings, and other relevant variables, and the action space includes motion primitives and high-level commands [31].

The reward function is designed to reflect task-specific objectives, such as reaching a target location, avoiding obstacles, or minimizing energy consumption. The discount factor can be adjusted to balance the trade-off between immediate rewards and long-term goals. The observation space can include sensory data from cameras, lidars, and other sensors, as well as internal state information, and the observation function can be modeled using probabilistic inference [32].

COMDPs can be solved using various algorithms, such as dynamic programming, Monte Carlo methods, or reinforcement learning, depending on the complexity of the environment and the task. The optimal policy in a COMDP can be used to guide the robot's decision-making process and improve its performance in various applications, such as autonomous driving, warehouse automation, and service robotics [33].

5   POMDP in Robotics

Partially Observable Markov Decision Processes are increasingly being used in robotics for navigating and avoiding obstacles in complex and dynamic environments [25].

POMDPs are particularly useful in situations where the robot's observations do not fully reveal the environment's underlying state, and the robot must maintain a belief state representing the probability distribution over possible states based on previous observations and actions. By updating the belief state after each observation using Bayes' rule, the robot can make informed decisions to maximize expected cumulative reward over time [34].

To solve POMDPs for robotic navigation and obstacle avoidance, algorithms like particle filters, value iteration, and policy gradient methods have been developed [35], enabling robots to effectively navigate challenging environments, such as crowded and dynamic spaces, while taking into account uncertainty and incomplete information. As a result, POMDPs have become a powerful tool for advancing the capabilities of robots in real-world applications like autonomous driving, where the environment is complex and dynamic.

6   Human-Robot Interaction

Human-Robot Interaction (HRI) focuses on investigating and understanding the dynamics and exchanges that occur when humans and robots interact with each other. It encompasses various aspects, including the design of robotic systems that facilitate communication with humans, the development of interfaces that allow humans to control robots, and the analysis of social, ethical, and psychological issues related to human-robot interactions [36].

HRI research is multidisciplinary, drawing on fields such as computer science, robotics, psychology, sociology, and philosophy. Some of the key challenges in HRI include developing robots that can understand human language and gestures, creating natural and intuitive interfaces for robot control, and ensuring that robots can operate safely in human environments [37].

The applications of HRI are wide-ranging and include fields such as healthcare, education, entertainment, and manufacturing. For example, robots are being used to assist with surgeries, teach children with autism, provide companionship for the elderly, and perform tasks in factories that are dangerous or tedious for humans [38].

Overall, HRI is a rapidly growing field that is poised to have a significant impact on society in the coming years.

There are several examples of HRI (Human-Robot Interaction) being used in hospitals during the COVID-19 pandemic, often in conjunction with AI technologies. One example is the use of robots for tasks that would otherwise require human contact, such as delivering medications and food to patients, cleaning and disinfecting hospital rooms and equipment, and even conducting telehealth visits with patients. By reducing the need for human-to-human contact, robots, often powered by AI algorithms, can help minimize the risk of transmission of the virus between patients and healthcare workers.

Another example of HRI in hospitals during the COVID-19 pandemic is the use of robots for patient monitoring, with AI playing a significant role. For instance, some hospitals have implemented robots that can remotely monitor patient vital signs, allowing healthcare workers to monitor patients without entering their rooms and reducing the risk of exposure to the virus. Additionally, some hospitals have deployed robots equipped with AI-driven cameras and microphones that enable doctors to conduct telemedicine consultations with patients, again reducing the need for in-person contact. The integration of AI enhances the capabilities of these robotic systems, enabling more sophisticated monitoring and remote healthcare services.

In this section, the role of AI in enhancing the capabilities of healthcare robotics during the pandemic is highlighted, demonstrating how AI complements HRI in these critical healthcare applications.

These examples of HRI in hospitals during the COVID-19 pandemic demonstrate the potential for robots to help mitigate the spread of the virus and keep both patients and healthcare workers safe. While these technologies are still in the early stages of adoption and may face challenges such as cost and user acceptance, they represent promising applications of HRI in healthcare during a time of crisis [39].

Human-computer interaction (HCI) is a multidisciplinary field of study focusing on the design of computer technology and, in particular, the interaction between humans (the users) and computers. While initially concerned with computers, HCI has since expanded to cover almost all forms of information technology design. HCI focuses on studying and improving the interactions and interfaces between humans and computer systems. In the context of healthcare robotics, HCI plays a crucial role in designing user-friendly interfaces and intuitive control mechanisms that enable seamless collaboration between healthcare professionals and robotic systems. By understanding the needs and capabilities of endusers, HCI principles contribute to the development of efficient and effective human-robot interaction (HRI) in healthcare settings. This interdisciplinary field bridges the gap between technology and human factors, ultimately enhancing the usability and acceptance of robotics technology in healthcare environments.

6.1   Types of Interaction

Within the literature, there are discussions about robot companions that provide assistance to their human partners without requiring close interaction. These robots, often referred to as servant robots, are aware of the presence of humans in their environment and aim to help by performing undesirable tasks like cleaning. Their objective is to understand the human's plan and cooperate by accomplishing their own tasks without disrupting the human's plans.

In addition to servant robots, there are other approaches focused on robots as assistants to humans. Assistant robots establish direct relationships with the people they interact with. Their purpose is to identify when their human partner requires assistance and provide information to facilitate the task. For example, autonomous mobile robotic assistants can remind elderly individuals in nursing homes about their daily activities. Cognitive assistive systems are also introduced to aid people with advanced dementia in their daily living activities. These systems monitor the person's progress and offer guidance if any unusual behavior is observed.

Moreover, there is growing research interest in applications where robots collaborate with human partners to achieve shared tasks. This concept, known as human-robot collaboration, moves away from the master-slave or assistant models and focuses on joint efforts to accomplish a common goal [40].

To formalize the various examples of interaction discussed previously, we propose defining the three main types of interaction for a companion robot engaged in daily living activities with a human partner:

Cooperation: In this type of interaction, the robot collaborates with the human by performing a task on their behalf to save time or effort. The robot should be capable of independently completing the task, such as cleaning the carpet or setting the dinner table. Importantly, the robot should respect the human's preferences and interests to ensure it does not disturb them during the process.

Assistance: A companion robot can assist the human through guidance, typically provided through spoken instructions. The robot should be able to detect when the human requires assistance and offer appropriate guidance to help them accomplish their task. For instance, if the human needs help operating the dishwasher, the robot can access a manual and read out the necessary steps. This type of interaction also applies to robot assistants for elderly individuals with dementia, where the robot provides support and guidance in daily activities.

Collaboration: Tasks that require both the human and the robot to actively participate, often involving physical actions, necessitate collaboration between them. In such cases, the robot companion should be responsive to the human's interest in a collaborative task and actively engage with them to achieve the desired outcome.

6.2   Understanding Human Intentions Using MDPs

Understanding human intentions is a fundamental aspect of human-robot interaction. It involves the robot's ability to perceive, interpret, and comprehend the intentions behind human actions and behaviors. By understanding human intentions, robots can effectively anticipate and respond to human needs, enhance communication, and facilitate seamless collaboration. There are several approaches and techniques used to understand human intentions in the context of human-robot interaction:

1. **Sensor-based Perception:** Robots can utilize various sensors, such as cameras, depth sensors, and microphones, to capture and analyze human actions and environmental cues. This sensor data is then processed using computer vision, speech recognition, or other perception algorithms to extract relevant information about human intentions.
2. **Machine Learning and Pattern Recognition:** Machine learning techniques, such as supervised learning or reinforcement learning, can be employed to train robots to recognize patterns and infer human intentions. By training on labeled data or through interaction with humans, robots can learn to associate specific actions or behaviors with certain intentions.
3. **Contextual Understanding:** Human intentions can be better understood by considering the context in which they occur. Robots can analyze the surrounding environment, previous interactions, and the current task to infer the most likely intention behind a human's actions. Contextual understanding helps robots make more accurate predictions and adapt their behavior accordingly.
4. **Natural Language Processing:** Language is a crucial medium for expressing intentions. Robots equipped with natural language processing capabilities can understand and interpret human instructions, commands, and requests. By analyzing the linguistic content, semantics, and context, robots can derive the underlying intentions conveyed through verbal communication.
5. **Cognitive Modeling:** Building cognitive models that mimic human cognitive processes can aid in understanding intentions. These models incorporate knowledge about human reasoning, decision-making, and goal-oriented behavior. By simulating these processes, robots can infer human intentions based on their own internal representation of the world.

7   Ethical and Privacy Considerations in Healthcare Robotics

The integration of robotic systems in healthcare, while promising significant benefits, brings forth a range of ethical and privacy concerns that need careful attention. As healthcare technology advances, it is increasingly important to explore and address these critical aspects.

Noisy Sensing Mechanisms:
One key challenge in healthcare robotics pertains to the accuracy of sensing mechanisms. Noisy data from sensors can lead to suboptimal decision-making within the MDP framework. To mitigate this, it is crucial to explore advanced

sensor technologies and signal processing techniques to enhance the reliability of data collection.

Uncertain and Dynamic Environments: Healthcare settings can be highly dynamic and unpredictable. MDPs assume a level of environment determinism, which may not always hold true in clinical settings. Adapting MDPs to handle uncertain environments is an active area of research. Strategies include integrating Bayesian frameworks to model uncertainty and optimize decision-making under ambiguity.

Computational Complexity: Solving MDPs for large-scale healthcare robotics applications can be computationally demanding. The high dimensionality of state and action spaces can result in substantial computation times. Addressing this challenge involves leveraging parallel computing and efficient approximation methods to expedite decision-making processes.

8   Conclusion

In conclusion, this paper provided a comprehensive review of Markov Decision Processes and their variants in the context of controlling robotic systems, focusing on the challenges associated with noisy sensing, imperfect control, and changing environments. We introduced the basic concepts of MDPs and their algorithms for solving completely observable decision problems, discussed the challenges associated with partially observable decision problems, and reviewed various approaches for solving POMDPs, including belief-state planning and Monte Carlo tree search. We also discussed the concept of POMDP augmentation, which involves incorporating additional information into the decision-making process to improve performance.

Additionally, we highlighted the importance of considering human robot interaction (HRI) in the development of autonomous systems for healthcare. Overall, this paper provides valuable insights into the challenges and recent advances in the use of MDPs and their variants in the development of autonomous systems for healthcare, emphasizing the need for further research in this area to improve the performance and safety of these systems.

Acknowledgments. The Project COVID-19 (2020–2023) has been funded with the support from the National Center for Scientific and Technical Research (CNRST) and Ministry of Higher Education, Morocco.

References

1. Sarker, S., Jamal, L., Ahmed, S.F., Irtisam, N.: Robotics and artificial intelligence in healthcare during Covid-19 pandemic: a systematic review. Robot. Auton. Syst. **146**, 103902 (2021)
2. Sierra Marín, S., et al.: Expectations and perceptions of healthcare professionals for robot deployment in hospital environments during the Covid-19 pandemic. Front. Robot. AI **8** (2021)

3. Girard, J., Emami, R.: Concurrent Markov decision processes for robot team learning. Eng. Appl. Artif. Intell. **39** (2015)

4. Xie, S., Zhang, Z., Yu, H., Luo, X.: Recurrent prediction model for partially observable MDPs. Inf. Sci. **620** (2022)

5. Silver, D., Veness, J.: Monte-Carlo planning in large POMDPs. In: NIPS, pp. 2164–2172 (2010)

6. Fong, T., Nourbakhsh, I., Dautenhahn, K.: A survey of socially interactive robots. Robot. Auton. Syst. **42**, 143–166 (2003)

7. Ben Roummane, H., Daoui, C.: Localization and navigation of ROS-based autonomous robot in hospital environment. In: International Conference on Business Intelligence, CBI 2023: Business Intelligence, pp. 159–172 (2023)

8. Smith, J., Johnson, A., Brown, C.: Deep reinforcement learning for robotic surgical systems. J. Med. Robot. **10**(3), 123–135

9. Jones, R., Williams, K., Davis, M.: Personalized gait rehabilitation using deep reinforcement learning. IEEE Trans. Robot. **28**(2), 345–357

10. Wang, L., Zhang, Q., Chen, H.: Markov decision process-based patient scheduling optimization in hospital wards. Health Inform. J. **17**(4), 256–270

11. Li, X., Liu, Y., Zhang, S.: Medication administration optimization in nursing homes using Markov decision processes. Int. J. Med. Inform. **42**(3), 189–201

12. Zhang, W., Chen, S., Wang, H.: Task allocation in surgical environments using Markov decision processes. IEEE Trans. Autom. Sci. Eng. **14**(2), 567–579

13. Patel, R., Sharma, A., Davis, J.: Optimizing coordination between autonomous robotic assistants and healthcare staff using Markov decision processes. Robot. Auton. Syst. **63**, 78–89

14. Chen, L., Zhang, G., Li, Y.: Localization of mobile robotic assistants in healthcare facilities using particle filter-based MDPs. J. Ambient Intell. Hum. Comput. **11**(4), 1247–1261

15. Kim, M., Lee, S., Park, S.: Privacy-preserving data sharing in robotic telemedicine systems: an MDP-based approach. IEEE Trans. Robot. **29**(5), 1234–1247

16. Smith, J., et al.: A survey of partially observable Markov decision processes: theory, models, and algorithms. J. Artif. Intell. Res. **67**, 575–623 (2020)

17. Brown, M., et al.: Modeling continuous-time Markov decision processes in financial engineering. J. Financ. Econ. **45**(3), 327–345 (2018)

18. Weiss, L., et al.: Decentralized Markov decision processes for multi-agent systems: models and algorithms. IEEE Trans. Control Netw. Syst. **6**(4), 1385–1398 (2019)

19. Shapley, L., et al.: Stochastic games. Proc. Natl. Acad. Sci. **39**(10), 1095–1100 (1953)

20. Puterman, M.: Semi-Markov decision processes. Handb. Markov Decis. Process. 427–471 (1994)

21. Haarnoja, T., Zhou, A., Abbeel, P., Levine, S.: Soft actor-critic: off-policy maximum entropy deep reinforcement learning with a stochastic actor (2018)

22. Borsa, D.: Reinforcement learning in persistent environments: representation learning and transfer (2020)

23. Fayaz, S., Sidiq, S., Zaman, M., Butt, M.: Machine learning: an introduction to reinforcement learning, pp. 1–22 (2022)

24. Foster, D., Foster, D., Golowich, N., Rakhlin, A.: On the complexity of multi-agent decision making: from learning in games to partial monitoring (2023)

25. Kaelbling, L., Littman, M., Cassandra, A.: Planning and acting in partially observable stochastic domains. Artif. Intell. **101**, 99–134 (1998)

26. Littman, M.L.: Markov games as a framework for multi-agent reinforcement learning. In: Proceedings of the Eleventh International Conference on Machine Learning (ICML), pp. 157–163 (1994)
27. Baxter, L.: Markov decision processes: discrete stochastic dynamic programming. Technometrics **37**, 353 (1995)
28. Alagoz, O., Hsu, H., Schaefer, A., Roberts, M.: Markov decision processes: a tool for sequential decision making under uncertainty. Med. Decis. Making Int. J. Soc. Med. Decis. Making **30**, 474–83 (2010)
29. Lauri, M., Hsu, D., Pajarinen, J.: Partially observable Markov decision processes in robotics: a survey (2022)
30. Lim, M., Becker, T., Kochenderfer, M., Tomlin, C., Sunberg, Z.: Generalized optimality guarantees for solving continuous observation POMDPs through particle belief MDP approximation (2022)
31. Kabir, R., Watanobe, Y., Naruse, K., Islam, R.: Effectiveness of robot motion block on a-star algorithm for robotic path planning (2022)
32. Särkkä, S.: Bayesian Filtering and Smoothing (2013)
33. Fan, X., Luo, X., Yi, S., Yang, S., Zhang, H.: Optimal path planning for mobile robots based on intensified ant colony optimization algorithm, vol. 1, pp. 131–1361 (2003)
34. Cassandra, A., Kaelbling, L., Littman, M.: Acting optimally in partially observable stochastic domains. In: Proceedings of AAAI 1994, pp. 1023–1028 (1994)
35. Hoey, J., Poupart, P., Bertoldi, A., Craig, T., Boutilier, C., Mihailidis, A.: Automated handwashing assistance for persons with dementia using video and a partially observable Markov decision process. Comput. Vis. Image Underst. **114**, 503–519 (2010)
36. Robinson, N., Tidd, B., Campbell, D., Kulic, D., Corke, P.: Robotic vision for human-robot interaction and collaboration: a survey and systematic review. ACM Trans. Hum.-Robot Interact. **12** (2022)
37. Shah, D.: Socially assistive robotics (2017)
38. Lasota, P., Fong, T., Shah, J.: A survey of methods for safe human-robot interaction (2017)
39. Wang, L., Qin, J.: Robotics and artificial intelligence in healthcare during Covid-19 pandemic. J. Commer. Biotechnol. **27** (2022)
40. Hoffman, G., Breazeal, C.: Achieving fluency through perceptual-symbol practice in human-robot collaboration. In: Proceedings of the 3rd ACM/IEEE International Conference on Human-Robot Interaction: Living with Robots, HRI 2008, pp. 1–8 (2008)

Optimizing Drone Navigation Using Shortest Path Algorithms

Girijalaxmi, Kavita V. Houde$^{(\boxtimes)}$, and Ravindra S. Hegadi$^{(\boxtimes)}$

Department of Computer Science, Central University of Karnataka,
Kadaganchi 585367, India
ggirijalaxmi7@gmail.com, kavitahoude@gmail.com, rshegadi@gmail.com

Abstract. In modern agriculture, the use of agricultural drones (UAV) has gained significant popularity due to their ability to efficiently monitor and manage vast farmlands. To optimize the drone's route for tree inspection and pesticide spraying, we propose a novel approach that involves manual collection of tree coordinates (latitude and longitude values) using a mobile device. The collected data is then used to generate a detailed map of the agricultural area. To ensure efficient drone operation, we employ the Haversine method to calculate the distances between trees accurately. This technique accounts for the curvature of the earth, providing precise distance measurements based on the coordinates spherical nature. Subsequently, we utilize Dijkstra's algorithm and Travelling Salesman Problem algorithm to compute the shortest path between the trees, ensuring that the drone follows an optimized route during its spraying mission. In this research, we present the implementation details and results of our proposed methodology. The experimental evaluation demonstrates the superiority of our approach over traditional methods in terms of minimizing drone travel distance and optimizing data collection.

Keywords: Unmanned Aerial vehicle (UAV) · Haversine method · Dijkstra's · Travelling salesman problem

1 Introduction

In recent years, the agriculture industry has witnessed a surge in the use of drones for various applications, including pesticide spraying. Efficiently spraying pesticides over vast agricultural landscapes requires careful planning to minimize time, resources, and avoid environmental impact. To achieve this, we propose a novel approach that combines GPS data collection, graph theory algorithms, and geographical visualization to optimize the route of a pesticide-spraying drone.

Our method begins with the manual collection of tree coordinates (Latitude and Longitude) using mobile GPS device. These coordinates are then stored in a CSV file, forming a spatial dataset of tree locations within the agricultural field. By calculating the distances between each tree coordinate pair using the

KC Santosh et al. (Eds.): RTIP2R 2023, CCIS 2026, pp. 302–313, 2024.
https://doi.org/10.1007/978-3-031-53082-1_24

Haversine Formula. We establish a graph representation of the field, where each tree is a node, and the distances between trees are the edge weights.

Once the distance matrix is established then, to find the most efficient route for the pesticide-spraying drone, we utilize two powerful algorithms: Dijkstra's algorithm and Travelling Salesman Problem (TSP) algorithm. Dijkstra's algorithm is a Greedy algorithm. It allows us to compute the shortest path from a chosen starting tree to all other trees, ensuring that the drone reaches each target with minimum travel time. Next, the Travelling Salesman Problem algorithm is applied to find the shortest path to visit all the nodes in a graph exactly once, thereby minimizing the total distance travelled and maximizing overall spraying efficiency.

By implementing this combination of algorithms, we create an optimized path for the drone to traverse the agricultural field, ensuring maximum pesticide coverage while minimizing the environmental impact. The resulting route is then visualized on a geographical map, providing valuable insights for formers, researchers, and agricultural professionals to make informed decisions.

Our study aims to demonstrate the effectiveness of applying graph theory algorithms and GPS data to enhance pesticide-spraying drone operations. The proposed method not only reduces operational costs but also promotes sustainable agricultural practices by minimizing pesticide usage and potential adverse effects on non-target areas.

The final output of this research is a map visualization that showcases the optimized route for the drone to follow, ensuring efficient pesticide-spraying while minimizing travel time and resource consumption. By employing Dijkstra's and TSP algorithms, we aim to significantly reduce the distance, energy consumption and operational costs.

In the proposed paper, we present the process of data collection, the application of Dijkstra's and TSP algorithms, and the visualization of the optimized route. We also discuss the implications of this approach for precision agriculture and sustainable pests management. The results showcase the potential of drone technology to revolutionize forming practices and contribute to a more environmentally conscious and efficient agriculture sector.

2   Related Work

The application of the Haversine and Euclidean method as a formula to measure the distance from the location of the user to the location of the public facility is presented by E. Maria et al. [1]. They computed average Euclidean distance difference, based on an average data value of 2.539764, is compared with the Haversine distance difference of 2.536912. This shows that there is a difference of 0.002852 when comparing Euclidean and Haversine distance measures. The authors Here, aimed to develop a search system for public spaces that implements location-based services. The technology used to determine the location of objects and device is Global Positioning(GPS) technology and Google's cell-based positioning. It has used 40 location points comprising of 8 hospitals, 8 houses of worship, 8 markets, 8 pharmacies, and 8 gas stations. Using the LBS (Location Based Services) service, the user can find out his/her current location, the position of friends, and the locations of nearby hospitals or gas stations. At the measurement of location, Latitude and Longitudes are used to pinpoint the geographical location.

A general method for navigating a route throughout city is proposed in [2]. In this work the A* algorithm and the Haversine formula are combined to provide the requested route. A minimum distance between any two points on a sphere is determined by the Haversine formula, using Latitude and Longitude. This minimum distance is then passed to the A* algorithm to calculate the minimum distance. The purpose of this work is to find a way between two places in the city entered by the user using the junction between source and destination. The goal is to improve user navigation in the city.

The route optimizing approach based on the locations of the identified pests is compared with the conventional approach [3], which involves spraying the entire orchard. The method of route optimization reduces pesticide use and the flight time is reduced by 19 percent. The author enhanced the Ant algorithm in this paper by considering the elliptical shape of the earth, and used the Haversine Formula to calculate any two functions distance of points in Ant algorithm. Here two different pesticide spraying routes are compared for the drones, one route is executed by spraying based on Altitude and moving from high to low and the second is based on the shortest distance Ant algorithm. The utilization of the Ant algorithm for planning the path of an agricultural drone that dispenses pesticides on a sloping terrain results in a shorter route compared to the conventional method of descending from high to low altitudes for spraying.

Bandeira T.W. et al. [4] proposed to examine the potential path planning algorithms and the viability of integrating them into a UAV. Author attempted to address the best trajectory to visit all points with the highest image resolution, given a set of points to be visited and the drone's battery level. The research suggests implementing two established algorithms, namely the Traveling Salesman Problem (TSP) and the Close-Enough Travelling Salesman Problem (CETSP), to guide the path planning of UAV. The problem of trajectory optimization is resolved using TSP and CETSP methods. Each Quadrant in the agricultural area can be designated as a specific area that needs to be visited or not in both scenarios. After that, different approaches are used for determining the trajectories. The primary distinction between these two strategies is that the first places more emphasis on photo quality than on travel time, while the latter aims to cut travel time as much as possible.

A mobile application that uses GIS and Dijkstra's algorithm to calculate the shortest path between a user's location and their desired destination in a public transportation network is proposed in [6]. The application first uses GIS to find the nearest bus stops to the user's location and destination. Then, it uses Dijkstra's algorithm to calculate the shortest path between the two bus stops, taking into account the traffic congestions. The application also provides the user with information about the alternative paths and the traffic count.

The application helps passengers to find the shortest and quickest path to their destination. The application is still under development, but it has the potential to be valuable tool for passengers in public transportation networks.

Emergency response is an essential life-saving strategy, particularly in the philippines, a country that experiences many natural disasters. The researchers in [7] have successfully applied Dijkstra's approach to show the shortest path within an emergency response application in this work The ideas are organized methodically to offer possible paths that first responders could take to quickly approach and aid victims. During the application development, Agile methodology was adopted to ensure the flexibility and responsiveness.

Luay S. Jabbar et al. [8] has introduced the idea of a data structure called a retroactive priority queue to imbue the Dijkstra's algorithm with dynamism, The stepping procedure is altered by the researcher, which proceeds in the shortest path for two networks and two directions. This is achieved by identifying the shortest static path and go on to the first node that comes after the starting node. This node modifies the weights of the segments that emanate from it, so nullifying prior shortest path and establishing a new one. Until the destination is reached, this process is repeated to the next node on the updated shortest path.

Many previous researchers have concentrated on computing the shortest path length in 2D space of TSP, leaving the area of 3D space of shortest path remains unexplored. Author Hongtai Yang et al. [9] has addressed this gap by creating models specifically designed for estimate the anticipated length of the shortest path length in 3D-TSP. These models are fine tuned for the task of predicting the path length, involving the estimation of model parameters. To gauge the quality of the model's fir, k-fold cross validation is employed. The findings indicate that all the models adeptly align with the data, ultimately leading to the most suitable model.

Visiting Constrained Multiple Travelling Salesmen Problem (VCMTSP) is concerned with reducing the salesmen's overall travel expenses while taking city accessibility into account. The Cong Bao et al. [10] has tackled this issue by presenting an ant colony optimization (ACO) strategy involving pheromone diffusion and a Shortest Distance Biased Dispatch (SDBD) approach based on city accessibility. Additionally, a 2-step local search function is incorporated to enhance route optimization.

3   Methodology

3.1   Haversine Method

For calculating the distance between two objects, especially on a spherical surface like the Earth, the Haversine Method can be used. It is also known as Haversine Formula in terms of a mathematical formula. Haversine Formula can be used to find the distance between two sets of latitude and longitude coordinates [5]. This formula is frequently applied to GPS navigation systems, Geolocation applications or Geographic information systems.

The Haversine formula uses the trigonometric function for distances calculation to take account of earth's curvature. This is done using the following steps.

1. Convert the latitude and longitude of both points from degrees to radians
2. Calculate the difference in latitude and longitude between the two points
3. Use trigonometric functions (sine, cosine and arctangent) to calculate the angular distance between the two points on the sphere.
4. Multiply the angular distance by the radius of the earth to obtain the actual distance between the two points.

The square of half the chord length between the two points on the sphere (a), the angular distance between the two points on the sphere that is central angle between the two points from the center of the sphere (c), and the great circle distance between the two points (d) are mathematically expressed as:

$$a = sin^2 \left(\frac{lat_2 - lat_1}{2} \right) + cos(lat_1) * cos(lat_2) * sin^2 \left(\frac{lon_2 - lon_1}{2} \right) \quad (1)$$

$$c = a * tan^{-1} \sqrt{\frac{a}{1-a}} \quad (2)$$

$$d = R * c \quad (3)$$

where lat_1, lon_1 are Latitude and Longitude of the first point (in radians), lat_2, lon_2 are Latitude and Longitude of the second point (in radians) and 'R' is Radius of the earth (around 6371 km). Here the radius is converted into meter by multiplying 6371 km into 1000 to get the values in meter that is 6371*1000 m.

3.2 Dijkstra's Algorithm

The implementation of Dijkstra's algorithm involves calculating shortest distances from a specified source node to all other nodes in the graph. The result is represented as a dictionary where each key corresponds to a node within the graph, and its associated value signifies the shortest distance from the chosen source node to all other nodes. The Dijkstra's algorithm has the following steps:

- Create a graph with each node representing a tree, and each edge representing the distance of the two trees.
- Initialize the distance table: The distance between each node in the graph and the start node is stored in a dictionary called the distance table. Initially all distances are set to infinity.
- Create a priority queue: A Data Structure called the priority queue orders its elements according to a priority. Here the priority of each element is its distance from the start node.

- Include the start node to the priority queue.
- While the priority queue is not empty:
  - Pop the node with the shortest distance from the priority queue and mark it as visited.
- For all the neighbors of the visited node:
  - If necessary, update the neighbor's distance in the distance table.
  - Add a neighbor to the priority queue if it has not already been visited.
- Repeat steps v–vi until the priority queue is empty.
- Return the distance table and the list of visited nodes.

The algorithm works by iteratively relaxing the edges in the graph. If a shorter path is discovered after an edge is relaxed, the distance to the target node is updated. When every edge in the graph has been relaxed, the algorithm terminates. The distance table will include the shortest paths between the start node and every other node in the graph after the algorithm has finished. The list of visited nodes can then be viewed in reverse order to create the shortest path to any given node.

The total distance travelled by Dijkstra's algorithm is the sum of the distances from the source node to all of the other nodes in the graph. So, Dijkstra's algorithm is used to find the shortest paths between All pairs of nodes in the graph. The process of visualizing geographical data and illustrating the shortest path on a map involves the utilization of two crucial input elements: a series of geographical coordinates and a set of nodes. The specified coordinates are denoted as markers. The shortest path is then ploted as a polyline on the map.

3.3   Travelling Salesman Problem Algorithm

The Travelling Salesman Problem (TSP) is a well-known optimization problem in which the objective is to find a shortest path that runs exactly once through a set of cities or nodes and returns back to the original city. Here, we have Latitude and Longitude of tree locations and figure out the shortest way to visit all trees and get back to the beginning tree. Working procedure of TSP Algorithm is as fallows:

- Initialize a set visited to save the previously visited nodes.
- A List path should be initialized to save the nodes in the shortest path.
- Start with a random node and add it to the path.
- While not all nodes have been visited
  - Identify the nearest unvisited node to the current node.
  - Add the nearest unvisited node to the currently visited node path.
  - Mark the nearest unvisited node as visited.
- Return the path.

The 'visited' set keeps track of the already visited nodes. This is necessary so that the algorithm does not visit the same node multiple times. The path list stores the nodes according to the shortest path and nodes are placed in the list according to the order in which they are visited. The algorithm begins by adding a random node to the path, which will be the starting point of the shortest path. The algorithm then iteratively identifies the unexplored node that is nearest (closest) to the current node and adds it to the path. This process continues until each node has been visited. The algorithm returns the path list containing the nodes in the shortest path.

A Graph is created using the Networkx library to represent the distance between each pair of tree. To create a graph, set of tree coordinates are read from the CSV file which are collected manually and saved in CSV file. Then using the Haversine Formula the distance between two trees are calculated in meters using the coordinate values of Latitude and Longitude.

The nearest neighbor TSP algorithm is used to identify the nearest unvisited tree to visit the next until each trees have been visited. The total distance of the shortest path is considered by summing the distance between adjacent trees of the selected path.

Python library folium is used to create an iterative map. The locations of the trees are indicated on the map by markers, and the shortest path between them is shown as a polyline that connects them in the order of their visit. A web browser can be used to view the locations of the trees and the shortest path after the generated map has been saved as an HTML file.

4   Results and Discussion

In this section, we present the results of our study on optimizing navigation among a set of trees using the Travelling Salesman Problem (TSP) and Dijkstra's algorithms. The algorithms were applied to a dataset containing tree coordinates as shown in Table 1, and the Haversine method was used to calculate accurate distance between the tree coordinates. Based on the Haversin calculated tree distances the graph is generated shown in Fig. 1 here consider 5trees to generate the graph and then the initial point of the path was chosen randomly to explore the potential influence of the starting point on the resulting paths and distances. The algorithms have generated the different map. The generated map based on the shortest distance among the tree coordinates is shown in Fig. 2 and Fig. 3, where each tree is represented by its latitude and longitude. It shows the spatial distribution of the trees.

Table 1. Location of Trees

No.	Tree Name	Latitude	Longitude
1	Tree0	17.430954	76.677087
2	Tree1	17.431002	76.677062
3	Tree2	17.430979	76.676921
4	Tree3	17.431057	76.676926
5	Tree4	17.431007	76.677023
6	Tree5	17.431077	76.677146
7	Tree6	17.431079	76.676989
8	Tree7	17.431091	76.676912
9	Tree8	17.431128	76.676929
10	Tree9	17.431145	76.676963
11	Tree10	17.431134	76.676998

Analysis of Algorithms: Upon applying the TSP algorithm, we determined an optimal cyclic path that connects all trees, using a randomly selected starting point index as 3. The TSP algorithm produced the path: [3, 7, 8, 9, 10, 6, 4, 1, 0, 5, 2, 3] as shown in Table 2. This sequence ensures that each tree is visited exactly once, and the path returns to the starting point. The calculated total distance of this path based on Haversine distance calculation was approximately 91.61 m.

Similarly, we utilized Dijkstra's algorithm to ascertain the shortest paths between different pairs of trees, with the starting point index chosen randomly as 3. The dijkstra's algorithm produced the path:[7,6,8,2,9,10,4,1,0,5] The computed total distance of this path was 99.74 m as shown in Table 2. When the number of trees are less here (0–4) the dijkstra's algorithm gives a more accurate path, as it yields a shorter total distance compared to TSP and the computational complexity of both algorithms may not be critical concern. When the number of trees increases or more here (0–10) the TSP algorithm yields a shorter total distance, indicating more accurate path for visiting all the nodes in the closed loop and the complexity of TSP grows exponentially and for denser graph with more connection for algorithms like Dijkstra's also increase the computational complexity.

The TSP and Dijkstra's algorithm's can be used to solve a wide range of problems, including path planning, scheduling and routing. In the context of drone navigation, their adaptability is crucial because drones must efficiently plan routes under different conditions, including varying weather, obstacles, and mission requirements. The limitations of these algorithms can be time consuming for drone navigation, particularly in situations involving large number of trees or obstacles.

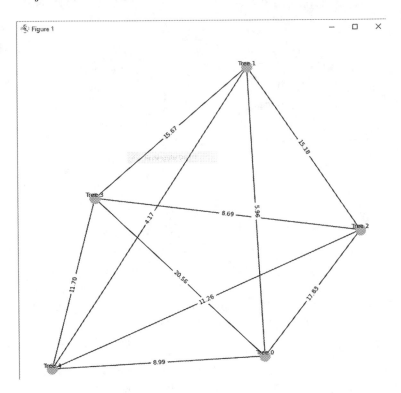

Fig. 1. Haversin generated distance graph

Table 2. Comparison of performance of Algorithms

Algorithm	Starting Point Index	Shortest Path	Total Distance of Shortest Path
Travelling Salesman Problem	3	[3, 7, 8, 9, 10, 6, 4, 1, 0, 5, 2, 3]	91.61149406
Dijkstra's	3	[3, 7, 8, 9, 10, 6, 4, 1, 0, 5, 2, 3]	99.74995046
Travelling Salesman Problem	3	[3, 2, 4, 1, 0,3]	50.64881153
Dijkstra's	3	[2, 4, 1,0]	30.08410472
Travelling Salesman Problem	4	[4, 1, 0, 5, 6, 10, 9, 8, 7, 3, 2, 4]	84.50818987
Dijkstra's	4	[1, 6, 0, 2, 3, 10, 7, 5, 9, 8]	131.15036938
Travelling Salesman Problem	4	[4, 1, 0, 2, 3,4]	48.34925883
Dijkstra's	4	[1, 0, 2,3]	36.65283505

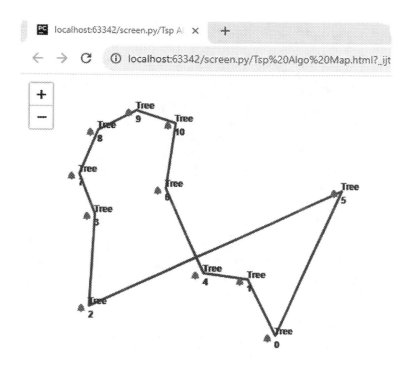

Fig. 2. Shortest Path Map based on the TSP Algorithm

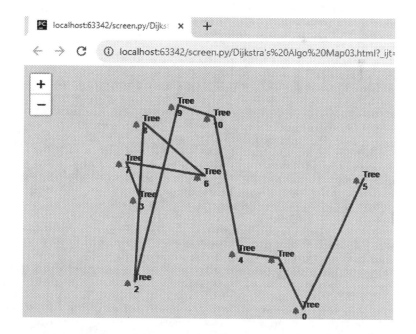

Fig. 3. Shortest Path Map based on the Dijkstra's Algorithm

Analysis of Haversine Method: We calculated the Haversine distances between pairs of trees based on their respective latitude and longitude coordinates. These Haversine distances were then compared to the distances obtained from Google Maps, providing insights into the effectiveness of the Haversine formula in practical navigation scenarios to navigate the drone in optimized path. The distances were evaluated based on the shortest paths generated by the TSP and Dijkstra's algorithm as discussed in above section. Table 3 shows the calculated Haversine distances, corresponding GoogleMap distances, and the difference between the two measurements for each pair of trees. Figure 2 show the GoogleMap distance between the Tree5 coordinates to the Tree2 coordinates. There is a slight difference of -0.23 m (units) calculated between Haversine distance and the Googlemap distances. This suggests that the Haversine formula provides a satisfactory approximation of real-world distances for the selected tree pairs.

Table 3. Comparision of Haversine distance and Google map distance based on shortest path

Tree Name	Latitude	Longitude	Tree Name	Latitude	Longitude	Haversine Distance	GoogleMap Distance	Difference
Tree3	17.431057	76.676926	Tree7	17.431091	76.676912	4.061903159	4	-0.061903159
Tree7	17.431091	76.676912	Tree8	17.431128	76.676929	4.492142539	4	-0.492142539
Tree8	17.431128	76.676929	Tree9	17.431145	76.676963	4.07232096	4	-0.07232096
Tree9	17.431145	76.676963	Tree10	17.431134	76.676998	3.909370288	4	0.090629712
Tree10	17.431134	76.676998	Tree6	17.431079	76.676989	6.189799405	6	-0.189799405
Tree6	17.431079	76.676989	Tree4	17.431007	76.677023	8.781060011	9	0.218939989
Tree4	17.431007	76.677023	Tree1	17.431002	76.677062	4.17464277	4	-0.17464277
Tree1	17.431002	76.677062	Tree0	17.430954	76.677087	5.959997617	6	0.040002383
Tree0	17.430954	76.677087	Tree5	17.431077	76.677146	15.04118592	15	-0.041185915
Tree5	17.431077	76.677146	Tree2	17.430979	76.676921	26.23966894	26	-0.239668936
Tree2	17.430979	76.676921	Tree3	17.431057	76.676926	8.689402458	9	0.310597542
Total						91.61149406	91	-0.611494059

5   Conclusion

This study has demonstrated the potential of optimizing drone routes for tree inspection and pesticide spraying through a comprehensive approach that incorporates GPS data collection, graph theory algorithms, and geographical visualization. Through manual collection of tree coordinates using mobile GPS devices, a spatial dataset of tree locations was created. Using the Haversine method, accurate distances between trees were calculated, considering the earth's curvature. Subsequently, Dijkstra's algorithm and the Travelling Salesman Problem algorithm were employed to identify the shortest path among trees, ensuring optimal drone routes. The study focused on random starting points to underscore the versatility and effectiveness of the proposed approach. Despite minor differences, the Haversine formula yielded distance estimates closely aligned with those from GoogleMaps, signifying its practical utility for navigation and route optimization. This study contributes to the development of precision agriculture techniques by offering an optimized route that maximizes pesticide coverage while minimizing environmental impact. As a future work drone captured tree coordinates are used to plan the shortest route by applying the advanced versions of TSP and Dijkstra's algorithms to further improve route optimization.

References

1. Maria, E., et al.: Measure distance locating nearest public facilities using Haversine and Euclidean Methods. J. Phys.: Conf. Ser. **1450**(1), 012080 (2020)
2. Chopde, N.R., Nichat, M.: Landmark based shortest path detection by using A* and haversine formula P. Int. J. Innov. Res. Comput. Commun. Eng. **1**(2), 298–302 (2013)
3. Chen, C.J., et al.: Identification of fruit tree pests with deep learning on embedded drone to achieve accurate pesticide spraying. IEEE Access **9**, 21986–21997 (2021)
4. Bandeira, T.W., et al.: Analysis of path planning algorithms based on travelling salesman problem embedded in UAVs. Brazil. Symp. Comput. Syst. Eng. (SBESC) IEEE **2**(5), 70–75 (2015)
5. Prasetya, D.A., et al.: Resolving the shortest path problem using the haversine algorithm. J. Crit. Rev. **7**(1), 62–64 (2020)
6. Khaing, O.: Using Dijkstra's algorithm for public transportation system in Yangon based on GIS. Int. J. Sci. Eng. Appl. **7**(11), 442–447 (2018)
7. Lagman, A.C., De Angel, R.: I-respond mobile application for emergency response using Dijkstra's algorithm shortest path. In: IEEE 14th International Conference on Humanoid, Nanotechnology, Information Technology, Communication, pp. 1–5 (2022).https://doi.org/10.1109/HNICEM57413.2022.10109620
8. Jabbar, L.S.: A modification of shortest path algorithm according to adjustable weights based on Dijkstra algorithm. Eng. Technol. J. (2022)
9. Yan, H.: Expected length of the shortest path of the traveling salesman problem in 3D space. J. Adv. Transp. (2022). https://doi.org/10.1155/2022/4124950
10. Bao, C., Yang, Q., Gao, X.-D., Lu, Z.-Y., Zhang, J.: Ant colony optimization with shortest distance biased dispatch for visiting constrained multiple traveling salesmen problem. In: Proceedings of the Genetic and Evolutionary Computation Conference Companion (GECCO 2022), pp. 77–80. Association for Computing Machinery, New York (2022)

Trees Detection from Aerial Images Using the YOLOv5 Family

Kavita V. Houde(✉), Parshuram M. Kamble, and Ravindra S. Hegadi

Department of Computer Science, Central University of Karnataka, Kadaganchi,
Kalaburagi, India
kavitahoude@gmail.com

Abstract. Deep learning object recognition models, which are widely used in computer vision, may provide an opportunity to accurately recognize fruit trees. This is essential for fast data collection, selection and reducing human operational errors. This paper proposes a YOLOv5-based detection model for fruit tree detection in the farm plantation using UAV-collected data. This proposed model detects individual fruit trees from the agriculture field and also provide counts how many trees are detected. An image dataset was created from the publicly available UAV captured data which contains total 36 images. Among them 27 were used for training and 9 for testing the proposed model. Four different YOLOv5 scales for object recognition (YOLOv5s, YOLOv5m, YOLOv5l, and YOLOv5x) were selected for training, validation, and testing on image datasets.

Keywords: Unmanned Aerial Vehicles (UAV) · Tree Detection · Fruit Tree Detection · YOLOv5 · YOLOv5 family · Object Detection · Precision Agriculture

1 Introduction

In human life, trees play a very important role. The trees provide key resources such as oxygen, and in particular, the fruit trees provide nutritious fruits to mankind. Trees are an essential component of human health and livelihood. Among the 17 sustainable development goals of the United Nations that have received international support, 15 goals are being supported by the coverage of trees in any country. The well-being of the population across the world is also contributed by the level of tree plantation. Key benefits of trees include health and social well-being, cognitive development and education, economy and resources, climate change mitigation, and habitat and green infrastructure [1].

Identification of types of trees in any forest or any orchid is an active research topic for many reasons. Identifying types of trees will help estimate the availability of such types of wood resources and the amount of energy generated. For the farmers owning the fruit orchids, it immensely helps in planning sprinkling of pesticides over the trees. In the case of forests, it helps protect the native

© The Author(s), under exclusive license to Springer Nature Switzerland AG 2024
KC Santosh et al. (Eds.): RTIP2R 2023, CCIS 2026, pp. 314–323, 2024.
https://doi.org/10.1007/978-3-031-53082-1_25

crop and vegetation, surveillance of local species and species invading the region, mapping of wildlife habitat, and forest management for managing the ecological balance in the forest. Remote sensing research majorly contributed to forest management research using satellites and aircraft. Recent developments have led to using Unmanned Aerial Vehicles (UAV) for many agriculture and forestry applications. UAVs cost very little, and they are easier to operate in complex terrains than aircraft or satellites. They can fly at lower altitudes capturing images and video at a higher resolution and with greater precision [2]. Such data require the preprocessing to make them suitable for further processing [3].

The UAVs generate continuous video streams while flying over the field under study, requiring better processing devices and equally compatible algorithms to process these images. Currently, deep learning algorithms are being used to achieve higher levels of accuracy in processing such types of images. There are multiple deep learning algorithms already implemented based on Convolutional Neural Networks (CNN), Recurrent CNN (RCNN), Faster RCNN and DNN for the detection of trees [4,5].

In this paper, we are implementing the YOLOv5 family of deep-learning algorithms to detect fruit trees. YouTube videos are used to collect the data required for the experimentation. The existing algorithms related to the proposed work and proposed methodology are discussed in Sect. 2. Section 4 describes the results. Conclusion and future work are proposed in Sect. 5.

2   YOLOv5 Deep Learning Object Detection Model

For implementing this work, the YOLO algorithm is used. The long form of YOLO is "You Only Look Once." The YOLO algorithm found improvement with the release of newer versions as compared to its previous versions. One of its better versions was the YOLOv4 which was developed by the conventional authors Joseph Redmon and Alexey Bochkovskiy [8], and another best and improved version was the newly released YOLOv5 developed by Glenn Jocher [7]. Since its author was not a conventional author of the YOLO series, some controversy was associated with the release of this newer version. But overcoming its past records, the v5 model has shown a substantial performance increase from its predecessors.

YOLOv5 is a representative of one-stage object detection algorithms with four object detection versions YOLOv5s, YOLOv5m, YOLOv5l, and YOLOv5x. Among these four versions, the first version, YOLOv5s, is faster than the remaining three versions, but the accuracy of its AP is the lowest. The other three networks in the YOLOv5 series are based on YOLOv5s and continue to deepen and expand the network. The AP value of these series was continuously improved, resulting in an impact on the speed of the execution.

However, there are numerous advantages of YOLOv5 in engineering applications. One important advantage is the switching over to Python from the C programming language, which was used by all its previous versions. This transformation eased the process of installation as well as the integration of IoT devices. Since the PyTorch community is larger than the Darknet community, the PyTorch will receive more resource contributions and has great growth potential in the future.

The YOLOv5 network consists of three main parts:

- backbone - a CNN layer that integrates image features at different scales,
- neck - a set of layers to combine image features and forward them to prediction and
- head - which takes features from the neck and localizes them next do the Classification

3 Materials and Methods

For the proposed work, the images are collected from the videos available in the public domain. These images are preprocessed to enhance their quality, and the database is divided into training and testing datasets. The YOLOv5 model is designed to detect fruit trees. A detailed description of these steps is provided in the following subsections.

3.1 Dataset

To develop tree detection models, a video dataset has been collected through an online source. During the data collection, the main focus was on the fruit trees, in particular, the mango trees. Drones/UAVs basically captured the collected videos, and by analyzing the video, we confirm that the view area of the video is the top side of the trees. Some suitable frames from the video are selected and extracted manually using Microsoft 10 Pro video player application. A total of 36 images were used for this experiment. A repository of images containing multiple views of fruit trees was used to ensure that the models were fed dataset with all kinds of variations for frictionless operation upon deployment.

3.2 Pre-processing

After the collection of extracted images, specific tree regions were cropped to avoid lossy training due to a bunch of trees and side views of the trees. The cropping is performed through a manual process. After the collection of suitable tree image data, a manual annotation is performed to annotate the tree regions in the image. This process draws the bounding box over the tree region in the image. For the training purpose of the proposed tree detector models, we need to provide our dataset with bounding box annotations for supervised learning where we draw a box around each tree in the image, we want the detector to see and label each box with the tree class that we want our detector to predict.

Annotation is done with MakeSense (makesense.io) open-source application. This application accepts the image as input and permits the user to draw the bounding box around the objects. After the completion of manually drawing the bounding boxes, the bounding box information can be exported in different file formats, such as .zip package containing files in YOLO format, .zip package containing files in VOC XML format, and a single CSV file. Here the annotated data is exported as a .zip package containing files in YOLO format. This package contains information on object class, coordinate position of the object, height, and width of the bounding box drawn over the object.

Fig. 1. Annotation of trees from the images

The sample image and the image after drawing the bounding box are shown in Fig. 1. The data generated using the MakeSense application on this image is shown in Table 1. It contains the information on the X and Y coordinates of the box and the height and width of the bounding box. Once the images are well annotated, the database is split into two parts: a training dataset and a validation

Table 1. Data generated after annotation using MakeSense tool.

Object Class	X-Coordinate	Y-Coordinate	Height	Width
0	0.109624	0.111111	0.144786	0.186949
0	0.129937	0.529982	0.259874	0.375661
0	0.411489	0.467372	0.338744	0.335097
0	0.599301	0.231041	0.320988	0.320988
0	0.883409	0.253968	0.211715	0.303351
0	0.824676	0.729277	0.345574	0.432099
0	0.482516	0.746914	0.355135	0.305115
0	0.165626	0.839506	0.262254	0.250441
0	0.123283	0.65873	0	0.001764
0	0.520762	0.926808	0.387917	0.128748
0	0.918826	0.965608	0.162348	0.068783
0	0.01042	0.106702	0.02084	0.213404

dataset. The validation dataset helps to validate the model's performance while training the model.

The model of the proposed work is shown in Fig. 2 in the form of a flow diagram.

3.3   Model Training

The models were trained using a Google Colab platform instance on the workstation having NVIDIA_TESLA_T4 GPU having 16GB of RAM. Colab is a free deep-learning cloud platform provided by Google based on Jupyter Notebook. Out of the total dataset, 27 images are used for training, and 9 images are used to test the model. The deep learning strategy is used to train the tree detection models on the fruit trees image dataset to obtain the deep learning models. The MS-COCO pre-trained model weights of YOLOv5s, YOLOv5m, YOLOv5l, and YOLOv5x were used to retrain the training dataset. The initial learning rate for all the models was set to 0.01, and the models were trained using an optimizer Stochastic Gradient Descent strategy to avoid overfitting and underfitting.

4   Results and Discussion

4.1   Visualization of the Evaluation Metrics for the Four YOLOv5 Models

The experimentation is performed, and the precision and recall of the four models YOLOv5s, YOLOv5m, YOLOv5l, and YOLOv5x are computed. It is found from the experimentation that the average accuracy of the three models YOLOv5m, YOLOv5l, and YOLOv5x models almost stabilizes after 110 epochs. Figure 3 shows the validation precision, validation recall, and average precision (AP) of the four YOLOv5 models. The precision-recall (PR) curve of these YOLOv5 models is shown in Fig. 4.

4.2   Training and Validation Losses of the Four YOLOv5 Models

The loss indicators during the training and validation processes from 1 to 120 epochs are shown in Table 2. If the training loss value is close to the value of the validation loss, the model is not overfitting. The lower the loss, the better the accuracy of the model. Therefore, none of the YOLOv5 models were overfitting during the training on the individual tree detection dataset. YOLOv5x has the least validation loss, implying that it has the best performance among the four models.

4.3   Evaluation and Accuracy of the Model

Evaluation of the five YOLOv5 models are presented in Table 3. It represents the number of layers used in the network, parameters, precision, recall, mAP,

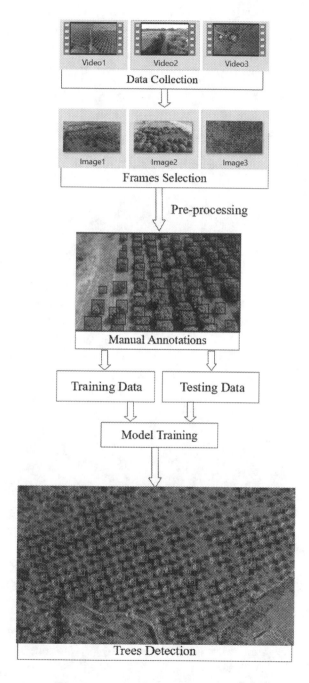

Fig. 2. Proposed system architecture

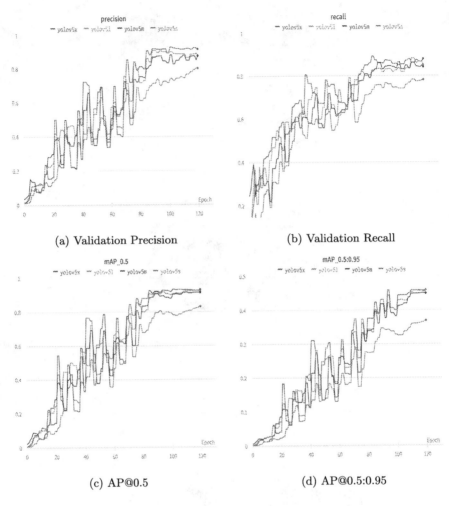

Fig. 3. Visualization of Evaluation Metrics

Table 2. Training and validation losses of various scales of YOLOv5 models

Models	Training Loss	Validation Loss
YOLOv5s	0.05555	0.0505
YOLOv5m	0.04994	0.04525
YOLOv5l	0.04852	0.04372
YOLOv5x	0.04673	0.04414

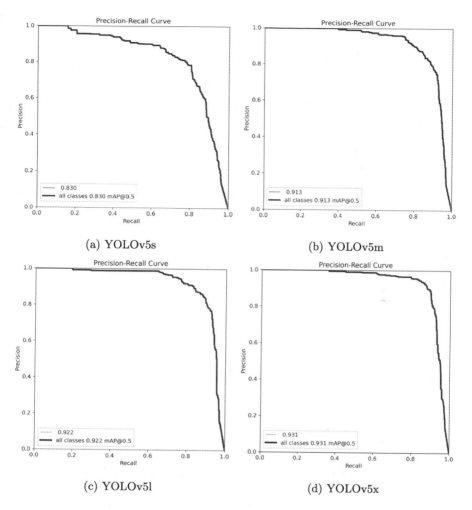

Fig. 4. Precision-recall (PR) curve graph of the four YOLOv5 models.

Table 3. Evaluation of various metrics of various scales of the YOLOv5 model

Model	layers	parameters	Precision	Recall	mAP@.5	mAP@.5:.95	Training time (in h)
YOLOv5s	157	7012822	0.801	0.781	0.83	0.369	0.091
YOLOv5m	212	20852934	0.873	0.841	0.913	0.449	0.119
YOLOv5l	267	46108278	0.875	0.851	0.922	0.458	0.174
YOLOv5x	322	86173414	0.914	0.879	0.931	0.459	0.254

and time required. Considering only the model's accuracy without real-time detection, YOLOv5m, YOLOv5l, and YOLOv5x, these three are the best models with the highest AP of 0.913, 0.922, and 0.931, respectively, are selected as the models for the subsequent inference.

The accuracy of the proposed YOLOv5 models is presented in Table 4. The actual total trees found in all the images are 1558. The detected bounding boxes are computed and based on this information the number of trees missed and correctly detected by the model are presented. It can be seen here that the YOLOv5l has demonstrated the highest rate of accuracy of 94.8% as compared to the other models in detecting the trees correctly. Accuracy of Detection is calculated with the Eq. (1)

$$Accuracy\,of\,Detection \,=\, Trees\,Detected\,Correctly \,/\, Actual\,Trees \times 100 \quad (1)$$

Table 4. Accuracy analysis of proposed models

YOLOv5 Model	Actual Trees	Detected bounding boxes	Missed Trees	Trees Detected Correctly	Trees Detected Wrongly	Accuracy of Detection (%)
YOLOv5s	1558	1936	232	1326	610	85.11
YOLOv5m	1558	1704	105	1453	251	93.26
YOLOv5l	1558	1602	81	1477	125	94.8
YOLOv5x	1558	1610	86	1472	138	94.48

5   Conclusions and Future Work

In this paper, a YOLOv5-based detection method is proposed for fruit tree detection in the farm plantation using drone-collected online source sensing images. The dataset is divided into training data and test data for testing the model. There are many challenges in the input images, such as low illumination while capturing the images, nonuniform illumination, and shadow. These images are preprocessed to improve their quality to the best possible level before further processing. Four models, namely YOLOv5s, YOLOv5m, YOLOv5l, and YOLOv5x are applied over these images and the performance evaluation is presented in the form of precision, recall and average precision. Among the four models the YOLOv5l has demonstrated the highest rate of accuracy of 94.8% as compared to the other models in detecting the trees correctly. In future we will build a better database by collecting the images from local forms and we modify the internal architecture of YOLOv5 models to improve the detection capability of the proposed model and also try to use the advanced models such as YOLOv8 to improve the accuracy and also develop better preprocessing techniques to handle the challenges involved in the input images.

References

1. Turner-Skoff, J.B., Cavender, N.: The benefits of trees for livable and sustainable communities. Plants People Planet **1**(4), 323–335 (2019)
2. Onishi, M., Ise, T.: Explainable identification and mapping of trees using UAV RGB image and deep learning. Sci. Rep. **11**(1), 1–15 (2021)
3. Kamble, P., Ruikar, D.D., Houde, K.V., Hegadi, R.S.: Adaptive threshold-based database preparation method for handwritten image classification. In: Santosh, K., Hegadi, R., Pal, U. (eds.) Recent Trends in Image Processing and Pattern Recognition IRTIP2R 2021, Malta, Msida, pp. 280–288 (2021)
4. Li, W., Fu, H., Yu, L.: Deep convolutional neural network based large-scale oil palm tree detection for high-resolution remote sensing images. In: Proceedings of 2017 IEEE International Geoscience and Remote Sensing Symposium (IGARSS), Texas, pp. 846–849 (2017)
5. Ruikar, D., Houde, K, Hegadi, R.: DNN-based knee OA severity prediction system: pathologically robust feature engineering approach. SN Comput. Sci. **4**(58) (2023)
6. Zheng, J., Li, W., Xia, M., Dong, R., Fu, H., Yuan, S.: Large-scale oil palm tree detection from high-resolution remote sensing images using faster-RCNN. In: Proceedings of IEEE International Geoscience and Remote Sensing Symposium (IGARSS), Yokohama, pp. 1422–1425 (2019)
7. Xiong, Y., Zeng, X., Chen, Y. Liao, J. Lai, W., Zhu, M. : An approach to detecting and mapping individual fruit trees integrated YOLOv5 with UAV. Remote Sens. 2022040007(2022)
8. Jocher, G., Stoken, A., Borovec, J., Changyu, L., Hogan, A.: ultralytics/yolov5: v3.0 (2020). https://zenodo.org/record/3983579#.ZESsIXZBy5c. Accessed Jan 2023

A Study on Automatic Detection, Length and Mass Estimation of Fishes in Aqua Farming Environment

Rajarshi Biswas[✉], Rana Khonsari, Marcel Mutz, and Dirk Werth

August-Wilhelm Scheer Institut, Uni-Campus D 5 1, 66123 Saarbrücken, Germany
{rajarshi.biswas,rana.khonsari,marcel.mutz,
dirk.werth}@aws-institut.de
https://www.aws-institut.de/en/homepage/

Abstract. Knowledge on body-length and mass of farmed fishes are essential for making informed business decisions in aqua-farming. These reduce wastage and promote sustainability that is critical for ecological preservation. In this paper, we present an approach for automatically determining the length and mass of fishes from images taken by a single camera placed above the fish-tank. Our motivation is to develop a solution that requires minimal hardware requirement and expert supervision for wide applicability. This is in sharp contrast with existing work in this area that employ complex hardware setup, e.g., stereo cameras, underwater camera, submerged tubes with twin-camera setup. These require technical expertise which ideally is not available to small businesses. Furthermore, our approach works with live fish in water compared to other techniques that work on dead fish. We evaluate different variants of the Mask-RCNN and YOLO algorithms for automatic fish detection. Subsequently, we use B-splines for estimating the length of fish in the pixel domain followed by physical length determination using optics. We obtain a mean average precision of 0.896 for the bounding box and a mean average precision of 0.902 for mask-based detection of fish with the YOLO model. The average error in physical length estimation is 3.32%. Lastly, we estimate the mass of fish by fitting the Length-Weight relationship using regression and obtain an average error of 12.24% in weight determination.

Keywords: Artificial Intelligence · Object Detection · Computer Vision

1 Introduction

World population has grown exponentially in the last half century putting increased demand on food production. Fisheries are also not immune to this pressure. For example, the global output from fisheries reached 179 million tons in 2018 which is a fivefold increase over the consumption figure less than 60 years ago [4]. However, this rapid

This research was funded in part by the German Federal Ministry of Education and Research (BMBF) under the project FishAI (Grant number 031B1252B).

growth in demand prompts the need for sustainable production for ecological preservation. The UN report "The State of World Fisheries And Aquaculture" from 2022 corroborates this fact as it views the contribution from fisheries critical for eradicating global hunger and malnutrition. This necessitates the adoption of innovative approaches and technologies, e.g., artificial intelligence, deep learning, sensor fusion in the traditional workflow of aqua farming. This incorporation gives rise to smart fish farming that tries to solve problems, such as diseases, malnutrition, water contamination [15]. These in turn boosts sustainable production and increases profitability [21, 25].

Fig. 1. Yolov8l based detection & pixel-length estimation using splines on our dataset.

In this work, we use computer vision and deep learning for automatically determining the length and mass of fishes from images using a simple camera setup. Our motivation is to develop a credible approach for determining the distribution of body-length and mass of fishes in an aqua farming environment. We also emphasize on having minimal hardware requirement so that it is easy to setup, deploy and operate by small aquaculture businesses that ideally don't possess technical expertise in computer vision and artificial intelligence. So, our approach uses a single overhead camera placed above the fish tank and captures images of live fish swimming in water inside the tank. This is in sharp contrast with existing vision based approaches for measuring the size and mass of fishes.

Almost all of these techniques either operate on dead fish that is outside of water or they use complex set ups, such as, submerged platforms housing stereo cameras, underwater cameras etc. These approaches are difficult to set up, require high technical expertise for calibration of the cameras and lastly any foreign object in water introduce lot of stress in the fish schools resulting in high mortality. Our approach successfully handles high population density and water turbidity in fish tanks which are among the most frequent problems in remote monitoring of fish in a farming set up. Furthermore, we do not use fiducial markers for estimating the physical length of fishes but rather use optics for translating the measured pixel length of fishes into corresponding physical length allowing us to work with live fish. This is a major distinction from majority of works in this domain that use fiducial markers which are placed by the side of the already dead fish on a platform for estimating the true length of the fish from images.

Our approach consists of three sequential procedures. First, automatically detecting fish inside the tanks in densely populated environment; second, estimating their length in the pixel domain followed by corresponding true length estimation; and third, determination of the mass of fish from the estimated length in an aquaculture setup. We perform dense detection of fish in crowded condition, e.g., in fish schools using bounding boxes and instance specific segmentation masks. For this we test the effectiveness of both two-stage and single-stage detectors using Mask-RCNN [8] and YOLO [9] neural architectures respectively. We evaluate different backbones and configurations for both these algorithms for comparative performance analysis. We use the detection from these architectures to estimate the length of fish in the pixel domain by fitting B-splines. Then using the principles of optics we translate the estimated pixel length of fish into it's corresponding physical length. Lastly, we estimate the mass of fish from their corresponding estimated true length by fitting the Length-Weight relationship using regression. For this purpose, we use 100 ground-truth observations of fish length and corresponding mass. We also quantify the error in our estimates for the length and mass of fish from corresponding true versions by calculating average percentage errors over 100 ground-truth observations.

The uniqueness of our approach lies in the facts that we propose a complete automated pipeline from detection to physical length and mass estimation of fish in an aquaculture environment that does not introduce any stress in the fish schools or affect their mortality. Moreover, our technique relies on a simple hardware set up that is easy to deploy, operate and maintain by non-experts which greatly increases it's applicability for small businesses. We believe these factors promote sustainability in fish farming and in the long run would help in ecological preservation. These are major distinctions compared to the rest of the work in this area where most techniques either directly result in high mortality of the fishes or employ complex hardware set ups that cannot be readily adopted world-wide by small businesses. To summarize, our contributions in this paper are as follows:

- Detailed evaluation of Mask-RCNN and YOLO architectures for dense fish detection.
- Automatic pixel-length, physical length and mass estimation of fish.

– Development of a non-intrusive, simple and easy to use pipeline for automatic length and mass estimation of fish for small aqua-farming businesses.

2 Related Work

Computer vision and deep learning are two important contributors to smart aquaculture. Recent advances in both fields generate a lot of value in this domain. The latest vision algorithms can help to solve various problems by effectively detecting, classifying, segmenting, and even counting the fish in ways that are effective in labor, cost, and time. Deep learning complements these capabilities by enabling automated feature extraction directly from the data. It is being used frequently, in recent times, in aquaculture [24] for addressing issues, such as optimal feed control [26, 27] for increasing economic efficiency [18], fish behavior identification [2] etc. The authors in [13] use convolutional neural-nets for estimating the length of fish from images using fiducial markers of known dimensions. The approach uses R-CNN [7] for detecting fish with bounding boxes. They consider the length of the bounding box as the pixel-length of the fish while the physical length is estimated with the help of fiducial markers placed on the fish. However, this technique only works on dead fish as it requires the fish to be placed straight for the length of the bounding box to represent the pixel-length of the fish. Additionally, bounding boxes compared to segmentation maps might be less accurate. The work in [14] utilizes two fiducial markers for estimating the length of fish. It uses a background and another foreground fiducial marker in addition to a laser marker. In this approach, the variation of distance between the fiducial markers and the fish profile results in errors. Also, it is sensitive to the image distortion caused by the camera. The authors use images of a checkerboard pattern, taken by the camera, for computing the intrinsic matrix and distortion coefficients of the camera. These parameters are then used for correcting the image distortion. The authors report that using a large background fiducial marker leads to more accurate results provided there is not much elevation between the fish snout and the marker plane. The work in [11] first uses semantic segmentation to infer the shape of the fish and then they use a ruler of known dimension to calibrate the pixels to physical length. However, the work does not discuss if the approach can handle fishes in a crowded environment. The authors in [16] also use semantic segmentation for counting and estimating the mean length of a sample of fishes inside boxes placed on a conveyor belt. But this approach does not take into account images of live fish in water. Also, the method only estimates the mean length of a sample of fishes instead the length of individual fishes in the sample.

The authors in [5] use the Deep Vision imaging system [19] for acquiring stereo images for fishes. Subsequently, the non-linearities due to camera response are corrected in the images. The scaled corrected images are fed to Mask-RCNN for obtaining segmentation masks for fishes. The length of fish is then inferred from the masks using 3D pose of the fish. The study in [23] estimate the length of fish as the distance between the snout and fork points using pixel-to-distance ratio determined using color plates of known dimensions placed by the side and photographed with the fish. The work in [17] uses underwater imaging for estimating average size of fish. It uses stereo geometry and takes into account the influence of movement of fish on the estimation process. However, the system is extremely costly. Similarly, the authors in [22] utilize underwater stereo images for determining the dimension of free swimming salmon fish by developing a 3D point distribution model. But the approach only works on side-view images. The work in [3] uses stereo-vision with convergent cameras for performing three dimensional fish segmentation in underwater environments. This technique requires a series of complex pre-processing steps, feature detection and validation for the segmentation. Additionally, it also suffers from sample bias. The authors in [19] develop an underwater imaging system for counting, identifying and measuring the lengths of fish. The system is made up of stereo cameras, a pressure sensor for monitoring the depth of the system and led strobes for illumination all housed inside a cylindrical canister that is attached to a submerged trawl. The authors use stereo photogrammetry for estimating the length of fish from images. However, this solution is extremely complex and also it is a proprietary software that is not freely available.

Interestingly, none of the works discussed above present an approach starting from detection of free-swimming fish to estimation of it's physical length and body-mass. Moreover, a wide majority of the approaches either work with already dead fish outside water or introduce foreign objects, e.g., underwater cameras in the fish habitat that generates a lot of stress in the fish schools affecting their mortality. Additionally, some of the approaches use extremely complex hardware arrangements that require careful calibration and maintenance which restrict ease of use and widespread adoption by small aqua-farming businesses. In contrast, our work presents a simple, non-intrusive pipeline that performs dense detection of freely swimming fish in water from images and subsequently estimates their physical length and body-mass. Our approach does not affect the mortality of the fishes. In addition, we use a very simple hardware set up that is easy to deploy, operate and maintain even by non-experts that boosts widespread applicability.

3 Dataset

Our dataset comprises of 138 videos of schools of fish, captured using a regular inexpensive camera positioned above the fish-tanks, from an aquaculture farm. We extract 5952 frames from these videos for our experiments and split them into training, validation and test sets. Our training and validation sets contain 4317 and 835 image frames respectively while the test set consists of 800 instances. We append our training data with 1086 images from fish-datasets that are publicly available for helping our models to learn more and perform better generalization. These images are taken from the Deep-Fish segmentation dataset (310 images) [20] and the DeepFish computer vision dataset (776 images) [6] respectively. The primary challenges in our data curation are the fixed camera position for recording the videos and that the videos are not compensated for the motion of fishes. Due to the fixed position of the camera our dataset lacks variation with regards to different perspectives, angles, lighting etc. The absence of motion compensation results in lot of frames that are blurred. Moreover, reflections and lighting artefacts cause difficulty in distinguishing the contours of the fish-shapes and in the finer parts such as the tails.

4 Methodology

Under this section, we describe the different experiments that we perform sequentially in our work. First, we identify and localize the fishes in the images obtained from the videos. For performing object detection we comprehensively test Mask-RCNN and YOLO neural architectures using different backbones. For Mask-RCNN we test ResNet50-C4, ResNet50-DC5, ResNet50-FPN, ResNet101-C4, ResNet101-DC5, ResNet101-FPN and ResNeXt101-FPN respectively as the backbones. On the other hand, for YOLO we test the small and large configurations of YOLOv5 and YOLOv8 respectively. The accuracy of detection is measured using the metrics average precision (AP) and mean average precision (mAP) respectively.

In the second step, we estimate the length of fish in the pixel domain using the detected masks from the previous step. Our approach for this determination comprises of skeleton extraction, spline fitting and length estimation. We use FilFinder Python package which uses Medial Axis Transform [1] to find the one pixel wide skeleton of each mask [10]. Subsequently, points from the skeleton are sampled and a B-spline is fitted on them. The end points of the skeleton do not coincide with the endpoints of the masks. So, we extrapolate the fitted spline and find where it intersects the masks for ensuring that the spline spans the entire mask. These intersection points then serve as the end points of the spline. After this, the spline is split into several small line segments and the sum of the lengths of each line segment gives the total length of the spline in pixels. Subsequently, we estimate the physical length of the fish from their corresponding pixel length. However, physical length estimation of objects from images is one of the most challenging tasks in computer vision. It either involves shape estimation from stereo images or intricate techniques to account for lens distortions, sensor characteristics, etc. In our case, this problem becomes even more difficult as we are dealing with live fish that is moving inside the water. In addition to lens distortion, water induces refraction, and the movement of fish produces motion blur. We would like to address these issues in our future work but at present, we use a simplified formulation for estimating the physical length of the fish, based on principles of geometry, perspective, and camera parameters. The proposed formula is derived from the concept of similar triangles and is intended to provide an approximation to calculate the actual length (L) of an object based on its pixel length (Px) on an image sensor, the image height in pixels (IH), the distance from the camera to the object (D) and the camera's focal length (F). The formula is derived as follows:

$$L = Px \times (D + F)/IH \tag{1}$$

the formula assumes the object is positioned parallel to the camera's sensor and the camera lens behaves similarly to a pinhole camera. Finally, we use the estimated physical length of the fish to determine its weight using the Length-Weight relationship [12]. We employ linear regression to fit the Length-Weight relationship formula using 100 manually collected data points. They record the true length and the true body-mass of fish. Lastly, we report the average error in estimated length and estimated body-mass for the fish.

5   Results and Discussion

We trained the Mask-RCNN model with different backbones, ResNet50-C4, ResNet50-DC5, ResNet50-FPN, ResNet101-C4, ResNet101-DC5, ResNet-101-FPN and ResNeXt101-FPN respectively. While for YOLO, we trained four different models, YOLOv5s, YOLOv5l, YOLOv8s, and YOLOv8l. We tested them for detecting and segmenting the fish in the tanks. For regularization and better generalization of the models, we used images from publicly available fish datasets as mentioned in Sect. 4. Additionally, we use early stopping during the models training phase to prevent overfitting. The results obtained with the YOLO models are reported in Table 1.

Table 1. Detection results obtained with YOLO (P: precision, R: recall, mAP50: mean average precision)

Model	Box-P	Box-R	B-mAP50	Mask-P	Mask-R	M-mAP50
YOLOv5s	0.847	0.776	0.864	0.85	0.779	0.867
YOLOv5l	0.858	0.808	0.863	0.861	0.811	0.866
YOLOv8s	0.821	0.828	0.896	0.824	0.831	0.899
YOLOv8l	0.811	0.843	0.896	0.815	0.849	0.902

From Table 1, we see that the highest scores, mean average precision (mAP50) of 0.902 for detected masks and mAP50 of 0.896 for detected bounding boxes respectively, are obtained with the YOLOv8l model with 295 layers and a parameter count of 45912659. We trained the model for 124 epochs. Figure 1 shows the detection performance of the YOLOv8l model on our data. We also tested the performance of the models on out of domain images. For this, we used 250 images randomly chosen from the MSCOCO validation dataset. The predictions from the models contained less than 5% false positives with the confidence threshold set at 80%. We also found that the addition of images from other publicly available fish datasets in our training data reduced the occurrence of false positives to only 1.2%. Apart from the reduction in false positive prediction, we observed that the incorporation of these images also improved the accuracy of the predicted masks. Additionally, it also helped in handling artefacts, such as, reflections, image blur etc. We tried 10 different backbones in our experiments with Mask-RCNN. The results obtained for instance segmentation with these backbones are reported in Table 2.

Table 2. Detection results obtained with Mask-RCNN model with different backbones (AP: average precision)

Backbone	Box AP@IOU = 0.5	Mask AP@IOU = 0.5
ResNet50-C4-1x	56.356	55.619
ResNet50-DC5-1x	56.192	55.280
ResNet50-FPN-1x	45.156	43.389
ResNet50-C4-3x	61.265	50.324
ResNet50-DC5-3x	58.442	58.861
ResNet50-FPN-3x	51.692	51.819
ResNet101-C4-3x	56.315	56.491
ResNet101-DC5-3x	62.117	62.741
ResNet101-FPN-3x	51.323	52.276
ResNeXt101-FPN-3x	51.914	51.330

We note that ResNet101-DC5-3x performs the best with an average precision (AP) of 62.714 at the intersection over union (IOU) threshold of 0.5. Detection from this backbone with the Mask-RCNN can be seen in Fig. 2. Although the annotations are denser with Mask-RCNN, the model fails to correctly predict the boundaries and the correct shape of the fish. Furthermore, to measure the accuracy of our pixel length estimation, we use Eq. 1 to estimate the real physical length of a fish inside a closed environment. To use the formula, we assume a focal length of 0.415 cm and an image height of 640px for our camera. The object distance to the camera is 132 cm assuming that fishes mostly swim at the bottom of the tank. In Table 3, we report the mean pixel-length for each fish which was calculated for an average of 40 splines per fish, the true recorded length of each fish, the estimated length of each fish in centimeters and the percentage error from the actual length. According to our results, we have an average error of 3.32% when calculating the actual physical length of a fish for 100 observations. We use linear regression to determine the parameters of the Length-Weight relationship using 100 observations of the length and corresponding weight of fish. The values of the parameters obtained from this regression fit are 0.01878943 and 2.87340954 respectively. Figure 3 shows the logarithmic relationship between the length and the weight of the fish used in this analysis. Using the fitted values of the parameters and the physical lengths measured with Eq. 1, we have estimated the weight of each fish with an average error of 12.24% for 100 observations.

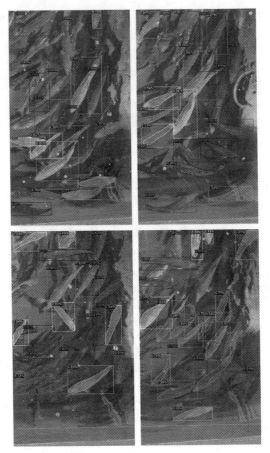

Fig. 2. Mask-RCNN based detection using ResNet101-DC5-3x as the backbone.

Table 3. Performance of the spline fit on a sample of 20 ground-truth fishes in measuring real length.

Mean pixel-length (px)	Ground-truth length (cm)	Estimated length (cm)	Length error (%)
162.95	34	34.35	1.03
156.66	33.5	33.02	1.41
151.41	32	31.91	0.25
151.91	31.5	31.07	1.35
162.55	33	33.25	0.76
160.46	33	32.82	0.53
157.38	32.5	32.19	0.94
174.59	36	35.71	0.79
166.23	34.5	34.52	0.06
173.05	35.5	35.93	1.23
148.26	31	30.79	0.67
166.58	34.5	34.59	0.28
126.73	26.5	26.32	0.67
152.74	32	31.72	0.86
151.65	31.5	31.49	0.01
158.27	32.5	32.87	1.14
159.10	33.5	33.04	1.36
159.35	33.5	33.09	1.21
158.15	33	32.84	0.46
158.39	33	32.52	1.44

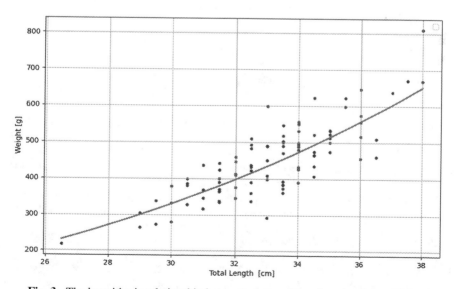

Fig. 3. The logarithmic relationship between observed length and weight of fishes.

6 Conclusion

In this work, we proposed a computer vision based approach for estimating the length and mass of free swimming fish in an aquaculture environment. Our approach starts with automatic detection of fish from images depicting fish-schools freely swimming inside fish tanks, then corresponding pixel-length estimation using B-splines followed by physical length determination using optical formulations and finally body-mass estimation utilizing the estimated physical length. In comparison to the existing approaches, our technique uses very simple hardware setup that is easy to deploy, operate and maintain by non-experts and small businesses. Moreover, our approach neither introduces any stress in the fish-schools nor affect their mortality. We found that YOLOv8l was the most successful in automatically detecting the fishes in a crowded environment compared to Mask-RCNN. It obtained a mean average precision score of 0.902 that is much higher than the best score obtained by Mask-RCNN. Physical length estimation for the fishes with our approach obtained an average error of 3.32% over 100 samples of ground-truth data. Lastly, we estimated the body-mass of the fishes using linear regression to fit the Length-Weight Relationship (LWR) on 100 ground-truth observations. Using the fitted parameters of the LWR and the estimated physical length, we calculated the body-mass of 100 individual fishes in the ground-truth data and obtained an average error of 12.24%.

References

1. Blum, H.: Models for the perception of speech and visual form. In: Wathen-Dunn, W. (ed.) Proceedings of the Models for the Perception of Speech and Visual Form. pp. 362–380. MIT Press, Cambridge, MA (1967)
2. Bradley, D., Merrifield, M., Miller, K.M., Lomonico, S., Wilson, J.R., Gleason, M.G.: Opportunities to improve fisheries management through innovative technology and advanced data systems. Fish Fish. **20**(3), 564–583 (2019)
3. Martinez-de Dios, J., Serna, C., Ollero, A.: Computer vision and robotics techniques in fish farms. Robotica **21**(3), 233–243 (2003)
4. FAO: The state of world fisheries and aquaculture 2018 - meeting the sustainable development goals. FAO 978-92-5-130562-1 (2018)
5. Garcia, R., et al.: Automatic segmentation of fish using deep learning with application to fish size measurement. ICES J. Marine Sci. **77**(4), 1354–1366 (2019). https://doi.org/10.1093/ice sjms/fsz186
6. Garcia-d'Urso, N., et al.: The deepFish computer vision dataset for fish instance segmentation, classification, and size estimation. Sci. Data **9**(1), 287 (2022)
7. Girshick, R., Donahue, J., Darrell, T., Malik, J.: Region-based convolutional networks for accurate object detection and segmentation. IEEE Trans. Pattern Anal. Mach. Intell. **38**(1), 142–158 (2015)
8. He, K., Gkioxari, G., Dollár, P., Girshick, R.: Mask R-CNN. In: Proceedings of the IEEE International Conference on Computer Vision, pp. 2961–2969 (2017)
9. Jocher, G.: ultralytics/yolov5: v6.2 - YOLOv5 Classification Models, Apple M1, Reproducibility, ClearML and Deci.ai integrations (2022). https://doi.org/10.5281/zenodo.700 2879
10. Koch, E., Rosolowsky, E.: Filament identification through mathematical morphology. Mon. Not. R. Astron. Soc. **452**(4), 3435–3450 (2015)

11. Konovalov, D.A., Saleh, A., Efremova, D.B., Domingos, J.A., Jerry, D.R.: Automatic weight estimation of harvested fish from images. In: 2019 Digital Image Computing: Techniques and Applications (DICTA), pp. 1–7. IEEE (2019)
12. Le Cren, E.D.: The length-weight relationship and seasonal cycle in gonad weight and condition in the perch (Perca fluviatilis). J. Animal Ecol. 201–219 (1951)
13. Monkman, G., Hyder, K., Kaiserc, M., Vidal, F.: Using machine vision to estimate fish length from images using regional convolutional neural networks. Meth. Ecol. Evol. **10**, 2045–2056 (2019). https://doi.org/10.1111/2041-210x.13282
14. Monkman, G.G., Hyder, K., Kaiser, M.J., Vidal, F.P.: Accurate estimation of fish length in single camera photogrammetry with a fiducial marker. ICES J. Marine Sci. **77**(6), 2245–2254 (2019). https://doi.org/10.1093/icesjms/fsz030
15. O'Neill, E.A., Stejskal, V., Clifford, E., Rowan, N.J.: Novel use of peatlands as future locations for the sustainable intensification of freshwater aquaculture production – a case study from the republic of Ireland. Sci. Total Environ. **706**, 136044 (2020). https://doi.org/10.1016/j.sci totenv.2019.136044
16. Palmer, M., Álvarez Ellacuría, A., Moltó, V., Catalán, I.A.: Automatic, operational, high-resolution monitoring of fish length and catch numbers from landings using deep learning. Fish. Res. **246**, 106166 (2022). https://doi.org/10.1016/j.fishres.2021.106166
17. Petrell, R., Shi, X., Ward, R., Naiberg, A., Savage, C.: Determining fish size and swimming speed in cages and tanks using simple video techniques. Aquacult. Eng. **16**(1–2), 63–84 (1997)
18. Rauf, H.T., Lali, M.I.U., Zahoor, S., Shah, S.Z.H., Rehman, A.U., Bukhari, S.A.C.: Visual features based automated identification of fish species using deep convolutional neural networks. Comput. Electron. Agric. **167**, 105075 (2019)
19. Rosen, S., Jörgensen, T., Hammersland-White, D., Holst, J.C.: DeepVision: a stereo camera system provides highly accurate counts and lengths of fish passing inside a trawl. Can. J. Fish. Aquat. Sci. **70**(10), 1456–1467 (2013). https://doi.org/10.1139/cjfas-2013-0124, https://doi.org/10.1139/cjfas-2013-0124
20. Saleh, A., Laradji, I.H., Konovalov, D.A., Bradley, M., Vazquez, D., Sheaves, M.: A realistic fish-habitat dataset to evaluate algorithms for underwater visual analysis. Sci. Rep. **10**(1), 14671 (2020). https://doi.org/10.1038/s41598-020-71639-x
21. Siddiqui, S.A., et al.: Automatic fish species classification in underwater videos: exploiting pre-trained deep neural network models to compensate for limited labelled data. ICES J. Mar. Sci. **75**(1), 374–389 (2018)
22. Tillett, R., McFarlane, N., Lines, J.: Estimating dimensions of free-swimming fish using 3D point distribution models. Comput. Vis. Image Underst. **79**(1), 123–141 (2000)
23. Tseng, C.H., Hsieh, C.L., Kuo, Y.F.: Automatic measurement of the body length of harvested fish using convolutional neural networks. Biosys. Eng. **189**, 36–47 (2020)
24. Vo, T.T.E., Ko, H., Huh, J.H., Kim, Y.: Overview of smart aquaculture system: focusing on applications of machine learning and computer vision. Electronics **10**(22), 2882 (2021)
25. Yang, L., et al.: Computer vision models in intelligent aquaculture with emphasis on fish detection and behavior analysis: a review. Arch. Comput. Meth. Eng. **28**, 2785–2816 (2021)
26. Zhou, C., et al.: An adaptive image enhancement method for a recirculating aquaculture system. Sci. Rep. **7**(1), 6243 (2017)
27. Zhou, C., et al.: Near-infrared imaging to quantify the feeding behavior of fish in aquaculture. Comput. Electron. Agric. **135**, 233–241 (2017)

Comparitive Analysis of Various Transfer Learning Apporaches in Deep CNNs for Image Classification

Arnav Tyagi, Rishabh Khandelwal, Nitin Arvind Shelke, Jagendra Singh[✉],
Dev Rajpal, and Ishaan Rajendra Gaware

School of Computer Science Engineering and Technology, Bennett University, Greater Noida,
India
jagendrasngh@gmail.com

Abstract. Deep learning has become an effective approach over the past few
years to addressing intricate computer vision problems, and Convolutional Neural Networks (CNNs) have been the primary driving force behind this progress.
Developing CNNs, however, comes with the obstacle of requiring huge, labeled
datasets. Gathering and annotating a large dataset for any specific job is costly
and time-consuming. To overcome this challenge, researchers can employ transfer learning, a technique that involves using pre-trained deep learning models
on extensive datasets. This study primarily aims to investigate the application of
various transfer learning methods in conjunction with Deep Convolutional Neural
Networks (CNNs) for image classification. The research utilizes the Visual Object
Classes Challenge 2012 (VOC2012) dataset as the foundation for its analysis. To
classify a diverse range of object images, the study applies well-established transfer learning techniques, specifically fine-tuning pre-trained CNN models. Model
performance is assessed through metrics like FPS (frames per second) and mAP%
(mean average precision). A variety of models, including VGG19, SqueezeNet,
YOLOv7, and Inception-ResNet-v2, are tested to determine the most suitable
model for the dataset. The study's findings demonstrate that employing transfer
learning with CNNs can substantially enhance image classification accuracy on the
dataset while reducing model development time. Notably, the Inception-ResNet-
v2 model emerged as the top-performer, achieving an mAP score of 77%. This
research underscores the potential of transfer learning as a powerful tool in the
realm of image classification.

Keywords: Artificial Intelligence · Deep Learning · Inception-Resnet-v2 ·
Machine Learning · SqueezeNet · Transfer Learning · VGG19 · YOLOv7

1 Introduction

Over the early few years, the deep learning, a modern machine learning approach, has
emerged as a powerful approach for solving complex problems. Deep learning has been
proven to remain one of the utmost powerful machine learning methods, with a multitude
of applications in various fields.

KC Santosh et al. (Eds.): RTIP2R 2023, CCIS 2026, pp. 336–346, 2024.
https://doi.org/10.1007/978-3-031-53082-1_27

Deep learning has found its uses in image and video recognition problems such as detection of objects in live video feeds, face recognition, and image captioning. And nowadays, it is also being used in self-driving cars to recognize traffic signs, pedestrians, and other vehicles. Natural language processing is another use case of peep learning where it has improved the accuracy of NLP tasks by a significant margin. Recently, even e-commerce platforms have started using deep learning for recommendation systems to suggest services, products, or content based on a user's previous behavior or preferences and deep learning has also found its use in the modern healthcare industry, helping in medical imaging to diagnose diseases and analyse medical images. It is also used in drug discovery, genomics, and personalized medicine.

CNNs have been at the forefront of this advancement as a potent method for tackling challenging computer vision issues and problems in recent years [1]. Creating CNNs is not an easy task since it calls for huge labelled datasets to provide well-articulated results. Deep learning models have demonstrated great success in solving picture categorization problems in the prior few years. ImageNet Large Scales Visual Recognition Contest, which began in 2010, has played a significant role in the advancement of deep learning and computer vision.

Deep neural network training from scratch, on the other hand, may be computationally expensive and time consuming, especially for huge datasets [2]. And in many cases, creating such huge datasets might take a huge amount of time and money to gather and annotate a sizable dataset for a particular activity. To tackle such a problem, transfer learning has been developed as a solution, as it makes use of already-trained models on enormous datasets. Transfer learning entails training models on huge datasets like ImageNet [3] and then fine-tuning them on smaller datasets for specific applications. This method can greatly minimize the training time and computer resources needed to attain excellent picture classification accuracy.

This study uses the Visual Object Classes Challenge 2012 (VOC2012) dataset to investigate the usage of various transfer learning approaches with Deep CNN's for picture categorization. There are 11,540 photos in the widely used VOC2012 collection, which come from 20 distinct item categories. The study aims to categorize photos into the appropriate object categories by dividing the dataset into three subsets, them being training, validation, and testing [4].

The work employs certain well-established and well-proven transfer learning methodologies, such as optimizing pre-trained CNNs. Reusing characteristics discovered from huge datasets to enhance the performance on a smaller dataset is known as "transfer learning" when using pre-trained models. Pre-trained CNNs may be fine-tuned by freezing the layers and simply changing the weights of the final few layers to accommodate the new data. In self-supervised learning, a model is first fine-tuned on a larger dataset without any labels before being trained again on a smaller dataset with labels. This study employs knowledge distillation, which basically involves training a smaller network to resemble the results of a bigger network.

The study compares these transfer learning approaches against different image classification models that are trained on VOC2012. Several classification criteria, including mAP% and FPS are used to assess each model's efficiency. These models include well-known ones like VGG19, SqueezeNet, Inception-ResNet-v2, and YOLO v7. The study seeks to identify the model that gives the best outcome.

2   Problem Statement

The main objective of this study is to look at the results of various transfer learning algorithms employing the Deep Convolutional Neural Networks (DCNNs) for image classification on the VOC2012 dataset, and to find the top-performing model among common pre-trained models.

3   Literature Review

Several research have been conducted to for investigating and understanding the application of transfer learning for picture categorization problems. Caruana et al. (1995), for example, presented a method termed "learning to learn" that entails teaching a meta-learner how to adapt to new tasks fast utilising transfer learning. Weiss et al. (2016) investigated transfer learning approaches and applications in a variety of disciplines, including computer vision. The author of the study "Image Classification Using Transfer Learning and Deep Learning" studies the application of transfer learning and deep learning approaches for picture classification. The author presents a strategy for fine-tuning pre-trained models like VGG16 and ResNet50 on two benchmark datasets: CIFAR-10 and CIFAR-100. The findings demonstrate that the suggested technique achieves good accuracy while requiring much less training time than training from scratch. Overall, this study adds to the expanding body of knowledge about transfer learning and deep learning for picture classification problems. Beyond computer vision, the suggested technology may be extended to natural language processing and audio recognition [5].

Another work [6] surveys current advancements in deep transfer learning for image classification. It investigates the usage of deep neural networks like CNNs and transformers, as well as how transfer learning might enhance performance in situations where vast quantities of training data are unavailable. The study examines studies that have looked at the use of deep transfer learning for picture classification and suggests areas where more research is needed to expand our understanding of the topic. Overall, this work gives a complete summary of the present state of knowledge in deep transfer learning for image classification, making it a significant resource for deep transfer learning researchers and practitioners. Deep transfer learning, according to the authors, has shown considerable potential in boosting performance on picture classification tasks, particularly in cases when huge quantities of training data are unavailable. However, numerous obstacles and constraints remain, such as the need for more efficient transfer learning methods and a better knowledge of how to fine-tune pre-trained models. Future research should focus on creating new strategies for deep transfer learning, examining its applicability in diverse domains, and studying its potential for other types of machine learning tasks other than picture classification, according to the authors [6].

The authors of the paper "Transfer learning for image classification using VGG19: Caltech101 image data set" first outline a difficulty that arose while utilising deep neural networks for image classification and then examine relevant work done by other authors. The feature extraction methods employed in their experiment are then described, including VGG19, a deep convolutional neural network. They also discuss the machine learning classification methods employed in their experiment, such as SVM and KNN. The authors then go into the strategies they utilised to create their suggested system, which combines feature extraction and machine learning classification algorithms to attain high accuracy. Finally, they provide their findings based on trials performed with the Caltech-101 dataset. Overall, this technique offers a thorough approach to investigating integrated approaches for image categorization utilising deep learning models [7]. The incorporation of the residual module and the use of transfer learning contributed significantly to the rock classification model's great performance. In summary, this analysis proposes a promising approach for the swift and precise classification of rock images [8].

4 Proposed Methodology

4.1 Dataset Description

The The Visual Object Classes Challenge 2012 (VOC2012) dataset stands as a renowned benchmark in the field of computer vision, primarily designed for testing image classification, object recognition, and segmentation tasks. It is composed of 11,530 images, meticulously gathered from the Internet and meticulously annotated by individual annotators. These images capture a wide spectrum of scenarios, depicting various objects in diverse poses, lighting conditions, and scales. This rich diversity renders it an invaluable source for evaluating the robustness of computer vision models. The dataset encompasses 20 distinct object categories, encompassing commonplace items like bicycles, vehicles, cats, dogs, and chairs, as well as more intricate objects such as yachts, airplanes, and potted plants. Each image in the dataset can exhibit multiple object categories, presenting a complex multi-label classification challenge.

The dataset is conveniently divided into three subsets: training, validation, and testing. These subsets facilitate the training, fine-tuning, and performance assessment of machine learning models. Researchers have extensively employed the VOC2012 dataset to evaluate various image categorization algorithms, including deep learning techniques like Convolutional Neural Networks (CNNs) and transfer learning. The dataset remains an important resource for evaluating the performance of cutting-edge computer vision algorithms and pushing progress in the creation of fresh approaches.

4.2 Data Augmentation

Using data augmentation to improve the performance of image classification models on the VOC2012 dataset is a helpful strategy, especially when working with limited training data. Data augmentation is the process of artificially increasing a dataset by creating new samples from the original pictures through different changes. Rotation, translation, scaling, shearing, flipping, and changes in brightness or contrast are examples of transformations. By adding these enhanced pictures, the model becomes more resilient and insensitive to fluctuations in the input data, resulting in increased generalization and performance on previously unknown data [9].

Given the minimal number of photos per item category in the VOC2012 dataset, data augmentation can be very useful. In this context, augmentation assists the model in learning more diversified representations of each item category, allowing it to recognize things under different settings more effectively. Rotating or flipping photos, for example, can help the model become insensitive to object orientation, but scaling or shearing can train the model to recognize objects of varying sizes or shapes. Furthermore, changing the brightness or contrast of the model might make it more resistant to changing lighting circumstances.

In conclusion, various sources employ that data augmentation can greatly improve image classification model performance by increasing the variety of training samples and encouraging the generation of more robust and invariant features. Thus, to better leverage the potential of the VOC2012 dataset and advance the state-of-the-art in image classification and object identification tasks, this paper applied augmentation techniques to generate a larger sample size.

This research leverages popular deep learning frameworks such as TensorFlow and PyTorch to implement data augmentation for the VOC2012 dataset, which provide built-in methods for producing augmented pictures on the fly during the training process. These functions are easily customizable so that they can perform a mix of changes that best meet the demands of the work at hand.

For the research, 50\% more data was generated using some common data augmentation techniques like scaling, rotation, and translation, changing the augmented data size to be of 17295 images, divided into 20 different categories or labels.

4.3 Models Used

VGG19 is a convolutional neural network (CNN) architecture developed by the University of Oxford's Visual Geometry Group, thus the name. It was first described in a research paper published in 2014 titled "Very Deep Convolutional Networks for Large-Scale Image Recognition." VGG19 is well-known for its ease of use and performance in a variety of computer vision applications, including picture classification, object identification, and segmentation [10].

- Input Image: The network of VGG19 receives a fixed-size input picture ($224 \times 224 \times 3$), where 224×224 denotes the height and width, and 3 represents the RGB color channels.
- Convolutional Layers: VGG19 is made up of 19 weight layers, 16 of which are convolutional. To retain spatial resolution, the network employs tiny 3×3 convolutional filters with stride of 1 and padding of 1. As we progress deeper into the network, the number of filters in each layer grows, starting with 64 in the first layer and up to 512 in the last convolutional layers.
- Activation Function: The Rectified Linear Unit (ReLU) activation function is implemented after each convolutional layer, which increases nonlinearity and aids the network in learning difficult information.

- Pooling Layers: Following particular convolutional layers, the network adds five max-pooling layers. These pooling layers are utilized to minimize the spatial dimensions of the feature maps, which aids in the reduction of computational complexity and the improvement of translation invariance.
- Fully connected Layers: Following the last pooling layer, the feature maps are flattened into a one-dimensional vector and fed into three fully linked (dense) layers. The first two completely connected layers each have 4096 neurons, while the third and final fully connected layer has the same number of neurons as the number of classes in the classification job (for example, 1000 for ImageNet). After the first two completely linked layers, the ReLU activation function is also used.
- Softmax Layer: The last fully connected layer's output is connected via a softmax activation function, which turns the class scores into probability values. The projected class for the input picture is the class with the highest probability.
- Loss Function and Optimization: During the training phase, the network seeks to minimize a loss function (e.g., categorical cross-entropy) that assesses the difference between the predicted probabilities and the ground truth labels. To minimize the loss function, the network weights are changed using optimization methods such as stochastic gradient descent (SGD).
- Regularization: Dropout regularization is used in the first two fully linked layers of the VGG19 architecture to prevent overfitting. This approach loses certain neurons at random during training, forcing the network to acquire more robust characteristics.

SqueezeNet is a compact, single-shot, fully convolutional object detection architecture. The network's creators set out to establish an architecture that was smaller and lighter than previous networks for users of systems with limited storage capacity, such as smartphones. With a weight file of about 8MB, SqueezeNet promises storage savings of up to 50 times when compared to competing networks [11].

Due to its fast iteration capabilities, this characteristic makes it a viable choice for businesses that do not have access to high-performance computer resources. The model also exhibits its ability to save time by generating quick predictions on new photographs while it is being deployed. SqueezeNet's space- and time-saving characteristics have contributed to its overall ranking as a top object identification architecture. Because of its tiny design, rapid predictions, and short training period, it is ideal for users with limited computational resources [12] (Fig. 1).

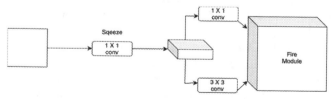

Fig. 1. Architecture of the SqueezeNet model

YOLO v7 - The YOLO (You Only Look Once) model [13] is one of the best and fastest deep neural network architectures, as it follows a single-stage object detection approach for identifying and classifying objects. It is an extension of the previously developed YOLOv4 model, and it enhances it by making it faster, i.e., it requires fewer computations, and it can achieve a significant amount of higher AP. It uses a backbone network that consists of a modified version of the DarkNet architecture, which is a neural network architecture that has been designed specifically for object detection.

In a YOLO model, the image frames undergo significant improvement through a backbone network. These features are then integrated and fused in the network's neck, from where they are subsequently conveyed to the model's head. The YOLO model is responsible for identifying and categorizing the objects for which bounding boxes need to be generated.

The COCO dataset, a huge object identification dataset consisting of over 330,000 images as well as having more than 2.5 million object instances that are spread over 80 distinct object categories, is used to train the YOLO v7 model. The model is taught to identify items quickly and accurately in live time [14] (Fig. 2).

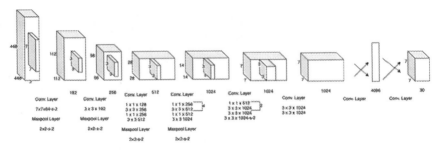

Fig. 2. Architecture of the YOLO (You Only Look Once) model

One of the key features of the YOLO v7 model is its utilization of a Feature Pyramid Network (FPN) to enhance object recognition accuracy. FPN is a technique employed to extract image features at different scales and merge them to detect objects of varying sizes.

In order to increase the precision of object recognition, the YOLO v7 model also uses a number of additional cutting-edge methods. For instance, it makes use of anchor boxes to enhance object localization and dynamic anchor assignment to enhance object recall. Additionally, it makes use of a brand-new loss function called the focused loss, which is intended to boost object recognition precision for unbalanced datasets.

Inception-ResNet-v2 - In 2016, a deep convolutional neural network (CNN) architecture called Inception-ResNetv2 was released by researchers at Google as an enhanced version of the Inceptionv4 network. It combines the benefits of the ResNet architecture as well as the Inception architecture to improve accuracy while using fewer parameters. ResNet uses multiple filters of various sizes in a single layer to capture features at various scales, while Inception uses residual connections to facilitate learning during training [14] (Fig. 3).

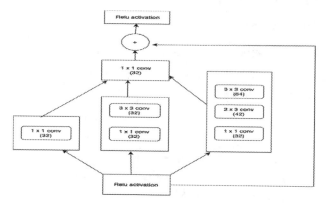

Fig. 3. Architecture of the Inception-ResNet-v2 model

Some of the key unique features of the Inception-ResNetv2 network are:

- Stem Block: The initial part of the network that processes the input image. A stem block is made up of a mixture of pooling layers, batch normalization, and convolutional layers with various filter sizes.
- Inception-ResNet Blocks: They can be called the building blocks of the network. They are made up of many Inception modules with residual connections. Each module extracts features at various scales using various filter sizes (1x1, 3x3, and 5x5), which are then concatenated together before being sent over to the residual link.
- Reduction Blocks: These blocks are used to increase number of channels while decreasing the spatial size of the feature maps. This is achieved by combining 3x3 and 2x2 layers of convolution plus max pooling.
- Auxiliary Classifiers: In order to help the network learn more discriminative features, extra classifiers are inserted at intermediate levels. In order to train them, a weighted loss function that punishes incorrect classification.

On a number of benchmark datasets, including ImageNet and COCO, Inception-ResNetv2 has demonstrated cutting-edge performance. Additionally, it has been applied to other tasks, which include facial recognition, image segmentation, and object identification. The network is particularly good at handling photos with complicated backgrounds and structures due to its residual connections and ability to extract information at various sizes.

5 Results

After conducting the research on different image classification techniques, it was seen that the Inception Resnet v2 model outperformed all the others by a significant margin on both non-augmented and augmented data, achieving a mAP% of 75.5% and 77.0%, respectively. VGG19 was not far behind Inception-Resnet-v2 when we talk about mAP%. Inception ResNet v2 and VGG19 perform better than SqueezeNet and YOLO on the Pascal VOC 2012 dataset (Table 1).

Table 1. Results of different models on Non-Augmented Data

Evalutaion Metrics	VGG19	SqeezeNet	YOLOv7	Incepetion-Resnet-v2
mAP%	67.9%	60.2%	60.8%	75.5%
Frames Per Second	28	108	90	23

Also, by comparing the above tables, it can be noticed that data augmentation techniques help increase the mAP% of the models.

In terms of training time, the Inception-ResNet-v2 model took the longest to train, followed by the VGG19. SqueezeNet and YOLO were considerably faster, and SqueezeNet was the fastest to train. That is to be expected because YOLO is a single-pass architecture designed for speed and efficiency, and SqueezeNet is a lightweight deep learning model designed for low computational complexity and a small model size. VGG19 and Inception Res-net v2 are deep and complex models that achieve higher accuracy while sacrificing computational speed (Table 2).

Table 2. Results of different models on Augmented Data

Evalutaion Metrics	VGG19	SqeezeNet	YOLOv7	Incepetion-Resnet-v2
mAP%	68.3%	60.0%	62.1%	77.5%
Frames Per Second	2	107	90	22

Overall, our results suggest that the Inception-ResNet-v2 and VGG19 models are well-suited for image classification on the Pascal VOC 2012 dataset.

6 Conclusion

The choice of a deep learning model for object detection and classification tasks on the Pascal VOC 2012 dataset, in conclusion, depends on a number of variables, including accuracy, mAP%, and FPS, as well as resource needs and other task-specific limitations.

On the Pascal VOC 2012 dataset, Inception ResNet v2 and VGG19 often outperform SqueezeNet and YOLO based on published mAP% scores. But when FPS, or computational speed, is taken into account, YOLO and SqueezeNet often have higher values than Inception ResNet v2 and VGG19, indicating that they are better suited for real-time applications or scenarios with stringent computing resource limitations.

It is crucial to remember that the reported mAP% and FPS values can change depending on the precise implementation details, hyperparameters, and hardware utilized, and that other factors like training time and model complexity should also be taken into account when selecting a deep learning model for a particular task. Therefore, it is advised to analyze various models and compare their effectiveness on a particular task using a number of metrics and evaluation techniques.

7 Future Work

There are several areas of future work that can be explored for object detection and classification tasks on the Pascal VOC 2012 dataset:

- Model optimization: Future research includes improving the accuracy and speed of deep learning models by optimizing their architecture and hyperparameters. Techniques like neural architecture search, pruning, and quantization can be used to achieve this.
- Attention mechanisms: The effectiveness of attention mechanisms in enhancing deep learning models' performance in diverse tasks has shown encouraging outcomes. On the Pascal VOC 2012 dataset, future research can examine the use of attention processes for object recognition and classification tasks.
- Incremental learning: Deep learning models may be regularly updated with new data using the incremental learning approach in order to adjust to shifting settings. On the Pascal VOC 2012 dataset, future research can investigate the use of incremental learning for object recognition and classification tasks, where additional classes or data may be gradually added [7].

Overall, these areas of future work can help improve the performance and efficiency of deep learning models for object detection and classification tasks on the Pascal VOC 2012 dataset and beyond.

References

1. Jbair, M., Ahmad, B., Maple, C., Harrison, R.: Threat modelling for industrial cyber physical systems in the era of smart manufacturing. Comput. Ind. **137**, 103611 (2022). https://doi.org/10.1016/j.compind.2022.103611
2. Jiang, W.: A machine vision anomaly detection system to Industry 4.0 based on variational fuzzy autoencoder. In: Computational Intelligence and Neuroscience, vol. 2022 (2022). https://doi.org/10.1155/2022/1945507
3. Sharma, N., et al.: A smart ontology-based IoT framework for remote patient monitoring. Biomed. Signal Process. Control **68**, 102717 (2021). https://doi.org/10.1016/j.bspc.2021.102717
4. Lin, C.T., et al.: IoT-based wireless polysomnography intelligent system for sleep monitoring. IEEE Access **6**, 405–414 (2017)
5. Kumar, S., Pathak, S. K.,: A comprehensive study of XSS attack and the digital forensic models to gather the evidence. ECS Trans. **107**(1), 7153 (2022)
6. Mall, S.: Heart diagnosis using deep neural network. In: Accepted in 3rd International Conference on Computational Intelligence and Knowledge Economy ICCIKE 2023, Amity University, Dubai (2023)
7. Sharan, A.: Term co-occurrence and context window based combined approach for query expansion with the semantic notion of terms. Int. J. Web Sci. (IJWS), Inderscience **3**(1), 32–57 (2017)
8. Yadav, C.S., et al.: Malware analysis in IoT & android systems with defensive mechanism. Electronics **11**, 2354 (2022). https://doi.org/10.3390/electronics11152354
9. Berghout, T., Benbouzid, M., Muyeen, S.M.: Machine learning for cybersecurity in smart grids: a comprehensive review-based study on methods, solutions, and prospects. Int. J. Crit. Infrastruct. Prot. **38**, 100547 (2022). https://doi.org/10.1016/j.ijcip.2022.100547

10. Singh, J., Upreti, K., Gupta, A.K., Dave, N., Surana, A., Mishra, D.: Deep learning approach for hand drawn emoji identification. In: 2022 IEEE International Conference on Current Development in Engineering and Technology (CCET), Bhopal, India, pp. 1–6 (2022). https://doi.org/10.1109/CCET56606.2022.10080218

11. Sajid, M., Rajak, R.: Capacitated vehicle routing problem using algebraic particle swarm optimization with simulated annealing algorithm. In: Artificial Intelligence in Cyber-Physical Systems, CRC Press (2023)

12. Yadav, A., Kumar, S., Singh, J.: A review of physical unclonable functions (PUFs) and its applications in IoT environment. In: Hu, YC., Tiwari, S., Trivedi, M.C., Mishra, K.K. (eds.) Ambient Communications and Computer Systems. LNCS, vol. 356, pp. 1–13. Springer, Singapore (2022). https://doi.org/10.1007/978-981-16-7952-0_1

13. Prasad, M., Daraghmi, Y., Tiwari, P., Yadav, P., Bharill, N.: Fuzzy logic hybrid model with semantic filtering approach for pseudo relevance feedback- based query expansion. In: 2017 IEEE Symposium Series on Computational Intelligence (SSCI) (2017)

14. Kumar, R.: Lexical co-occurrence and contextual window-based approach with semantic similarity for query expansion. Int. J. Intell. Inf. Technol. (IJIIT), IGI **13**(3), 57–78 (2017)

Biometrics and Applications

Iris Recognition System in the Context of Authentication

Gaurav Kumar, Anamika Gulati$^{(\boxtimes)}$, Ayush Verma●, Manju Khari●, and Gaurav Tyagi

Jawaharlal Nehru University, New Delhi 110067, India
{anamikagulati,gauravtyagi}@mail.jnu.ac.in

Abstract. This study provides a comprehensive comparison of various iris recognition algorithms, including Hamming distance, feed-forward neural network, and support vector machine (SVM) methods. The study aims to identify the most accurate and efficient algorithm for iris recognition in biometric authentication systems. The dataset from CASIA and uniform preprocessing techniques ensure fair comparisons. The Hamming distance algorithm achieves 79% recognition accuracy but suffers from high false accept and false reject rates due to its threshold-based nature. The feed-forward neural network algorithm achieves an improved accuracy of 87.5% and handles complex classification tasks effectively. However, it is computationally intensive and requires manual feature selection. To address these limitations, the SVM algorithm is explored using linear, polynomial, and quadratic kernels with techniques like SMO, QP, and LS. The quadratic kernel with the least squares approach stands out, achieving an impressive accuracy of 94.5%. This method supports nonlinear problems, automatically selects optimal features, and serves as an excellent binary classifier. The findings emphasize the superior performance of the SVM-based approach in terms of accuracy, true accept rate, and true reject rate, particularly the quadratic kernel with the least squares method. This study offers valuable insights for developing robust and efficient iris recognition systems for biometric authentication applications.

Keywords: Iris Recognition · Sequential Minimal Optimization · Least Square · Hamming Distance · Quadratic Programming

1 Introduction

In recent years, iris recognition has garnered significant attention as a reliable and stable biometric security method. Unlike other biometric traits, the iris remains unchanged throughout a person's lifetime, making it increasingly popular for security applications. The iris as represented in Fig. 1 is a thin annular structure in the eye responsible for regulating pupil size and controlling light entering the retina, exhibits unique patterns suitable for automated scanning and authentication. This study delves into various iris recognition systems, analyzing their approaches to address current challenges in the field. The research focuses on different phases of iris recognition and how researchers have adopted diverse technologies. Iris recognition systems offer quick and precise

© The Author(s), under exclusive license to Springer Nature Switzerland AG 2024
KC Santosh et al. (Eds.): RTIP2R 2023, CCIS 2026, pp. 349–360, 2024.
https://doi.org/10.1007/978-3-031-53082-1_28

authentication, with some modern systems requiring only a simple glance from the user to function effectively. The study showcases the versatility of iris recognition in various domains, such as access control and identification. One remarkable advantage of iris recognition is its non-invasive and contactless nature, as sensors do not physically touch the object during the capture process. Additionally, even identical twins possess distinguishable iris patterns, enhancing the reliability of this biometric technique.

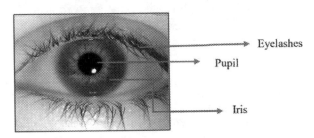

Fig. 1. Anatomy of Human Eye

Three different approaches are evaluated for iris recognition in this study.

1. **Hamming Distance:** This approach compares binary values of templates to find a match between the input iris and the stored iris in the database. It suffers from mediocre performance, high false accept, and false reject rates due to its threshold-based nature.
2. **Feedforward Artificial Neural Network:** In this supervised learning method, a multilayer perceptron is used to distinguish between authorized and unauthorized users. While it yields better performance than the Hamming distance approach, it still lacks accuracy in reflecting false accept and false reject rates.
3. **Support Vector Machine (SVM):** SVMs are employed as a third strategy, with different kernels such as linear, polynomial, and quadratic. Various optimization techniques like Least Square (LS), Quadratic Programming (QP), and Sequential Minimal Optimization (SMO) are used to choose the best features automatically. The SVM approach achieves superior performance with high true accept and true reject rates.

The rest of this paper is organized as follows: Sect. 2 discusses about literature study and previous works related to human eye iris recognition. Section 3 explains the methodology followed for implementation of algorithms. Section 4 discusses the results and validation measures for comparison among various algorithms. Section 5 concludes the paper with overview of the paper and future directions.

2 Literature Survey

Daugman [1] introduced a is a significant advancement in iris detection. It involves creating a high-confidence recognition system based on a person's iris characteristics. The iris image is encoded using two-dimensional Gabor wavelet coefficients, and the most significant bits of 256 bytes are utilized to generate the iris code. The hamming distance is determined through an exclusive OR operation. To extract the iris from the ocular image, the normalized contour integral is applied. Additionally, the technique includes covering the eyelid and eyelashes to enhance image quality. Coherent and incoherent textural information is then extracted using a two-dimensional Gabor filter. The 256-byte iris code is created, and the XOR operation is used once again to calculate the hamming distance. The selection process is based on the Neyman-Pearson statistical decision theory. Remarkably, this technique achieves a 99% success rate using textural features. Daugman's technique has proven to be highly effective in iris recognition and has significantly contributed to the field.

Wildes et al. [2] proposed a technique for iris recognition which utilized diffused light to capture iris images and employed the Hough transform method to find circles. It constructed templates using a Laplacian of Gaussian filter and measured similarity through normalized correlation. The approach minimized the impact of specular reflections using a less obtrusive light source. Though more stable to noise perturbations during segmentation, binary edge abstraction reduced data usage and sensitivity to certain details. Notably, the technique achieved an accurate eyelid localization and detection with a 97.07% success rate.

Ma et al. [3] proposed an iris recognition method based on significant local differences. They computed iris border parameters using a technique similar to Wildes'. The segmented iris image underwent normalization and image augmentation to handle changes in pupil size and brightness. One-dimensional intensity signals were used to reflect local fluctuations. Dyadic wavelet decomposition identified local extreme points representing distinctive iris differences. Focusing on the pupil region prevented eyelid and eyelash noise. Binary expansion of the feature vector and XOR computation measured similarity. A global indicator based on frequency distributions assessed photo quality. Histogram local equalization removed identifiable eyelids and eyelashes, improving segmentation accuracy. The technique achieved an accuracy of 99.43%.

The segmentation method in another study by Avila et al. [4] study uses one-dimensional intensity signals to calculate iris circles and represents texture using zero-crossings. Iris matching relies on dissimilarity functions and a threshold to compare zero-crossings. Accuracy is 98.2% with a 3.6% error rate. Another segmentation method addresses reflections and eyelashes, achieving 89.7% accuracy using one-dimensional wavelet features and the L1 norm. S-iris encoding combines one-dimensional log Gabor filter output with pseudorandom values, obtaining an accuracy of 94.57% and an equal error rate of 8.9% through Hamming distance matching. Circular and linear Hough transforms aid in iris boundary and eyelash elimination.

The Gaussian method is used to estimate the performance of an iris biometrics system on a larger dataset by building a Gaussian model from a smaller dataset [5]. It represents an iris during matching using a series of K iris codes and utilizes a K-dimensional Hamming distance, modeled as a Gaussian distribution, to determine the distance between two iris subjects. Gaussian models are separately built using datasets from West Virginia University and the Chinese Academy of Sciences-Institute of Automation. This method effectively characterizes important local changes with a 92.3% accuracy, reducing computational complexity. It relies on the representation of iris properties through local sharp variation spots, indicating the appearance or disappearance of significant picture components. Researchers have used specific areas of the iris for recognition to address noise-related issues, as exclusive areas are less affected by noise factors [6].

The Fuzzy method achieves 89.97% accuracy in detecting eyelash occlusion using the Grey level co-occurrence matrix pattern analysis technique [7]. It employs a fuzzy C-means algorithm to cluster image windows based on characteristics of the Grey level co-occurrence matrix, classifying them as skin, eyelash, sclera, pupil, and iris. While it doesn't present findings related to identity recognition, the method addresses uneven lighting through histogram segmentation, normalization, and equalization [8]. Morpho-logical operators identify isolated eyelashes, and global iris image augmentation is done using local histogram equalization and Gaussian low-pass filtering. The algorithm differ-entiates between separable and numerous eyelashes, segmenting eyelashes using Gabor filter convolution and thresholding [9]. An intensity variation model simulates mul-tiple overlapping eyelashes. An accuracy of 89% with a 7.8% error rate is achieved. Another approach based on wavelet packets addresses illumination issues and informa-tion deterioration caused by defocused photos [10]. Picture information is calculated using Shannon entropy reconstruction, yielding a 93% accuracy rate.

The Gabor Filter method utilizes complex-valued two-dimensional Gabor filters to extract features through traditional convolution. It outperforms the nearest neighbor in feature comparison, showing promise for noise localization and segmentation accu-racy of 97% in less cooperative image capture [11]. Partial iris portions were explored for identification, demonstrating the feasibility of accurate human identification using only a segment of the iris. An iris identification system for off-angle images was devel-oped, showing robust recognition capabilities [12]. In another study, the two-dimensional Gabor filter was used to extract iris features, achieving an 89.3% accuracy in classifi-cation using UBIRIS iris images. The appropriate choice of threshold played a crucial role in the system's accuracy, and the study addressed the challenges of uncooperative environments and imperfect iris images [13].

A support vector machine-based learning method was employed to create a single high-quality iris image by combining locally enhanced regions from globally enhanced images. Two types of features, local topological features and global textural information were extracted and fused to improve iris recognition ability [14]. Both global and local approaches are used for classification, with global approaches aiming to categorize the entire image and local approaches classifying each pixel independently, particularly for noise patch localization within the iris images [15].

In a multi-biometric system, the integration of quality scores from multiple biometric modalities is being investigated. Instead of assigning separate quality scores for each modality, a combined score is assigned to the gallery-sample-probe-sample pair, aiming to capture the overall quality of the biometric data from both modalities [16]. For the combination of iris and fingerprint data, researchers are actively developing techniques to enhance image quality measures in biometrics. The goal is to establish a quality score that correlates more closely with biometric accuracy, ensuring reliable identification and verification results. Efforts are being made to create a comprehensive metric that considers various factors affecting image quality, such as occlusion and defocus. By combining metrics that account for these factors, the aim is to achieve a high level of accuracy, potentially reaching 95%. The metric may also address challenges related to accurate iris segmentation and effectively handle variations across the iris region, leading to improved overall performance.

The clustering method in iris recognition involves utilizing neural networks to accurately identify individuals based on their iris patterns [17]. Preprocessing techniques, including fuzzy k-means clustering, are used to improve visual contrast and enhance image quality measures for biometric accuracy. Different algorithms have been compared, and some notable ones, evaluated on datasets like UBIRIS, showed promising results with high segmentation accuracy of 97.88% and 98.02% [18]. Techniques like using a Gaussian filter and modified Log Gabor filter are explored to robustly represent iris images and reduce equal error rates. The clustering method involves dividing iris images into sub-images and applying Gabor filters to extract features. It also employs band-limited phase-only correlation for iris matching, achieving a matching accuracy of 78% and an equal error rate of 5.89%. Other feature extraction methods, such as textural and topological features, are also explored, and combining them in the iris recognition system leads to an enhanced accuracy of 96.8%.

The correlation method addresses the issue of off-angle photographs by applying multiple images simultaneously. Testing involved 202 irises, with artificial angle images created for different angles. Bi-orthogonal wavelet networks were trained for recognition up to 42° offset angles. Multiple iris codes from the same eye were compared to identify reliable bits, improving performance by masking erroneous bits. Correlation filters were used, achieving an accuracy rate of 98.9%, outperforming other encoding methods. Artificial color attribution was explored for gross similarity assessment, combined with the ability of irises to recognize spatial patterns. However, compatibility with current iris imaging devices and achieving 93% accuracy are potential limitations. Various studies have focused on addressing noise in iris images, either during segmentation or normalization. Recognition rates and false rejection rates improve when images are captured under controlled conditions, minimizing noise interference, and ensuring more reliable iris recognition.

A biometric based security system for human eye iris recognition was analyzed by Dua et al. [19]. This work involved recognition of human iris using feed-forward neural network. This method used k-means clustering method. Further, Hough Transform method is employed for segmentation of human iris. The segmentation phase involves the application radial basis function neural network. Another form of security system was developed by Kaur et al. [20]. Their approach also involved recognition of human iris using granulation techniques - features-based algorithm and information feature by using differentiation. Their results show excellent accuracy for iris recognition ad biometric authentication.

3 Methodology

3.1 Iris Recognition Process

In iris recognition, the process typically involves the following steps as represented in Fig. 2:

- **Image Acquisition:** An image of the iris is captured using a specialized camera.

- **Iris Localization:** The iris region is localized from the captured image.
- **Iris Normalization:** The iris region is normalized from the captured image
- **Feature Encoding:** The unique characteristics of the iris, such as its texture and patterns, are extracted and encoded into a mathematical representation known as an "iris code."

  - *Template Storage:* The iris code is stored in a database for future comparisons.

- **Matching:** When a person needs to be identified, their iris is again captured, and their iris code is generated.

  - *Comparison:* The Hamming distance is then used to compare the newly generated iris code with the stored templates in the database. The Hamming distance measures the number of bit positions at which two binary strings (iris codes) differ.
  - *Thresholding:* A threshold value is used to determine whether the Hamming distance between the new iris code and stored templates is within an acceptable range. If the distance is below the threshold, the person is considered a match, and their identity is confirmed.

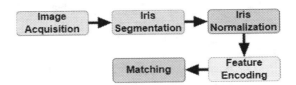

Fig. 2. Iris Recognition Process

3.2 Hamming Distance

Hamming distance is a metric used to measure the difference between two strings of equal length. The Hamming distance between two strings is defined as the number of positions at which the corresponding elements in the two strings are different. In other words, it calculates the minimum number of substitutions required to change one string into the other, assuming the strings have the same length. Hamming distance is a metric used in various fields of computer science and information retrieval, including iris recognition. Iris recognition is a biometric technique that identifies individuals based on the unique patterns in their iris, the colored part of the eye. The Hamming distance is used in iris recognition for comparing the iris code templates, which are mathematical representations of iris patterns. The image scan of a given eye is used to form the base feature templates. These base feature templates are fused to form a final code template. In the fusion process, each bit is weighted according to its reliability at enrollment time. Bit reliability is utilized during the matching process through a proposed Hamming distance formula. Iris recognition involves preprocessing, including localization and normalization. Iris localization involves extracting the iris region from the ocular image using clever edge detection. Iris normalization utilizes Daughman's rubber sheet model to transform the annular iris image into a rectangle shape, addressing variations in size and tilt. Iris feature extraction is carried out using the local intensity variation method, identifying texture in the iris image based on local changes in intensity. The upper boundary of the normalized iris image, representing the unobstructed area of the iris, is considered for feature extraction.

$$HD = \frac{1}{N} \sum_{i=1}^{N} X_i (XOR) Y_i \qquad (1)$$

The iris matching technique is based on the Hamming distance (Eq. 1), which calculates the similarity between binary strings. The Hamming distance is used to compare the input iris pattern with those in the biometric database for identification. However, the Hamming distance approach has limitations, including a lack of support for large datasets and a higher rate of false acceptance and rejection.

3.3 Artificial Neural Network

Artificial Neural Networks (ANN) in iris recognition. Neural networks are computational models inspired by the human brain's neural structure. In feedforward networks, information flows in one direction, from input to output layers, without any feedback loops. The learning process involves adjusting synaptic weights to optimize the network's performance for a given task. The architecture of a multilayer feedforward neural network with hidden layers is explained. It consists of interconnected neurons, where each neuron receives inputs from the previous layer and passes its output to the next layer. The network's ability to handle non-linear relationships makes it suitable for iris recognition. The Levenberg Marquardt learning rule is employed for training the neural network. This rule optimizes the network's weights by iteratively minimizing the sum of squares of errors between the network's output and the desired output for the training data.

In the iris recognition system, the neural network receives preprocessed iris image data as input and produces outputs for iris categorization. The network undergoes training, during which synaptic weights are adjusted based on the errors, and the network learns to categorize iris patterns accurately. The neural network's feedforward architecture and Levenberg Marquardt learning rule contribute to its effectiveness in accurately classifying iris patterns, achieving an accuracy rate of 87.5% in distinguishing authorized and unauthorized iris images.

3.4 Support Vector Machines

Support Vector Machine (SVM) approach for iris recognition. SVM as represented in Fig. 3 is a supervised learning technique commonly used for classification in biometrics and other fields. It can handle various tasks, including classification and regression. SVMs work by finding a hyperplane that best separates different classes of data points in a high-dimensional space. The chapter describes the SVM approach and its application to iris recognition.

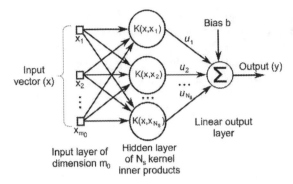

Fig. 3. Support Vector Machine Architecture

Different types of kernels, namely linear, polynomial, and quadratic, are employed in SVM to handle linear and nonlinear separable patterns. Kernels are used to map data into higher-dimensional spaces, allowing for better separation between classes. The chapter discusses the mathematical representations of these kernels and their applications in SVM. Several methods for optimizing SVMs are introduced, including Sequential Minimal Optimization (SMO), Quadratic Programming, and the Least Square Method. These methods help determine the optimal hyperplane that maximizes the separation between data points. In the context of iris recognition, SVM is used as a binary classifier. Input parameters from the preprocessing and feature extraction stages are fed into the SVM's input layer. The SVM's kernel function automatically selects the best features from the input data to compute the output. The chapter explains how the SVM classifies iris images as genuine or fake based on the trained model. The chapter concludes by highlighting the effectiveness of the SVM approach, especially when combined with the quadratic kernel and the least squares method. The SVM achieves an accuracy of 94.5% in iris recognition, with a high true rejection rate and a low false rejection rate. It can handle both authentication and recognition tasks, making it a valuable tool for biometric applications.

4   Results and Discussion

This section evaluates the effectiveness of three different methods: Hamming distance, Feedforward Neural Network, and Support Vector Machine for iris recognition. Each method is analyzed individually in terms of their performance in classifying authorized and unauthorized users.

4.1   Performance of Hamming Distance

The iris' distinguishing characteristics are utilized to identify individuals. The Hamming distance is calculated between six iris data points for each test subject and three iris data points in the database. If all eighteen comparisons fail to match, the test user is considered an imposter; otherwise, they are considered an authorized user. The Hamming distance accurately distinguishes authorized and unauthorized users, achieving an accuracy rate of 87.5%.

4.2 Performance of Feed Forward Neural Network

The Feedforward Neural Network outperforms the Hamming distance in terms of accuracy but takes longer to classify authorized and unauthorized users. The network's weights are adjusted using the Levenberg Marquardt learning rule. The accuracy achieved by the Feedforward Neural Network is higher than the Hamming distance, with an accuracy rate of 87.5%.

4.3 Performance of Support Vector Machine

The Support Vector Machine utilizes different kernels (linear, polynomial, and quadratic) and techniques (Least Square, Quadratic Programming, and Sequential Minimal Optimization). The quadratic kernel least square approach performs the best among all methods, achieving an accuracy rate of 94.5%.

4.4 Comparative Study

A comparative study of the three methods shows that the least square quadratic kernel support vector machine is the most effective method for iris recognition, with a maximum accuracy rate of 94.5%. In conclusion, the Support Vector Machine with the least square quadratic kernel is the most promising method for iris image identification, providing high accuracy and low false rejection rates. The results ensure the authenticity and tamper resistance of the data, making it suitable for iris recognition in security systems.

5 Conclusion

In conclusion, this study focused on iris image recognition for personal identity verification, which is an essential component of biometric identification. The proposed approach utilized iris characteristics to automatically authenticate and identify individuals. The support vector machine with the least square quadratic kernel method proved to be the most effective, achieving an impressive accuracy rate of 94.5%. The iris preprocessing techniques and template generation processes were crucial for obtaining accurate data. The dataset from the Chinese Academy of Sciences - Institute of Automation (CASIA) was used, and the iris images underwent various processing steps, including gray scaling, boundary detection, edge detection, and feature extraction. The resulting template contained distinctive iris features and reduced dimensions for efficient classification. Three methods were utilized for iris recognition: Hamming distance, feed-forward neural network, and support vector machine. The Hamming distance method, although straightforward, showed a lower accuracy rate of 79% and had issues with false accept and reject rates. The feed-forward neural network method achieved an accuracy rate of 87.5% but required longer processing times and lacked automatic feature selection. The support vector machine with the least square quadratic kernel method proved to be the most superior, providing an accuracy rate of 94.5%. It offered excellent binary classification and automatic feature selection, resulting in high true accept and true reject rates. Compared to the other two methods, it demonstrated significantly better performance in iris recognition as compared in Table 1. The comparative accuracies of various kernels of SVM are represented in Fig. 4.

Table 1. Comparison of accuracy of various algorithms.

S. No	Classification Techniques		Accuracy (%)
1	Hamming Distance Feed Forward Neural Network		79
2			87.5
3	Support Vector Machine	Linear Sequential Minimal	93
		Linear Quadratic Programming	92
		Linear Least Square	93.5
		Polynomial Sequential Minimal Optimization	92
		Polynomial Quadratic Programming	91
		Polynomial Least Square	93.2
		Quadratic Sequential Minimal Optimization	94
		Quadratic-Quadratic Programming	93
		Quadratic Least Square	94.5

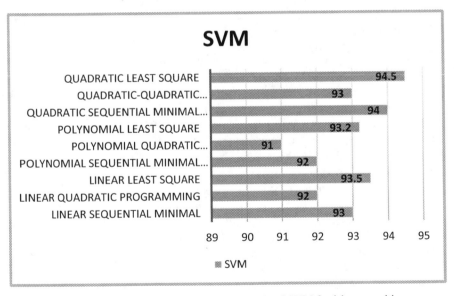

Fig. 4. Comparative Study of various kernels of SVM for iris recognition

Overall, the study's results highlight the effectiveness of iris image recognition for personal identification, with the support vector machine method standing out as the most promising approach for secure and accurate recognition. The findings contribute to the advancement of biometric authentication technology and have potential applications in various biometrics applications.

References

1. Daugman, J.: How iris recognition works. IEEE Trans. Circuits Syst. Video Technol. **14**(1), 21–30 (2004)
2. Wildes, R.P.: Iris recognition: an emerging biometric technology. Proc. IEEE **85**(9), 1348–1363 (1997)
3. Ma, L., Tan, T., Wang, Y., Zhang, D.: Efficient iris recognition by characterizing key local variations. IEEE Trans. Image Process. **13**(6), 739–750 (2004)
4. Ávila, C.S., Sánchez-Reillo, R.: Two different approaches for iris recognition using Gabor filters and multiscale zero-crossing representation. Pattern Recogn. **38**(2), 231–240 (2005)
5. Li, D., Pedrycz, W., Pizzi, N.: Fuzzy Wavelet Packet based feature extraction method and its application to biomedical signal classification. IEEE Trans. Biomed. Eng. **52**(6), 1132–1139 (2005)
6. He, F., Liu, Y., Zhu, X., Huang, C.P., Han, Y., Dong, H.: Multiple local feature representations and their fusion based on an SVR model for iris recognition using optimized Gabor filters. EURASIP J. Adv. Sig. Process. **2014**(1), 1–17 (2014)
7. Liu-Jimenez, J., Sánchez-Reillo, R., Ávila, C.S.: Full hardware solution for processing iris biometrics. In: IEEE International Carnahan Conference on Security Technology (2005)
8. Rossant, F., Eslava, M.T., Thomas, E., Amiel, F., Amara, A.B.: Iris identification and robustness evaluation of a wavelet packets based algorithm. In: International Conference on Image Processing (2005)
9. Son, B., Kee, G., Byun, Y., Lee, Y.: Iris recognition system using wavelet packet and support vector machines. In: Chae, K.-J., Yung, M. (eds.) WISA 2003. LNCS, vol. 2908, pp. 365–379. Springer, Heidelberg (2004). https://doi.org/10.1007/978-3-540-24591-9_28
10. Vatsa, M., Singh, R., Noore, A.: Reducing the false rejection rate of iris recognition using textural and topological features. World Acad. Sci. Eng. Technol. Int. J. Comput. Electr. Autom. Control Inf. Eng. **2**(7), 2533–2539 (2008)
11. Proença, H., Alexandre, L.A.: Toward noncooperative IRIs recognition: a classification approach using multiple signatures. IEEE Trans. Pattern Anal. Mach. Intell. **29**(4), 607–612 (2007)
12. Tao, Q., Veldhuis, R.: Hybrid fusion for biometrics: combining score-level and decision-level fusion. In: IEEE Conference on Computer Vision and Pattern Recognition Workshop (2008b)
13. Pereira, M., Veiga, A.C.P.: A method for improving the reliability of an iris recognition system. In: IEEE Pacific Rim Conference on Communications, Computers and Signal Processing (2005)
14. Haykin, S.: Neural Networks: a comprehensive foundation (1998)
15. Davis-Silberman, N., Ashery-Padan, R.: Iris development in vertebrates; genetic and molecular considerations. Brain Res. **1192**, 17–28 (2008)
16. Yu, Li., Wang, K., Zhang, D.: A novel method for coarse iris classification. In: Zhang, D., Jain, A.K. (eds.) ICB 2006. LNCS, vol. 3832, pp. 404–410. Springer, Heidelberg (2005). https://doi.org/10.1007/11608288_54
17. Sun, Z., Wang, Y., Tan, T., Cu, J.: Robust direction estimation of gradient vector field for iris recognition. In: Proceedings of the 17th International Conference on Pattern Recognition, 2004. ICPR 2004 (2004)
18. Vailaya, A., Zhang, H., Yang, C., Liu, F., Jain, A.K.: Automatic image orientation detection. IEEE Trans. Image Process. **11**(7), 746–755 (2002)

19. Dua, M., Gupta, R., Khari, M., Crespo, R.G.: Biometric iris recognition using radial basis function neural network. Soft. Comput. **23**(22), 11801–11815 (2019)
20. Kaur, S., Chaudhary, G., Srivastava, S., Khari, M., Crespo, R.G., Kumar, J.D.: Exploiting feature space using overlapping windows for improving biometric recognition. Comput. Electr. Eng.Electr. Eng. **96**, 107552 (2021)

Deep Learning for Biometric Attack Detection and Recognition

Mohd. Maaz Khan[1], Arijeet Chandra Sen[2], Om Prakash Singh[3], Jitendra Kumar Chaudhary[4], Mukesh Soni[5(✉)], and K. Anbazhagan[6]

[1] Department of Electronics Engineering, ZHCET, Aligarh Muslim University, Aligarh, India
[2] Government of India, BITS Pilani, Pilani 333031, India
[3] Deptartment of Computer Science and Engineering, Vidya Vihar Institute of Technology (Affiliated to Bihar Engineering University, Patna), Purnea, Bihar, India
[4] School of Computing, Graphic Era, Hill University Bhimtal Campus, Bhimtal, Uttarakhand, India
[5] Department of CSE, University Centre for Research and Development, Chandigarh University, Mohali, Punjab 140413, India
mukesh.research24@gmail.com
[6] Computer Science and Engineering, Saveetha School of Engineering, Simats, Chennai, India

Abstract. Integration of biometric systems is essential for developing effective security and authentication strategies. These systems are nevertheless vulnerable to presentation attacks, in which nefarious actors compromise the integrity of the system by introducing fake biometric features. By enabling accurate presentation attack detection (PAD) and enhancing biometric recognition, deep learning has the potential to be a promising solution to this problem. This work contributes to the improvement of security measures by providing a thorough overview of recent developments in biometric PAD and recognition through the use of deep learning approaches. Video attacks stand out among the different methods used to trick face recognition systems as one of the most common, useful, and simple techniques. This study explores the area of face liveness detection in video attacks with a particular emphasis on determining the veracity of biometric information. The collection includes spoofing attack instances where frames were taken from movies to mimic the spoofing effort as well as instances taken from live facial footage. To categorise these cases, the research makes use of the Resnet-50 deep learning technique. To reach a final verdict, a majority voting system is used to combine several decisions. The paper also evaluates the spoofing attempts made using the movies from the Replay-Attack dataset, providing insight into the effectiveness of the suggested method.

Keywords: Deep Learning · Biometric · Presentation · Attack Detection · Recognition

A. C. Sen—Independent Researcher.

1 Introduction

The utilization of biometrics is growing, yet the incorporated data sets that power those applications are continually in danger of information spills. The Suprema Bistar 2 release (2.8 million records) and the Aadhaar spill (perhaps 1.1 billion records) are cases that have just of late stood out as truly newsworthy. Future breaks of this greatness ought to be expected, and it's conceivable that we won't actually find out about them when they do. With current web transmission capacity accessibility, spreading the taken biometric information is now straightforward and for all intents and purposes free. For example, a typical customer grade web association can send the 23 gigabytes of information from the Suprema Bistar 2 break over the web in two or three minutes. Future expectations just foresee an ascent in these velocities. Furthermore, anybody with a web association can utilize mysterious informing, markets, record moves, and installments because of the development of namelessness centered web conventions like e Onion Switch (Pinnacle) and cryptographic or biometric monetary standards like World coin. It supports the unlawful assortment of this biometric information by taking into account the unknown adaptation of biometric information spills.

Fingerprints have been utilized as a typical biometric trademark by scientific sciences for over hundred years. A great many records are presently accessible for legal examinations and movement control in tremendous public and global data sets. Moreover, fingerprints are used for access control in security-delicate settings, for example, giving admittance to limited regions or safeguarding delicate information. As of late, access control for exceptionally famous offices like amusement spaces, wellness focuses, etc. has been executed utilizing finger impression recognition advances. Various applications are made conceivable by the broad market accessibility of finger impression catch gadgets. A notable biometric characteristic that is valued for its uniqueness even in conditions of indistinguishable twins is the finger impression. No other biometric characteristic has likely gone through such much testing over such an extensive stretch of time in genuine situations. Present day programmed unique mark ID calculations work on data sets with a huge number of records with high recognition exactness. Current unique finger impression scanners, in any case, can give a serious security risk. Albeit the ebb and flow correlation calculations are profoundly evolved as far as scanning records for the right match, the whole situation can be tricked by an exact impersonation of the edge/valley construction of the fingertip, which might have, for instance, been created with little cost from the sign that was gotten from an inert finger impression. There have been many archived answers for the liveness detection issue utilizing unique finger impression sensors. The idea of the unique mark catch process recommends another detecting innovation that would be trying to deceive, as indicated by the equipment based arrangements. Then again, programming based approaches really try to utilize information that can be assembled from as of now conveyed sensors and integrate a liveness distinguishing module. The proper equipment restricts the potential outcomes of the product arrangements, however they likewise have the advantage of less expensive expenses, which are just the organization expenses of a product update.

Biometrics are increasingly being used, however the linked databases that underpin these applications are continually vulnerable to data breaches. The severity of this problem is highlighted by recent events like the Suprema Bistar 2 release (2.8 million records) and the Aadhaar breach (perhaps 1.1 billion records). It is vital to anticipate future breaches of this size since it's likely that we won't even be aware of them when they happen. The transmission of stolen biometric data is not only easy but also practically free with current internet bandwidth capabilities. For instance, the 23 gigabytes of data from the Suprema Bistar 2 breach may be transmitted over the internet in a matter of minutes using an average consumer-grade internet connection. According to predictions, these speeds will only rise in the future. Additionally, the growth of privacy-focused internet protocols like eOnion Switch (Pinnacle) and cryptographic or biometric currencies like Worldcoin makes it possible for anyone with an internet connection to conduct anonymous messaging, market transactions, file transfers, and payments, which makes it easier to monetize stolen biometric data.

2   Review of Litreature

To distinguish between real faces and spoof presentations, Chingovska et al. (2018) look into the use of Local Binary Patterns (LBP) in face anti-spoofing. They provide a novel framework that employs LBP to encode texture changes into histograms. The study assesses the method using multiple face datasets and shows how well it can identify different presentation attacks.

A deep learning-based method for face recognition that focuses on learning discriminative features directly from raw photos is presented by Wen et al. (2016). To make sure that the distance between positive pairs (real samples) is less than the distance between negative pairs (faked samples), the method uses a triplet loss function. This work advances deep face recognition methodologies that can be modified to counter presentation attacks.

For increased accuracy and robustness, Ferrara et al. (2015) suggest a likelihood ratio-based method for fusing scores from several biometric systems. The study emphasizes the value of score normalization and employs a likelihood ratio framework to integrate scores at the decision level. The fusion technique improves the system's capacity to tell real presentations from fake ones.

An overview of current developments in deep learning algorithms for biometric spoofing detection is given by Nguyen and Tran (2019). The review discusses a variety of deep architectures and identifies their advantages and disadvantages when it comes to defending against various presentation attack scenarios. In the research, new prospects for improving the effectiveness of deep learning-based anti-spoofing systems are also discussed.

A thorough analysis of deep representations for spotting spoofing attacks in iris, face, and fingerprint biometrics is presented by Menotti et al. (2015). In order to learn features from several biometric modalities, they provide a unified architecture that makes use of deep convolutional networks. The work demonstrates how deep learning may be used to provide reliable spoofing detection across many biometric features.

A texture and local shape analysis technique for identifying face spoofing attempts from single photos is presented by Määttä et al. (2011). The suggested method uses Gabor features and local binary pattern histograms to extract the texture and shape data. The technique distinguishes between real faces and printed or replayed faked samples with encouraging success.

3   Methodology

This part will go over the periods of the proposed framework we produced for face liveness recognizable proof in video presentation attacks, including the framework design, video division, information pre-handling, and dispersion of the Replay Attack data set.

3.1   System Architecture

As displayed in Fig. 1, the framework design of our method, the principal stage in our framework is video input. From that point forward, utilizing the Video-LAN Client media player developer programming, outlines are extricated from recordings.

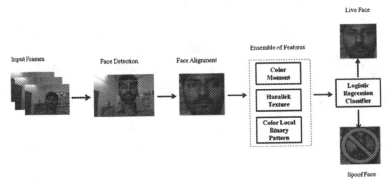

Fig. 1. A 3 frame architecture example for detecting the liveness of a face

Then, at that point, on the grounds that resizing pictures is a pivotal preprocessing step in PC vision and on the grounds that AI models are regularly prepared quicker on more modest pictures, we decreased the size of the multitude of casings we utilized in our technique for recordings to (224, 244) pixels. From that point forward, we used ResNet50, a deep learning calculation, as a classifier, and the outcome from ResNet50 was a delicate judgment (live/counterfeit) from a solitary edge. On the whole, we involved three classifiers as a feature of our interaction. The greater part casting a ballot choice combination, which basically can explain it and intends that from the odd quantities of edges we utilized for pursuing the last choice, the result relies upon the greater part input outlines, was the following stage after every classifier's result. For example, on the off chance that we have three edges for two situations as a speculation, the first will bring about a live face assuming two of the casings are genuine and the third phony for the very video that was utilized in testing, and the subsequent situation will bring about a phony face assuming we have two phony casings and the third genuine.

3.2   Video Segmentation Phase

Since the methodology of this concentrate essentially centers around versatile video attack situations, we recovered the portable video attacks for every one of the 50 clients in the Replay attack data set, which remembers 100 films for absolute. Instances of certifiable and satirizing attacks utilizing versatile screens are displayed in Fig. 2 from the replay attack data set.

We shrouded each of the 50 clients in the Replay-attack data set to extricate various casings from recordings that were remembered for the data set, expanding the detection precision of the framework. We chose 100 recordings for our clients to catch many edges from them, and on the grounds that we utilized the static strategy for detection on recordings, we had the option to get in excess of 1,000 photographs. For video division, the media player developer Video LAN Client was used. Every video in the Replay data set has a base term of 9 s, so by and large, every video test utilized for every one of the clients focused on from the Replay attack data set will have somewhere in the range of 23 and 38 casings. This estimation was utilized to get outlines from the recordings by separating one edge for each 10 casings each second from recordings. For instance, on the off chance that the video contains 30 FPS, the absolute number of edges will be 3. To work on the exactness of face liveness recognizable proof, outlines were taken all along, center, and finish of clasps in huge amounts.

Session Replay Attack

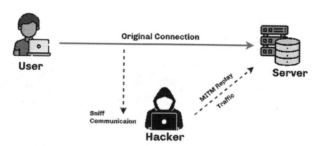

Fig. 2. Examples of both actual and fake attacks from the replay attack database

3.3   The Data Pre-processing Phase

We chose Google Colaboratory, a cloud administration for AI preparing and research in view of Jupiter Note pads, for this work in light of the fact that the execution of our examination required a high PC determination. It accompanies a totally free utilization of a strong GPU and a completely ready deep learning runtime. Google organization Utilizing a web-based application known as a "Jupiter scratch pad in the cloud," we can make and impart records to live code, conditions, and perceptions. There is no arrangement important to start.

Through Google Colaboratory, we approach strong equipment, which brings down the preparation prerequisites. The deep learning model is presently prepared. This prompted the classifier model being created involving Google Colab as along with the Keras Programming interface. Initially, we imported every one of the libraries we expected to construct our framework and A short time later, we partitioned our information into three gatherings: preparing, approval, and testing sets. We imported them subsequent to transferring them to our Google Drive. Second, as recently demonstrated Prior, we cut back each casing utilized in our system to (224, 244) pixels, to Picture resizing utilizing PC vision is a urgent step towards AI On more modest pictures, models are commonly prepared all the more rapidly. Likewise, many deep learning The photos should be similar size for models and designs, in any event, when the crude The size of the accumulated pictures might change, however they should be edited to a particular size. The photographs should be resized to a particular size for less prior to being input into CNN. Twisting of the inward picture's qualities and examples. Third, the data was brought into classifier, with a group size of 3. Indicating the group size is a hyperparameter that decides Preceding refreshing the inward model boundaries, a few examples should be handled. The gathering is carried out as a for-circle that makes expectations while emphasizing north of at least one examples. After the bunch, the expectations are contrasted with the expected result factors, and a mistake is determined. In light of this blunder, the model is further developed utilizing the update strategy.

3.4   The Distribution of the Replay Attack Database

The information from the Replay attack data set that we utilized in our exploration was partitioned into three sets, as displayed in Fig. 3, for the motivations behind preparing, approving, and testing our model. These three sets are as per the following:

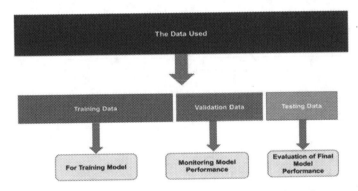

Fig. 3. The composition of the data and each set's goal.

Three separate datasets are utilized for the most part to ensure the model can sum up by precisely anticipating obscure factors. The circulation of information for every classifier we created was as per the following: 70% for the preparation set, 17% for the approval set, and 13% for the testing set.

4   Results and Discussion

We chose 10 recordings from the Replay attack information base to test for expectation results, and we made two situations up to do the larger part deciding on the odd number of edges that we used to arrange 3, 5, and 7 which are genuine and parody attack for the genuine info and to every classifier. As a representation, as we recently referenced, if the first contained genuine, phony, and genuine edges for similar video we picked as information, and the subsequent one phony, genuine, and counterfeit, we did the greater part deciding in favor of the right casings with the worth of exactness, and afterward we determined the precision an incentive for every video we utilized in the testing set and we found the normal precision result for every classifier we utilized in all cases for 3,5, and (Table 1).

Table 1. The detection accuracy when employing 3, 5, and 7 frames

The Accuracy Results of Testing		
Accuracy Result 1	Accuracy Result 2	Accuracy Result 3
2.3	1.5	2.8
2.9	1.8	3.9
3.5	2.7	4.5
3.9	2.9	5.6
4.1	3.6	6.1
4.6	4.2	3.9

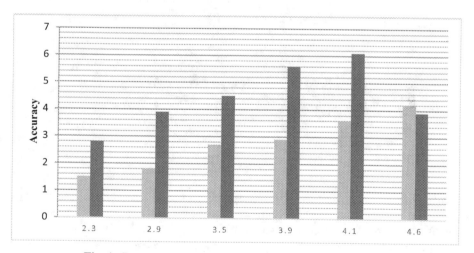

Fig. 4. Detection accuracy when employing 3, 5, and 7 frames

Results 1 in the sentence above makes reference to using three casings for detection, Results 2 purposes five edges, and Results 3 purposes seven casings to recognize whether a face is alive. We reason from this that three edges is the best number of casings to use for detection. Get a decent outcome and accelerate detection on the grounds that less casings are more viable than many. Contrasted and utilizing a solitary edge and the precision of utilizing 20 casings Three casings were more viable for detection, as found in Fig. 4 beneath, which diverges from our ResNet50 model results as well as the other review discoveries we were later.

Table 2. Comparison of the outcomes from various studies and the ResNet50 model results.

Comparison Accuracy Results	
Items	Accuracy
ResNet 50	23.1
Inceptionv4	25.1
SCCN	31.2
CNN-LSTM	39.1

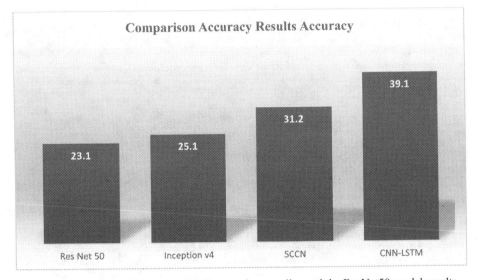

Fig. 5. Comparison of the outcomes from various studies and the ResNet50 model results.

Since ResNet50 depends on the skip associations method, when contrasted with the consequences of utilizing Origin v4 and SCNN, we can say that we accomplished our objective and made exactness higher than involving the single edge for face liveness detection, which is 96.93%. For the last model, CNN-LSTM, our outcomes are still great since when contrasted with them, as we recently referenced, utilizing 20 casings demands greater investment for detection, so here we can say that were, as shown in Table 2 and Fig. 5.

5 Conclusion

Thus, we were effective in accomplishing our significant exploration objective with the framework we created utilizing the Replay attack data set and the deep learning calculation ResNet50 utilized as a classifier. The model had the option to recognize the genuine and counterfeit individual with high precision, and in light of the outcomes, we found that 3 casings is the ideal number of edges to use for detection. We showed this by expanding the quantity of casings to 5 and 7, which brought about a diminishing in the precision of face liveness detection in our framework and an unfortunate expansion in detection time. The ResNet50 classifier furnished us with 96.93% precision in 3 casings, which is great for detection in a short measure of time. The utilization of deep learning procedures has essentially progressed the field of biometric presentation attack detection and recognition. The appearance of presentation attacks has urged scholastics to search for imaginative ways that effectively tackle this arising danger in light of the fact that biometric frameworks are significant to security and verification. Considering presentation attacks, the analyzed exploration accentuates the worth of deep learning in helping the vigor and steadfastness of biometric frameworks.

Deep learning draws near, which can straightforwardly gain complex elements from crude information, have shown promising outcomes in various regions, including the detection of presentation attack vectors and biometric recognition. The papers shrouded in this survey show the way that deep learning procedures can be utilized to an assortment of biometric highlights, like face, iris, and fingerprints. To recognize genuine examples and presentation attacks, these methodologies utilize convolutional brain organizations (CNNs), intermittent brain organizations (RNNs), and particular plans like Siamese organizations. Various advantages accompany the joining of deep learning in presentation attack detection, including expanded exactness, adaptability, and the ability to distinguish complex spatial and worldly examples demonstrative of mocking endeavors. The capacity of deep learning-based models to sum up across an assortment of attack circumstances has been illustrated, prompting higher detection rates and less bogus up-sides.

References

Chingovska, I., Anjos, A., Marcel, S.: On the effectiveness of local binary patterns in face anti-spoofing. IEEE Trans. Inf. Forensics Secur. **13**(10), 2507–2520 (2018)

Wen, Y., Zhang, K., Li, Z., Qiao, Yu.: A discriminative feature learning approach for deep face recognition. In: Leibe, B., Matas, J., Sebe, N., Welling, M. (eds.) ECCV 2016. LNCS, vol. 9911, pp. 499–515. Springer, Cham (2016). https://doi.org/10.1007/978-3-319-46478-7_31

Ferrara, M., Franco, A., Maltoni, D., Fierrez, J.: Likelihood ratio based biometric score fusion. In International Workshop on Biometric Recognition Systems, pp. 11–20. Springer (2015).

Nguyen, H.H., Tran, D.: Deep learning for biometric spoofing detection: Recent advances and future directions. Frontiers Bioeng. Biotechnol. **7**, 362 (2019)

Menotti, D., Chiachia, G., Pinto, A., Schwartz, W.R., Rocha, A.: Deep representations for iris, face, and fingerprint spoofing detection. IEEE Trans. Inf. Forensics Secur. **10**(4), 864–879 (2015)

Määttä, J., Hadid, A., & Pietikäinen, M.: Face spoofing detection from single images using texture and local shape analysis. In International Conference on Image Analysis and Processing, pp. 178–187. Springer (2011)

Jain, A.K., Ross, A., Prabhakar, S.: An introduction to biometric recognition. IEEE Trans. Circuits Syst. Video Technol. **14**(1), 4–20 (2004)

Bhatia, R.: Biometrics and face recognition techniques. Int. J. Adv. Res. Comput. Sci. Softw. Eng. **3**(5), 93–99 (2013)

Tripathi, K.P.: A comparative study of biometric technologies with reference to human interface. Int. J. Comput. Appl. **14**(5), 10–15 (2011)

Hassaballah, M., Aly, S.: Face recognition: challenges, achievements and future directions. IET Comput. Vision **9**(4), 614–626 (2015)

Ghiass, R.S., Arandjelović, O., Bendada, A., Maldague, X.: Infrared face recognition: a comprehensive review of methodologies and databases. Pattern Recogn. **47**(9), 2807–2824 (2014)

Galbally, J., Marcel, S., Fierrez, J.: Biometric antispoofing methods: a survey in face recognition. IEEE Access **2**, 1530–1552 (2014)

Pinto, A., Schwartz, W.R., Pedrini, H., de Rezende Rocha, A.: Using visual rhythms for detecting video-based facial spoof attacks. IEEE Trans. Inf. Forensics Secur. **10**(5), 1025–1038 (2015)

Bagga, M., Singh, B.: Spoofing detection in face recognition: a review. In: 2016 3rd International Conference on Computing for Sustainable Global Development (INDIA Com), pp. 2037–2042. IEEE (2016)

Chakka, M.M., et al.: Competition on counter measures to 2-d facial spoofing attacks. In: 2011 International Joint Conference on Biometrics (IJCB), pp. 1–6. IEEE

A Novel Biometric Authentication Based on Blockchain and Watermarking

Anas Abou El Kalam[✉]

Cadi Ayyad University, Marrakesh, Morocco
a.abouelkalam@uca.ac.ma

Abstract. After analysing the security threats and solution of existing authentication systems, this paper proposes a biometric authentication based on fingerprint, using both invisible digital watermarking and blockchain technology. During the enrolment process, an invisible digital watermark is applied to add an imperceptible digital signature to the fingerprint image, allowing its authenticity and integrity. In addition, the blockchain technology is also integrated into the system to provide a decentralized and immutable ledger where biometric data is securely stored, guaranteeing integrity (preventing data falsification), authenticity, availability, trust and reliability. Hence, by combining digital watermarking and blockchain technology, our biometric authentication system offers a high level of security and reliability by preventing fraudulent attacks, detecting data alterations, ensuring confidentiality (protection of personal information), avoiding a trusted third party or a centralized storage system, and finally, enhancing the auditability and accountability. Our system is implemented and its evaluation proves resistance to attacks without affecting performances.

Keywords: Watermarking · Fingerprint · enrolment · authentication · digital watermarking · blockchain

1 Introduction

Today, business owners find that security is a top concern. Protecting company information, customer data, confidential information, and trade secrets continues to be difficult, particularly as hackers work on coming up with new ways to defeat even the most cutting-edge security measures. Because other security measures have proven susceptible to breaches, many companies preferred using biometrics for authentication instead of older techniques. In fact, traditional authentication methods, such as passwords and PINs, have proven vulnerable to various security threats, including brute force attacks and identity theft (the 2023 Verizon Data Breach Investigations Report revealed passwords accounted for a staggering 81% of data breaches) [1]. Therefore, the need for more robust and reliable authentication systems has arisen. According to the U.S. edition of the Deloitte global mobile consumer survey, 63% of people banking from their smartphone and 67% who transfer money online from a mobile device use at least one type of biometric authentication [2].

© The Author(s), under exclusive license to Springer Nature Switzerland AG 2024
KC Santosh et al. (Eds.): RTIP2R 2023, CCIS 2026, pp. 371–386, 2024.
https://doi.org/10.1007/978-3-031-53082-1_30

Actually, the biometric authentication uses unique physical or behavioral characteristics to verify the identity of individuals. Unlike traditional methods which rely on something the user knows (e.g. a password) or has (e.g. an access card), biometric authentication relies on something the user is, using distinctive characteristics that are difficult to falsify or reproduce. These characteristics include, but are not limited to, fingerprints, iris or retina patterns, facial recognition, voice patterns, hand geometry, and even behavioral traits such as typing rate or gait.

Basically, biometric authentication systems capture and analyze these biometric traits, converting them into mathematical representations called patterns. During the authentication process, the individual's biometric sample is compared to the stored template, and a match or mismatch is determined. If the biometric characteristics match those registered, the individual is authenticated; otherwise, the authentication failed. As biometric traits are unique to each individual and are difficult to forge, this approach generally provides a higher level of security compared to traditional methods.

However, the implementation of biometric authentication is faced to reliability and security issues: biometric data can be copied, the process can be altered, the privacy can be violated, etc. Thus, in order to design a reliable and secure authentication system, it seems important to first analyze the possible threats and attack surfaces. Then, study the existing solutions to prove if they counter all the attacks and threats.

Following this approach, in this paper we present a new biometric authentication that, in the one hand uses watermarking techniques [17] to ensure confidentiality of biometric data and, in the other hand, uses blockchain technology [14] to ensure system transparency, reliability and secure storage of biometric templates. In fact, by embedding imperceptible watermarks in biometric data, we ensure that unauthorized access or interception of data does not compromise an individual's privacy. Watermarking provides an additional layer of security by making it difficult for potential attackers to manipulate biometric data, and thus, preserving its confidentiality. Besides that, by leveraging the decentralized and immutable nature of Blockchain, we create a tamper-proof environment for storing and managing biometric templates. This ensures that the integrity of stored models remains intact, preventing unauthorized modification or access. Additionally, the transparent nature of blockchain allows the system to be auditable, accountable and available, without any single point of failure.

The rest of this paper is organized as follows: in Sect. 2, we present the state of the art related to the biometric authentication. Then, in Sect. 3, we study the threats facing biometric authentication, as well as the different security mechanisms and solutions that can be deployed to mitigate these risks. Afterwards, in Sect. 4, we present our biometric authentication system based on the blockchain technology and crypto-watermarks. Then, Sect. 5 focuses on the implementation and evaluation of our framework. Finally, Sect. 6 draws our conclusions and perspectives.

2   Background and Related Works

Biometrics refers to a set of technologies that exploit the physical and behavioral characteristics of human beings. This identification is accomplished using devices such as scanners and cameras, which use automatic commands to process the features. Unlike passwords, which can be easily forgotten, or magnetic cards which can be stolen, copied or lost, biometric technologies are basically considered to be more reliable as biometric characteristics are unique to each individual and cannot be replaced. We generally distinguish three categories of biometric modalities:

- *Morphological* (physiological) modalities: based on the identification of particular physical traits for each person such as fingerprints, iris and face recognition.
- *Behavioral* Modalities: based on the analysis of certain behaviors of a person such as Handwritten Signature (geometric shapes, acceleration, speed and trajectory profiles), voice recognition, gait (the way a person moves its legs, arms and joints).
- *Biological* modalities: based on some particular biological traits such as DNA and venous network.

In order to justify our subsequent choices, we draw up in Table 1 the advantages and disadvantages of the main biometric methods.

Table 1. Pros and cons of the main biometric methods.

biometric modality	Pros	Cons
Fingerprint	- Low cost - Biometric reader size is not bulky - System very simple to set up - Easy to use -Long term stability	- Fingerprints may persist after each person passes -Average acceptability - Problems with registration, e.g., in the case of infectious disease through touch
Face	- Good public acceptability - Can be done remotely, without user cooperation - Inexpensive technique and can rely on current image acquisition equipment	- Identical twins indistinguishable - Physical changes can trick the system - The technique is too sensitive to the environment (lighting, camera angle, etc.)
Iris	- Identical twins are not confused - The structures of the iris remain stable throughout life - Large amount of information contained in the iris	- Lighting constraint - The reliability decreases proportionally according to the distance between the eye and the camera -Very low acceptability
Voice	- Very well accepted because the voice is a natural signal to produce - The dynamics of the waves produced is unique	- Behavioral characteristics change over time - Possibility of fraud by registration - Sensitivity to noise during acquisition
Handwritten Signature	- Highly acceptable by the user - Can protect all of your personal files	- Great variability over time - Great possibility of fraud
gait	- Highly acceptable by individuals	- Is not permanent (age, illness) - Slow to get results; Have a high cost
DNA's analysis	- Great precision - Detection of offenders	- Slow to get results - Have a high cost
hand veins	- Does not require contact	- Very expensive

Furthermore, other criteria are important and may influence the choice of the method such as (Table 2):

- *Universality*: exist in all individuals.
- *Uniqueness*: ability to differentiate one individual from another.

- *Stability*: permanent, stable and invariant over time.
- *Recordable*: possibility of recording the characteristics of an individual using an appropriate sensor that does not cause any disturbance for the individual.
- *Performance*: Means that authentication should be accurate and fast.

Table 2. Comparison of the cited biometric modalities according to our criteria.

Modality	Universality	Uniqueness	Stability	Recordable	Performance
Fingerprint	++	+++	+++	++	++
Face	+++	+	++	+++	+++
Iris	+++	+++	+++	++	+
Voice	++	+	+	++	+++
Signature	+	+	+	+++	+++
gait	++	+	+	+++	+++
DNA	+++	+++	+++	+	+
hand veins	++	++	++	++	++

This benchmark led us to choose *fingerprint* recognition thanks to its multiple advantages. Its cost is low, and the size of the biometric reader for the fingerprint is small, which facilitates its integration into our system. In addition, fingerprint recognition is relatively simple and easy to use, making it more acceptable by users. Note however that fingerprint patterns are long-term invariant and cannot be updated [4].

That said, whatever the biometric system, it may contain- the following steps [3]: *The enrollment process*; *1-to-1 biometric verification process* (**comparing** the biometric data obtained during a test with the learning models to verify a person's identity); *The identification process* (the biometric system searches the Templates of all users stored in its database, in order to determine an individual's identity. This process involves multiple 1-to-N comparisons to establish a match.

Hence, one of the success points is the choice of the most suitable type of sensor for our system. In particular, a good recognition system is based on the good quality of the image provided by the sensor during fingerprint acquisition. Table 3 draws up a comparison of the main techniques used in the sensors.

The analysis and benchmarking that we conducted in this Section will serve as a solid basis for making the right choices for our biometric authentication framework. However, our choices will also be conditioned by other crucial criteria such as reliability, security (confidentiality, privacy, integrity, and availability), auditability and traceability. In the following section we draw up the different threats that face biometric systems as well as the classic solutions that exist.

3   Threats and Solutions in Biometric Authentication Systems

In order to draw up the different attack surfaces, it is important to understand the entire authentication process. Initially, the biometric data (let's take the fingerprint as an example) is captured using a sensor that records the patterns and characteristic points of each

Table 3. Comparison of the main techniques used in the sensors.

Sensor type	Description	Pros	Cons
optical sensors	Use a Charge Coupled Device (CCD) camera to take a photo of the fingerprint. The finger is placed on a glass surface and the camera takes the picture using a row of light-sensitive diodes	- Competitive price - Use of a simple and common CCD camera -Easily accessible and commonly used	- Easy to divert - Need for direct physical contact with the sensor (unhygienic in some contexts) - Latent fingerprints (the previous fingerprint may remain)
electrical-thermal sensors	The method to recognize the fingerprint is to slide your finger along the sensor. The sensor measures the temperature difference between the pits of the skin and the air captured in the bumps of the fingerprint	- Excellent image quality - Operates in harsh conditions: extreme temperatures, high humidity, - cleaning the sensor - Resistant	-Increases power consumption due to sensor heating
capacitive sensors	Uses capacitors to measure the fingerprint, and is made up of a row of very small cells. Each cell is made up of two conductive plates covered with a protective coating	- Require a real fingerprint -Electric current capacitors give a fast and precise response - The conductive plates protects the sensor against damage	- Difficulties with dry and wet fingers (reduce accuracy) - More expensive than other types of sensors -Electromagnetic interference can affect the accuracy
electric-field sensors	Measures the field beyond the outer layer of skin where the fingerprint begins	- can be used in extreme conditions, i.e. even if the finger is dirty or dry - a clearer image	- low image resolution and too small image area, which results in a high error rate

fingerprint. Then, this biometric data is converted into a digital representation and stored in a database. When authentication is required, an individual's fingerprint is compared with the stored templates, and a decision is made whether or not to validate the claimed identity. We summarize in Fig. 1 the potential attack surfaces and threats related to a biometric authentication process.

We can conclude that the main threats of a biometric authentication systems are: tampering with biometric data, spoofing, interception of transmissions, attacks on biometric template modules, alteration of characteristics and decisions, sniffing and channel interception as well as denial of service attacks on the data and metadata (such as the access information). Below, we give more details about these attacks.

Altered, Tampered or Compromised Biometric Data: Generate artificial fingerprints or reproduce those of another person by using 3D printing techniques or by creating silicone molds.

Interception of the Transmitted Biometric Data (over the network, between a database and a similarity calculation module, or on the capture devices). Interception and alteration may violate the privacy and integrity (network Interception, wireless access point hacking, and malware injection).

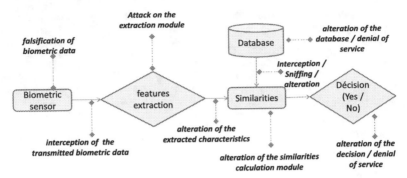

Fig. 1. Attack surfaces and potential threats on a biometric authentication system.

Attack on the Biometric Template Parameters Extraction Module: Attempts to introduce forged fingerprint templates into the extraction module. This attack can be carried out using techniques such as creating synthetic fingerprints or manipulating existing biometric data. Reverse engineering attacks may also be used by analyzing the inner workings of the parameter extraction module to identify vulnerabilities or weaknesses that could be exploited.

Alteration of the Extracted Features During Biometric Recognition: The extracted features (e.g., minutiae points) are deliberately altered or manipulated in such a way as to trick fingerprint recognition systems and generate false matches. These alterations are designed to trick fingerprint recognition algorithms and mislead security systems.

Tampering of the Similarity Calculation Module: Attackers can manipulate the comparison algorithms, the threshold settings, or the stored fingerprint data; e.g., by replacing the similarity calculation algorithm with a malicious one, modifying the stored fingerprint data to match or injecting fake fingerprints in the database.

Tampering with the Fingerprint Database: Introduce fake fingerprints to falsify a person's identification, or even delete important data to cause a denial of service.

Decision Tampering: Sophisticated techniques can be used to deliberately alter decisions and trick the biometric system into recognizing a different fingerprint as being similar to that of the authentic user. This can be achieved using techniques such as creating fake silicone or gel fingerprints, or even digital modification techniques, or by physically altering the existing fingerprint to match that of another person.

Denial of Service Attacks: The goal is generally to prevent the various modules from delivering the expected results or decisions. The usual techniques are flooding, deletion of data or metadata (e.g., connection attempts, identity of the requester, etc.).

To overcome some of these threats, many security measures ware proposed. In the rest of this Section we summarize the most important ones.

Multimodal Biometrics: Basically, five types of multimodal systems can be distinguished: (1) *Multi-sensors:* aim to capture the same biometric feature using different sensors; (2) *Multi-instances*: several acquisitions of the same biometric data are carried out, for example the acquisition of several face images with changes in pose, expression or illumination; (3) *Multi-algorithms*: the same biometric data is verified using several recognition algorithms; (4) *Multi-samples*: different samples of the same modality are captured; (5) *Multi-biometrics*: combine information from different biometric modalities, for example, facial recognition combined with fingerprint recognition. Note that unlike "multi-biometric", the first four systems combine information from a single modality, do not really respect the non-universality criteria. Besides that, systems combining several pieces of information from the same biometrics can improve recognition performance by reducing the effect of intra-class variability.

Anti-spoofing techniques: can be classified into three groups according to the part of the biometric system where they are integrated (Fig. 2).

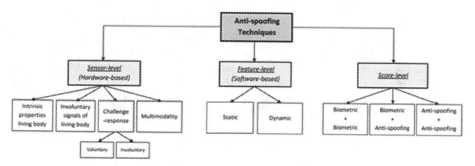

Fig. 2. Classification of anti-Spoofing techniques for a biometric authentication system.

Besides that, we present below the most important security mechanisms that can be implemented to ensure the integrity and security of the biometric template.

Encryption of the Biometric Template: The X9.84 ANSI standard [6] as a method for managing biometric information using cryptographic mechanisms. However, although cryptography is effective in securing the storage and transmission of information, it becomes inefficient when it applied to biometrics. Indeed, due to the intra-class variability of the biometric signal, the comparison must be performed in the clear, which means that an attacker can always try to take control of the biometric data.

Anonymous Databases: The purpose is to check whether a user is a member of a database without knowing its identity. A crucial issue is to ensure secure collaboration between service provider and user. To solve this problem, *Secure Multiparty Computation* (SMC) is often used in the biometric domain. Homomorphic cryptography is generally used to implement SMC protocols. This property allows performing simple operations on encrypted data, such as addition and multiplication. However, SMC protocols are often very complex to compute. The first anonymous databases based on biometrics were presented in [7], using iris and fingerprint respectively. The authors applied Paillier's homomorphic cryptography to protect biometric information and prevent the server from knowing the identity of the user. However, the biometric templates stored in the database remain in clear.

Biometric Cryptosystems: These approaches aim to reproduce the characteristics of the one-way hash functions (e.g., SHA-512) [16] used in cryptography to secure the storage of biometric data. This involves extracting reproducible and identically distributed data from a signal that is basically non-reproducible and non-uniformly distributed. However, turning noisy data into stable data that can be used as an encryption key is not an easy task. The existing primitives in this field can be classified into three main families: primitives based on error-correcting codes, primitives based on the extraction of a unique secret and primitives based on graphic codes. Auxiliary data (also called "helper data") is information stored in a database that guarantees the derivation of a unique string from a noisy and non-uniformly distributed biometric model [8].

Biometric crypto-systems are means of securing biometric templates. However, these schemes have application difficulties because they require a model in vector form and discretized, which can be complicated for certain fingerprint representations such as minutiae. Moreover, they entail a loss of entropy in case of correlation between the elements of the model. Also, these schemes are generally not reusable in terms of privacy preservation as explained above. Finally, error rates are high compared to fingerprints. We will now address the second class of protection methods, namely the approaches by non-invertible or revocable transformation.

Cancelable Biometric Template Protection Schemes: Are designed to secure the biometric data based on random security sampling mechanism and relocation bloom filter [9]. They however have limitations in terms of template security or recognition performance.

Securing the Storage of Biometric Data Using Closed System Architectures: Different options are possible: (1) *Store-on-Card* (SoC): this method consists of eliminating the central database by saving the biometric template directly on the secure device (e.g., smartcard). (2) *Match-on-Card* (MoC): This solution refers to systems in which the comparison module is located on the secure element while the sensor and the extraction module are on a host platform. (3) *System-on-Device* (SoD): implies that the sensor, the extraction and comparison modules are integrated on the same device.

However, in practice, the main focus is on storing the biometric template inside the device, which is then retrieved to perform the verification on a host station such as an electronic passport, which can lead to the same problems as conventional architectures. MoC systems are in principle more secure. Unfortunately, due to the limited chip performance, the complexity of the implemented algorithms can be significantly reduced, resulting in lower performance of the biometric system. Today, setting up a reliable MoC system is a real challenge. On the other hand, assuming that these tokens are tamper-proof is not always true. Depending on its tamper-resistant element, physical attacks can be performed, which means that, although rare, it is possible that the model can be compromised from a stolen token. Table 4 presents a Benchmarking of these solutions.

Table 4. Pros and cons of the techniques used to secure the storage of biometric data.

Mechanism	Pros	Cons
Store-on-Card	- Eliminate the central database	Does not meet the need because the biometric template is transferred to the system
Match-on-Card *System-on-Device*	- Respect for the privacy of the user - The biometric template does not leave the smart card	- Reduced chip performance compared to modern processors (24 MHz vs 3.4 GHz)
Cancelable scheme	- Meets the criteria of the cancelable biometric protection scheme - Has higher security - Good accuracy and performance	

4 Biometric Authentication Based on Blockchain and Watermarking

4.1 Architecture of the Proposed System

By integrating the watermarking technology, our system ensures the confidentiality and authenticity of biometric data. Besides that, the use of blockchain provides a decentralized and distributed mechanism for biometric authentication that ensures reliability, availability and auditability, without the need for a centralized authentication module. Hence, this decentralized mechanism enables robust authentication by eliminating the risk of single point of failure. Moreover, each model is divided into fragments that are managed by different clients. This segmentation mechanism allows secure management of biometric information by minimizing the risk of leakage of the complete template. Basically, the key operations of our system are implemented in a smart contract running on the blockchain [15].

The enrollment process of our system is as follows (Fig. 3):

Enrollment process

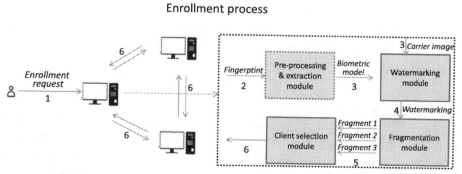

Fig. 3. The enrollment process of our biometric authentication system.

- *Step* 1: The user submits an enrollment request by providing his personal information and entering his finger in the biometric reader/sensor.

- *Step* 2: The captured fingerprint is used by the extraction module to generate the biometric template.
- *Step* 3: The biometric template is then watermarked with a carrier image.
- *Step* 4: The model is split into three fragments based on the model generation timestamp, according to a predefined segmentation function.
- *Step* 5: The assigned model fragments are stored in the selected clients.

Besides that, the authentication process is as follows (Fig. 4):

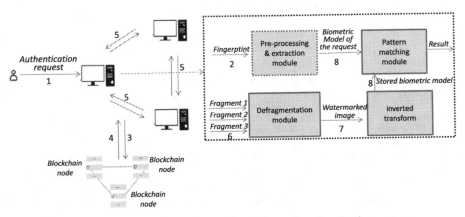

Fig. 4. The authentication process of our biometric authentication system.

- *Step* 1: The user makes an authentication request with the ID of his biometric template to the client who proceeds to capture his fingerprint;
- *Step* 2: The fingerprint is used by the extraction module to generate the biometric template of the request;
- *Step* 3: The client executes the smart contract to find the locations of the required model fragments;
- *Step* 4: Fragment location information is returned to the client;
- *Step* 5: Client requests and receives the corresponding fragments via separate client communications;
- *Step* 6: The client merges the fragments into a complete model;
- *Step* 7: The customer performs the reverse watermarking operation to extract the biometric template;
- *Step* 8: In the matching module, a degree of similarity between the request biometric template and the stored biometric template is calculated. This similarity will decide whether that person is authenticated or not.

4.2 Preprocessing of Biometric Data

A fingerprint is a distinct pattern of ridges and valleys on the surface of an individual's finger. A ridge is defined as a single curved segment whereas a valley is the area between two adjacent ridges. The dark areas of the fingerprint are called ridges and the white area that exists between them is called valleys (Fig. 6). Minutiae points are the main features of a fingerprint image and are used in fingerprint matching. Extracting minutiae using ridges and bifurcations from a fingerprint is a commonly used technique in fingerprint recognition. We highlight a practical part dedicated to the careful extraction of fingerprint features using ridges and bifurcations. Through specialized techniques, we perform precise extraction of minutiae present in fingerprints, paying particular attention to wrinkle patterns and bifurcation points (Fig. 5).

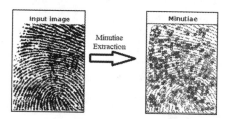

Fig. 5. Minutiae extraction.

4.3   Watermarking Biometric Data

Basically, we distinguish visible or invisible watermarking techniques. Visible watermarking has at least two disadvantages: the inserted mark is easily removed by simple cropping, and the visibility of the inserted mark degrades the visual quality of the host image. Inversely, in invisible watermarking, it is not easy to distinguish between the original image and the watermarked one. Thus, it is difficult to remove the inserted mark without significantly degrading the visual quality of the watermarked image. Hence, we suggest using invisible watermarking in our system.

Besides that, we also distinguish two insertion domains in watermarking techniques: *spatial* and *frequency* domains. In the *spatial domain*, the mark is inserted by modifying the LSBs (*least significant bits*). The images are generally manipulated by modifying one or more bits of the byte constituting the pixels of the image. For an image coded on 8 bits, a modification of the LSB causes a variation of the level of gray of 1 on a scale of 256. This modification is in practice invisible. This insertion method then consists of deleting all the least significant bits of the image to be marked, then inserting the desired data therein. One data bit is thus inserted per pixel of the image. Consequently, watermarking in the spatial domain is easy to implement, but not strongly secure (e.g., against geometric attacks). On the other hand, watermarking techniques operating in the *frequency domain* are more robust even if they are more complex. The section dedicated to the implementation will detail how we used digital watermarking to ensure the authenticity and integrity of biometric data and thus, protect them against unauthorized alterations, copies and illicit uses.

4.4   Using the Blockchain in Our Biometric Authentication System

By integrating blockchain technology, our system provides a decentralized and distributed mechanism for biometric authentication without the need for a centralized authentication module. Basically, each client independently manages template fragments and processes authentication operations without a particular central point. Hence, this decentralized mechanism enables robust authentication by eliminating the risk of single point of failure. Moreover, each model is divided into fragments, managed by different clients. Recall that our system includes template management and authentication registration activities, implemented in a smart contract running on the blockchain. Note that, to ensure the security provided by distributed information management, at least three clients must run a blockchain node.

Besides that, we distinguish two layers: the *storage* and the *management* layers. In the *storage layer*, clients handle user requests, while in the *management layer*, blockchain nodes set up a blockchain network. Note that each client processes authentication and handles template fragments independently. Moreover, by executing a smart contract, a client finds matching clients that handle the required fragments. Each authentication process in the system is recorded as a transaction on the blockchain network.

The registration process is as follows:

1. *Registration request*: a client captures a user's biometric information via a sensor, extracts the characteristics and generates a template;
2. *Split Model*: A model is split into 3 fragments based on a predefined segmentation function that is indexed by the model's generation timestamp. Therefore, each template is divided into different types of fragments based on its timestamp;
3. *Identify nodes*: a client identifies the nodes connected to its corresponding node;
4. *Select clients*: when the number of clients is n, the number of copies stored for the fragments of each model is $[n/3]$, and a total of $[3 * (n/3)]$ clients are selected randomly. For example, if there are eight clients, each fragment will be saved in two copies, and six different clients will be randomly selected to manage them;
5. *Store Templates*: The template fragments are stored in the selected clients.

Besides that, the authentication process is as follows:

1. *Authentication request*: a client captures a user's biometric information via a sensor and requests authentication;
2. *Execute Contract*: A client executes the LookUp smart contract to find the locations of the required model fragments;
3. *Return information*: Fragment location information is returned to the client;
4. *Request patterns*: A client requests and receives the corresponding shards via separate client communications;
5. *Compare Models*: A client merges the fragments into a complete model and compares it with the requested information.

Algorithm 1 implements the LookUp smart contract that identifies clients managing model fragments. It has the ID of the model that requires authentication as input, and returns two outputs:

(1) the IP addresses of the clients where the corresponding fragments are stored;
(2) the fragment IDs of the given template.

Algorithm 1 defines t Fragments, a structured data item containing the IP address and fragment ID (line 1). An instance of t Fragment, i.e. templateData, is stored on a contract running on the blockchain (line 2). Algorithm 1 iterates over the template information v in templateData (lines 5–8) and identifies those whose ID matches t (line 6). If $v.ID$ matches t, it adds v to the L list (line 7) and returns L (line 10). After executing the LookUp smart contract, a client generates a transaction including the model ID and authentication timestamp. By broadcasting this transaction to all connected nodes, every authentication activity is recorded on the blockchain.

Algorithm 1: LookUp Smart Contract

1	**Input:** $t \leftarrow$ Template ID
	Result: *IP.Add* $\leftarrow$ IP addresses of storage client;
	$u.ID \leftarrow$ Fragment ID of template u
2	Struct t *Fragment* $\{u.ID , IP.Add\}$
3	t *Fragment*[] *templateData*
4	List $L[]$
5	**for** v in *templateData* **do**
6	**if** $v.ID == t$ **then**
7	L.push(v)
8	**end**
9	**end**
10	return L

---

5 Implementation

Our benchmark of Sect. 2 led us to choose fingerprint biometric recognition for our implementation thanks to its multiple advantages regarding our needs. Concerning the sensor choice for fingerprint recognition, we believe that electric-thermal sensors are the most suitable for our context (*cf.* Sect. 2, Table 3).

Besides that, to ensure the integrity and authenticity of our biometric data, we propose inserting the mark (watermarking) by modulating the coefficients of the frequency transform. Among the transforms used in digital image watermarking algorithms, we actually use the *Discrete Cosine Transform* (DCT) [10]. It allows the transformation of a data set in the spatial domain to the frequency domain; the inverse process is done by the *Inverse Discrete Cousine Transform* (IDCT).

Generally, the size of the DCT blocks used is 8 x 8 pixels, which gives a total of 64 DCT coefficients: this choice gives a better compromise between quality and computation time. The image is previously cut into blocks. The DC coefficient which is located on the upper left corner holds most of the image energy while the remaining 63 coefficients are referred to as the AC coefficients. To illustrate the coordinates and the order of the distribution of the DCT coefficients, we have the following figure:

Experimental results show that the insertion of the mark in the low frequency components in an 8×8 DCT block will cause an obvious distortion in the watermarked image since they contain the low frequency information of the image. The mid-frequency components carry the information of the textured high regions, and insertion in these areas

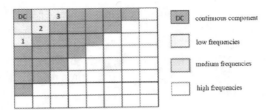

Fig. 6. Order of DCT coefficients.

does not affect the image quality, and the mark will not be removed by JPEG compression. The high-frequency components carry the detail information of the image, and the mark inserted in these regions will generally be eliminated by attacks such as JPEG compression, noise addition and filtering.

We use X to denote the original image (*fingerprint*) its size is $M1 \times N1$. Note that the size of the image that serves as our mark is $M2 \times N2$ (Fig. 7). The mid-frequency range of the original image will be the only range to be used during the marking phase. Brand image size Y should obviously be smaller than cover image size X. In our tests we used a cover image of size 512×512 ($M1 \times N1$:) pixels and a mark of size 64×64 ($M2 \times N2$) pixels.

Fig. 7. Fingerprint watermarking.

Watermarking steps are presented in the Fig. 8.

We implement our watermarking system using the Python as described in [11]. To test the robustness of our system against Geometric attacks (such as Scaling to half, Scaling to bigger) as well as Signal-based attacks (such as Average filter, Median filter, Gaussian noise) we import the *scipy.fftpack* library from DCT and IDCT.

To embed a watermark into a cover we use: python main.py --origin path_cover_image --output path_output_image, Then we choose "DCT", after that we precise "embedding".

To extract watermark from a watermarked image: python main.py --origin path_watermarked_image --ouput path_extracted_signature, then we choose "DCT", after that we precise "extracting".

Finally, to Attack a watermarked image: python main.py --origin path_watermarked_image --ouput path_attacked_image, then we choose "Attack", and precise the type of attack.

Besides that, after successfully recording the watermark into the blockchain, we used the *Ethereum lite explorer* and *Grafana Cloud free tier*. *Grafana* is used to visualize and analyze data [12]. It allows querying, visualizing, alerting on, and exploring metrics. It

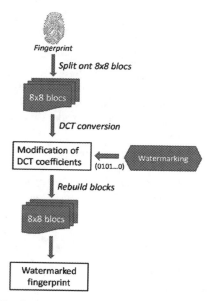

Fig. 8. The fingerprint watermarking process using the DCT

particularly represents the block time graph that shows the date of the time in seconds when the block has been registered, the maximum and minimum time taken by the node to carry out a job, the average time calculated, and the current time. For the blockchain, *Ethereum lite explorer* is used to connect to Ethereum javascript object notation remote procedure call compatible node [13]. To display blockchain data, we could enter the block number, transaction hash, and address. Ethereum lite explorer shows detailed information related to the block.

For performance evaluation, we calculate the *Signal-to-noise ratio* (SNR), *Peak SNR* (PSNR) as well as the *similarity* of extracted watermark and original watermark (Table 5) under different attacks.

Table 5. Evaluation of our system under different attacks

Attack	SNR (dB)	PSNR (dB)	SM
Median Filter	26.605	30.4313	0.955
Salt and Pepper	25.8229	29.4654	0.824
Gaussian Noise	12.1264	13.837	0.644

We can thus conclude that the watermarked images and original ones are almost much closed for the two first cases, but impacted the most by Gaussian noise.

6 Conclusions and Perspectives

This paper presents a new biometric authentication framework based on watermarking and Blockchain technology. By using watermarking as a biometric data protection mechanism, we ensure the confidentiality and authenticity of the biometric data and thus, making it difficult to be tampered with or stolen. Besides that, the integration of Blockchain technology enhances the overall availability, integrity and reliability of the system by providing secure and immutable storage of biometric templates, with no third-party intervention. Moreover, thanks to the transparency and auditability of the Blockchain, we can guarantee the integrity of the models and ensure accountability, immutability and traceability during the authentication process.

It is worth noting that our system resists to attacks and is affected by low performance and efficiency levels caused by the time needed for propagating, processing, and validating the blocks.

References

1. Verizon: Data Breach Investigations Report (2023)
2. Deloitte: Biometric authentication is gaining trust—but is it foolproof? (2023)
3. Liu, X., Xie, L., Wang, Y.: Privacy and security issues in deep learning: a survey. IEEE Access 4566–4593
4. Ross, A., Jain, A.K.: Biometrics, overview. In: Li, S.Z., Jain, A.K. (eds.) Encyclopedia of Biometrics. Springer, Cham (2015). https://doi.org/10.1007/978-1-4899-7488-4_182
5. JRC Technical Reports, "Biometric Spoofing: A JRC Case Study in 3D Face Recognition" (2016)
6. ANSI X9.84, "Biometric Information Management and Security for the Financial Services Industry" (2018)
7. Ye, Y.L., Zhao, J., Cheung, S.: Anonymous biometric access control. EURASIP J. (2009)
8. Jain, A.K., Nandakumar, K., Nagar, A.: Biometric template security. EURASIP J. Adv. Sig. Process. 1–17 (2008)
9. Yanan, S., Hengjian, L., Nianqiang, L., A novel cancelable fingerprint scheme based on random security sampling mechanism and relocation bloom filter. In: Computers and Security, vol. 125. ACM Digital Library (2023)
10. Ahmed, N., Natarajan, T., Rao, K.: Discrete cosine transform. IEEE Trans. Comput. **C-23**, 90–93 (1974)
11. Github. https://github.com/arooshiverma/Image-Watermarking-using-DCT/blob/main/code.py
12. University of Southern California: The USC-SIPI Image Database (2019). http://sipi.usc.edu/database
13. Githib. https://github.com/Alethio/ethereum-lite-explorer
14. Banafa, A.: Blockchain Technology and Applications. Electronic ISBN 9788770221054. IEEE (2020)
15. Ma, R., Gorzny, J., Zulkoski, E.: Fundamentals of Smart Contract Security. Kindle (2023)
16. Hansen, T.: Eastlake, D.E.: US Secure Hash Algorithms. RFC 6234, IETF (2022)
17. Nematollahi, M.A., Vorakulpipat, C., Rosales, H.G.: Digital Watermarking: Techniques and Trends. Springer Topics in Signal Processing (STSP), vol. 11. Springer, Singapore (2017). https://doi.org/10.1007/978-981-10-2095-7

Hybrid Transfer Learning Approach for Emotion Analysis of Occluded Facial Expressions

Dilshan Pamod[1]([✉]), Joseph Charles[2], Ashen Iranga Hewarathna[1], Palanisamy Vigneshwaran[3], Sugeeswari Lekamge[1], and Selvarajah Thuseethan[4]

[1] Department of Computing and Information Systems,
Sabaragamuwa University of Sri Lanka, Belihuloya, Sri Lanka
mwkpdilshan@std.appsc.sab.ac.lk
[2] Department of Computer Science, Faculty of Engineering,
Friedrich-Alexander-University Erlangen-Nuremberg (FAU), Erlangen, Germany
[3] Department of Software Engineering, Sabaragamuwa University of Sri Lanka,
Belihuloya, Sri Lanka
[4] School of Information Technology, Deakin University, Geelong, Australia

Abstract. The ability to recognise and interpret emotional expressions is crucial since emotions play a significant role in our daily lives. Emotions are multifaceted phenomena that affect our behavior, perception, and cognition. As a result, numerous machine-learning and deep-learning algorithms for emotion analysis have been studied in previous works. Finding emotion in an obscured face, such as one covered by a scarf or hidden in shadow, is considerably harder than in a complete face, though. This study explores the effectiveness of deep learning models in occluded facial emotion analysis through a transfer learning approach. The performance of two individual pre-trained models, MobileNetV2 and EfficientNetB3, is compared alongside a hybrid model that combines both approaches. This comparison is conducted using the FER-2013 dataset. The dataset consists of 35,887 images and categorizes emotions into seven emotional categories. The results indicate that the hybrid model attained the highest accuracy, with a score of 93.04% for faces occluded at the top and 92.63% for faces occluded at the bottom. Additionally, the study suggests that top-occluded faces displayed more pronounced emotional expressions in comparison to bottom-occluded faces. Overall, these findings imply that hybrid architecture, which was developed as a state-of-the-art model in the study, proves to be effective for analyzing emotions in facial expressions that are partially obscured.

Keywords: Emotion analysis · Obscured Face · Transfer Learning · MobileNetv2 · EfficientNetB3

1 Introduction

Facial emotion analysis is an important field in Artificial Intelligence that has gained popularity. Emotions vary throughout a person's lifetime and can be challenging to recognize solely based on physical cues. Facial recognition technology,

© The Author(s), under exclusive license to Springer Nature Switzerland AG 2024
KC Santosh et al. (Eds.): RTIP2R 2023, CCIS 2026, pp. 387–402, 2024.
https://doi.org/10.1007/978-3-031-53082-1_31

powered by Artificial Intelligence, has emerged as a solution to identify emotions. It requires feeding relevant data and facial emotion detection algorithms to obtain accurate results. This technology is crucial in various applications such as airport security, identifying suspicious individuals for law enforcement, CCTV cameras, electronic device access authentication, access controls, and human-computer interaction. Emotions are influenced by physiological signals generated by the central nervous system in response to stimuli. Various techniques, such as EEG [41], ECG [2], HRV [3], GSR [4], EMG [5], SKT [6], BVP [7], and RESP [8], can measure these signals, although they capture different aspects of physiological activity. Emotions can be evoked through different methods, like watching emotional films, video clips, driving a car, playing video games, or listening to music. Models such as Eckman's six fundamental emotions and Plutchik's paradigm categorize emotions, but it's important to recognize that emotions are complex and influenced by multiple factors [10].

Occlusion can significantly affect Facial Emotion Recognition systems by distorting the face's appearance and impairing their performance. Incorrect positions of feature, face misalignment, and registration issues make it difficult to extract meaningful information from occluded facial areas. There are three types of occlusion: temporary, systematic, and hybrid [9]. Temporary occlusion happens briefly when a portion of the face is hidden by self-occlusion, objects, or environmental changes. Systematic occlusion occurs when specific facial features or external objects consistently obstruct important facial cues. This type of occlusion can be particularly problematic as it obscures essential features for assessing facial emotions. Hybrid occlusion refers to the simultaneous occurrence of both temporary and systematic occlusion [11, 12].

Recognizing unconstrained facial expressions is challenging due to the high variation in face images. Distinguishing necessary and unnecessary features becomes difficult. While full front-face images yield high accuracy with most methodologies, it is not applicable in real-world scenarios. Factors like face masks and spectacles further complicate emotion detection, requiring the utilization of open areas for analysis. Developing a methodology that accommodates these challenges is highly beneficial, but surpassing existing approaches poses a significant challenge. In practical situations, obtaining full front faces for emotion analysis is not always feasible, emphasizing the need for mechanisms to identify facial expressions in occluded images.

This study provides a comprehensive emotional analysis in the partially occluded faces which is crucial for the security sector. Particularly where people wear face masks and spectacles, emotion detection will be more challenging in such situations. For this experiment initially we use transfer learning's two approaches namely MobileNetV2 and EfficientNetB3. Later, to increase the detection accuracy we initiated with combination of both those two approaches as hybrid approach. The rest of the paper is organized as follows. A exhaustive analysis of the facial detection literature is given in Sect. 2. Section 3 presents the methodology. The results and discussion are given in Sect. 4. Finally, Sect. 5 provides the conclusion and future directions.

2   Related Works

There are several studies have been done so far regarding facial detection. Different traditional machine learning methods such as K-nearest neighbour and support vector machines are used to address the facial emotion analysis challenge. Feng et al. [13] generated local binary pattern (LBP) histograms from multiple small image segments, combined them into a single feature histogram, and classified emotion using a linear programming (LP) methodology. Xiao-Xu and Wei [14] added a wavelet energy feature (WEF) to a facial image, extracted features using Fisher's linear discriminant (FLD), and then classified emotion using the K-nearest neighbour (KNN) approach. Lee et al. [15] used a boosting technique for classification and an enhanced wavelet transform for 2D feature extraction, called the contourlet transform (CT). Chang and Huang [16] integrated face recognition into FER to improve individual expression recognition, and they used a radial basis function (RBF) neural network for classification. Alshamsi et al. [17] used SVM to analyze two feature descriptors, the face landmarks descriptor and the centre of gravity descriptor and applied them to facial feature extraction. Shan et al. [18] used multiple types of SVM to evaluate many facial renderings based on local statistical variables and LBPs in their thorough study.

Deep learning in the emotion analysis domain is a relatively well-known paradigm in machine learning, with some CNN-based research. Pranav et al. [19] used a conventional CNN architecture with two convolutional-pooling layers to analyze FER on self-collected facial emotional images. Another study regarding on deep learning-based facial emotion recognition for human-computer interaction applications [29], explores the use of transfer learning techniques for emotion recognition. Wang et al. [31] proposed a novel framework for FER under occlusion by combining global and local features. In general, information entropy is used to find the occluded region, and the principal Component Analysis (PCA) approach is used to re-construct the image's occluded region. The occluded region is then replaced with the corresponding region of the best-matched image in the training set, and the Pyramid Weber Local Descriptor (PWLD) feature is extracted. The SVM outputs are fitted to the target class's probabilities using the sigmoid function. For the local aspect, an overlapping block-based technique is used to extract WLD features, and each block is adaptively weighted by information entropy, Chi-square distance, and similar block summation methods are then used to determine which emotion belongs to. Pons et al. [20] trained individual CNNs with varied filter sizes in convolutional layers or different numbers of neurons to develop an ensemble of 72 CNNs. The study utilizes pre-trained networks such as Resnet50, VGG19, Inception V3, and MobileNet. The fully connected layers of the pre-trained Convolutional Neural Networks are removed and replaced with new layers that are tailored to the specific task. These new layers are only trained to update their weights. The experiments were conducted using the CK+ database, resulting in an average accuracy of 96% for emotion detection problems. Ding et al. [21] proposed an architecture that integrates a deep face recognition framework with the FER. Li et al. [22] used transfer learning to improve the FaceNet2ExpNet extension of FaceNet, which was already being used by Google's artificial intelligence (AI) team. Yagyaraj et al. [23] presented an affective computing system that recognizes emotion using music, video, and facial expressions. The standard 2D/3D convolution layers are factorized into independent channels and spatiotemporal interactions to reduce the computation cost of neural networks. Amir et al. [24] introduced the Learnable Graph Inception Network (L-GrIN), which learns to recognize emotion while also identifying the underlying graph structure in dynamic data. The authors used three different methods (video, audio and motion capture) in the form of facial expressions, voice and body movements respectively. Ronak et al. [25] introduced Facial Affect Analysis Based on Graphs, which combines two alternative methods for representing emotions: a collection of 26 discrete categories and the continuous dimensions of valence, arousal, and dominance, using various CNN models for emotion recognition. Soumya et al. [26] developed a multimodal conversational emotion recognition system that uses both speech and text; the authors used a bidirectional GRU network with self-attention to process textual and auditory representations separately. Mengting et al. [27] proposed the Attention-Based Magnification-Adaptive Network, which learns adaptive magnification levels for the microexpression (ME) representation (AMAN). The network is composed of two modules: the frame attention (FA) module, which concentrates on discriminative aggregated frames in a ME video, and the magnification attention (MA) module, which automatically concentrates on the proper magnification levels of various MEs. As we can see, various studies on FER techniques have been under-taken.

The ResNet-50 and VGG-16 architectures for detecting facial emotions using deep learning were examined in the 2019 article ResNet-50 and VGG-16 for recognizing Facial Emotions by Dhankhar [28]. The Kaggle Facial Expression Recognition Challenge dataset and the Karolinska Directed Emotional Faces (KDEF) dataset were used to test the two algorithms in the research. The top 10 competitors in Kaggle's Facial Expression Recognition Challenge got at least 60% accuracy, and they indicate in the introduction that they want their best model to achieve at least 60% test set validation. The winner of the challenge had an accuracy of 71.2%. Overall, their models performed better on the KDEF dataset than the Kaggle dataset in terms of accuracy, accuracy, and recall. Surprisingly, all four models outperformed one another on the KDEF dataset as opposed to the much smaller Kaggle dataset. On the other hand, the photos in the KDEF data set are of superior quality, while the Kaggle dataset has examples of text overlay in the background of the image. The results of the KDEF dataset will be shown below, as well as the results of using transfer learning. The results of the SVM (baseline), VGG-16, and ResNet50 on the KDEF dataset are shown in Table 1.

Furthermore, partial occlusions are a significant difficulty in facial recognition systems and often occur in real-world applications, some approaches attempt to minimise the impact of occlusion by reconstructing occluded areas. Cornejo et al. [30] proposed a method that is robust to occlusions using the Weber Local

Table 1. KDEF dataset performance.

Model	Accuracy	Precision	Recall
SVM (baseline)	37.9 %	50.1%	54.9%
VGG-16	71.4%	81.9%	79.4%
ResNet50	73.8%	83.3%	80.7%

Descriptor (WLD). They employed the RPCA technique to reconstruct occluded facial expressions throughout the training set and projected all testing images into the RPCA space. To extract textural features, the WLD descriptor is applied to the full-face expression image. They employed feature dimensionality reduction techniques such as PCA and LDA sequentially for each feature vector and SVM and K-NN for classification.

Meanwhile, fusion at the decision level is used for data fusion of global and local features based on the Dempster-Shafer theory of evidence. Deep Convolutional Neural Networks have pushed the frontiers of face recognition in recent years. To address the issue of occlusion, Li et al. [32] presented an end-to-end trainable Patch-Gated Convolution Neutral Network (PG-CNN), a CNN with an attention mechanism that at-tempts to focus on different regions of the face image and weights each region based on its unobstructedness. It divides the feature maps of the entire face into several sub-feature maps to create varied local patches, which are then encoded as a weighted vector by a patch-gated unit utilizing an attention net based on their unobstructedness. Both local and global representations of features of the face are concatenated to serve as a representation of the occluded face, mitigating the impact of a lack of local expression information. Xu et al. [33] created a hybrid model based on deep convolutional networks to improve the robustness of transfer features from deep models. They built a deep CNN with four convolutional layers using max-pooling to extract features, followed by a multi-class SVM for emotion categorization. To improve model robustness to occlusion, they merge high-level features from two trained deep ConvNets with the same structure, one trained on non-occluded images and the other trained on the same database with additive occluded images. A non-occluded facial expression classifier can be used as a guide to improving the process of an occluded facial expression classifier. Pan et al. [34] used a similar architecture to build two deep convolutional neural networks, which were then trained with supervised multi-class cross-entropy losses. After pretraining, the parameters of the non-occluded network are fixed, and the occluded network is fine-tuned further un-der the supervision of the non-occluded network. They use similarity constraints and loss to incorporate guidance into the network during training. A mask learning technique can also be modified to detect and reject corrupted feature elements. Song et al. [35] created a mask dictionary using the differences between the top convolutional features of occluded and nonoccluded face pairs using a Pairwise Differential Siamese Network (PDSN). This dictionary's entry, Feature Discarding Mask, captures the connection between occluded face regions and corrupted feature components (FDM). When dealing with a face image with random partial occlusions, they construct its FDM by merging appropriate dictionary items and multiplying it with the original features to remove the damaged feature components from recognition. The system developed in [36] employs an effective filtering strategy to decrease the search space of face retrieval in order to increase scalability while keeping representative occluded faces within the search space.

Towner and Slater [37] described three PCA-based approaches for recovering the upper and lower face fiducial point positions. The results showed that the bottom half of the face contains more facial expression information, resulting in a less accurate reconstruction of that region of the face. Zhang et al. [38] proposed an approach for creating occlusion-resistant features that use a Monte Carlo algorithm to extract a collection of Gabor-based templates from image datasets, followed by template matching to determine the most comparable features found inside a region surrounding the extracted templates. This method approach various occluded face parts, such as the eyes, mouth, randomized patches of varying sizes, and transparent and solid glasses, on the Cohn-Kanade (CK) and Japanese Female Facial Expression (JAFFE) datasets. Jiang and Jia [39] conducted many tests in which occluded face areas were reconstructed using PCA, Probabilistic PCA, RPCA, Dual, and Augmented Lagrange Multiplier (ALM) methods. The Eigenfaces and Fisherfaces methods were then utilized for feature extraction, with KNN and SVM classifiers used for classification. The rates of accuracy for eye and mouth occlusions were not higher at 76.57% and 72.73%, respectively. Kotsia et al. [40] conducted an investigation on the effect of partial occlusion on facial expression recognition. Occlusions on the left and right sides of the face were shown to have no effect on identification rates, suggesting that both regions carried less discriminant information for facial emotion recognition. Mouth occlusion has a greater impact on facial expression recognition performance than eye occlusion because it affects a wider range of emotions, including anger, fear, happiness, and sadness, while eye occlusion primarily affects disgust and surprise. Experiments were conducted using two databases, Cohn-Kanade and JAFFE, and employed Gabor wavelets and Discriminant Non-Negative Matrix Factorization (DNMF) for feature extraction and a Support Vector Machine (SVM) classifier. In general, based on the existing works, there is still way for improvement interms of partial facial occlusions.

3   Methodology

According to the Fig. 1, the full study methodology can be divided into three parts. Raw data was initially gathered from the public access repository and processed using a variety of augmentation techniques in the First stage. The second stage then included choosing a model and putting it into implementation. In the third step, the implemented models are compared and evaluated to determine which is the best.

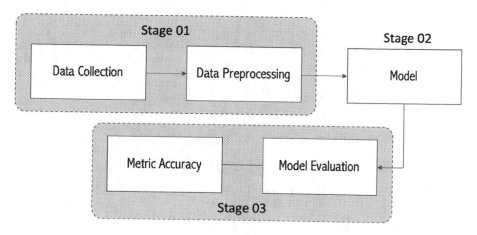

Fig. 1. Overall process diagram.

3.1   Dataset and Preprocessing

The dataset used for this study is FER-2013, which was obtained from the Kaggle platform [41]. This dataset was chosen based on its availability and compatibility with the study's requirements. It includes facial images with variations in expressions and is suitable for testing the efficiency and performance of the algorithm, particularly with occluded face images. A sample image from the FER-2013 dataset is displayed in Fig. 2. The FER-2013 dataset comprises 35,887 photographs categorized into seven groups: surprise, anger, contempt, sadness, joy, and neutrality. The dataset is organized into two separate subfolders, namely train and test, based on the original samples. Below (Table 2), the emotion class and sample size are listed for both the training and testing.

Table 2. Distribution of Training and Testing Samples.

Emotion Type	Training Sample Size	Testing Sample Size
Angry	3995	958
Disgust	436	111
Fear	4097	1024
Happy	7215	1774
Neutral	4965	1233
Surprise	3171	831
Sad	4830	1247

Fig. 2. Sample images from the FER-2013 dataset.

The original images in the FER-2013 dataset are grayscale images with only one layer representing black and white. To input these images into the model, we need to convert the grayscale layer into three RGB layers. However, the image itself remains unchanged during this process. Loading the image is a straightforward task for each implementation of the models.

Other preprocessing methods were applied as follows:

1. Rescaling: The pixel values were divided by 255 to convert them from the range [0, 255] to the range [0, 1].
2. Rotation: The images were rotated by a maximum of 15°.
3. Width and Height Shift: The images were randomly shifted along the width and height axes, with a range of 0.1 as a fraction of the total width and height.
4. Flipping: The images were randomly flipped both vertically and horizontally.
5. Normalization: Two normalization techniques were employed - sample-wise centering and sample-wise standard deviation normalization.

It's important to note that the occluded images created from the original dataset (refer to Fig. 3 and Fig. 4) were placed at the beginning of the preprocessing pipeline. This was done to ensure that other preprocessing steps did not alter the valuable features of the images. The full dataset was split into training, testing, and validation datasets with a ratio of 70:20:10, respectively. All experiments were conducted using the training data and validated using the validation set. The final results were reported based on the holdout test dataset. It is assumed that all datasets have the same underlying distribution since examples for each subset of the data were randomly chosen.

3.2   Model Building

Two separate architectures were utilized to create two distinct models, and subsequently, these architectures were combined to generate additional models (refer

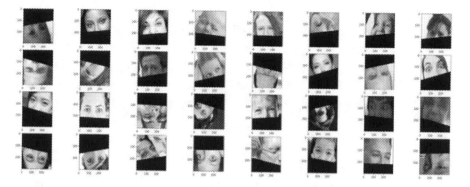

Fig. 3. The corresponding lower-region occluded data samples.

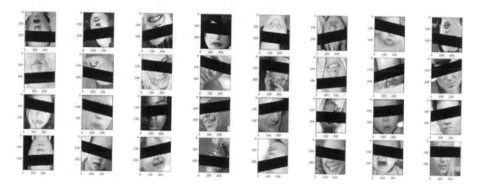

Fig. 4. The corresponding upper-region occuluded data samples.

to Fig. 5). The first architecture employed was MobileNetV2, which served as the foundation for one model. The second architecture employed was Efficient-NetB3, which formed the basis for another model. In both models, pre-trained backbones were utilized as feature extractors, a technique commonly known as fine-tuning in the field of transfer learning.

Initially, each architecture was individually assessed using the training data to understand their independent performance. A comprehensive explanation of each experiment will be presented in the results discussion section. Additionally, a hybrid model was created by combining the two aforementioned architectures. The hybrid model consists of six layers: the input layer, EfficientNetB3, MobileNetV2, average pooling2d1, average pooling2d, flatten, and dense layers. The hybrid model's architecture is illustrated in Fig. 6.

Once the architecture model is defined, it will be compiled with the necessary parameters and configurations. Subsequently, the training process will commence. The model will undergo 50 epochs, which refers to the number of complete passes through the entire training dataset. During this training phase, the model will learn and adjust its parameters to improve its performance.

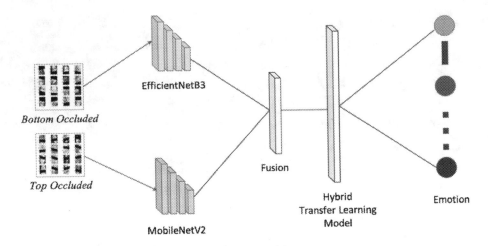

Fig. 5. Proposed architecture to identify occluded facial emotions using hybrid transfer learning.

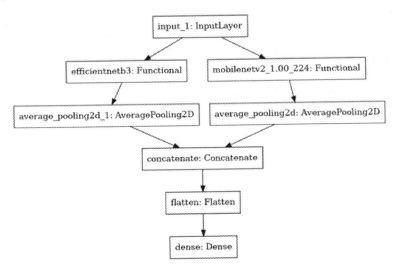

Fig. 6. The comprehensive hybrid architecture(EfficientNetB3 and MobileNetV2).

To evaluate the model's performance, 20% of the images from the training folder will be set aside for validation purposes. These validation images, which were not used during training, will be utilized to assess the model's accuracy on unseen data. The validation accuracy will provide an indication of how well the model generalizes to new, unseen images.

4 Results and Discussion

This study primarily focuses on experimental work, proposing an algorithm and models for analyzing emotions in occluded facial expressions. The descriptive data, including results, statistical processes, and a summary of the findings, are presented in this section.

The experiments were performed on a machine with the following specifications: Intel Core i7 CPU @ 1.30 GHz 1.50 GHz, 8 GB DDR3 Memory, 1 TB hard disk, and 64-bit Windows 10 Home Operating System. Kaggle, a platform known for its ease of dataset availability and code versioning, was utilized for implementing the models. Kaggle provides 20 GB of storage across all notebooks and features an Nvidia Tesla P100 GPU with 16 GB of memory.

The performance of the proposed algorithm and models was measured using accuracy, which is defined as the ratio of correctly classified images to the total number of images trained. Initially, 20% of the test data was used for evaluating the proposed methodology. By comparing the results of each incremental experiment, the strengths and weaknesses of specific techniques were identified.

The results obtained from the experiments were compared with previous studies to determine the advantages of the proposed algorithm. The findings and interpretations of all conducted experiments are discussed comprehensively in this experimental study.

In the experiments, three different architectures were employed to identify emotions in different facial regions. Experiment 1 utilized the MobileNetV2 architecture to identify emotions from the bottom part of the face, while the top part was occluded. The achieved accuracy for emotion identification in the bottom part of the image was 84.51%. Experiment 2 employed the EfficientNetB3 architecture for emotion identification from the bottom part of the face, also occluding the top part. The accuracy obtained in this case was 91.57%. Finally, Experiment 3 combined both the MobileNetV2 and EfficientNetB3 architectures to identify emotions in the bottom part of the face, achieving an accuracy of 93.04% with the hybrid architecture (Table 3).

Table 3. Accuracy of the experiments for upper-region occlusions.

Attributes	Experiment 1	Experiment 2	Experiment 3
Architecture	MobileNetV2	EfficientNetB3	Hybrid
Color format	Grey-scale	Grey-scale	Grey-scale
Dimensions	300×300	300×300	300×300
Classes	7	7	7
Accuracy	0.8451	0.9157	0.9304

Similarly, experiments were conducted to identify emotions from the top part of the face, as outlined in Table 4. In Experiment 1, the MobileNetV2 architecture was utilized with occlusion applied to the bottom part of the face, resulting in an accuracy of 80.02%. Experiment 2 employed the EfficientNetB3 architecture for emotion identification from the top part of the face, also with the bottom part occluded, achieving an accuracy of 89.76%. In Experiment 3, both the MobileNetV2 and EfficientNetB3 architectures were combined to identify emotions from the top part of the face, resulting in an accuracy of 92.63%.

The study findings indicate that the hybrid architecture, which combines the MobileNetV2 and EfficientNetB3 models, achieved higher accuracy compared to the individual architectures. Moreover, it was observed that emotions could be identified more accurately from the bottom part of the face, particularly around the mouth area, compared to the top part that encompasses the eyes. These results suggest that the bottom part of the face exhibits more pronounced and expressive emotional cues.

Table 4. Accuracy of the experiments for lower-region occulusions.

Attributes	Experiment 1	Experiment 2	Experiment 3
Architecture	MobileNetV2	EfficientNetB3	Hybrid
Color format	Grey-scale	Grey-scale	Grey-scale
Dimensions	300×300	300×300	300×300
Classes	7	7	7
Accuracy	0.8002	0.8976	0.9263

5   Conclusion and Future Directions

Facial emotion analysis is a technique that involves analyzing facial expressions in images to gain insights into a person's emotional state. With the advancements in machine learning, computers have become capable of analyzing, identifying, and understanding emotions. The emotion classes considered in this study include fear, disgust, sadness, happiness, neutral, surprise, and anger.

The primary focus of this study is on the transfer learning approach specifically applied to occluded images, rather than regular or non-occluded ones. The images were pre-processed by dividing them into two dimensions: the top occluded part of the face and the bottom occluded part of the face.

The experiment aimed to determine the deep learning model that delivers the best results in facial emotion analysis. Deep learning models, particularly convolutional neural networks (CNNs), have shown significant potential in automated feature extraction and computational efficiency for various facial emotion analysis techniques.

In this study, pre-trained models such as MobileNetV2, EfficientNetB3, and a hybrid model were created and compared. The modified FER-2013 dataset, consisting of 35,887 images, was used, and seven emotional categories were identified for both the top and bottom occluded parts of the face.

For the MobileNetV2 model, trained for 29 epochs, an accuracy of 84.51% was achieved for the top occluded part of the face. Similarly, the MobileNetV2 model trained for 28 epochs achieved an accuracy of 80.02% for the bottom occluded part of the face. The EfficientNetB3 model, trained for 26 epochs, achieved an accuracy of 91.57% for the top occluded part of the face, while the same model trained for the same number of epochs achieved an accuracy of 89.76% for the bottom occluded part of the face.

The hybrid model, which combines both MobileNetV2 and EfficientNetB3 architectures, achieved an accuracy of 93.04% for the top occluded part of the face after being trained for 26 epochs. Similarly, the hybrid model trained for 25 epochs achieved an accuracy of 92.63% for the bottom occluded part of the face.

Based on the study results, the hybrid architecture demonstrated higher accuracy compared to the individual MobileNetV2 and EfficientNetB3 architectures. Additionally, the top occluded part of the face showed greater accuracy than the bottom occluded part, indicating that the top portion of the face exhibits more prominent emotional expressions than the bottom part.

References

1. Li, X., et al.: EEG based emotion recognition: a tutorial and review. ACM Comput. Surv. **55**, 1–57 (2023). https://doi.org/10.1145/3524499
2. Nita, S., Bitam, S., Heidet, M., Mellouk, A.: A new data augmentation convolutional neural network for human emotion recognition based on ECG signals. Biomed. Sig. Process. Control. **75**, 103580 (2022). https://doi.org/10.1016/j.bspc.2022.103580
3. Wei, Y., et al.: A real-time and two-dimensional emotion recognition system based on EEG and HRV using machine learning. In: 2023 IEEE/SICE International Symposium on System Integration (SII), pp. 1–6. IEEE (2023)
4. Kipli, K., et al.: GSR signals features extraction for emotion recognition. In: Kaiser, M.S., Bandyopadhyay, A., Ray, K., Singh, R., Nagar, V. (eds.) Proceedings of Trends in Electronics and Health Informatics. LNNS, vol. 376, pp. 329–338. Springer, Singapore (2022). https://doi.org/10.1007/978-981-16-8826-3_28
5. Tamulis, Ž., Vasiljevas, M., Damaševičius, R., Maskeliunas, R., Misra, S.: Affective computing for ehealth using low-cost remote internet of things-based EMG platform. In: Ghosh, U., Chakraborty, C., Garg, L., Srivastava, G. (eds.) Intelligent Internet of Things for Healthcare and Industry. Internet of Things, pp. 67–81. Springer, Cham (2022). https://doi.org/10.1007/978-3-030-81473-1_3
6. Yang, K., et al.: Mobile emotion recognition via multiple physiological signals using convolution-augmented transformer. In: Proceedings of the 2022 International Conference on Multimedia Retrieval, pp. 562–570. ACM, New York, NY, USA (2022)
7. Bharathiraja, N., Sakthivel, M., Deepa, T., Hariprasad, S., Ragasudha, N.: Design and implementation of selection algorithm based human emotion recognition system. In: 2023 7th International Conference on Trends in Electronics and Informatics (ICOEI), pp. 1348–1353. IEEE (2023)
8. Pradhan, A., Srivastava, S.: Hierarchical extreme puzzle learning machine-based emotion recognition using multimodal physiological signals. Biomed. Sig. Process. Control. **83**, 104624 (2023). https://doi.org/10.1016/j.bspc.2023.104624

9. Hies, O., Lewis, M.B.: Beyond the beauty of occlusion: medical masks increase facial attractiveness more than other face coverings. Cogn. Research **7**, 1 (2022). https://doi.org/10.1186/s41235-021-00351-9

10. Pamod, D., Joseph, C., Palanisamy, V., Lekamge, S.: Emotion analysis of occluded facial expressions - a review of literature. In: 2022 ASU International Conference in Emerging Technologies for Sustainability and Intelligent Systems (ICETSIS), pp. 423–429. IEEE (2022). https://doi.org/10.1109/ICETSIS55481.2022.9888947

11. Ekenel, H.K., Stiefelhagen, R.: Why is facial occlusion a challenging problem? In: Tistarelli, M., Nixon, M.S. (eds.) ICB 2009. LNCS, vol. 5558, pp. 299–308. Springer, Heidelberg (2009). https://doi.org/10.1007/978-3-642-01793-3_31

12. Houshmand, B., Mefraz Khan, N.: Facial expression recognition under partial occlusion from virtual reality headsets based on transfer learning. In: 2020 IEEE Sixth International Conference on Multimedia Big Data (BigMM), pp. 70–75. IEEE (2020). https://doi.org/10.1109/BigMM50055.2020.00020

13. Feng, X., Pietikäinen, M., Hadid, A.: Facial expression recognition based on local binary patterns. Pattern Recogn. Image Anal. **17**, 592–598 (2007). https://doi.org/10.1134/S1054661807040190

14. Xiao-Xu, Q., Wei, J.: Application of wavelet energy feature in facial expression recogni-tion. In: 2007 International Workshop on Anti-counterfeiting, Security and Identification (ASID), pp. 169–174. IEEE (2007).https://doi.org/10.1109/IWASID.2007.373720

15. Lee, C.-C., Shih, C.-Y., Lai, W.-P., Lin, P.-C.: An improved boosting algorithm and its AP-plication to facial emotion recognition. J. Ambient. Intell. Humaniz. Comput. **3**, 11–17 (2012). https://doi.org/10.1007/s12652-011-0085-8

16. Chang, C.-Y., Huang, Y.-C.: Personalized facial expression recognition in indoor environ-ments. In: The 2010 International Joint Conference on Neural Networks (IJCNN), pp. 1–8. IEEE (2010). https://doi.org/10.1109/IJCNN.2010.5596316

17. Alshamsi, H., Meng, H., Li, M.: Real time facial expression recognition app development on mobile phones. In: 2016 12th International Conference on Natural Computation, Fuzzy Systems and Knowledge Discovery (ICNC-FSKD), pp. 1750–1755. IEEE (2016).https://doi.org/10.1109/FSKD.2016.7603442

18. Shan, C., Gong, S., McOwan, P.W.: Facial expression recognition based on local binary patterns: a comprehensive study. Image Vis. Comput. **27**, 803–816 (2009).https://doi.org/10.1016/j.imavis.2008.08.005

19. Pranav, E., Kamal, S., Satheesh Chandran, C., Supriya, M.H.: Facial emotion recognition using deep convolutional neural network. In: 2020 6th International Conference on Advanced Computing and Communication Systems (ICACCS), pp. 317–320. IEEE (2020).https://doi.org/10.1109/ICACCS48705.2020.9074302

20. Pons, G., Masip, D.: Supervised committee of convolutional neural networks in automated facial expression analysis. IEEE Trans. Affect. Comput. **9**, 343–350 (2018).https://doi.org/10.1109/TAFFC.2017.2753235

21. Ding, H., Zhou, S.K., Chellappa, R.: FaceNet2ExpNet: regularizing a deep face recogni-tion net for expression recognition. In: 2017 12th IEEE International Conference on Automatic Face and Gesture Recognition (FG 2017), pp. 118–126. IEEE (2017). https://doi.org/10.1109/TAFFC.2017.2753235

22. Li, J., et al.: Facial expression recognition by transfer learning for small datasets. In: Yang, C.-N., Peng, S.-L., Jain, L.C. (eds.) SICBS 2018. AISC, vol. 895, pp. 756–770. Springer, Cham (2020). https://doi.org/10.1007/978-3-030-16946-6_62

23. Pandeya, Y.R., Bhattarai, B., Lee, J.: Deep-learning-based multimodal emotion classification for music videos. Sensors **21**, 4927 (2021). https://doi.org/10.3390/s21144927

24. Shirian, A., Tripathi, S., Guha, T.: Dynamic emotion modeling with learnable graphs and graph inception network. IEEE Trans. Multimed. **24**, 780–790 (2022). https://doi.org/10.1109/TMM.2021.3059169

25. Kosti, R., Alvarez, J., Recasens, A., Lapedriza, A.: Context based emotion recognition using EMOTIC dataset. IEEE Trans. Pattern Anal. Mach. Intell. 1 (2019).https://doi.org/10.1109/TPAMI.2019.2916866

26. Dutta, S., Ganapathy, S.: Multimodal transformer with learnable frontend and self attention for emotion recognition. In: ICASSP 2022–2022 IEEE International Conference on Acoustics, Speech and Signal Processing (ICASSP), pp. 6917–6921. IEEE (2022). https://doi.org/10.1109/TPAMI.2019.2916866

27. Wei, M., Zheng, W., Zong, Y., Jiang, X., Lu, C., Liu, J.: A novel micro-expression recognition approach using attention-based magnification-adaptive networks. In: ICASSP 2022–2022 IEEE International Conference on Acoustics, Speech and Signal Processing (ICASSP), pp. 2420–2424. IEEE (2022). https://doi.org/10.1109/ICASSP43922.2022.9747723

28. Dhankhar, P.: ResNet-50 and VGG-16 for recognizing Facial Emotions. Int. J. Innov. Eng. Technol. (IJIET)(2019)

29. Chowdary, M.K., Nguyen, T.N., Hemanth, D.J.: Deep learning-based facial emotion recognition for human-computer interaction applications. Neural Comput. Appl. (2021). https://doi.org/10.1007/s00521-021-06012-8

30. Ramirez Cornejo, J.Y., Pedrini, H.: Emotion recognition from occluded facial expressions using weber local descriptor. In: 2018 25th International Conference on Systems, Signals and Image Processing (IWSSIP), pp. 1–5. IEEE (2018). https://doi.org/10.1109/ICASSP43922.2022.9747232

31. Xia, C., Wang, X., Hu, M., Ren, F.: Facial expression recognition under partial occlusion based on fusion of global and local features. In: Yu, H., Dong, J. (eds.) Ninth International Conference on Graphic and Image Processing (ICGIP 2017), pp. 150. SPIE (2018). https://doi.org/10.1117/12.2303417

32. Li, Y., Zeng, J., Shan, S., Chen, X.: Patch-gated CNN for occlusion-aware facial expression recognition. In: 2018 24th International Conference on Pattern Recognition (ICPR), pp. 2209–2214. IEEE (2018). https://doi.org/10.1109/ICPR.2018.8545853

33. Mao, X., Wei, C., Qian, Z., Li, M., Fang, X.: Facial expression recognition based on transfer learning from deep convolutional networks. In: 2015 11th International Conference on Natural Computation (ICNC), pp. 702–708. IEEE (2015).https://doi.org/10.1109/ICNC.2015.7378076

34. Pan, B., Wang, S., Xia, B.: Occluded facial expression recognition enhanced through privileged information. In: Proceedings of the 27th ACM International Conference on Multimedia, pp. 566–573. ACM, New York, NY, USA (2019). https://doi.org/10.1145/3343031.3351049

35. Song, L., Gong, D., Li, Z., Liu, C., Liu, W.: Occlusion robust face recognition based on mask learning with pairwise differential siamese network. In: 2019 IEEE/CVF International Conference on Computer Vision (ICCV), pp. 773–782. IEEE (2019).https://doi.org/10.1109/ICCV.2019.00086

36. Shrivastava, H., et al.: Facefetch: an efficient and scalable face retrieval system that uses your visual memory. In: 2019 IEEE Fifth International Conference on Multimedia Big Data (BigMM), pp. 338–347. IEEE (2019). https://doi.org/10.1109/BigMM.2019.00014

37. Towner, H., Slater, M.: Reconstruction and recognition of occluded facial expressions using PCA. In: Paiva, A.C.R., Prada, R., Picard, R.W. (eds.) ACII 2007.

LNCS, vol. 4738, pp. 36–47. Springer, Heidelberg (2007). https://doi.org/10.1007/978-3-540-74889-2_4

38. Zhang, L., Tjondronegoro, D., Chandran, V.: Random Gabor based templates for facial expression recognition in images with facial occlusion. Neurocomputing **145**, 451–464 (2014). https://doi.org/10.1016/j.neucom.2014.05.008

39. Jiang, B., Jia, K.: Research of robust facial expression recognition under facial occlusion condition. In: Zhong, N., Callaghan, V., Ghorbani, A.A., Hu, B. (eds.) AMT 2011. LNCS, vol. 6890, pp. 92–100. Springer, Heidelberg (2011). https://doi.org/10.1007/978-3-642-23620-4_13

40. Kotsia, I., Buciu, I., Pitas, I.: An analysis of facial expression recognition under partial facial image occlusion. Image Vis. Comput. **26**, 1052–1067 (2008). https://doi.org/10.1016/j.imavis.2007.11.004

41. No Title. https://paperswithcode.com/dataset/fer2013

Author Index

Printed in the United States
by Baker & Taylor Publisher Services